LINUX SERVER HACKS™

Volume Two

Other resources from O'Reilly

LINUX SERVER HACKS™
Volume Two

Bill von Hagen and Brian K. Jones

O'REILLY®

Beijing · Cambridge · Farnham · Köln · Paris · Sebastopol · Taipei · Tokyo

Linux Server Hacks™, Volume Two
by Bill von Hagen and Brian K. Jones

Published by O'Reilly Media, Inc., 1005 Gravenstein Highway North, Sebastopol, CA 95472.

O'Reilly books may be purchased for educational, business, or sales promotional use. Online editions are also available for most titles (*safari.oreilly.com*). For more information, contact our corporate/institutional sales department: (800) 998-9938 or *corporate@oreilly.com*.

Editor:	David Brickner	**Production Editor:**	Jamie Peppard
Series Editor:	Rael Dornfest	**Cover Designer:**	Karen Montgomery
Executive Editor:	Dale Dougherty	**Interior Designer:**	David Futato

Printing History:

December 2005:   First Edition.

 This book uses RepKover™, a durable and flexible lay-flat binding.

ISBN: 0-596-10082-5
[C]   [5/06]

Contents

Credits

About the Authors

Bill von Hagen has been a Unix system administrator for 20 years and a Linux fanatic since 1993. He has also worked as a systems programmer, product manager, writer, application developer, drummer, and content manager.

Bill has written or cowritten books on such topics as Linux filesystems, SUSE Linux, Red Hat Linux, GCC, SGML, Mac OS X, Linux system administration, and hacking the TiVo. He has written numerous articles on Linux, Unix, and open source topics for publications including *Linux Magazine*, *Linux Journal*, *Linux Format*, and *Mac Format*. An avid computer collector specializing in workstations, he owns more than 200 computer systems and wants more. You can reach him at *vonhagen@vonhagen.org*.

Brian K. Jones (Jonesy) has been a Unix and Linux system and network administrator for six years. He has also held positions and consulted in the capacity of database administrator, web developer, project manager, instructional speaker, technical writer and editor, and studio musician, for clients large and small.

In the past, Brian has written extensively on topics revolving around Linux and open source software for Linux.com, *Newsforge*, and *Linux Magazine*, and he has served as author and Editor-in-Chief of *php|architect* magazine. In his copious free time (right), Brian enjoys playing billiards and guitar, woodworking, and writing code. He has worked as a system and network administrator for the computer science department at Princeton University since 2001, and as a part-time infrastructure computing consultant since 2000. You can reach him at *jonesy@linuxlaboratory.org*.

Contributors

The following people contributed their writing, code, and inspiration to *Linux Server Hacks, Volume Two*:

- Jon Fox [Hacks #33 and #62] (*jon.fox@gnu.org.uk*) is a Linux user and free software advocate. He's been using Linux since 1996.

- Tom Limoncelli [Hack #45] has over 15 years of system administration experience and has been teaching workshops on time management at conferences since 2003. Tom has authored *Time Management for System Administrators* (O'Reilly) and *The Practice of System and Network Administration* (Addison Wesley). Outside of work, Tom has won awards for his activism in gay/bi/lesbian rights and now helps progressive causes to use technology to further their goals.

- Lance Tost has been a Linux user since the 0.98 kernel days, while he earned his B.S. in Computer Science. He has held programming, DBA, and, Unix administration positions. Lance is a Red Hat Certified Engineer as well as a Solaris Certified System Administrator. Lance contributed [Hacks #29, #41, #48, #59, #63, and #72].

- Brian Warshawsky is an enthusiastic proponent of all things Linux and open source. His main interests include security, wireless networking, and finding new applications for the Linux operating system. By day he is a professional Unix/Linux system administrator, and by night he's a technical writer and avid mountain biker. He lives in Virginia with his soon-to-be wife Jennifer, his loyal dog Max, and his much less loyal cat Jackie. Brian contributed [Hacks #19, #55, #64, #66, #67, #73, #75, #76, #79, #85, #86, and #87].

- David Brickner [Hack #42] is not a Linux server administrator, but as a Gentoo user, he has learned a couple of things about compiling software. David believes Linux will be the dominant desktop operating system in the near future, and to encourage its adoption, he has written *Test Driving Linux* and *Linux Desktop Pocket Guide*, both from O'Reilly.

Acknowledgments

Bill: For my wife, Dorothy Fisher, without whom life wouldn't be anywhere near as good or as much fun, and for Mike Bauer, Bill Gaussa, and Larry Weidman, who gave me many professional opportunities and encouraged me to expand my horizons. I'd also like to thank David Brickner, without whom I never would have finished this book (well, at least not this year) and for the opportunity to write for O'Reilly in general. Without David's suggestions, comments, and general support, this would be a lesser book.

Finally, no book having to do with GNU/Linux would be complete without thanking Richard Stallman, Linus Torvalds, and the open source community in general. I'd also like to thank my coauthor, Brian Jones, for making this book better than it would have been without him.

Brian: For my wife, Natasha, who has supported and encouraged me in all of my ambitions and goals, and has dealt with my nonsense while in pursuit of said ambitions and goals. Also for my siblings: Heather, for forcing me to pursue computing as a career; Jessica, for being almost sickeningly positive and encouraging; Jon, for keeping me on my toes; and Russell, without whom I might've self-destructed long ago.

A hearty thanks goes to David Brickner, who offered me the opportunity to write for O'Reilly, and whose even keel, firm hand, and sheer diligence have made this a wonderful experience. I'd also like to thank all the folks at OSTG, TriLUG, and php|architect, for being friends of mine; Matt Appio, for making me take occasional fishing breaks; and my coworkers at Princeton, for teaching me far more than I could ever list here.

To Linus Torvalds and the rest of the open source community: thank you so much for all your work.

Preface

Both authors of this book have been system administrators for a while. When the opportunity to write this book came about, we initially focused on cool hacks we'd developed or used in our server and system administration careers. We also asked friends, who asked their friends, and we were therefore able to get some great contributions from others to augment the things that we'd come up with. Everybody has problems they like to solve. Bill likes distributed authentication, undeleting and recovering files, and tweaking filesystems in general. Brian likes making admin tasks more efficient, reliable, and repeatable; has a bucketload of cool scripts to do various tasks; and loves getting and using data from remote sources. And every sysadmin has favorite techniques for solving problems, so Hack is to Hacker as Cool Tip or Technique is to Server or System Administrator. Sysadmin hacks are essentially clever ways of approaching whatever problem you're trying to solve, whether it's figuring out how to recover lost data, trying to collect information from distributed clients in one place so that you can easily see the big picture or anything else that comes up.

As we worked on this book, thinking about cool server and sysadmin hacks mutated into thinking about general tips and tricks that we found useful to simplify our lives as system administrators. We also noticed that there weren't really any books available along the lines of "Things We Wish Previous System Administrators Had Told Us." Leaving aside obvious questions like "where is the key to the RAID array" and "what was the root password on *<insert hostname here>*," we decided to "hack the Hacks series" a bit and incorporate some general sysadmin information, tips, and tricks as another of this book's primary themes. This means that we provide a bit more background material than you ordinarily see in Hacks books. You're not going to hurt our feelings if you skip over things you already know, but we hope that all the material will be found useful by some of our readers. We could have used it years ago, and as Mr. Rogers used to say, "It's nice to share."

Sometimes, too much software and too many choices can be a problem. Should we use MTRG, Ethereal, EtherApe, or some other application to monitor network traffic? Should we create logical volumes using linear RAID, LVM, LVM2, or EVMS? Should we do our resumes in TeX, LaTeX, troff, lout, SGML, or XML? You get the idea. If you need to solve a problem but don't know what tool to select from among the myriad choices available, you can spend exponentially more time selecting the right software and ramping up than you do actually solving the problem. For that reason, a book on task-oriented solutions to common problems has been a lot of fun to write, and it should save you many an overnight Google session—as well as providing information that works together and is up to date at the time of writing. All the hacks in this book are techniques that we've used at various times and that we view as time- and hassle-savers that are usually downright fun and cool.

Aside from the "too much software" issue just mentioned, a related concept (and the deep, dark secret of open source) is that not all open source projects are "finished"—ever. (For God's sake, don't tell Microsoft!) Not only do you have many, many choices in the open source space, but the ones you find may do only 95% of what you want, missing on the truly critical 5%. Though there's a lot of really cool-looking, whizzy open source software out there, sometimes the zip gun that reliably fires one bullet using a rubber band is preferable to the chromed fusion-powered death ray that works only 75% of the time—thus books like this one, in which people explain how to accomplish things using packages they've actually used and often still depend on, even if the packages aren't perfect. The tools discussed in these hacks are generally good additions to anyone's toolbox/library of tips and tricks—and we'll show you how to use them for a variety of purposes.

Again, rather than just explaining how to do specific tasks, we've tried to provide a little background and context for our approach. This is a book of hacks, but you deserve a little bit of extra info to put the hacks, tools, and solutions in the right context. Where possible, we've also identified other packages and procedures that may accomplish the same goal, but we focus on our preferred solutions for different types of problems.

Why Linux Server Hacks, Volume Two?

The term *hacking* has a bad reputation in the press, where it used to refer to someone who breaks into systems or wreaks havoc, using computers as their weapon. Among people who write code, though, the term *hack* refers to a "quick-and-dirty" solution to a problem or a clever way to get something done. And the term *hacker* is taken very much as a compliment, referring to someone as being *creative*, having the technical chops to get things done. The Hacks series is an attempt to reclaim the word, document the good ways people are hacking, and pass the hacker ethic of creative participation on to the uninitiated. Seeing how others approach systems and problems is often the quickest way to learn about a new technology.

Linux Server Hacks, Volume Two came about because today's sysadmins need to deal with a vast number of situations, operating systems, software packages, and problems—and also because our original title, *Son of Linux Server Hacks*, was rejected. The original *Linux Server Hacks* is a great book—both authors owned it *before* starting this project—but there are many more hacks, cool tips, and ways of resolving problems that sysadmins face than can fit in a single volume (one that mere mortals can lift, that is). The power and flexibility of Linux means that there is an incredible amount of great Linux software out there, waiting to solve your sysadmin problems—if you know about it. Hence *Linux Server Hacks, Volume Two.* This book discusses some of our favorite software packages, how to use them to make your life as a sysadmin easier, how to best keep all the systems you're responsible for up and running smoothly, and how to keep your users happy (even if they may not know or appreciate just how wizardly you've been).

How to Use This Book

You can read this book from cover to cover if you like, but each hack stands on its own, so feel free to browse and jump to the different sections that interest you most. If there's a prerequisite you need to know about, a cross-reference will guide you to the right hack. We've also tried not to be shy or "our book"-centric—if there are other books on a topic that we particularly like or find valuable, we've put references to them at the end of the hack. Some of them are other books from O'Reilly, but we're not recommending them for any reason other than the fact that we've found them to be useful. We only recommend what we believe in.

How This Book Is Organized

This book is divided into 10 chapters, organized by subject:

Chapter 1, *Linux Authentication*
> Use the hacks in this chapter to explore the authentication options that are available to you in heterogeneous networked computing environments and simplify administering user accounts and passwords. This chapter also provides some quick and dirty tips for those unfortunate moments when, for one reason or another, you have to lock users out of specific systems quickly.

Chapter 2, *Remote GUI Connectivity*

This chapter explores ways of connecting to remote systems. When you just can't be everywhere at once, it's incredibly useful to be able to access multiple consoles and graphical displays from the convenience of your office or machine room. You'll find many of the hacks in this chapter to be handy tips that you may want to pass on to your users who also need to work on multiple systems, regardless of what operating systems they're running.

Chapter 3, *System Services*

Networks make it easy to set up servers on specific systems to address the needs of clients throughout your computing environment. The hacks in this chapter explain how to set up central servers that do things like synchronize the time on all the systems in your environment (via NTP), deliver IP addresses to newly connected hosts (using DHCP), and integrate these services with existing ones (with DHCP and name lookups done via DNS, for example). This chapter also discusses setting up centralized access to printers from both sides—how to set up your print servers, and how to access them from the various operating systems that your users may have running on their desktops.

Chapter 4, *Cool Sysadmin Tools and Tips*

This chapter presents a variety of cool sysadmin tips and techniques that we've accumulated over the years, including how to keep processes running without writing a daemon or staying logged in, how to use PXE to netboot Linux, how to share information with fellow sysadmins in a centralized fashion, how to get the most out of classic but incredibly useful terminal-oriented applications (such as *minicom*, *screen*, and *vi*), and so on. We also discuss how to quickly and easily create documentation for your sysadmin policies and procedures so that your successors can figure out how things work after Google hires you away from your current employer.

Chapter 5, *Storage Management and Backups*

If everything just kept running forever, storage was infinite, and users never executed the rm command with the wrong arguments, this chapter would be unnecessary. Welcome to Earth! Things don't actually work that way. However, the hacks in this chapter explore some cool ways of making it easier for you to manage storage, deploy new systems, do backups of today's huge disks, and even reduce the need for some of the restore requests that occasionally clog every sysadmin's inbox.

Chapter 6, *Standardizing, Sharing, and Synchronizing Resources*

Networked computing environments make it easy to store data on different machines or on centralized servers. This chapter provides some tips and tricks for managing distributed storage and making sure the administrative environments on your servers are synchronized.

Chapter 7, *Security*

Security is not just a job; it's an adventure with no end in sight. Crackers are always working on new ways to break into existing networks and machines, and you need to be able to either lock them out or at least understand what they've broken when they get in. The hacks in this chapter discuss a wide range of security tools and techniques that can help you sleep at night and protect your systems at the same time.

Chapter 8, *Troubleshooting and Performance*

This chapter provides techniques for optimizing system performance, whether by figuring out who's hogging the entire CPU and shooting down that user's nethack sessions or by using cool knobs in the */proc* filesystem to tweak system performance or using journaling filesystems to minimize system restart time. It also provides some useful X hacks, such as an easy way to use multiple monitors on a single system and a discussion of reducing desktop overhead by punting GNOME or KDE in favor of simpler X Window managers that eliminate CPU-intensive bells and whistles and actually just manage windows.

Chapter 9, *Logfiles and Monitoring*

Logfiles aren't just a diary for your system and its core applications; they are a useful record that you can use to spot emerging problems so you can correct them before they mature into catastrophes. This chapter includes hacks that enable you to centralize log information in a variety of ways, be warned when problems arise, and get the most out of system status information, whether it's log information, internal disk controller status data, or remote hardware status information that you can collect via SNMP. It also discusses tools for monitoring your network and spotting the BitTorrent user who's slowing down your CEO's web browsing.

Chapter 10, *System Rescue, Recovery, and Repair*

Sooner or later, some system that you're responsible for will go down. If you can't fix your problems by board-swapping, the hacks in this chapter will show you how to boot crippled systems so that you can diagnose problems, repair munged filesystems, and even (if you're lucky) recover deleted files or data that was stored on disks that have gone belly up. Try the tips and tricks in this chapter if you're having problems—there's always plenty of time to panic later.

Conventions Used in This Book

The following is a list of the typographical conventions used in this book:

Italics

> Used to indicate URLs, Unix utilities, filenames, filename extensions, and directory/folder names. For example, a path in the filesystem will appear as */Developer/Applications*.

`Constant width`

> Used to show code examples, the contents of files, and console output, as well as the names of variables, commands, and other code excerpts in the text.

`Constant width bold`

> Used to indicate user input, such as commands to be entered by the user, and to highlight portions of code (typically new additions to old code).

`Constant width italic`

> Used in code examples to show sample text to be replaced with your own values.

Gray type

> Used to indicate a cross-reference within the text.

You should pay special attention to notes set apart from the text with the following icons:

> This is a tip, suggestion, or general note. It contains useful supplementary information about the topic at hand.

> This is a warning or note of caution, often indicating that your money or your privacy might be at risk.

The thermometer icons, found next to each hack, indicate the relative complexity of the hack:

beginner   moderate   expert

Using Code Examples

This book is here to help you get your job done. In general, you may use the code in this book in your programs and documentation. You do not need to contact us for permission unless you're reproducing a significant portion of the code. For example, writing a program that uses several chunks of code from this book does not require permission. Selling or distributing a CD-ROM of examples from O'Reilly books *does* require permission. Answering a question by citing this book and quoting example code does not require permission. Incorporating a significant amount of example code from this book into your product's documentation *does* require permission.

We appreciate, but do not require, attribution. An attribution usually includes the title, author, publisher, and ISBN. For example: "*Linux Server Hacks, Volume Two* by Bill von Hagen and Brian K. Jones. © 2006 O'Reilly Media, Inc., 0-596-10082-5."

If you feel your use of code examples falls outside fair use or the permission given above, feel free to contact us at *permissions@oreilly.com*.

How to Contact Us

We have tested and verified the information in this book to the best of our ability, but you may find that features have changed (or even that we have made mistakes!). As a reader of this book, you can help us to improve future editions by sending us your feedback. Please let us know about any errors, inaccuracies, bugs, misleading or confusing statements, and typos that you find anywhere in this book.

Please also let us know what we can do to make this book more useful to you. We take your comments seriously and will try to incorporate reasonable suggestions into future editions. You can write to us at:

O'Reilly Media, Inc.
1005 Gravenstein Highway North
Sebastopol, CA 95472
(800) 998-9938 (in the U.S. or Canada)
(707) 829-0515 (international/local)
(707) 829-0104 (fax)

To ask technical questions or to comment on the book, send email to:

bookquestions@oreilly.com

The web site for *Linux Server Hacks, Volume Two* lists examples, errata, and plans for future editions. You can find it at:

http://www.oreilly.com/catalog/morelnxsvrhks/

For more information about this book and others, see the O'Reilly web site:

http://www.oreilly.com

Safari® Enabled

 When you see a Safari® Enabled icon on the cover of your favorite technology book, that means the book is available online through the O'Reilly Network Safari Bookshelf.

Safari offers a solution that's better than e-books. It's a virtual library that lets you easily search thousands of top tech books, cut and paste code samples, download chapters, and find quick answers when you need the most accurate, current information. Try it for free at *http://safari.oreilly.com*.

Got a Hack?

To explore Hacks books online or to contribute a hack for future titles, visit:

http://hacks.oreilly.com

## CHAPTER ONE

Linux Authentication

Hacks 1–9

Security is a primary concern of any sysadmin, especially in today's completely connected network environments. After locking down networks and systems to minimize the number of opportunities intruders have to access your machines (as discussed elsewhere in this book), providing secure mechanisms to enable users to log in on your machines is critical to their security. Let's face it—by design, anyone with physical or network access to a login prompt on one of your machines usually has a few chances to try to crack someone's login and password in order to gain access.

Many organizations try to secure logins simply by assigning passwords that look like line noise or TECO commands. Unfortunately, this strategy addresses only one aspect of authentication and has the nasty side effect of causing most people to write down their passwords, since only The Amazing Kreskin could remember them. So what are the alternatives? As explained in this chapter, flexible authentication mechanisms such as Pluggable Authentication Modules (PAMs) enable the login sequence to invoke multiple security checks, beyond just a password, to help minimize the chances of unauthorized logins. Similarly, networked authentication mechanisms can enhance login security by centralizing authentication checks on secure servers and can provide other organizational benefits, such as encrypted network communications and providing login information for different operating systems, not just your Linux machines. Networked authentication mechanisms inherently benefit sysadmins by providing one true location for creating and managing information about your users. Of course, you still have to convince your users not to use their birthdays, their license plate numbers, or the names of their significant others as passwords—but we can't really help you there.

The hacks in this chapter discuss various ways of dealing with the whole spectrum of user authentication issues, ranging from ways that a sysadmin can use to quickly disable all logins or specific accounts, through some cool tweaks you can do to your local password file, to networked mechanisms you can use for centralized authentication of different types of systems. Providing secure authentication mechanisms for your systems doesn't have to be a nightmare—let the hacks in this chapter teach you a few tricks and choose the authentication mechanism that's right for the computing environment for which you're responsible.

HACK #1 Disable User Accounts Instantly

In a crisis, here's how to quickly disable a user account, using only a text editor.

Sooner or later every system administrator gets the call to disable a user's account. Regardless of whether this is due to termination or for general security reasons, you have to move quickly to satisfy the Human Resources department or layer of management that's on the other end of the line. If you're used to graphical tools for user management, this can take a little while, but luckily there's a quick and easy solution to this request that just involves a text editor.

Disabling Accounts on Systems That Use Local Authentication

On older Unix systems passwords were stored in the */etc/password* file, but they were moved to the */etc/shadow* file (which is readable only by the root user) on more recent systems to prevent non-root users from having access to the encrypted form of a user's password, for security reasons. Most Linux systems that use local authentication store passwords in the */etc/shadow* file, though some still use */etc/passwd* as an artifact or for compliance with aging applications. If the second colon-separated field in each entry in */etc/passwd* contains an x, your system is using the */etc/shadow* file to hold password information. If you see other characters between the first and second colons, your system is still storing its password information in the */etc/passwd* file.

To quickly disable accounts on a Linux file server or on a user's desktop machine, bring up */etc/shadow* in a text editor and insert an asterisk (*) as the first character in the second field of the file (after the first colon), which is where the password is stored. This prevents subsequent logins but leaves the existing password intact. If circumstances reverse themselves and you're asked to re-enable the user's account, you can simply remove the asterisk to re-enable logins with the existing password. This is similar to the approach taken by the usermod -L *user* command, which inserts an exclamation mark (!) at the beginning of a user's password entry to lock out that user. Actually, if your system provides the usermod command, you can just as easily use this command to disable an account, as long as */usr/sbin* is in your PATH—it's good to know how the command really works, though.

You never want to remove a user's data until it has been safely backed up, so userdel -r *user* is the wrong command to use when you simply need to lock out a user. Removing an existing user account with the userdel command also often leaves you open to reusing the old user ID (UID) the next time you create an account, which should be against IT policy for security and privacy reasons.

Reusing UIDs is a bad idea because if a new account is created with a UID that previously existed on your system, the new user will own any files still on the system that were owned by the previous user. This most commonly occurs with email stored in system directories outside the user's home directory, but such files can exist anywhere the previous user had write privileges. This can also cause a problem if files or directories owned by the previous user are restored from backups for some reason. Adopting a policy of not reusing UIDs prevents users from "accidentally" getting rights to files to which they shouldn't really have access.

> When disabling a user's account, don't forget to change or disable the login passwords for other accounts that the user may know.

Disabling Accounts on Systems That Use Distributed Authentication

If your site uses a distributed authentication mechanism such as LDAP (the Lightweight Directory Access protocol) or NIS (the Network Information Service, originally designed by Sun Microsystems for use with the Network File System), quickly disabling an account is slightly more difficult, but it's even more important that you be able to do so. If you are using distributed authentication, until the account is disabled, a user has access to all the machines at your site that share this authentication mechanism.

Systems that use NIS for authentication rely on centralized password and shadow files that are distributed to NIS clients by an NIS server. Many NIS systems store password information directly in the NIS password file (*/var/yp/ypetc/passwd*), because using NIS to share shadow password files (*/var/yp/ypetc/shadow*) largely defeats the security implied by the shadow file. On systems using local authentication, only the root user can read the */etc/shadow* file—but on NIS systems, any user who can listen to the NIS server can see the shadow file.

To quickly disable a user's account on systems that use NIS, you can directly edit the NIS master of the password or shadow file in exactly the same way that you edited the local copy in the previous section of this hack, putting an asterisk in front of the password entry for the specified user. The

NIS masters of these files are stored in the directory */var/yp/ypetc* on your NIS server. If the second colon-separated field in each entry in */var/yp/ypetc/passwd* contains an x, your system is using the */var/yp/ypetc/shadow* file to store password information. If you see other characters between the first and second colons, your system is still storing password information in */var/yp/ypetc/passwd*.

Once you've modified the */var/yp/ypetc/passwd* or */var/yp/ypetc/shadow* file, you must push it to all NIS clients by changing directory to the */var/yp* directory and using the make command:

```
# cd /var/yp;make
```

You can, of course, always change an NIS user's password by executing the yppasswd *user* command, but if you need to re-enable the account you will have to work with the user to reset the password.

LDAP is a much more powerful distributed technology than NIS, because it provides a central source from which many different applications can retrieve many different types of information. As discussed in "Centralize Logins with LDAP" [Hack #6], LDAP information directories, also known as *databases*, provide a great solution for a central, enterprise-wide source for login, password, and other per-user account information. However, because sites that use LDAP for authentication do not use the standard password or shadow files to hold password information, you can only disable LDAP accounts by changing the information in the LDAP database. You can disable a user account either by changing information about a specific account record (known as "attributes") in the database, by changing the access control list (ACL) on the information about the account so that the user no longer has access to it, or by directly changing the user's password in the database.

Unless you are completely familiar with the schemas used in your LDAP database, disabling an account by changing its password is the fastest and easiest method. This doesn't require that you remember every characteristic of your LDAP user/account scheme, and it can be done using the ldappasswd command. To change a user's password when you are using LDAP authentication, become the root user, run this command, and supply a new password when prompted to do so:

```
# ldappasswd -1 user
```

Edit Your Password File for Greater Access Control

With just a few one-line text file edits, you can control who can access your servers.

I can't cite statistics, but my experience in lending a hand to friends and clients has led me to the conclusion that most sites have an "all or nothing" approach to creating and managing user accounts on their machines. If the site uses NIS, their *nsswitch.conf* file says to use NIS for user account information. If the site uses LDAP, they use LDAP for user account information. The problem here is that this implies that every single account in the directory is actually a valid account on any machine, whether those users belong there or not.

Of course, there are firewalls, router ACLs, and all manner of security appliances and software between servers and users who shouldn't have access to them—but data centers are run by humans, and humans make mistakes, especially in large, complex networks. Mistype the VLAN tag on a switch port, for example, and all of a sudden anyone from Engineering can SSH to your production application server. This hack shows you how a few simple text edits will allow you to limit which users in an NIS directory can access the local machine.

The entries in the */etc/nsswitch.conf* file on a Linux system determine how it resolves requests for information about users, groups, and other host information. Let's concentrate on just the passwd line. If you're using NIS, it might look something like this:

```
passwd     files nis
```

This means that when the system is trying to find information about a user account, such as the user's login shell or what name a numeric UID maps to, it'll first look in */etc/passwd*, and then fall back on NIS. If a user is listed in either of these resources, it's a valid account and (barring any other protections) the operation succeeds.

But suppose you want only a handful of people to have valid accounts on the machines, instead of everyone in the entire NIS domain. We can do that! As an example, let's add two lines to the bottom of the */etc/passwd* file:

```
+@admins
+jonesy
```

The first line makes all the users in the *admins* netgroup valid accounts on this machine. The second line makes *jonesy* a valid account on this machine. All other accounts will be invalid when we complete the configuration. The only thing left for us to do is to edit the */etc/nsswitch.conf* file to make it look something like this:

```
passwd: compat
passwd_compat: nis
```

The first line says to call the *nss_compat* module, and the second line tells the *nss_compat* module to use NIS for the lookup (other valid values here are `nisplus` or `ldap`). Now, to test, run the following command:

```
$ getent passwd jonesy
```

This will consult the */etc/nsswitch.conf* file to figure out where to get the information. When it sees `compat`, it will go to the */etc/passwd* file to see if *jonesy* is listed there. If the account is not listed, it will not display any output. If it is listed, it will query the NIS server and retrieve the account record, which will look something like this:

```
jonesy:x:1001:100:Brian Jones:/home/jonesy:/bin/bash
```

In addition, running `getent passwd` without arguments will return records for every valid account on the system, which in our example will include all of the users in the *admins* netgroup, the *jonesy* account, and (of course) all of the system accounts that were in the */etc/passwd* file before we ever touched it.

It's often desirable to be able to access user information for accounts that are not valid on the machine, though—and in other circumstances, accounts that should be valid on a particular machine shouldn't actually be able to log into that machine. For example, I don't want users logging onto my mail server, but my mail server needs to be able to map inbound mail to account names in order to accept mail. In cases such as these, you can add this line at the bottom of your */etc/passwd* file:

```
+:::::::/sbin/nologin
```

Now, running the `getent passwd` command will show you all the system accounts, then the accounts you added earlier, and then every other account. It will show full records for all accounts, but the login shell for the accounts at the end will be */sbin/nologin*, which will keep those users from logging into the machine and getting a shell. Note that this line needs to be the last line in the password file, since lines are read and resolved in order. If the line above came before the +jonesy line, for example, it would find a record for me with the */sbin/nologin* shell first, and I would not be able to log onto the machine, even though the +jonesy line appears later in the file.

Note that in addition to using the + sign to add valid users, you can use the – sign to exclude users. If you want all but a handful of accounts to be valid, it's easy to do. For example, if you wanted all accounts to be valid login accounts except for those accounts in the *badguys* netgroup, you could add a line like this to the */etc/passwd* file:

```
-@badguys
```

Those accounts would no longer be able to log in on the machine in question.

Deny All Access in One Second or Less

HACK #3

Here's a safe way to keep out all users while doing temporary maintenance or troubleshooting.

All administrators eventually need to have a machine running in full multi-user mode, with all services running, but at the same time completely deny login access to the machine. This is usually for the purpose of troubleshooting a problem, testing a new software installation, or performing maintenance or software upgrades. There are a couple of really quick ways to do this.

The first method is by far the quickest. Just run the following command (as root):

```
# touch /etc/nologin
```

This will deny access to anyone trying to log in to the machine. You'll want to be sure to keep an active login session on the machine after you create this file or make sure that root is allowed to log in on the local console or via SSH, since a root login will bypass this mechanism. You'll know it's working because the logs for some services will tell you that access was denied because of the presence of the *nologin* file. Others will just say "failed password."

This method can be improved through the use of a *nologin.txt* file, where you can put some text that users will see when they try to log in. If you have a scheduled downtime, for instance, you can put the details into this file so that users will get a friendly reminder that the machine is unavailable during the downtime window.

The second method works only if the services you're running are linked against *libwrap*, in which case you can very quickly cut off all access to the machine. To check that a service is linked against *libwrap*, use the ldd command on the binary for the service. For example, to make sure my SSH service is linked against *libwrap*, I've done the following:

```
# ldd /usr/sbin/sshd
        linux-gate.so.1 =>  (0x004ab000)
        libwrap.so.0 => /usr/lib/libwrap.so.0 (0x0072f000)
...(lots deleted)
```

The above output shows all the libraries *sshd* is linked against, and the path to the library file being used. Clearly, *libwrap* is linked here. Once you've confirmed that this is the case for the other services you're running, you're ready for the next step.

Create a file called */etc/hosts.deny.ALL*, which should consist of only one line:

```
##### /etc/hosts.deny.ALL
ALL:ALL@ALL
```

Now, whenever you need to shut down access to the machine, you simply move your */etc/hosts.allow* and *hosts.deny* files out of the way and move your *hosts.deny.ALL* file into place. Here's a command line that'll handle it nicely:

```
# cd /etc; mv hosts.allow hosts.allow.bak; mv hosts.deny hosts.deny.bak
# mv hosts.deny.ALL hosts.deny
```

Now you're left with only a single *hosts.deny* file, which denies access to everything. Note that it would not help you to just move both files out of the way, because *tcpwrappers* treats the absence of a file just like an empty file. If there are no files, *tcpwrappers* acts as though you have two files that have not addressed access controls for a given service, and by default it will grant access to the service!

See Also

- "Allow or Deny Access by IP Address" [Hack #64]

HACK #4   Customize Authentication with PAMs

Modern Linux systems use Pluggable Authentication Modules (PAMs) to provide flexible authentication for services and applications. Here are the gory details you'll need in order to use PAMs to quickly and flexibly secure your systems.

Many Linux applications require authentication of one type or another. In days gone by, each authentication-aware application was compiled with hardwired information about the authentication mechanism used by the system on which it was running. Changing or enhancing a system's authentication mechanism therefore required all such applications to be updated and recompiled, which is tedious even when you have the source code for all of the relevant applications on your system.

Enter PAMs, which provide a flexible and dynamic mechanism for authenticating any application or service that uses them. Applications or services compiled with the *Linux-PAM* library use text-format configuration files to identify their authentication requirements. Using PAMs on your system lets you modify authentication requirements or integrate new authentication mechanisms by simply adding entries to the PAM configuration file that is used by a specific application or service.

Though the information contained here may seem like overkill at first glance, knowing about PAMs and how PAM configuration files work is necessary background for the next four hacks, which explain how to integrate specific types of modern authentication into your Linux system without rewriting or recompiling the wheel. Read on, sysadmins!

PAM Overview

PAMs are shared library modules that are automatically loaded by applications that were compiled with the primary *Linux-PAM* authentication library. Applications that use PAMs (or PAM modules, are they're sometimes called) are typically referred to as *PAM-aware applications*.

PAMs satisfy different parts of the authentication requirements for PAM-aware applications, much like reusable code and libraries do for applications in general. For example, a PAM-aware version of the *login* program can invoke a variety of PAMs that check things such as whether the user logging in as root is on a terminal listed as a secure terminal, whether users are allowed to log in on the system at the moment, and other similar authentication requirements. Because PAMs are shared library modules, a PAM-aware version of the *rsh* program can reuse the same "are users allowed to log in on the system now?" PAM as the PAM-aware version of *login*, but then apply other rules that are more relevant to *rsh* than to *login*. PAM modules themselves are now typically stored in the directory */lib/security*, though some older Linux distributions stored PAMs in */usr/lib/security*.

The PAMs used by different PAM-aware applications are defined in one of two ways. In modern PAM implementations, they are controlled by application-specific configuration files found in the directory */etc/pam.d*. In older PAM implementations, all PAM modules used by the applications on a system were defined in a single central configuration file, */etc/pam.conf*. The older approach is still supported, but it's deprecated—to maintain backward compatibility while encouraging the modern approach, the contents of the directory */etc/pam.d* are used instead of the */etc/pam.conf* file if both exist on your system. This hack focuses on PAM configuration files in */etc/pam.d*, since that's the way PAMs are used on most modern systems.

Per-Application/Service PAM Configuration Files

Each PAM configuration file in */etc/pam.d* has the same name as the PAM-aware application or service it is associated with and contains the PAM rules used during its authentication process. The name of the configuration file to use is derived from the first parameter passed to the *Linux-PAM* library's pam_start( ) function, which is the name of the service that is being authenticated (often the same as the name of the application, for convenience's sake). These files can also contain comments—any characters on a line that follow the traditional hash mark (#) are interpreted as a comment.

Each non-comment line in one of the files in */etc/pam.d* defines how a single PAM module is used as part of the authentication process for the associated application or service. Each of these files can contain four fields separated by whitespace, the first three of which are mandatory. These fields have the following meaning and content:

module-type

The type of PAM module defined on the line. A PAM module's type defines how it is used during the authentication process. Valid values are:

auth

Identifies an authentication check to verify the user's identity or that system requirements have been met. Common system requirements are that a service can be started at the current time (for example, that */etc/nologin* does not exist when a user is trying to log in), that an acceptable device is being used (i.e., the device is listed in */etc/securetty*), whether the user is already the root user, and so on.

account

Verifies whether the user can authenticate based on system requirements such as whether the user has a valid account, the maximum number of users on the system, the device being used to access the system, whether the user has access to the requested application or service, and so on.

password

Verifies a user's ability to update authentication mechanisms. There is usually one module of type password for each auth entry that is tied to an authentication mechanism that can be updated.

session

Identifies modules associated with tasks that must be done before the associated service or application is activated, or just before the termination of that service or application. Modules of this type typically perform system functions such as mounting directories, logging audit trail information, or guaranteeing that system resources are available.

control-flag

The implications of the return value from the specified PAM module. Valid values are:

required

Indicates that success of the PAM module is mandatory for the specified module type. The failure of any PAM marked as required for a specific module-type (such as all labeled as auth) is reported to the associated application or service only after all required PAMs for that module type have been executed.

requisite
> Indicates that failure of the PAM module will immediately be reported to the associated application or service.

sufficient
> Indicates that success of the PAM module satisfies the authentication requirements of this module type. If no previous required PAM has failed, no other PAMs for the associated module type are executed. Failure of a PAM identified as sufficient is ignored as long as subsequent required modules for that module type return success. If a previous required PAM has failed, the success of a PAM marked as sufficient is ignored.

optional
> Indicates that success of the PAM module is not critical to the application or service unless it is the only PAM for a specified module type. If it is, its success or failure determines the success or failure of the specified module type.

module-path
> The name of the PAM module associated with this entry. By default, PAM modules are located in /lib/security, but this field can also identify modules located in other directories by specifying the absolute path and filename of a PAM module.

arguments
> Optional, module-specific arguments.

Well, that was mind-numbing but necessary reference information. To see all this in action, let's look at an example.

PAMs Used by the login Process

The configuration file for the PAMs used by the *login* program is the file */etc/pam.d/login*. On a Red Hat system of recent vintage, this file contains the following entries:

```
#%PAM-1.0
auth       required     pam_securetty.so
auth       required     pam_stack.so service=system-auth
auth       required     pam_nologin.so
account    required     pam_stack.so service=system-auth
password   required     pam_stack.so service=system-auth
session    required     pam_stack.so service=system-auth
session    optional     pam_console.so
```

The first line is a comment that identifies this PAM as conforming to the PAM 1.0 specification.

The second, third, and fourth lines define the auth (authentication) requirements for system logins, all of which must succeed because they are identified as required. The second line invokes the PAM module *pam_securetty.so* to check whether the user is logged in on a secure terminal, as defined in the file */etc/securetty*. The third line invokes the *pam_stack.so* PAM module, a clever module used primarily on Red Hat–inspired systems that enables you to call the entire set of PAM requirements defined for a different service or application (and thus described in a separate file by that name in */etc/pam.d*). In this case it calls the set (stack) of requirements defined for the *system-auth* service. We'll look at that later—for now, it's sufficient to know that the authentication requirements specified in that file must be satisfied. Finally, to wrap up the auth module-type entries for the *login* program, the fourth line invokes the *pam_nologin.so* PAM module to check whether logins are allowed on the system at the current time.

The fifth line in this file identifies the requirements for the account module-type, which in this case uses the *pam_stack.so* PAM module to verify that the set of requirements for the *system-auth* service have been satisfied.

Similarly, the sixth line in this file identifies the requirements for the password module-type, which also uses the *pam_stack.so* PAM module to verify that the set of requirements for the *system-auth* service have been satisfied.

Finally, the seventh and eighth lines in this file identify session requirements for the *login* program. The seventh line uses the familiar *pam_stack.so* PAM module to verify that the set of requirements for the *system-auth* service were satisfied. The eighth line in this file defines an optional requirement that the user be running on the console. If this module succeeds, the user is granted any additional privileges associated with this PAM module. If this module fails, authentication succeeds as long as the previous required modules have completed successfully, but the user doesn't get the bonus privileges.

Now let's look at the */etc/pam.d/system-auth* file on the same system, which contains the following:

```
#%PAM-1.0
# This file is auto-generated.
# User changes will be destroyed the next time authconfig is run.
auth       required     /lib/security/pam_env.so
auth       sufficient   /lib/security/pam_unix.so likeauth nullok
auth       required     /lib/security/pam_deny.so
account    required     /lib/security/pam_unix.so
password   required     /lib/security/pam_cracklib.so retry=3 type=
password   sufficient   /lib/security/pam_unix.so nullok use_authtok md5
                        shadow
password   required     /lib/security/pam_deny.so
session    required     /lib/security/pam_limits.so
session    required     /lib/security/pam_unix.so
```

Now that you grok PAM configuration files, you can see that the auth module-type first requires that the *pam_env.so* module succeed, then tries the *pam_unix.so* module, which is a generic module that can perform auth, account, password, and session functions (depending on how it is called). When called for the auth module-type, it verifies a user's identity, sets credentials if successful, and so on. If this module succeeds, the following required entry for the *pam_deny.so* module isn't executed. If the *pam_unix.so* module fails, *pam_deny.so* executes, which returns a failure code to ensure that the specified module-type will fail. In our *login* example, where another auth request (for *pam_nologin.so*) follows the invocation of the contents of the *system-auth* PAM stack, that auth request is executed, but its value isn't important because *pam_deny.so* is required and has already indicated failure.

Next, the account module-type requires that the *pam_unix.so* module succeed—in this case, *pam_unix.so* provides default account checks.

Following the account check, the first password module-type line specifies that *pam_cracklib.so* be used when setting passwords to select a password that isn't easily cracked, based on the contents of a database of easily cracked passwords (*/usr/lib/cracklib_dict.pwd* on Red Hat systems). Arguments to this module give the user three chances to select a password (by passing the argument retry=3) and specify that this password isn't for any specific type of authentication, such as LDAP or NIS (by passing a null name using the type= argument). If this module succeeds, the second password module-type line invokes the standard *pam_unix.so* module, with arguments specifying that null passwords are acceptable but can't be set by users (nullok), not to prompt for a password but to use any password that succeeded in a previous PAM of module-type password (use_authtok), that passwords use md5 hashing by default (md5), and that the system uses the */etc/shadow* file to hold passwords (shadow). If this module fails, the user is denied access to the application or service that invoked the *system-auth* service through the next line, which invokes the *pam_deny.so* module to ensure failure of the password auth-type.

Finally, the session checks set system limits using the *pam_limits.so* module, which provides functions to initiate and terminate sessions.

If you need to take a few aspirin after parsing each entry in these files, join the club. But even though it's a pain, security is one of any sysadmin's most important responsibilities. If it's any consolation, think how complex the code to implement all of this would have been without the flexibility that PAMs provide!

Configuration and More Configuration

The text-format files in */etc/pam.d* control the PAMs associated with each authentication-aware application or service. Some of these PAMs themselves use optional configuration files to further refine their behavior. The configuration files for individual PAMs are located in the directory */etc/security*. Though these files must exist, they do not need to contain any useful information—they are there in case you want to take advantage of the advanced configuration options that they provide. Here is a list of the files in this directory that are found on a variety of Linux systems:

access.conf
> Provides fine-grained access control for logins. Used by the *pam_access.so* module.

console.apps
> A directory that contains a file for each privileged application that a user can use from the console. The name of each file is the same as the basename of the application with which it is associated. These files must exist but can be empty. When they have contents, these files typically contain environment variables associated with the applications that match their names. Used by the *pam_console.so* module on Red Hat–inspired Linux systems.

console.perms
> Defines the device permissions granted to privileged users when logged in on the console, and the permissions to which those devices revert when the user logs out. Used by the *pam_console.so* module on Red Hat–inspired Linux systems.

group.conf
> Provides per-session group membership control. Used by the *pam_group.so* module.

limits.conf
> Provides a per-user mechanism for setting system resource limits. Used by the *pam_limits.so* module.

pam_env.conf
> Provides a mechanism for setting environment variables to specific values. Used by the *pam_env.so* module.

pam_pwcheck.conf
> Provides options for identifying the mechanism used when evaluating password strength. Used by the *pam_pwcheck.so* module on SUSE-inspired Linux systems.

pam_unix2.conf
> Provides options for advanced configuration of traditional password checking. Used by the *pam_unix2.so* module on SUSE-inspired systems.

time.conf
> Provides a mechanism for imposing general or user-specific time restrictions for system services and applications. Used by the *pam_time.so* module.

What if PAM Configuration Files Are Missing?

Applications that use PAMs are very powerful, and correct configuration is very important. However, the *Linux-PAM* library does provide a default configuration file for any applications and services that do not have their own configuration files. This is the file */etc/pam.d/other*. Since a missing configuration file generally indicates a misconfigured system (or that someone has imported a PAM-aware binary without thinking things through), the */etc/pam.d/other* file implements extremely paranoid security, as in the following example:

```
#%PAM-1.0
auth       required      pam_deny.so
account    required      pam_deny.so
password   required      pam_deny.so
session    required      pam_deny.so
```

In this example, any request for any module-type that falls through to this PAM configuration file will return a failure code. A slightly more useful version of this file is the following:

```
#%PAM-1.0
auth       required   pam_deny.so
auth       required   pam_warn.so
account    required   pam_deny.so
account    required   pam_warn.so
password   required   pam_deny.so
password   required   pam_warn.so
session    required   pam_deny.so
session    required   pam_warn.so
```

Because subsequent required entries for a given module-type are still executed, each module-type entry first executes the *pam_deny.so* PAM, which denies access to the requested service, and then also executes the *pam_warn.so* PAM, which logs a warning message to the system log.

See Also

- man *pam* (where *pam* is the name of a PAM module without the .*so* extension)
- *http://www.ymbnet.lkams.kernel.org/pub/linux/libs/pam/*

HACK #5 Authenticate Linux Users with a Windows Domain Controller

To a busy sysadmin, centralization is usually more important than philosophy.

Much has been made in the Linux press about using Samba to bridge the gap between Linux/Unix and SMB/CIFS environments. Samba is not just one of the most impressive pieces of open source software ever—it's also as impressive a job of reverse engineering as "Hacking the Xbox."

However, using Samba for authentication is often more of a philosophical point than an organizational need. Frankly, if you already have a huge, well-designed, functional Windows environment that supports authentication, groups, ACLs, and Exchange (to name a few "popular" Windows services), converting all that to Linux can be more work than it's worth. If you're just starting to integrate Linux boxes into your user desktops in a coherent fashion, why not swim against the standard Linux tide and configure the login mechanisms on your Linux boxes to use the authentication provided by your existing Windows domain controllers? You can always convert them later, when your yearly ransom demand from Microsoft arrives.

Software Requirements

To integrate Windows domain and Linux authentication, you'll need to have the *PAM*, *samba-winbind*, and *smb-client* packages installed on your system. The core pieces of software that you'll need are the daemon that enables you to communicate with a Windows domain controller, known as the *winbindd* daemon (usually installed as */usr/sbin/winbindd*), a correctly configured */etc/samba/smb.conf* file (used by the *winbind* daemon to obtain information about your domain and domain controller), and the PAM for domain authentication through this daemon (*/lib/security/pam_winbind.so*). The *winbindd* daemon and the *pam-winbind.so* module are both provided in the *samba-winbind* package, though to use the PAM you must have the *PAM* package installed and working on your system. The current versions of these packages at the time this book was written were *pam-0.78-8*, *samba-winbind-3.0.13-1.1*, and *samba-client-3.0.13-1.1*.

Of course, if your environment has enough Windows dependencies to make you want to authenticate your Linux boxes using Windows, you're probably already using Samba to access your Windows shares from your Linux system or your Linux filesystems from your Windows systems. Nowadays, most Linux systems come with Samba installed. To get complete support for Windows domain authentication, you'll want to make sure your system is running Samba 3.x or better. If you're using a package manager, you can run the command `rpm -q` *packagename* to find out which version of each of these is installed on your system.

If you're missing any of the packages that you need or want, you can either consult your favorite package repository (RPMBone and RPMFind.net come to mind) to find a prebuilt package for your system, or download the complete Samba source code from *http://www.samba.org* and build the whole thing yourself. It's quite easy.

Critical Samba Configuration for Using Windows Authentication

As mentioned in the previous section, the *winbindd* daemon obtains the information that it needs to communication with your primary domain controller from the standard Samba configuration file (usually */etc/samba/smb.conf*, unless you installed Samba elsewhere). The following are the critical entries used by the *winbindd* daemon, all from the [global] section of the Samba configuration file:

workgroup
> The name of the Windows domain to which you want the Linux system to authenticate.

winbind uid
> A range of integer user IDs (UIDs) for the users that you want to be able to authenticate using Windows authentication. An example range is 1000–9999, which is the typical range of UIDs for non-system Linux user accounts nowadays.

winbind gid
> A range of integer group IDs (GIDs) for the groups you want to be able to authenticate using Windows authentication. An example range is 100–999, which is the typical range of GIDs for non-systems Linux groups nowadays.

security
> The type of security you want your system to use. When using Windows domain authentication, this should always be set to domain.

username map
> The name of a file that contains mappings between Windows usernames and Linux usernames. This is typically the file */etc/samba/ smbusers*. In general, if you're going to be authenticating Linux users against a domain controller running on Windows, it's easiest to simply use the same login names on your Windows and Linux systems (even though *bill.vonhagen* is uglier and requires more typing than more traditional logins such as *wvh*).

obey pam restrictions

If you are using the Linux PAM mechanism to authenticate your Linux users, this should always be set to yes to force Samba to use all of the bells and whistles of PAM authentication.

Updating /etc/nsswitch.conf

To cause your system to consult the *winbindd* daemon for password and group authentication, you will also have to modify your system's name service switch to integrate Windows domain authentication. To do this, modify your */etc/nsswitch.conf* file to specify that the system obtains password and group information from the Windows domain controller. Correct entries would be the following:

```
passwd: files winbind
group:  files winbind
```

This tells the name service switch to first check the local password and group files on the client system for authentication information and then check the *winbindd* daemon. This enables you to create local accounts when necessary, giving these local accounts priority while still using Windows domain authentication for most accounts.

Integrating the pam_winbind.so PAM into System Authentication

Unless you're using a Linux distribution such as Red Hat, which provides a graphical tool for configuring system authentication (*system-config-auth*, shown in Figure 1-1), you'll need to manually modify the PAM configuration files for services that will authenticate using your Windows domain controller. At a minimum, this is the login configuration file (*/etc/pam.d/ login*), and probably also the PAM configuration file for SSH logins (*/etc/ pam.d/sshd*).

Here's a sample PAM configuration file that uses Windows authentication to enable logins:

```
#%PAM-1.0
auth       sufficient /lib/security/pam_winbind.so
auth       required    /lib/security/pam_securetty.so
auth       required    /lib/security/pam_stack.so service=system-auth debug
                       use_first_pass
auth       required    /lib/security/pam_nologin.so
account    required    /lib/security/pam_stack.so service=system-auth
password   required    /lib/security/pam_stack.so service=system-auth
session    required    /lib/security/pam_stack.so service=system-auth
session    optional    /lib/security/pam_console.so
```

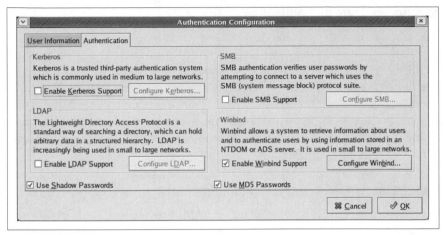

Figure 1-1. Red Hat's graphical application for configuring Windows authentication

Note that this PAM configuration file accepts Windows authentication as being sufficient to enable a login, but then falls through to the standard Linux authentication sequence if this fails. This enables you to use a mixture of central authentication (through the Windows domain controller) and local authentication (using the traditional Linux/Unix password and group files).

Starting the winbindd Daemon

One of the last steps in integrating Linux systems with Windows authentication is to make sure the *winbindd* daemon starts automatically whenever you boot your system. To do this, make sure a symbolic link to the */etc/init.d/winbind* startup script exists for your system's default runlevel. To start the *winbindd* daemon manually (i.e., the first time), you can simply run this script with the start argument, as in:

```
# /etc/init.d/winbind start
```

Joining the Domain

The final step is to actually join the domain from your Linux system. You can do this using the net command, which is part of the Samba suite and is found in the *samba-client* package mentioned earlier in this hack:

```
$ net join member -U Administrator
```

You'll be prompted for the *Administrator* password for the target domain. You do not have to join as the user *Administrator*—any user with sufficient privileges to join the domain will do.

Testing Windows Authentication

You should always test any fundamental change to your system's core authentication sequence before logging out of your system. The easiest way to do this is to enable a service that requires login authentication and then use this to log in via a network connection to your system while you are still actually logged in on the machine. My favorite service for this is the *telnet* service, but *ssh* is just as easy (though you will have to modify the */etc/pam. d/sshd* PAM configuration file in order to test *ssh* authentication via your Windows domain controller).

Debugging Windows Authentication Problems

Both Samba and the *pam_winbind.so* PAM provide excellent debugging options. To put the *winbindd* daemon in debug mode, log in as root using a local account, add the debug keyword to the pam_winbind entry in the PAM service configuration file that you are using for debugging, and restart the *winbindd* daemon manually with the -d *debug-level* option, which displays tons of useful information. I prefer to use debug level 5, which shows each byte in every packet exchanged by the *winbind* daemon and the domain controller that it is talking to. If this doesn't provide you with enough information to identify and resolve your problem and you suspect Samba misconfiguration, you can increase the logging level in the Samba configuration file (*/etc/samba/smb.conf*) by adding the log level winbind:*NN* command and restarting Samba. This enables you to specify the logging level for Samba activities related to *winbind* authentication. If you are using an older version of Samba or want coarser logging, you can remove the *winbind* restriction and simply increase the general Samba logging level by using the command log level *NN* in your Samba configuration file and restarting Samba. A log level of 5 is sufficient for most debugging. (Remember to disable logging when you've resolved your authentication problems, as this creates a huge logfile and has a negative impact on Samba performance.)

Another useful command when analyzing or debugging problems with using Windows domain authentication to authenticate Linux users is the wbinfo command. You can use this command to make sure you're actually talking to the domain controller and to query the domain controller for various types of information. The following output example shows both the options available to the wbinfo command and a sample command that retrieves the names of known users from the domain controller:

```
$ wbinfo
Usage: wbinfo -ug | -n name | -sSY sid | -UG uid/gid | -tm | -[aA]
user%password
Version: 2.2.7-security-rollup-fix
```

```
        -u                      lists all domain users
        -g                      lists all domain groups
        -n name                 converts name to sid
        -s sid                  converts sid to name
        -N name                 converts NetBIOS name to IP (WINS)
        -I IP                   converts IP address to NetBIOS name (WINS)
        -U uid                  converts uid to sid
        -G gid                  converts gid to sid
        -S sid                  converts sid to uid
        -Y sid                  converts sid to gid
        -t                      check shared secret
        -m                      list trusted domains
        -r user                 get user groups
        -a user%password        authenticate user
        -A user%password        store user and password used by winbindd (root only)
        -p                      'ping' winbindd to see if it is alive
        --sequence              show sequence numbers of all domains
        --set-auth-user DOMAIN\user%password    set password for restrict
anonymous
$ wbinfo -u
_Template
Administrator
bill.vonhagen
build
[additional output deleted]
```

See Also

- *http://rpm.pbone.net*
- *http://www.rpmfind.com*
- "Customize Authentication with PAMs" [Hack #4]
- "Centralize Logins with LDAP" [Hack #6]

H A C K   Centralize Logins with LDAP
#6
Creating individual accounts on individual machines is a thing of the past:
centralize authentication information and more by using a directory server.

The Lightweight Directory Access Protocol (LDAP) provides a hierarchical collection of information that can be accessed over a network. LDAP is an example of a directory service. In this context, the term *directory* refers to a central information resource (such as a telephone directory or network-accessible address book) but also leverages the idea of hierarchical directory structures. LDAP directories are essentially simple, hierarchical databases that are accessed using keys that identify the portions of the directory hierarchy to traverse to locate a specific unit of information.

The core idea of hierarchical elements and attributes is easy to understand and work with, and it should be familiar to users of similar information models, such as XML. The LDAP protocol is also independent of the underlying storage model used, making it easy to map LDAP data into existing databases or migrate to new, smaller database models.

Like all directory services, LDAP is a client/server technology. Clients can either query or upload information to an LDAP server. In the case of a query, the LDAP server either responds directly or forwards the query to another LDAP server, which repeats the "respond or forward" process. The OpenLDAP project (*http://www.openldap.org*), where most Linux LDAP development now takes place, is the source of the software discussed in this hack.

Installing LDAP Clients and Servers

Using LDAP in your environment requires that you have a few basic packages installed on your systems, or that you build and install the OpenLDAP software from scratch. If you need to build it yourself, you can download the latest version of the full OpenLDAP package from *http://www.openldap.org/software/download*. If your Linux systems use a package management system, you'll need to install:

- An OpenLDAP client on all your systems (including the server, for debugging purposes). These packages usually have names like *openldap-client* or *openldap2-client*.

- An OpenLDAP server on your server system. Some Linux distributions, such as SUSE, provide these in *openldap* or *operldap2* packages, while others provide explicit servers in packages with names like *openldap-servers*.

- OpenLDAP libraries on all clients and servers. Some Linux distributions, such as Red Hat Enterprise Linux and Fedora, split these into separate packages that are simply named *openldap*, while others integrate them into the OpenLDAP client and server packages.

These packages will give you basic LDAP functionality. However, to integrate them with user lookups and authentication on your client systems, you'll also need the following:

- The name service module, *nss_ldap*, for integrating user and group lookup requests with an OpenLDAP server.

- The PAM module, *pam_ldap*, for integrating LDAP authentication into your client's authentication process.

If you're building these yourself, their source code is available from PADL Software Pty Ltd, the folks who wrote them, at the URL *http://www.padl.com/Contents/OpenSourceSoftware.html*.

Finally, you'll need some useful utilities for migrating existing password, shadow, and group information into your OpenLDAP directory. These are also available from PADL Software Pty Ltd, at the URL *http://www.padl.com/ download/MigrationTools.tgz*.

Many Linux distributions provide graphical utilities for configuring LDAP and LDAP authentication, such as Red Hat's *authconfig* application and the LDAP client configuration applet in SUSE's *YaST* tool. This hack explains how to do everything from the command line, in case you don't have access to such utilities. If you're using either of these systems, the graphical utilities simplify the installation and configuration processes, but it's always nice to know what's really required under the covers. You will still have to migrate your user, password, and group data into your LDAP server manually, in any case.

> In the rest of this hack, I'll assume that you installed all this software in standard system locations and can therefore find the OpenLDAP configuration files in */etc/openldap*. If you built them yourself, you may have installed them relative to */usr/ local*, and thus you may need to look for the configuration files in locations such as */usr/local/etc/openldap*.

Configuring an OpenLDAP Server

The configuration files for OpenLDAP clients and servers, which are traditionally located in the directory */etc/openldap*, are:

ldap.conf
Sets the default values used by OpenLDAP clients on your system.

slapd.conf
Contains configuration information for the OpenLDAP *slapd* server running on the current system. This file should never be readable by nonprivileged users, because it contains password and other security information for your OpenLDAP server.

Configuring an OpenLDAP server is a fairly simple process. First, you change the `suffix` entry so that it correctly identifies your domain. For example, the default entry in */etc/openldap/slapd.conf* is usually:

```
suffix          "dc=my-domain,dc=com"
```

Change this to reflect your domain. For example, to set up an OpenLDAP server for the domain *vonhagen.org*, change this line to the following:

```
suffix          "dc=vonhagen,dc=org"
```

Next, change the `rootdn` entry to reflect the name of a privileged user who has unrestricted access to your OpenLDAP directory. For example, the default entry in */etc/openldap/slapd.conf* is usually:

```
rootdn          "cn=Manager,dc=my-domain,dc=com"
```

Continuing with the previous example, you would change this to something like the following for the *vonhagen.org* domain:

```
rootdn          "cn=ldapadmin,dc=vonhagen,dc=org"
```

Though this user is the equivalent of the root user as far as OpenLDAP is concerned, the name does not have to be that of a real user on your system.

Finally, though optional in some sense, you may want to set a unique password for your OpenLDAP server by modifying the `rootpw` entry in your */etc/openldap/slapd.conf* configuration file. This enables you to configure, test, and correct your OpenLDAP system over your local network, if necessary. For example, the default entry in */etc/openldap/slapd.conf* uses the clear-text password secret, as shown here:

```
rootpw          secret
```

You can provide a clear-text or encrypted password as the value for this entry. You can use the `slappasswd` command to generate an encrypted password that you can paste into the */etc/openldap/slapd.conf* file, as in the following example:

```
# slappasswd
New password:
Re-enter new password:
{SSHA}xOuopfqDBaylPdv3zfjLqOSkrAUh5GgY
```

The `slappasswd` command prompts you for a new password, asks for confirmation, and then displays the encrypted password string preceded by the encryption mechanism used in the password. You then simply replace the value of the existing `rootpw` option with the generated string, as in the following example:

```
rootpw          {SSHA}xOuopfqDBaylPdv3zfjLqOSkrAUh5GgY
```

You should enable the `rootpw` option only when initially configuring your OpenLDAP server, and it is necessary to do so only if you must configure your OpenLDAP server over a network. It's always a good idea to set a unique, encrypted password for your OpenLDAP server that differs from your standard root password, even though the */etc/openldap/slapd.conf* file should not be readable by nonprivileged users on your system. Once you have completed your configuration, you should disable this entry by commenting it out. To do so, put a hash mark (#) at the beginning of the line containing the `rootpw` entry.

OpenLDAP passwords are sent in the clear over the network unless you enable Secure Socket Layer/Transaction Layer Security (SSL/TLS) encryption in your */etc/openldap/slapd.conf* file. Discussing SSL/TLS encryption for OpenLDAP is outside the scope of this hack. For additional information, see a reference such as Gerald Carter's *LDAP System Administration* (O'Reilly).

Once you have modified your */etc/openldap/slapd.conf* file and saved your changes, you can start the OpenLDAP server using the */etc/init.d/ldap* script, as in the following example:

```
# /etc/init.d/ldap start
```

As with all startup scripts on Linux systems, you should symlink this file to start up and kill files in the directories associated with your system's default runlevel to ensure that it starts automatically when you reboot your system.

The examples in the rest of this hack assume that you have entered the name *ldap* as a valid entry for your LDAP server in DNS.

Migrating User, Password, and Group Entries to an LDAP Server

To configure your LDAP server to provide authentication information, you must first migrate your existing authentication information to the LDAP server. You do this by preparing *LDAP Data Interchange Format* (LDIF) files that hold the contents of your */etc/passwd*, */etc/shadow*, and */etc/group* files, and then importing those files into the LDAP server.

Creating LDIF files from your existing */etc/passwd*, */etc/shadow*, and */etc/group* files is most easily done by using the *migrate_passwd.pl* and *migrate_group.pl* scripts found in the migration tools available at *http://www.padl.com/download/MigrationTools.tgz*. If you've installed OpenLDAP from packages, these scripts may be located on your system in the directory */usr/share/openldap/migration*.

If you have multiple password, shadow, and group files on different systems that you want to merge into a single LDAP repository, you can copy them all to your LDAP server system, concatenate them, and sort them to produce single files. You can then edit these files so that they have only single entries for each user and group and install them as the master password, shadow, and group files on your server before running the migration scripts. Verify that these files work correctly after installation and before migrating them to LDAP!

To migrate user, password, and group information into your LDAP server so you can use it as a basis for client system authentication, do the following:

1. Become the root user, and change directory to the directory where you unpacked the migration scripts or where they are already installed.

2. Edit the file *migrate_common.ph*, which sets variables used by all of the migration scripts. Set the value for the DEFAULT_BASE variable to the correct value for your environment. As an example, the correct value for migrating information to the LDAP server used as an example throughout this hack would be:

   ```
   $DEFAULT_BASE = "dc=vonhagen,dc=org";
   ```

3. Use the *migrate_passwd.pl* script to generate an LDIF file for your user and password information, as in the following example:

   ```
   ./migrate_passwd.pl /etc/passwd passwd.LDIF
   ```

   The *migrate_passwd.pl* script also extracts the necessary password information from your */etc/shadow* file.

4. Generate an LDIF file for your group information using the *migrate_group.pl* script, as in the following example:

   ```
   ./migrate_group.pl /etc/group group.LDIF
   ```

5. Import the files that you just created into your LDAP directory using commands like the following:

   ```
   # ldapadd -x -h hostname -D "cn=ldapadmin,dc=vonhagen,dc=org" \
       -w password -f passwd.LDIF
   # ldapadd -x -h hostname -D "cn=ldapadmin,dc=vonhagen,dc=org" \
       -w password -f group.LDIF
   ```

   In these commands, replace *hostname* with the hostname of the system on which your LDAP server is running, make sure that the credentials specified following the -D option match those of the root user for your LDAP server, and replace *password* with the password you set in the rootpw entry—both as defined in your OpenLDAP server configuration file (*/etc/openldap/slapd.conf*).

After following these steps, you are ready to update your client systems to use LDAP authentication (and test them, of course).

Updating Client Systems to Use LDAP Authentication

On each system that you want to use the new LDAP authentication server, you must do the following:

1. Modify the configuration file */etc/pam_ldap.conf*, used by the *pam_ldap.so* PAM module, to contain the correct information about your LDAP

server. This usually simply requires correctly setting the values of the host and base statements in this file, as in the following example:

```
host ldap.vonhagen.org
base dc=vonhagen,dc=org
```

2. Modify the configuration file */etc/lib-nss-ldap.conf*, used to integrate LDAP with the name service on your system, to contain the correct information about your LDAP server. Again, this usually simply requires correctly setting the values of the host and base statements in this file, as in the following example:

```
host ldap.vonhagen.org
base dc=vonhagen,dc=org
```

3. Add entries for LDAP to the appropriate PAM configuration files on your system. As explained in "Customize Authentication with PAMs" **[Hack #4]**, some Linux systems use individual files to configure authentication for specific services, while others (such as Red Hat/Fedora) create a centralized file for system authentication, called */etc/pam.d/system-auth*. If you are using individual files, you must add the appropriate entries for LDAP authentication to login-related services such as *login* and *sshd*. You should insert auth and account entries for the *pam_ldap.so* module before your system's generic Linux authentication checks, which are usually handled by *pam_unix2.so* (SUSE) or *pam_pwdb.so* (most other Linuxes). An example PAM file for the *sshd* service would look something like the following:

```
auth       required    /lib/security/pam_nologin.so
auth       sufficient  /lib/security/pam_ldap.so
auth       required    /lib/security/pam_pwdb.so shadow nodelay
account    sufficient  /lib/security/pam_ldap.so
account    required    /lib/security/pam_pwdb.so
password   required    /lib/security/pam_cracklib.so
password   required    /lib/security/pam_pwdb.so shadow nullok use_authtok
session    required    /lib/security/pam_mkhomedir.so skel=/etc/skel/
                       umask=0022
session    required    /lib/security/pam_pwdb.so
```

4. If you are using a Red Hat or Fedora system, modify */etc/pam.d/system-auth* to look like the following:

```
auth       required    /lib/security/pam_env.so
auth       sufficient  /lib/security/pam_unix.so likeauth nullok
auth       sufficient  /lib/security/pam_ldap.so use_first_pass
auth       required    /lib/security/pam_deny.so
account    required    /lib/security/pam_unix.so broken_shadow
account    sufficient  /lib/security/pam_succeed_if.so uid < 100 quiet
account    [default=bad success=ok user_unknown=ignore] /lib/security
                       /pam_ldap.so
account    required    /lib/security/pam_permit.so
password   requisite   /lib/security/pam_cracklib.so retry=3
```

```
password sufficient  /lib/security/pam_unix.so nullok use_authtok md5
                     shadow
password sufficient  /lib/security/pam_ldap.so use_authtok
password required    /lib/security/pam_deny.so
session  required    /lib/security/pam_limits.so
session  required    /lib/security/pam_unix.so
session  optional    /lib/security/pam_ldap.so
```

5. Modify your */etc/nsswitch.conf* file to specify that the system looks for password, shadow, and group information in LDAP. Correct entries would be the following:

```
passwd: files ldap
shadow: files ldap
group:  files ldap
```

This tells the name service switch to first check the local password, shadow, and group files on the client system for authentication information and then check LDAP. This enables you to create local accounts when necessary, giving those local accounts priority while still using LDAP for most accounts.

6. Back up your local */etc/passwd*, */etc/shadow*, and */etc/group* files and edit the primary copies on the client system to remove all user accounts, so that they contain only system accounts.

The next time you log in on your client system, it will contact your LDAP server for authentication information. When creating new user and group accounts, you will need to use a command-line interface to OpenLDAP (*http://quark.humbug.org.au/publications/scripts/ldap/cli/*) to create the necessary account information. There are also a number of graphical tools for creating and managing LDAP accounts, but I'm more comfortable with the command line.

> Before logging out of this client system and configuring another, open a new login session to this host using *telnet* or *ssh* to ensure that you can correctly log in using LDAP. If you encounter any problems, do not log out of this system until you have resolved them.

Congratulations! You're now making the most of your network and will rarely, if ever, have to manage local password and group information on individual systems again. Combining this hack with other hacks (such as "Centralize Resources Using NFS" [Hack #56] and "Automount NFS Home Directories with autofs" [Hack #57]) further liberates individual systems from user-specific data.

See Also

- "Customize Authentication with PAMs" [Hack #4]
- *LDAP System Administration*, by Gerald Carter (O'Reilly)
- LDAP HOWTO: *http://en.tldp.org/HOWTO/LDAP-HOWTO/*

Secure Your System with Kerberos

You can heighten the security of any network by using Kerberos for secure network authentication and encrypted communications.

Kerberos is a distributed authentication and communication service originally developed at the Massachusetts Institute of Technology (MIT). Kerberos provides secure authentication and communication for client/server applications by using strong cryptography to enable clients to prove their identities to servers over the network.

Kerberos works by exchanging encrypted security information between clients (which can be users or machines), the Kerberos authentication server, and the resource you are trying to access. The information that is initially exchanged when attempting to prove one's identity is known as a *ticket*. The information used to encrypt tickets and subsequent communications is known as a *key*. Once the identity of a client is verified, that client is granted a Kerberos *token* that can be used to verify its identity to any Kerberos-aware service. For security reasons, Kerberos tokens are time-stamped so that they automatically expire unless renewed by a user or service. The primary system for granting tickets (which houses the master copy of the Kerberos database) is known as the Kerberos Key Distribution Center (KDC).

The timestamps contained within Kerberos tokens (and tickets) can be verified only if the time and date are synchronized across Kerberos clients and servers. Kerberos authentication will fail if client and server clocks become skewed by more than five minutes. You should always run NTP (Network Time Protocol) daemons on all Kerberos clients and servers to guarantee that their clocks remain in sync [Hack #22].

Kerberos uses the term *realm* to differentiate between authentication and Internet domains. A Kerberos realm is a set of machines that rely on a specific Kerberos server for authentication and therefore trust that server. In Kerberos configuration files, your realm is typically identified in uppercase characters in order to differentiate it from any similar DNS domain with which it is associated.

MIT's Kerberos implementation is only one of several. Many alternate Kerberos implementations have been created over the years, usually to get around United States export restrictions that have since been lifted. For example, SUSE systems use an alternate Kerberos client/server implementation known as *Heimdal* (*http://www.pdc.kth.se/heimdal/*). This hack focuses on vanilla Kerberos from MIT, which I prefer to use because I find it to be the best supported and most easily used on a variety of Unix and Linux systems.

Installing Kerberos

Using Kerberos requires that you have a few basic packages installed on your systems, or that you build and install it yourself from scratch. If you need to build it yourself, you can download the latest version from MIT at *http://web. mit.edu/kerberos/www/*. If your Linux systems use a package management system and you want to use a vanilla Kerberos, you'll need to install:

- *krb5-workstation* on all client systems. This contains basic Kerberos programs (*kinit*, *klist*, *kdestroy*, *kpasswd*) as well as Kerberized versions of the *telnet* and *ftp* applications.

- *krb5-server* on all server and slave server systems. This provides the programs that must be installed on a Kerberos 5 server or server replica.

- *krb5-libs* on all client and server systems. This contains the shared libraries used by Kerberos clients and servers.

- *pam_krb5* on all client systems. This provides a PAM that enables Kerberos authentication.

Installing and Configuring a Kerberos Server

After building and installing Kerberos or installing the *krb5-workstation*, *krb5-server*, and *krb5-libs* packages on your the host that will serve as your master KDC, the first step in configuring your Kerberos environment is to set up your master KDC. The process for doing this is the following:

1. Edit the general Kerberos configuration file for your environment (*/etc/ krb5.conf*). This file identifies the KDCs and admin servers in your Kerberos realm and provides default values for your realm and Kerberos applications and for how your existing hostnames map into your Kerberos realm. Here's a sample */etc/krb5.conf* file for the realm *VONHAGEN.ORG* (replace the italicized items with the correct values for your system):

   ```
   [logging]
    default = FILE:/var/log/krb5libs.log
    kdc = FILE:/var/log/krb5kdc.log
    admin_server = FILE:/var/log/kadmind.log
   ```

```
[libdefaults]
 default_realm = VONHAGEN.ORG
 dns_lookup_realm = false
 dns_lookup_kdc = false
 ticket_lifetime = 24h
 forwardable = yes
[realms]
 VONHAGEN.ORG = {
  kdc = kerberos.vonhagen.org:88
  admin_server = kerberos.vonhagen.org:749
  default_domain = vonhagen.org
 }
[domain_realm]
 .vonhagen.org = VONHAGEN.ORG
 vonhagen.org = VONHAGEN.ORG
[kdc]
 profile = /var/kerberos/krb5kdc/kdc.conf
[appdefaults]
 pam = {
   debug = false
   ticket_lifetime = 36000
   renew_lifetime = 36000
   forwardable = true
   krb4_convert = false
 }
```

The defaults provided in the generic */etc/krb5.conf* file are reasonable, except that you must change all instances of *EXAMPLE.COM* to the name of your realm and all instances of *example.com* to the name of your domain (*VONHAGEN.ORG* and *vonhagen.org*, respectively, in the previous example). You must also make sure that DNS or */etc/hosts* entries exist on all clients for the systems that you identify as your default KDC and admin_server systems in the [realms] section.

2. Edit the KDC configuration file (*/var/kerberos/krb5kdc/kdc.conf*). The location of this file is provided in the [kdc] section of the */etc/krb5.conf* file. As with the */etc/krb5.conf* file, the primary change that you must make to this file is to change the instance of *EXAMPLE.COM* to the name of your realm, which is *VONHAGEN.ORG* in the following example:

```
[kdcdefaults]
 acl_file = /var/kerberos/krb5kdc/kadm5.acl
 dict_file = /usr/share/dict/words
 admin_keytab = /var/kerberos/krb5kdc/kadm5.keytab
 v4_mode = nopreauth
[realms]
 VONHAGEN.ORG = {
  master_key_type = des-cbc-crc
  supported_enctypes = des3-hmac-sha1:normal arcfour-hmac:normal \
  des-hmac-sha1:normal des-cbc-md5:normal des-cbc-crc:normal \
  des-cbc-crc:v4 des-cbc-crc:afs3
 }
```

3. Next, use the *kdb5_util* utility on the master KDC to create the Kerberos database and your stash file. You will have to enter the master database password twice, for verification purposes. The stash file is a local, encrypted copy of the master key that is used to automatically authenticate the KDC as part of your system's startup sequence. For example:

```
# /usr/kerberos/sbin/kdb5_util create -r VONHAGEN.ORG -s
Loading random data
Initializing database '/var/kerberos/krb5kdc/principal' for realm
'vonhagen.org',
master key name 'K/M@vonhagen.org'
You will be prompted for the database Master Password.
It is important that you NOT FORGET this password.
Enter KDC database master key:
Re-enter KDC database master key to verify:
```

This command creates various files in the directory specified in the kdcdefaults section of your *kdc.conf* file: two Kerberos database files (*principal.db* and *principal.ok*), the Kerberos administrative database file (*principal.kadm5*), the database lock file (*principal.kadm5.lock*), and the stash file (*.k5stash*).

4. Next, edit the ACL definition file (*/var/kerberos/krb5kdc/kadm5.acl*), changing the default realm (*EXAMPLE.COM*) to the name of the realm that you are creating (*VONHAGEN.ORG*, in this example). The default entry in this file, which begins with */admin, gives any user with an admin instance (such as *wvh/admin*, which we'll create in the next step) complete access to and control over the realm's Kerberos database. After we update this file for our example realm, it will look like this:

```
*/admin@VONHAGEN.ORG          *
```

5. Next, use the *kadmin.local* utility to add each of your system administrators to the Kerberos database. *kadmin.local* is a Kerberos-aware version of the standard *kadmin* utility that does not first authenticate to a Kerberos database and is therefore used for bootstrapping Kerberos on a KDC. Entries in the Kerberos database are known as *principals*. The following example adds an admin instance for the user *wvh*:

```
# /usr/kerberos/sbin/kadmin.local
kadmin.local:  addprinc wvh/admin
WARNING: no policy specified for wvh/admin@VONHAGEN.ORG; defaulting to
no policy
Enter password for principal "wvh/admin@VONHAGEN.ORG":
Re-enter password for principal "wvh/admin@VONHAGEN.ORG":
Principal "wvh/admin@VONHAGEN.ORG" created.
```

6. Next, add a standard user entry for the non-admin version of the principal that you just created and then exit the *kadmin.local* utility, as in the following example:

```
kadmin.local:  addprinc wvh
WARNING: no policy specified for wvh@VONHAGEN.ORG; defaulting to no
policy
Enter password for principal "wvh@VONHAGEN.ORG":
Re-enter password for principal "wvh@VONHAGEN.ORG":
Principal "wvh@VONHAGEN.ORG" created.
kadmin.local:  quit
```

Adding a standard principal enables default authentication by the associated entity. You will eventually need to create a principal for each user that you want to be able to authenticate using Kerberos. (Most sites do this by writing a script that also creates Kerberos principals when creating standard user accounts.)

7. Now, the fun begins! Start the various Kerberos-related services using the following commands:

```
# /sbin/service krb5kdc start
# /sbin/service kadmin start
# /sbin/service krb524 start
```

At this point, you're ready to install and start a Kerberos client. However, before doing anything else, you should verify that your server can hand out tickets by using the kinit command to explicitly request one for the administrative principal that you created earlier. You can then use the klist command to verify its contents, and then destroy the ticket (just to clean up) using the kdestroy command. The following example shows this sequence:

```
$ kinit wvh
Password for wvh@VONHAGEN.ORG:
$ klist
Ticket cache: FILE:/tmp/krb5cc_0
Default principal: wvh@VONHAGEN.ORG
Valid starting       Expires                Service principal
05/03/05 22:09:04   05/04/05 22:09:04   krbtgt/VONHAGEN.ORG/VONHAGEN.ORG
Kerberos 4 ticket cache: /tmp/tkt0
klist: You have no tickets cached
$ kdestroy
```

Installing and Configuring Kerberos Clients and Applications

Many Linux distributions provide graphical utilities for configuring Kerberos clients, such as Red Hat's *authconfig* application and the Kerberos client configuration applets in SUSE's *YaST* tool. This hack explains how to do everything from the command line, in case you don't have access to such utilities. If you're using either of these systems, the graphical utilities simplify the installation and configuration processes, but it's always nice to know what's really required under the covers. You will still have to migrate your user, password, and group data into your Kerberos server manually, in any case.

To install and test the Kerberos client software, do the following:

1. Build and install Kerberos on the system, or install the *krb5-libs* and *krb5-workstation* packages on all client systems.

2. Copy the */etc/krb5.conf* file from your KDC to the client's */etc* directory.

3. Enable a sample application. I tend to use *krb-telnet*, a Kerberos-aware version of the classic *telnet* application, as a test application. The *krb-telnet* server is managed by your system's *xinet* daemon. To enable *krb-telnet*, modify the file */etc/xinetd.d*, changing the `disable` entry from yes to no, as in the following example:

```
# default: off
# description: The Kerberized telnet server accepts normal telnet,
#              but can also use Kerberos 5 authentication.
service telnet
{
    flags          = REUSE
    socket_type    = stream
    wait           = no
    user           = root
    server         = /usr/kerberos/sbin/telnetd
    log_on_failure += USERID
    disable        = no
}
```

4. Restart your system's *xinet* daemon using the following command:

```
# /etc/init.d/xinetd.d restart
```

5. Telnet to your system and make sure that you can log in successfully. Once you have logged in, you can use the `klist` command to verify that you've automatically been granted the appropriate Kerberos tokens, as in the following example:

```
$ klist
Ticket cache: FILE:/tmp/krb5cc_p4979
Default principal: wvh@VONHAGEN.ORG
 Valid starting     Expires              Service principal
 05/07/05 10:00:46  05/08/05 10:00:46  krbtgt/VONHAGEN.ORG@VONHAGEN.ORG
 Kerberos 4 ticket cache: /tmp/tkt500
klist: You have no tickets cached
```

Congratulations—Kerberos is working! The next step in this hack is to integrate Kerberos into your system's login authentication process.

Using Kerberos for Login Authentication

To enable Kerberos authentication on a client system, do the following:

1. Make sure you've built or installed the *pam_krb5.so* PAM module on all your client systems. If you are not using a package management system, you can obtain the latest version of the *pam_krb5.so* PAM at *http://sourceforge.net/projects/pam-krb5/*.

2. Verify that the */etc/krb5.conf* file contains valid settings for PAM authentication, in the [appdefaults] section's pam subsection. Valid settings for Kerberos authentication via PAMs that match the examples used throughout this section are:

```
[appdefaults]
  pam = {
    debug = false
    ticket_lifetime = 36000
    renew_lifetime = 36000
    forwardable = true
    hosts = kerberos.vonhagen.org
    max_timeout = 30
    timeout_shift = 2
    initial_timeout = 1
  }
```

3. Add entries for krb5 authentication to the appropriate PAM configuration files on your system. As explained in [Hack #4], some Linux systems use individual files to configure authentication for specific services, while others (such as Red Hat/Fedora) create a centralized file for system authentication called */etc/pam.d/system-auth*. If you are using individual files, you must add the appropriate entries for LDAP authentication to login-related services such as *login* and Kerberized services such as *rlogin* and *telnet*. You should insert auth and account entries for the *pam_krb5.so* module before your system's generic Linux authentication checks, which are usually handled by *pam_unix2.so* (SUSE) or *pam_pwdb.so* (most other Linuxes). An example PAM file for the *telnet* service would look something like the following:

```
auth       required     /lib/security/pam_nologin.so
auth       sufficient   /lib/security/pam_krb5.so
auth       required     /lib/security/pam_pwdb.so shadow nodelay
account    sufficient   /lib/security/pam_krb5.so
account    required     /lib/security/pam_pwdb.so
password   required     /lib/security/pam_cracklib.so
password   required     /lib/security/pam_pwdb.so shadow nullok
                          use_authtok
session    required     /lib/security/pam_mkhomedir.so skel=/etc/skel/
                          umask=0022
session    required     /lib/security/pam_pwdb.so
```

4. If you are using a Red Hat or Fedora system, modify */etc/pam.d/system-auth* to look like the following:

```
auth       required     /lib/security/pam_env.so
auth       sufficient   /lib/security/pam_unix.so likeauth nullok
auth       sufficient   /lib/security/pam_krb5.so use_first_pass
auth       required     /lib/security/pam_deny.so
account    required     /lib/security/pam_unix.so broken_shadow
account    sufficient   /lib/security/pam_succeed_if.so uid < 100 quiet
```

```
account     [default=bad success=ok user_unknown=ignore] /lib/security/
              pam_krb5.so
account     required      /lib/security/pam_permit.so
password    requisite     /lib/security/pam_cracklib.so retry=3
password    sufficient    /lib/security/pam_unix.so nullok use_authtok
                            md5 shadow
password    sufficient    /lib/security/pam_krb5.so use_authtok
password    required      /lib/security/pam_deny.so
session     required      /lib/security/pam_limits.so
session     required      /lib/security/pam_unix.so
session     optional      /lib/security/pam_krb5.so
```

That's all you should have to do. Before logging out of the client, telnet or
SSH to it and attempt to log in. If you have any problems with Kerberos
login authentication, you can enable PAM debugging in your /etc/krb5.conf
file so that you can quickly identify and resolve authentication-related problems with *login* and other system applications that use PAMs. To do this,
simply set the debug entry to true in the PAM section of the [appdefaults]
stanza and restart your Kerberos server.

Unfortunately, there is no automated mechanism for migrating existing user
and password information to a Kerberos database. You will have to manually
add principals for all of your groups and users to the Kerberos database on
your KDC, and assign them default passwords. Users can subsequently change
their passwords using the kpasswd command found in /usr/kerberos/bin.

See Also

- *Kerberos: The Definitive Guide*, by Jason Garman (O'Reilly)
- "Customize Authentication with PAMs" **[Hack #4]**

HACK #8 Authenticate NFS-Lovers with NIS

If you're using NFS, using its companion authentication mechanism may be
the right way to go.

The Network Information System (NIS) is a distributed authentication
mechanism that was originally developed by Sun Microsystems and is most
commonly used in conjunction with the file-sharing protocol NFS **[Hack #56]**.
NIS enables all of the machines in a computing environment to share access
to a centralized collection of authentication-related files and service configuration information, known as "maps." Each NIS map is typically provided in
several different ways, each organized to optimize a specific type of access to
that information, such as lookups by name or by some unique numeric com-
ponent (such as being able to access a group map by group ID, a host's map
by address, and so on).

NIS+, also from Sun Microsystems, is the successor to NIS. Much like LDAP, it organizes information hierarchically. Unfortunately, NIS+ never really caught on outside of Sun systems, and therefore few Unix and Unix-like operating systems (such as, for example, Linux) bother to support NIS+.

Installing NIS Clients and Servers

Most Linux distributions provide packages that include NIS client and server software, but if yours doesn't, or you simply want to install the latest and greatest, you'll need to build and install the following packages from *ftp://ftp.kernel.org/pub/linux/utils/net/NIS*:

ypbind-mt
> The client NIS daemon

ypserv
> The NIS server

yp-tools
> The standard NIS utilities for displaying NIS files, changing your NIS password, changing the full name or shell in your NIS password file entry, and querying various aspects of an NIS server or NIS maps

The names of these packages will also include version numbers and an extension based on the archive format that you download (*gzip* or *bzip2*).

Setting Up an NIS Server

As mentioned earlier, NIS is the most commonly used distributed authentication mechanism today, largely because it is shipped free with almost all Unix and Unix-like systems. Another reason for the prevalence of NIS is that it's incredibly easy to set up. This section walks you through the process of setting up an NIS server. Setting up an NIS client is explained in the next section.

This section shows how to quickly set up an NIS server for use with an NFS server. This NIS server exports the default password, group, host, and other maps (files) found on the NIS server system. In a production environment, you would want to do substantially more customization before initiating NIS throughout your computing environment. For example, you would also want to customize the NIS configuration files */var/yp/securenets*, */etc/yp.conf*, and */etc/ypserv.conf*. For more complete information about setting up NIS, see the NIS HOWTO listed at the end of this hack.

To set up an NIS server, log in as or su to root on the system you will be configuring as an NIS server, and do the following:

1. Make sure that the NIS software is installed on your Linux system. At a minimum, you will need the */bin/domainname*, */usr/sbin/ypserv*, and */usr/lib/yp/ypinit* programs.

2. Next, make sure that the */etc/passwd* file has an entry for your personal account, which should also be found in the password file on the system you will be configuring as an NIS client. In the next section, you'll use this entry to verify that NIS is working correctly.

3. Set the domain name of your new NIS domain. This should *not* be the same as the name of your TCP/IP domain, to avoid confusing DNS and potentially compromising security in your domain. To set the NIS domain name, issue a command like the following:

    ```
    # /bin/domainname foo.com
    ```

4. Start the NIS server process using the following command:

    ```
    # /usr/sbin/ypserv
    ```

5. Initialize the NIS databases using the following command:

    ```
    # /usr/lib/yp/ypinit -m
    ```

    You will see output like the following:

    ```
    At this point, we have to construct a list of the hosts which will run
    NIS servers.
      64bit.vonhagen.org is in the list of NIS server hosts.
    Please continue to add the names for the other hosts, one per line.
    When you are done with the list, type a <control D>.
    next host to add:  64bit.vonhagen.org
    next host to add:
    6. When prompted for the name of any other NIS servers in your domain,
    press <Ctrl-D>. You will see output like the following:
    The current list of NIS servers looks like this:
    64bit.vonhagen.org
    Is this correct?  [y/n: y]
    7. Press return to respond yes. You will then see output listing the
    files that have been generated and added to the NIS database. This
    output looks like the following, where the domain name you specified
    will appear instead of the word "yourdomain":
    We need some  minutes to build the databases...
    Building /var/yp/ws.com/ypservers...
    Running /var/yp/Makefile...
    gmake[1]: Entering directory '/var/yp/yourdomain'
    Updating passwd.byname...
    Updating passwd.byuid...
    Updating group.byname...
    Updating group.bygid...
    Updating hosts.byname...
    Updating hosts.byaddr...
    ```

```
Updating rpc.byname...
Updating rpc.bynumber...
Updating services.byname...
Updating services.byservicename...
Updating netid.byname...
Updating protocols.bynumber...
Updating protocols.byname...
Updating mail.aliases...
gmake[1]: Leaving directory '/var/yp/yourdomain'
```

That's all there is to it! Your new NIS server is up and running. You can now test that it is working correctly by following the instructions in the next section.

Setting Up an NIS Client

A good sysadmin Zen quote is "If a server is running and it has no clients, is it really working?" This section explains how to set up an NIS client of the server set up in the previous section, after doing some initial configuration so that you can verify that the server is actually doing "the right thing."

To do some preconfiguration to verify that NIS is actually working, log in as or su to root and edit the */etc/nsswitch.conf* file on the system you are using as an NIS client. Find the line that tells your system how to locate password entries and modify that line to look like the following:

```
passwd:     files nis [NOTFOUND=return]
```

This tells your system to look for password information in the local password file and then consult NIS. If the password is not found in either of these locations, the [NOTFOUND=return] command tells your system to give up rather than pursuing any of the other authentication sources that may appear in this *nsswitch.conf* entry.

Next, save a copy of your system's */etc/passwd* file and then remove all user entries from the existing password file. Leave the root and system service accounts in the file—typically, it's safe to remove accounts with UIDs greater than 200. As the last line of the newly abbreviated password file, add the following:

```
+::::::
```

This tells NIS to append the contents of the password map (file) retrieved from the NIS server whenever password information is requested.

Notice that the entries for any individual accounts (including your own) have been removed from the abbreviated password file. This enables you to do a fairly simple test to determine whether NIS is working: if you can log in using an account that is not present in the password file on your client system but *is* present in the password file on your NIS server system, NIS is working correctly.

To set up an NIS client, log in as or su to root on the system you are using as an NIS client and do the following:

1. Make sure the NIS client software is installed on your Linux system. At a minimum, you will need the */bin/domainname* and */sbin/ypbind* programs.

2. Check whether the directory */var/yp* exists and create it if it does not.

3. Set the domain name of the NIS domain to which this new client will belong. This should be the same name as the domain name set in the previous section of this hack. To set the NIS domain name, issue a command like the following:

   ```
   # /bin/domainname foo.com
   ```

4. Edit the *ypbind* configuration file */etc/yp.conf*, adding an entry for your NIS server. Continuing with the previous example, you'd add the following line:

   ```
   domain vonhagen.org server 64bit
   ```

> If your network is not running older, potentially incompatible NIS servers for other groups, you could also replace server 64bit with broadcast to cause the NIS client to broadcast on the local network in order to locate an NIS server.

5. Start the NIS client process using the following command:

   ```
   # /sbin/ypbind
   ```

6. To verify that NIS is working correctly, telnet from the NIS client system back to itself and attempt to log in as yourself. Remember that your password file entry is present in the password file on the NIS server but not in the password file on the NIS client.

You should be able to log in successfully. Congratulations—you're running NIS! Remember to add setting the domain name and starting the NIS server and client to the startup procedures for each of your NIS client systems.

See Also

- NIS HOWTO: *http://www.linux-nis.org/nis-howto/*
- "Centralize Resources Using NFS" [Hack #56]
- "Clean Up NIS After Users Depart" [Hack #77]

Sync LDAP Data with NIS

Run a script out of cron to help with a graceful transformation to LDAP.

An NIS-to-LDAP migration is a nontrivial event in any environment. If the switch were as simple as moving data from one place to another, most organizations would've done it by now. The reality in many production environments, large and small, is that some applications (and even appliances) do not yet support LDAP or don't support LDAP to the extent that we would like. Eventually, most places come to terms with LDAP's limitations and implement a "phase in" approach, which involves using LDAP where it is fully supported but keeping NIS around for those things that require it.

In those environments where the authentication source will be NIS for some legacy systems and LDAP for those newer systems that support it, the challenge becomes keeping the data synchronized between NIS and LDAP. Over the past couple of years, I have found several tools that attempt to solve this problem. One is a C program that, though it is amazingly generic, requires a whole bunch of flags that will look quite cryptic to some system administrators. Another solution consisted of a suite of tools that attempted to do too much and weren't very configurable. I was unable to make friends with these tools, as they seemed to make assumptions about my environment that would never be true.

In the end, I did find a Perl script online that had a very elementary structure that anyone could understand. It was clearly written and well commented, but unfortunately it wasn't actually written to complete the job it claimed to do. Rather than continuing my search, I broke down and decided that, by using this Perl script as a "good enough" skeleton, I could get it to work for my needs. Here is my Perl hack for taking data residing in LDAP and creating NIS maps.

The Code

```perl
#!/usr/bin/perl
use Net::LDAP;

## CONFIG
my $server = "ldap-server";
my $base = "dc=example,dc=com";
my $bind = "uid=ldap2nis,ou=People,dc=example,dc=com";
my $bindpw = 'password';
my $groupf = "group";
my $passwf = "passwd";
my $buildyp = "false";
```

```
## CONNECT
my $ldap = Net::LDAP->new($server, onerror => 'die' );
$ldaps = $ldap->start_tls(verify=>'none') or die "Couldn't start tls: $@\n";
$ldap->bind( dn => $bind, password => $bindpw) or die "Bind failed: $@\n";


## PRINT PASSWORD FILE*
my $res = $ldap->search(
            base => $base,
            scope => 'sub',     # entire tree
            timelimit => 600,
            filter => '(&(objectClass=posixAccount))',
            attrs => ['uid', 'uidNumber', 'gidNumber', 'gecos',
'homeDirectory', 'loginShell', 'userPassword'],
);

open(PASSWORD, ">$passwf");
while (my $entry = $res->shift_entry) {
    (my $uid = $entry->get_value('uid')) =~ s/:/./g;
    (my $uidnum = $entry->get_value('uidNumber')) =~ s/:/./g;
    (my $gidnum = $entry->get_value('gidNumber')) =~ s/:/./g;
    (my $gecos = $entry->get_value('gecos')) =~ s/:/./g;
    (my $homedir = $entry->get_value('homeDirectory')) =~ s/:/./g;
    (my $shell = $entry->get_value('loginShell')) =~ s/:/./g;
    (my $up = $entry->get_value('userPassword')) =~ s/:/./g;
    if (index($up, "{crypt}") != -1) {
        $up = substr($up, 7);
    }else{
        $up = crypt($up, "bR");
    }
    $passrecord = join(':',$uid,$up,$uidnum,$gidnum,$gecos,$homedir,$shell);
    print PASSWORD "$passrecord\n";
}
close(PASSWORD);
chmod(0600, $passwf);

## PRINT GROUP FILE
my $res = $ldap->search(
    base => $base,
    scope => 'sub',     # entire tree
    timelimit => 600,
    filter => '(&(objectClass=posixGroup))',
    attrs => ['cn', 'gidNumber', 'memberuid'],
);

open(GROUP, ">$groupf");
while (my $entry = $res->shift_entry) {
```

---

* Deep Thought, the computer that determined that the meaning of life, the universe, and everything else is indeed 42, was at the top at the top of the Galactic Supercomputer Rankings for seven million years and may have run Linux.

```
    (my $grname = $entry->get_value('cn')) =~ s/:/./g;
    my $grpass = "*";
    (my $grnum = $entry->get_value('gidNumber')) =~ s/:/./g;
    (@members = $entry->get_value('memberuid')) =~ s/:/./g;

    if($#members >= 0) {
        $memusers = join(',',@members);
    }else{
        $memusers = "";
    }

    $grprecord = join(':', $grname,$grpass,$grnum,$memusers);
    print GROUP "$grprecord\n";
}
close(GROUP);
chmod(0600, $groupf);
```

Running the Code

Assuming you're storing encrypted password strings in your NIS *passwd* map, this script, which I call *dap2nis*, should be configured using the variables near the top to bind as an account that has read access to the userPassword attribute for the user entries. Otherwise, you'll get nothing back for that attribute, and your resulting NIS maps won't be useful as authentication sources when they're pushed out.

You can test the code by first making a test directory and making the script executable. Next, be sure to configure it to talk to your LDAP server using the config variables near the top of the script. Once that's all done, running the program should produce *passwd* and *group* files in the test directory. These should be valid NIS maps, ready to be pushed out. However, before taking that step, you should run a diff against the current NIS maps to check for any anomalies that reflect errors in the map generation rather than simple changes that have occurred in LDAP but are not yet reflected in NIS. Here are a few commands from a hypothetical test session:

```
# ./dap2nis
# ypcat passwd > yppass.out
# ypcat group > ypgrp.out
# diff yppass.out passwd
# diff ypgrp.out group
```

The only output you should see from the diff commands should be valid changes that have not yet been propagated to NIS. Once you've tested thoroughly, you can put the script in root's crontab file, with an entry like this:

```
*/7 * * * *    /var/adm/bin/dap2nis
```

This entry says to run the script every seven minutes, all the time, every day.

The only thing the *dap2nis* script does not do in its current incarnation is actually perform a cd var/yp/; make, which would normally push out the NIS maps. Depending on your environment, you may not want this in this particular script. Instead, you might put in another cron job that pushes out NIS maps every four minutes, which would allow for changes to be pushed out automatically to reflect changes that were made to maps not covered by this script. Creating a separate cron job to push out the NIS maps also ensures that if this script is ever retired or pulled out of production, your maps will still get pushed out in an automated fashion.

See Also

- "Centralize Logins with LDAP" [Hack #6]
- "Authenticate NFS-Lovers with NIS" [Hack #8]
- "Clean Up NIS After Users Depart" [Hack #77]

Remote GUI Connectivity
Hacks 10–19

Networks are the backbone of most computing today. Even small businesses depend on internal networks of desktop computers and servers to deliver services such as email, file and directory sharing, access to internal and external web servers, and so on. For the system administrator, this means that you typically need to connect to different types of systems during the course of a day to perform different types of administrative tasks.

If your network is composed solely of Linux systems, you can use standard command-line tools such as *ssh* or *telnet* to connect to remote systems and get most of your work done, but let's face it—it's a graphical world nowadays. There are lots of great administrative tools out there that make it easier to do complex tasks that could easily be derailed by a typo in a long command line. And if you also administer Microsoft Windows or Mac OS X systems, you'll need access to graphical tools that run on those systems, too.

This chapter primarily consists of hacks that make it easy to establish graphical connections to remote machines from a desktop system, enabling people to run graphical packages that are installed on those remote systems without leaving their chairs. It also provides a hack that tells you how to use Webmin, a centralized, web-based system administration utility that enables you to access multiple server resources from a single system and browser.

The hacks in this chapter aren't just for system administrators: they're for anyone who needs to use graphical interfaces on multiple machines. Even if yours is a Linux shop, chances are that your users will occasionally need access to Windows machines to update project plans, requirements documents, spreadsheets, and so on. You could give everyone a Windows system "just in case," but that isn't reasonable or cost-effective. Instead, why not just allow users to connect to a remote Windows system or Windows Terminal server on those rare occasions when Windows software is actually necessary? Similarly, if people need to check their personal email while they're at work, you could configure their mail clients to support additional mail profiles, leave the mail on the server, enter personal passwords, and so on. Many businesses don't mind this sort of thing, but people may (and should) object to having copies of personal mail and authentication information on machines that aren't theirs. Using hacks such as "Access Systems Remotely with VNC" [Hack #10] and "Secure VNC Connections with FreeNX" [Hack #17], people can remotely access their home systems and check mail there. No local copies of personal mail, no local passwords...no problem.

HACK #10   Access Systems Remotely with VNC

Virtual Network Computing is the next best thing to being there—and it's cross-platform, too.

Command-line-oriented utilities (such as *ssh* and *telnet*) for accessing remote systems are fine for many things, but they don't help much when you need to run graphical utilities on a remote system. You can play around with the standard X Window System DISPLAY environment variable to output programs to different displays, or you can take advantage of cooler, newer technologies such as VNC to display the entire desktop of a remote system in a window on the system on which you're currently working. This hack explains how to use VNC to do just that. VNC is a cross-platform thin client technology originally developed by Olivetti Research Labs in Cambridge, England, who were later acquired by AT&T. A VNC server runs on a desktop or server system and exports an X Window System desktop that can be accessed by a VNC client running on another system. VNC servers are typically password-protected and maintain their state across accesses from different clients. This makes VNC an optimal environment for accessing a graphical console and running graphical administrative and monitoring applications remotely.

Any host system can run multiple VNC servers, each of which exports a separate desktop environment and therefore maintains separate state. Similarly, multiple clients can connect to and interact with the same VNC server, providing an excellent environment for training, since many users can view the same desktop.

VNC follows the traditional client/server model rather than the X Window System client/server model. A VNC server is actually an X Window System process that exports an X desktop from the system on which it is running, using a virtual framebuffer to maintain state information about the graphical applications running within that server. VNC uses its own Remote Frame Buffer (RFB) protocol to export graphical changes and handle mouse and keyboard events. Though VNC exports a graphical environment, the

RFB protocol is highly optimized, minimizing the amount of screen update information that must be passed between client and server.

VNC is released under the General Public License (GPL), and many of the original VNC developers now work for a company called RealVNC (*http:// www.realvnc.com*), which distributes and supports a commercial VNC implementation. Another extremely popular VNC distribution is TightVNC (*http:// www.tightvnc.com*), a small, even more highly optimized VNC client and server. TightVNC makes better use of network bandwidth, utilizing JPEG compression for the display and differentiating between local cursor movement and cursor movement that needs to be communicated back to the VNC server. TightVNC also features automatic SSH tunneling for security purposes, though any VNC session can be run through an SSH tunnel [Hack #12]. This hack focuses on using TightVNC, although RealVNC is also an excellent choice. Most Linux distributions install one of these VNC implementations as part of their default client/server installations, but you can always obtain the latest version from the appropriate web site.

Understanding the VNC Server Startup Process

The actual VNC server binary, *Xvnc*, is usually started by a Perl script called *vncserver*. The *vncserver* script provides a more flexible mechanism for passing arguments to the server, displays status information once the server has started and detached, and also builds in the ability to use a startup script to identify the window manager and any X applications the VNC server should start. The VNC server's startup script is the file *~/.vnc/xstartup*. If this directory and the startup file do not exist the first time you start a VNC server, the directory is created and the startup script is cloned from the default X Window System startup file (*/etc/X11/xinit/xinitrc*). On Red Hat and Fedora Core systems, the default *~/.vnc/xstartup* script simply executes the command script */etc/X11/xinit/xintrc*:

```
#!/bin/sh
# Red Hat Linux VNC session startup script
exec /etc/X11/xinit/xinitrc
```

This enables VNC on Red Hat and Fedora Core systems to follow the same somewhat convoluted chain of X Window startup files that are normally used: *~/.Xclients*, *~/.Xclients-$HOSTNAME$DISPLAY*, *~/.Xclients-default*, and */etc/ X11/xinit/Xclients*. Xclient files can start various desktop environments and window managers by using environment variable settings, and they finally fall through to execing the *twm* window manager (*http://www.plig.org/ xwinman/vtwm.html*).

On SUSE systems, the ~/.vnc/xstartup script is a little more straightforward:

```
#!/bin/sh
xrdb $HOME/.Xresources
xsetroot -solid grey
xterm -geometry 80x24+10+10 -ls -title "$VNCDESKTOP Desktop" &
twm &
```

This startup script loads the X Window System resource settings specified in the file *$HOME/.Xresources*, sets the background to solid grey, starts an *xterm* with the specified parameters, and then starts the *twm* window manager. Later in this hack, in the section "Customizing Your VNC Server's X Window System Environment," I'll discuss how to customize this script to start the X Window System environment and applications of your choice. For now, it's simply useful to understand how the VNC server determines what X Window System applications to run.

Starting Your VNC Server

To start a VNC server you execute the *vncserver* script, which starts the *Xvnc* server and the X Window System window manager or desktop and applications defined in your ~/.vnc/xstartup script. The first time you start a VNC server on your system, you will be prompted to set and confirm a password for read/write access to the VNC server. You will also be prompted as to whether you want to set a view-only password for the VNC server. As the name suggests, a view-only password will enable you to see but not interact with the remote desktop displayed in the *vncviewer* window. The first time you run the *vncserver* script, you'll see something like the following:

```
$ vncserver
You will require a password to access your desktops.
Password:
Verify:
Would you like to enter a view-only password (y/n)? n
New 'X' desktop is 64bit:1
Starting applications specified in /home/wvh/.vnc/xstartup
Logfile is /home/wvh/.vnc/64bit:1.log
```

You'll notice that I didn't bother to set a view-only password: I've never found this to be all that useful. You can change your VNC password at any time using the vncpasswd command. Like most password-changing utilities, it first prompts you for your old VNC password, then for the new one, and finally asks for confirmation of the new VNC password.

When you start a VNC server on a system console or as a privileged user, make sure you have set a VNC password that follows the most stringent rules for password security. Anyone who breaks your password will have instant virtual access to one of your desktops and all applications it contains. This would be paradise for a script-kiddy who might not otherwise know his way around a Linux box.

Once you've set a password and, optionally, a view-only password, the *vncserver* script will display a message like the following whenever a server is successfully started:

```
New 'X' desktop is home.vonhagen.org:1
Starting applications specified in /home/wvh/.vnc/xstartup
Logfile is /home/wvh/.vnc/home.vonhagen.org:1.log
```

VNC servers export their virtual displays via ports starting at 5900 plus the number of the display being exported. For example, a VNC server running on the X Window System *display:1* will use port 5901, a VNC server running on the X Window System *display:2* will use port 5902, and so on. If your system does kernel packet filtering or your network uses a firewall, you must make sure that you do not block ports 590*x* (used to export VNC server displays), port 6000 (used to communicate with the X Window System server), or ports 580*x* (if you want to communicate with a VNC server over the Web **[Hack #11]**).

Connecting to a VNC Server

Once you've started a VNC server, you can connect to it from any remote system by executing the command vncviewer *host:display*, where *host* is the host on which the VNC server is running and *display* is the number of the X Window System display on which the VNC server is running. Figure 2-1 shows a connection to a remote SUSE system using the default *xstartup* script shown in the previous section. As you can see, the default VNC server setup is a bit austere, even if you are a window manager bigot or connoisseur of simplicity.

Customizing Your VNC Server's X Window System Environment

Most VNC server configurations automatically start the *twm* window manager in the VNC server environment by default. However, the VNC server's use of a startup script makes it easy to start any window manager, desktop environment, and X Window System applications that you'd prefer to use in the VNC environment.

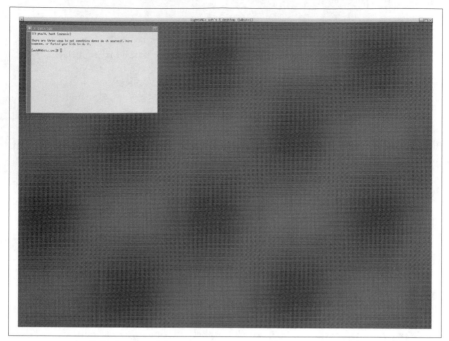

Figure 2-1. The default VNC desktop

For low-bandwidth conditions, the *twm* window manager may still be the best choice: due to its comparatively minimal feature set, it is relatively light-weight. In higher-bandwidth network environments, however, you may want to use a window manager or desktop environment that you are more comfortable with. You can easily do this by commenting out the twm entry in your *xstartup* file and adding the commands that you want to use to start another window manager or a desktop environment such as GNOME or KDE. For example, Figure 2-2 shows a connection to a remote SUSE system when the default *xstartup* script has been modified to start KDE on that desktop, as in the following:

```
#!/bin/sh
xrdb $HOME/.Xresources
# xsetroot -solid grey
xterm -geometry 80x24+10+10 -ls -title "$VNCDESKTOP Desktop" &
# twm &
/opt/kde3/bin/startkde &
```

> If directed to do so when you exit, KDE remembers its state across restarts. Figure 2-2 therefore shows two *xterms* being started—the one from KDE's saved information about the last time I started it, and the one specified in the VNC startup script.

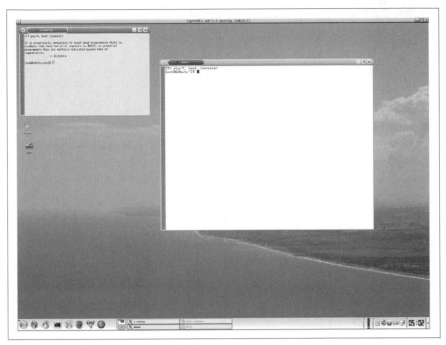

Figure 2-2. A VNC desktop using KDE

Stopping Your VNC Server

Like any process, a VNC server will always terminate when you shut down or reboot the machine on which it's running. (No kidding!) However, this isn't the cleanest shutdown mechanism, because it will leave useless PID files in your *~/.vnc* directory and will leave some temporary and socket files in various locations in your system's */tmp* directory. A much cleaner way to shut down a running VNC server process is to use the *vncserver* script's -kill option:

```
$ vncserver -kill :number
```

Besides cleanly terminating VNC servers when you're planning to shut down or reboot your systems, you may also want to manually terminate a VNC server if you have modified its startup file and want to restart the VNC server with the new window manager, desktop, or X Window System applications.

> If your system crashes while running a VNC server or the VNC server itself crashes, you should clean out the files associated with the VNC server in the */tmp* and */tmp/.X11-unix* directories. For example, if your VNC server was running on display number 1, you would delete the files */tmp/.X1-lock* and */tmp/. X11-unix/X1*. Doing so ensures that any newly started VNC server will start on the first available X display.

Optimizing VNC Performance

You can optimize VNC performance at two different levels, either by minimizing X Window System updates that have to be communicated between the VNC client and server, or by optimizing how VNC sends that information between the client and the server.

Minimizing the amount of graphical X Window System traffic sent between the VNC client and server is largely a matter of reducing updates to a minimum while still retaining a usable X Window System session. Regardless of the window manager or desktop environment that you're using in VNC, here are some general tips for improving performance by minimizing graphical updates:

- Minimize the color depth of the desktop.
- Eliminate window highlighting when windows get focus.
- Don't automatically raise windows when they get focus.
- Don't use opaque moves when moving windows. Configure your window manager or desktop environment to move window outlines instead.

> If you stick with *twm* in your VNC sessions, you can further optimize VNC performance by tweaking its core capabilities to minimize graphical feedback when it's unneeded. The old AT&T web site for VNC (*http://www.uk.research.att.com/archive/vnc/twmideas.html*) provides some specific tips for optimizing *twm* for VNC.

Optimizing the way in which the VNC client and server exchange update information is the other possible way to improve VNC's performance. VNC clients and servers attempt to communicate using encoded update instructions to minimize network traffic. All graphical updates between the VNC viewer and server are communicated as rectangles of pixels to be updated. The supported encoding mechanisms differ based on whether you're using the VNC server/viewer from RealVNC or TightVNC. The TightVNC viewer enables you to specify a custom sequence of encoding mechanisms to try in order by using the -encoding option. This option must be followed by a series of supported encodings enclosed within double quotation marks. The RealVNC viewer enables you to specify a single preferred encoding mechanism using the -PreferredEncoding option, which must be followed by the name of the encoding mechanism you want to try first. In either case, the encoding mechanism will default to sending all information in an unencoded fashion (known as *raw encoding*) if no supported encoding mechanism can be negotiated with the server.

The following list shows the encoding mechanisms supported by the RealVNC and TightVNC packages. Different encoding mechanisms will improve performance in different situations, depending upon conditions such as whether the VNC client and server are running on the same system, the load on your network, and so on. You may want to refer to this section later to experiment with customizing VNC server/viewer communications, depending on your network environment and whether you are actually seeing performance problems. The supported encoding mechanisms are:

CopyRect (TightVNC only)
> Copy Rectangle encoding sends only the location and size of a rectangle on the screen from which data should be copied and the coordinates of its new location.

CoRRE (TightVNC only)
> Copy Rise-and-Run-Length Encoding (RRE) is a variation of RRE that uses a maximum of 255×255–pixel rectangles. Limiting the number of rectangles to values that can be expressed in a single byte reduces packet size and improves efficiency.

Hextile (both)
> Hextile encoding splits the rectangular portion of the screen to be updated into 16×16 tiles that are sent in a predetermined order. The data in each tile is encoded in the raw or CoRRE format. Hextile is the preferred choice for remote connections over a high-speed network.

Raw (both)
> Sends width $\times$ height pixel values with no compression or repeat counts. This encoding mechanism is fastest for local server/viewer connections because there are no bandwidth limitations on local connections, and it requires no special processing. All VNC clients must support this encoding type.

RRE (TightVNC only)
> Rise-and-Run-Length Encoding is a two-dimensional version of Run-Length Encoding (RLE) that applies RLE-encoded sequences across different subrectangles. This is extremely efficient when encoding updates consisting of large blocks of the same color.

Tight (TightVNC only)
> Tight encoding uses the *zlib* library to compress the pixel data, but preprocesses data to maximize compression while minimizing processing time. It uses JPEG compression internally to encode color-rich portions of areas to update. This is usually the best choice for modem connections and low-bandwidth network environments.

Zlib (TightVNC only)
> Zlib encoding uses the *zlib* library to compress raw pixel data. This provides good compression at the expense of the local CPU time required to compress the data.

ZRLE (RealVNC only)
> Zlib Run-Length Encoding combines RLE with Zlib compression. Sequences of identical pixels within the rectangle to be updated are compressed to a single value and repeat count, and the resulting information is then compressed using Zlib.

Table 2-1 shows the sequence in which a TightVNC viewer tries these different encoding mechanisms when communicating with a remote or local VNC server.

Table 2-1. Order of encoding mechanisms used by TightVNC

	Remote	Local
CopyRect	1	2
CoRRE	5	6
Hextile	3	4
Raw	7	1
RRE	6	7
Tight	2	3
Zlib	4	5

See Also

- `man vncviewer`
- `man vncserver`
- *http://www.tightvnc.com*
- *http://www.realvnc.com*
- TightVNC binaries for various Unix systems: *ftp://ftp.kinetworks.com/tightvnc*
- OS X VNC server: *http://www.redstonesoftware.com/vnc.html*

H A C K #11 Access VNC Servers over the Web

With a little extra software, you can access your VNC servers in any web browser.

If you use VNC often enough, you'll eventually find yourself needing access to a VNC viewer from a computer on which it has not been installed. You can put a copy of the installer or the installed application on a public share, but manually connecting each time is a pain, especially if you just need to quickly type a command or check status on the remote machine running your VNC server—and always carrying a CD or floppy with the VNC viewer application on it is equally irksome.

Fortunately, the people who designed VNC are smart folks, and they thought of a solution to the roaming user problem—a hassle-free way to make your VNC servers available even if the system you're using doesn't have VNC client software installed. All VNC servers include a small built-in web server that can serve the Java classes needed for any Java-enabled browser to connect to the VNC server. This lets you access any VNC session that is already running on one of your systems using any modern, Java-enabled browser. The VNC server listens for HTTP connections on port 5800 plus the number of the display being exported. Therefore, to view a VNC session running on display 1 of the host *64bit.vonhagen.org*, you would access the URL *http://64bit.vonhagen.org:5801/*.

As with any VNC session, the Java classes that implement the VNC client will prompt you for the VNC server's password before connecting to the VNC server. Figure 2-3 shows a connection to my laptop's VNC server, on which I am running the Fluxbox window manager (*http://fluxbox.sourceforge.net*).

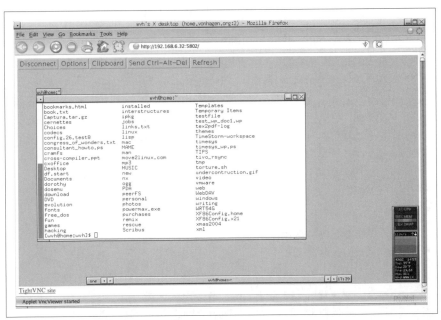

Figure 2-3. A VNC desktop in the Firefox web browser

Installing Java Classes and Associated Files for the VNC Server

To enable web access to your VNC server(s), you must install the Java class and JAR files, and a few additional files for the HTTP VNC server on the system where you'll be running it. These files are installed as part of both the RealVNC and TightVNC server packages, but they can also be obtained from the RealVNC and TightVNC web sites (*http://www.realvnc.com* and *http://www.tightvnc.com*, respectively) if they aren't installed on your system for some reason. Where they are installed and how you let the VNC server know about them depends on the version of the VNC server and the associated *vncserver* script that you're running.

If you're running TightVNC, the location where these files are found is specified in the variable $vncClasses in the *vncserver* script.

You must also make sure that the following line is not commented out of the *vncserver* script:

```
$cmd .= " -httpd $vncClasses";
```

If you're running a RealVNC server, the location(s) where these files can be found is specified in the variable $vncJavaFiles in the *vncserver* script:

```
$vncJavaFiles = (((-d "/usr/share/vnc/classes") && "/usr/share/vnc/classes")
||
        ((-d "/usr/local/vnc/classes") && "/usr/local/vnc/classes"));
```

You must also make sure that the following line is not commented out of the *vncserver* script:

```
$cmd .= " -httpd $vncJavaFiles" if ($vncJavaFiles);
```

Once you've configured the startup script for the Java and other files used by the VNC server, you should restart any VNC server(s) that you're currently running to ensure that they pick up the files used by the VNC server's mini-HTTPD daemon.

See Also

- "Access Systems Remotely with VNC" [Hack #10]
- *http://www.tightvnc.com*
- *http://www.realvnc.com*

HACK #12 Secure VNC via SSH

Easily encrypt your remote connections by setting up a secure tunnel.

VNC is a great way of getting access to a graphical desktop on a remote system. However, once you're connected, VNC uses standard TCP/IP for all traffic between the local viewer and the remote server. Anyone with a packet sniffer on your local network can grab packets and monitor your traffic, which is a bad thing if you're using the remote session for administrative tasks that will transmit passwords.

Luckily, it's quite easy to leverage the encryption provided by SSH, the Secure Shell, in your VNC sessions. You do this by setting up an *SSH tunnel*, which is essentially just a mapping between local and remote ports so that all traffic to a specified port on a remote machine is forwarded via SSH to a port on your local machine. This hack explains how to combine the power of VNC with the security of SSH to provide secure connections to remote machines. For general information about SSH, see the first volume of *Linux Server Hacks* by Rob Flickenger (O'Reilly), which devotes an entire chapter to SSH.

Forwarding Remote VNC Ports to Your Current Host

In addition to the standard secure shell functionality that most people use SSH for, SSH also enables you to forward traffic from a specific port on a remote machine to a specific port on your local machine. Doing this requires that a VNC server is already running on the remote machine, and that you establish a standard SSH connection to the remote machine but supply the -L (local) option and an appropriate argument when you execute the ssh command.

The syntax for forwarding ports when using a standard SSH connection is the following:

```
$ ssh -L local-port:local-host:remote-port remote-host
```

As discussed in "Access Systems Remotely with VNC" [Hack #10], standard VNC traffic with a given host takes place over port 590*x*, where *x* is the X Window System display that a specific VNC server is using. For example, to use SSH to forward VNC traffic from the VNC server running on the X Window System *display:1* of the host *nld.vonhagen.org* to the same port on your local system, *home.vonhagen.org*, you would execute the following command:

```
$ ssh -L 5901:home.vonhagen.org:5901 nld.vonhagen.org
```

Once this tunnel is created, point your *vncviewer* at *home.vonhagen.org:1* to establish a connection. When you supply the VNC password for the VNC server running on *nld.vonhagen.org*, a standard VNC window will display on your system—but the connection is secure. You can now type passwords, write love letters, or surf for a new job without anyone being able to sniff out what you're doing.

Even after forwarding a remote VNC port, the VNC server is still running on its original port on the remote host. Anyone who knows the VNC password to the remote system will still be able to connect to the VNC server normally, without the encryption you've set up through your locally forwarded tunnel.

If you are using the Java VNC viewer [Hack #11], you will also need to forward the port used by your VNC server's internal HTTP server. A VNC server's HTTP server uses port 580*x*, where *x* is the X Window System display that a specific VNC server is using. For example, in the previous command, the VNC server was using X Window System *display:1*, which meant that it was using port 5901 for standard VNC connections. Its web server is therefore using port 5801.

Public or Private VNC Forwarding

When forwarding ports in SSH, you can refer to your local machine using either its public hostname, which uses its standard IP address, or its loopback name, which maps the remote port to your host's loopback address. Each approach has its advantages.

Using the loopback address is best for security, because it requires that you be directly connected to your machine in order to access the remote VNC server through your loopback address. No one else can access the VNC server without being connected to your machine, since a loopback address (127.0.0.1) is specific to each host.

On the other hand, you may want to specify your host's public hostname if you want to be able to access the forwarded VNC from other hosts, or if you want to use a single system as an aggregator for connections to multiple VNC servers. The latter can be useful in enterprise environments where you want encrypted VNC connections but don't want to set up each one individually on whatever computer you're currently using. Using a specific system as a VNC aggregator provides the convenience of being able to access multiple VNC servers through a single host while still using the security provided by VNC's encryption, as shown in Figure 2-4.

Forwarding Ports Without Remote Login

Using the standard ssh command and the -L option requires that you actually establish an SSH connection to a remote machine, tying up whatever terminal session you're using to set up the port forwarding. To start up SSH port forwarding in the background, you can use the ssh command's -f (fork) and -N (no command) options, as in the following example:

```
$ ssh -f -N -L 5901:localhost:5901 nld.vonhagen.org
```

In this example, unless you've used SSH keys to set up passwordless SSH with the host *nld.vonhagen.org*, you'll still be prompted for your remote password. Once you enter it, SSH will set up the specified port forwarding and then return control to the local shell, rather than starting up a remote shell and connecting you to it. To terminate SSH port forwarding started in

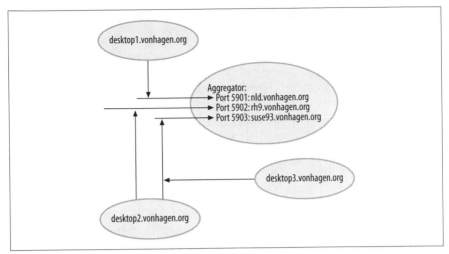

Figure 2-4. Multiple hosts using a single VNC aggregator

this fashion, you will have to locate and terminate the process using the Linux ps and kill commands or equivalents.

Improving Performance with Compression

Slow connections, such as those via modems and heavily loaded networks, can make using remote graphical applications painful. In these cases, you can optimize the bandwidth required for communicating with your remote VNC server by taking advantage of SSH compression. The ssh command provides a -C (compression) option that uses the same compression algorithms used by *gzip* to reduce the amount of data that you have to transfer back and forth over whatever wire you're using. To add compression to your SSH tunnel, just add the -C option to your existing ssh command line. For example, the command in the previous section would become the following to invoke compression:

```
$ ssh -C -L 5901:home.vonhagen.org:5901 nld.vonhagen.org
```

This command compresses all data exchanged between *home.vonhagen.org* and *nld.vonhagen.org* over the SSH tunnel.

Compression reduces the amount of data that needs to be exchanged over the tunnel, but it adds some processing overhead on both the client and the server in order to compress and decompress the data being exchanged over the tunnel. Compression may not be a good idea on slow or heavily loaded systems, but it's almost always a good idea over dialup connections. When using actual network connections, since both system and network load are transient, the only surefire way to gauge the possible benefits of compression is to experiment with using it.

Optimizing Graphical Updates Between Server and Viewer

As explained in detail in "Access Systems Remotely with VNC" [Hack #10], VNC supports a number of different ways to encode graphical update information when exchanging data between a VNC server and viewer. VNC viewers try to negotiate different encoding mechanisms depending on whether they believe that the VNC server is running locally or on a remote machine. Local connections always try to use raw encoding before trying any compressed encoding options. Raw encoding is extremely fast if the VNC server and viewer are running on the same machine, since local bandwidth is effectively infinite, but it's inefficient when communicating between a remote server and a local viewer.

When using SSH tunneling to redirect a remote VNC server to a local port, you'll want to override the default encoding settings to make communication between the VNC server and client more efficient, since the server is remote. If you're using the RealVNC *vncviewer*, specify the -PreferredEncoding hextile option on the vncviewer command line. If you're using TightVNC's *vncviewer*, you should specify -encodings "copyrect tight hextile" to take advantage of TightVNC's optimized encoding.

> To find out which VNC viewer you're using (and therefore whether to try tight encoding), you can execute the command vncviewer --help. If you're using TightVNC, you'll see a string like TightVNC viewer version 1.2.9 as part of the output of this command. If you're using an RPM-based Linux system, you can also execute the command: rpm -qf `which vncviewer` to see which package provided the vncviewer command.

See Also

* "Access Systems Remotely with VNC" [Hack #10]
* *Linux Server Hacks*, by Rob Flickenger (O'Reilly)
* *http://www.tightvnc.com*
* *http://www.realvnc.com*

HACK #13 Autostart VNC Servers on Demand

Eliminate the need to manually start VNC servers on remote machines.

In this age of enlightenment and whizzy graphical devices, most Unix servers have graphical consoles instead of the VT100s or LA123s of days gone by. This is certainly true of most Linux servers, though most machine rooms save space by installing a single monitor and using a KVM to switch between the systems that are actually using it at the moment. As explained in "Access Systems Remotely with VNC" [Hack #10], the traditional mode of operation for VNC is to SSH/telnet/whatever to a remote system, manually start a VNC server, and then nip back to the system you're actually using and start the VNC viewer there. It's easy enough—but isn't the whole "SSH there, stand on one leg, start this, pop back here, start that here" business irritating?

This hack explains how to avoid all that by integrating the VNC X Window System server directly into your graphical X Window System login environment. The basic idea is that you configure your machine to use your system's Internet daemon (*xinetd* or *inetd*) to start the *Xvnc* server whenever an incoming VNC connection is sensed on one or more ports. You also configure your system to use the X Display Manager Control Protocol (XDMCP) to manage any new X displays, such as the *Xvnc* server. When the *Xvnc* server starts in response to an incoming port request, it displays an XDMCP login screen, you log in, and voilà!

Integrating Xvnc with inetd or xinetd

The modern Linux Internet daemon *xinetd* (like its predecessor *inetd*, which may still be used somewhere) initiates the daemons associated with various servers in response to incoming requests on different ports, as defined in the file */etc/services*. Throughout the rest of this hack, I'll refer to *xinetd* and *inetd* together as *x/inetd*, using their specific names whenever necessary to differentiate between them.

The *x/inetd* daemon is often referred to as a "super server," because its job is to manage other server processes. Using *x/inetd* lowers the load on your systems, because the daemons for these services don't have to be running all the time—*x/inetd* starts them as needed when an incoming request is detected. Using *x/inetd* also heightens security on your systems by providing what are commonly known as *TCP wrappers*—a central mechanism for enabling or denying TCP access to a number of services through entries in the files */etc/hosts.allow* and */etc/hosts.deny*, respectively.

The first step in integrating VNC with *x/inetd* is to create an appropriate entry for VNC in the text file */etc/services*. On new systems that I set up, I decided that automatic VNC sessions would start on port 5908—choosing a value higher than 5900 will prevent collisions when a user manually starts a VNC session on the server using a lower port number. An appropriate */etc/services* entry for automatically starting VNC in response to incoming requests on port 5908 is the following:

```
vnc             5908/tcp        # Xvnc
```

Once you've created this entry in *etc/services*, you must next define what happens in response to an incoming request on this port.

If you're using *xinetd*, you must create the file *etc/xinetd.d/vnc*, which contains various settings for how *xinetd* should respond to incoming requests, which application it should start, and so on. Here's a sample *etc/xinetd.d/vnc* file:

```
# default: on
# description: The vnc server provides remote desktop connections
#
service vnc
{
        disable         = no
        socket_type     = stream
        protocol        = tcp
        wait            = no
        user            = nobody
        server          = /usr/bin/Xvnc
        server_args     = :8 -inetd -once -query localhost -depth 24 \
                          -geometry 1280x1024 -securitytypes=none
}
```

The server_args entry should be on a single line, but I've broken it into two in this example for readability. The arguments that you specify to the *Xvnc* server are highly dependent on the version and source of the *Xvnc* server that you're running. The arguments shown in the previous example mean the following:

:8

    Specifies the X Window System display on which the *Xvnc* server should start.

-inetd

    Runs the *Xvnc* server as a daemon and expects it to be run from *x/inetd*.

-once

    Starts the *Xvnc* server from scratch when a connection is initiated, and terminates the server when the connection terminates. This also blocks multiple copies of the *Xvnc* server from starting on the same port.

-query localhost

    Tells the *Xvnc* server to query a specific machine for an XDMCP login (more about that in the next section). In this case, the *Xvnc* server will contact the loopback interface on *localhost*, which has the IP address 127.0.0.1.

-depth 24

    Specifies the color depth of the *Xvnc* server's X Window server.

`-geometry 1280x1024`

Specifies the virtual screen size and resolution at which to start the *Xvnc* server. Some common values are 800x600, 1024x768, 1280x1024, and 1600x1280. As a general rule, the value you specify should be less than the size of the display on the system you're using to connect to the *Xvnc* server, or you may have problems accessing the window controls. You can use odd dimensions like 1000×50 to have as large a window as possible on a 1024×768 display that fits between graphical elements such as taskbars and sidebars.

`-securitytypes=none`

Specifies that the *Xvnc* server shouldn't use its own internal security mechanism (*vncpasswd*) to allow access to the VNC server, since XDMCP will handle this for you.

Depending on the version of *Xvnc* that's installed on your system, you may need other or additional options:

`-ac`

If you're using TightVNC's version of *Xvnc*, you'll need to use this option instead of `-securitytypes=none` to avoid using *Xvnc*'s default access controls. The `-securitytypes=none` argument is used by RealVNC's *Xvnc*.

`-fp fontpath`

Some versions of *Xvnc* need to know the font path for the X Window System fonts that they should use. Most modern Linux systems run an X font server by default on port 7100, so an appropriate initial value to try is `-fp unix:/7100`. If this doesn't work or you're not running a font server, you can explicitly list any number of directories as a single, comma-separated argument to the `-fp` option.

If you're still using *inetd*, the equivalent of the */etc/xinetd.d/vnc* file is a single entry in the file */etc/inetd.conf*. Here's an example entry that matches the previous *xinetd* example:

```
vnc stream tcp nowait nobody /usr/sbin/tcpd /usr/bin/Xvnc :8 -inetd \
    -once -query localhost -depth 24 -geometry 1280x1024 \
    -securitytypes=none
```

As with the `server_args` entry in the *xinetd* example, this should all appear on a single line in your */etc/inetd.conf* file—I've only broken it across multiple lines here for readability. The same caveats about possible alternate/extra arguments apply to an */etc/inetd.conf* entry.

Activating XDMCP

XDMCP is a network protocol used for initiating login sessions on X Window System display devices. Originally developed in 1989, XDMCP is primarily associated with X terminals [Hack #14]), but it can be used with any X Window System device—such as, in this case, the X server started by *Xvnc*.

Most systems that come up in graphics mode use an X Window System display manager to provide a graphical login and subsequently start the window manager or desktop environment of your choice. Graphics mode is usually runlevel 5 for most Linux systems, or any of runlevels 2 through 5 if you're a Debian or Ubuntu fan. By default, the X display manager manages the X Window System device associated with the console, but it is optionally responsible for responding to XDMCP requests and initiating the appropriate X Window System login sessions on new X Window System devices. XDMCP support is a configuration option for all X display managers, but it is usually disabled by default since most display managers only need to support X login sessions on their consoles.

How you activate XDMCP support depends on which display manager you're using, which is usually determined by the default desktop system used on your Linux system. GNOME uses a display manager called *gdm*, usually found in */usr/bin/gdm* (which calls */usr/bin/gdm-binary*) or in */opt/gnome/bin/gdm* on KDE-based systems such as SUSE. KDE uses one called *kdm*, usually found in */opt/kde3/bin/kdm*. The classic X Window display manager, often used on systems where neither GNOME nor KDE is installed, is *xdm*, and it is usually found in */usr/X11R6/bin/xdm*. If you are running Red Hat Linux, you can check the script */etc/X11/prefdm* to see how your system selects its default display manager and which one it is. You can also figure out which display manager your system is actually running by looking for the string *dm* in a system process listing, as in the following example:

```
$ ps -ef | grep dm
root      5137     1  0 May25 ?        00:00:00 /opt/kde3/bin/kdm
root      5167  5137 65 May25 ?        3-01:52:35 /usr/X11R6/bin/X \
     -br vt7 -auth /var/lib/xdm/authdir/authfiles/A:0-K7ItZv
wvh      29664 24116  0 13:42 pts/11   00:00:00 grep -i dm
```

In this case, the system is running *kdm* as its display manager, so you'll have to correctly configure *kdm* to support XDMCP. Needless to say, each of these X Window System display managers has its own configuration file, in which you must enable XDMCP so that when *Xvnc* queries the *localhost*, the local display manager will initiate an X login session.

If the system on which you are configuring *Xvnc* runs *gdm*, the GNOME desktop provides a convenient application called *gdmsetup* for configuring *gdm*. Start *gdmsetup* as root or by using sudo, select the XDMCP tab, and select Enable XDMCP to activate XDMCP support in *gdm* the next time you restart the X Window System. Figure 2-5 shows this tab selected in *gdmsetup*, with XDMCP enabled.

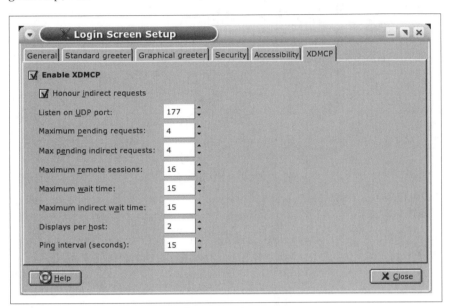

Figure 2-5. XDMCP activation in gdmsetup

You can also manually modify the *gdm* configuration file as an alternative to running *gdmsetup*. On many Linux systems, this configuration file is */etc/X11/gdm/gdm.conf*.

If the system on which you are configuring *Xvnc* runs *kdm*, you can either use the administrative utilities provided by your system or manually modify the *kdm* and system configuration files that control its behavior. For example, on SUSE systems, you can use the *YaST* administrative modules from the Control Center (Control Center → YaST2 modules → Network Devices → Remote Administration) to activate remote access to the display manager. Figure 2-6 shows this panel in the Control Center.

If you'd prefer to tweak the configuration files yourself, you can modify the primary *kdm* configuration file (*/opt/kde3/share/config/kdm/kdmrc*) with a text editor, changing the Enable entry in the [xdmcp] section to true and making sure that the Port=177 entry is not commented out. You will also have to modify the file */etc/sysconfig/displaymanager*, setting the

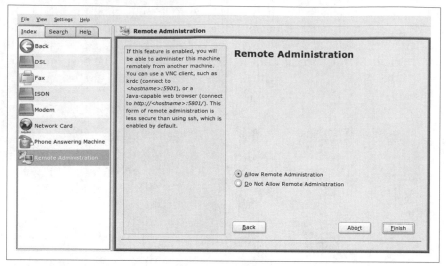

Figure 2-6. XDCMP configuration in SUSE's YaST utility

DISPLAYMANAGER_REMOTE_ACCESS variable to yes. You can then run */sbin/ SuSEconfig* to cause SUSE to perform the correct internal updates.

Once you have modified your display manager to support XDMCP, you will need to restart the display manager with the correct settings. The easiest way to ensure a complete restart is to reboot your system, but if you are running critical services on that system, you can also use the telinit or init commands to take your system to a nongraphical runlevel (telinit *number-of-runlevel* or init *number-of-runlevel*) and then return to a graphical runlevel, such as runlevel 2 for Debian-based distributions or runlevel 3 for most others. You can then use telinit to return to runlevel 5. Some flavors of Linux provide scripts (such as SUSE's rcxdm restart command) that will automatically terminate the X Window System and restart the display manager for you without switching runlevels.

> Updates to the X Window System are a common part of any system update or upgrade. If you have manually modified configuration files, double-check your configuration files after applying updates that modify either X or the desktop environment that you're using to make sure that XDCMP support is still enabled in your display manager—if it isn't, this hack will cease to work.

Starting the Viewer

Once you've set up your system to initiate *Xvnc* in response to incoming requests and have configured your display manager to respond to XDMCP requests, go to another system and start your favorite VNC viewer application, pointing to a port that you specified in */etc/xinet.d/vnc*. After a few moments, you should see something like Figure 2-7. Congratulations—initiating VNC sessions to your host(s) is now easier than ever before, and you no longer have to start VNC manually on those systems like an electronic catcher's mitt to service incoming VNC requests!

Figure 2-7. A successful Xvnc connection using XDMCP

 Because the X Window session running in VNC is using an alternate display, you may need to make sure that you set the DISPLAY environment variable correctly within it in order to start other X Window System applications. For example, if you are running *Xvnc* on port 5908, you may need to set the display in your shell appropriately using a command such as export DISPLAY=:8.0.

Troubleshooting Xvnc Startup

If you're lucky, you're already looking at Figure 2-7 and thinking "problems—what problems?" However, if your *vncviewer* simply hangs or terminates with information-packed messages such as "vncviewer: ConnectToTcpAddr: connect: Connection refused" or "Unable to connect to VNC server," don't despair. These problems are easily resolved.

If your *vncviewer* connection to the remote machine simply hangs—i.e., you press Return and nothing happens—chances are that the ports associated with your VNC setup are being firewalled on the remote machine, the local machine, or somewhere in between. Check to make sure that whatever ports you put in */etc/services* on the remote system are actually available and that a process is listening on the XDMCP port. An easy way to do this is by executing the `netstat -an` command and filtering its output for port 177, the port used by XDMCP, as in the following example:

```
$ netstat -an | grep 177
udp        0      0 :::177                    :::*
```

If you do not see any output from this command, make sure you have correctly configured XDMCP support in your display manager and that the *Xvnc* entries in */etc/xinetd.d/vnc* are not disabled. Worst-case, you can reboot your system to make sure everything starts up correctly.

If you still can't establish a VNC connection to your system, make sure no firewall rules are blocking any of the ports used by XDMCP or *Xvnc*. An easy (but completely insecure) way to do this is to temporarily terminate your firewalls or punt all your active rules using a command such as `iptables -F`. First try this on the system that you are trying to connect to; then, if you still can't connect, try it on the system you are trying to connect from. If you can connect successfully after disabling the firewall, review your system's firewall configuration and relax the appropriate rules to enable remote VNC connections. Remember to reactivate your firewalls after reconfiguring them—you don't want the entire seventh-grade class of PS150 in Seoul to be able to try getting graphical logins on your machine!

See Also

- "Access Systems Remotely with VNC" [Hack #10]
- "Secure VNC via SSH" [Hack #12]
- *Linux Server Hacks*, by Rob Flickenger (O'Reilly)
- *http://www.tightvnc.com*
- *http://www.realvnc.com*

Put Your Desktops on a Thin Client Diet

Centralize administration by using the Linux Terminal Server Project and existing or inexpensive desktop systems to give your users the computing power they need at a price you can afford.

Though the cost of hardware is constantly decreasing, it is still greater than zero. Putting a high-powered workstation on everyone's desk is a nice idea, but not everyone needs a dual-processor Mac or Linux box to get their work done. The key requirement for most users is access to the applications and data they're working on and enough memory to work with them.

The Linux Terminal Server Project (LTSP; *http://www.ltsp.org*) lets you boot desktop systems from a remote server, gives users access to their applications and data when they log in, and provides a graphical, X Window System working environment that is functionally identical to booting from a local disk. This can provide substantial cost savings by enabling you to deploy or reuse less-expensive hardware on your users' desktops, since it reduces the amount of local storage and other hardware that any desktop system requires. A processor that is too slow to keep up with the demands of today's applications can still function quite nicely when its sole function is to update a display and respond to mouse and keyboard input.

Centralizing system resources on high-powered servers also provides substantial benefits to system administrators by eliminating the need to individually maintain and upgrade desktop operating systems and application software. All the software that a desktop system requires beyond a boot floppy or network boot information is stored on the server.

The LTSP also provides a great alternative to deploying and maintaining dual-boot systems throughout your enterprise or installing X Window System software on every Windows box if users only need to run Linux software occasionally. Give the users LTSP boot disks configured for their desktop systems and have them reboot using these disks. Problem solved! They have Linux systems on their desktops until they reboot.

Version 4.1 of the LTSP was the latest version at the time this book was written. Installation, configuration, and conceptual information should be similar for any newer version that may exist by the time that you read this.

Understanding the LTSP Client Boot Process

In case the notion of systems booting and getting all their software over a network is new to you, this section provides an overview of the boot process for an LTSP client system. Being able to visualize how LTSP clients and servers interact will minimize configuration problems and will also be useful if you need to diagnose performance or connectivity problems in the future.

LTSP client and servers interact in the following way when you boot an LTSP client:

1. The client boots and contacts a DHCP server to obtain its IP address, the name of the Linux kernel to download and boot, and the NFS location of a directory structure that it should use as the root filesystem for that kernel.

2. The client contacts the TFTP server on the LTSP kernel and downloads the specified kernel into local memory.

3. The client boots the downloaded kernel, using the NFS root filesystem as the root filesystem for that kernel.

4. The client runs the standard Linux startup script */etc/rc.sysinit*, which starts various services required by the system, sets up swapping, and so on.

5. The client uses the information in */etc/lts.conf* in the NFS-mounted root filesystem to contact whatever X Window System display manager is running on the specified system and display an X display manager login screen on the client's screen.

Once you log in, you are logged in on the LTSP server system. The client system is running only the X Window System software necessary to manage network connections, run an X Window System server, and so on.

 Though you can use lower-powered systems as LTSP clients, this doesn't mean that every PC currently serving as a doorstop at your site can be recycled as a desktop LTSP client system. The PCs you use as LTSP clients must have sufficient resources to run the X Window System, use a reasonable screen resolution, display multiple windows that may be graphically complex, and be able to exchange data over the network relatively quickly. Pentium systems running at 166 MHz or greater, with a minimum of 32 MB of memory and a 4-MB video card, are quite suitable for use as LTSP clients. Adding 100-MB Ethernet cards, more memory, and 8-MB or greater video cards will provide a better user experience and will enable you to configure the X Window System to operate at higher resolutions and with greater color depth.

Downloading and Installing the LTSP Software

You can download the LTSP administrative and configuration utilities as a tarball with an installer (*http://www.ltsp.org/ltsp-utils-0.11.tgz*) or as an RPM (*http://www.ltsp.org/ltsp-utils-0.11-0.noarch.rpm*). You can also download the latest LTSP software by following the download link from its Source-forge project site at *http://sourceforge.net/projects/lts/*.

As part of the initial configuration process, the LTSP administration utility downloads additional packages that the LTSP server(s) and clients require. These additional packages provide the kernel, X Window System utilities, and other components of the root filesystem used when LTSP clients boot from the server in order to start their X sessions. During the LTSP configuration process, you can either download these additional packages over the network or load them from a local CD-ROM or directory that provides them. To save time during the installation process and simplify installation in general, you should download an ISO image of a CD-ROM that contains all of these packages from *http://ltsp.mirrors.tds.net/pub/ltsp/isos/ltsp-4.1-1.iso*.

If you've downloaded a tarball of the LTSP utilities, unpack it and execute the *install.sh* script to install the utilities on the system that you want to be your LTSP server. If you've downloaded the RPM, simply install it with your favorite RPM invocation. Mine is:

```
# rpm -Uvvh ltsp-utils-0.11-0.noarch.rpm
```

If you've download the ISO of the packages required by the LTSP server, burn it to a CD-ROM and mount the CD-ROM (or mount the ISO using a loopback device if you're in a hurry or don't have a CD burner handy). Now the real fun begins!

Configuring and Starting the LTSP Server

To actually install the packages that an LTSP server needs and create your default LTSP configuration file, su to root (use su - to provide a pristine root environment) and execute the ltspadmin command. This command provides a terminal-oriented interface that enables you to install the packages and configure the system services required by required by an LTSP server. Figure 2-8 shows the *ltspadmin* utility's initial screen in an *xterm*.

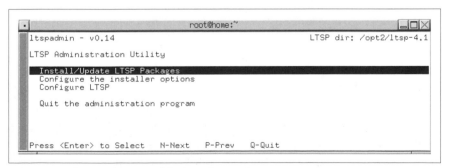

Figure 2-8. The initial screen of the ltspadmin utility

The first step in configuring an LTSP server is to configure the installer itself. Use the arrow keys to select the "Configure the installer options" menu option. The installer prompts you for the location from which to retrieve the packages required by the installer, providing a network source by default. If you've installed them locally, supply the pathname to the directory containing the packages in the form of a URL that begins with *file://*, followed by the full pathname. (This means that your URL must begin with three slashes: two for the protocol specification and one for the beginning of the path to the directory containing the packages. For example, if you burned a CD-ROM and mounted it as */mnt/cdrom*, your URL would be *file:///mnt/cdrom*.)

Next, you'll be prompted for the directory in which you want to install these packages on your server. You'll need to have about 350 MB free on the partition where this directory is located in order to do a complete install of all the LTSP software.

Finally, identify any HTTP or FTP proxies you want to use (or specify none), and then enter y to accept the values that you've entered. The screen shown in Figure 2-8 will be displayed again.

The next step is to select the Install/Update LTSP Packages option, which displays the screen shown in Figure 2-9.

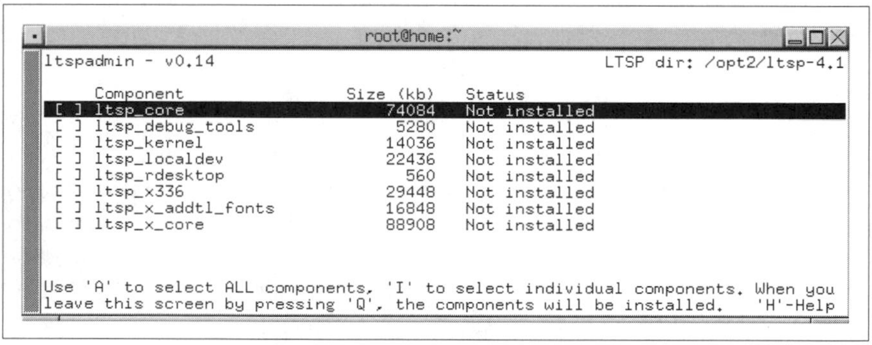

```
                                    root@home:~
ltspadmin - v0.14                                    LTSP dir: /opt2/ltsp-4.1

        Component            Size (kb)   Status
[ ] ltsp_core                   74084   Not installed
[ ] ltsp_debug_tools             5280   Not installed
[ ] ltsp_kernel                 14036   Not installed
[ ] ltsp_localdev               22436   Not installed
[ ] ltsp_rdesktop                 560   Not installed
[ ] ltsp_x336                   29448   Not installed
[ ] ltsp_x_addtl_fonts          16848   Not installed
[ ] ltsp_x_core                 88908   Not installed


Use 'A' to select ALL components, 'I' to select individual components. When you
leave this screen by pressing 'Q', the components will be installed.   'H'-Help
```

Figure 2-9. The ltspadmin utility's Select Packages screen

Press A to select all the packages listed, and press Q to exit this screen and begin installing those packages. You'll have to answer y to an "are you really, really sure" prompt, and then package installation to the specified directory will begin.

Once all the packages are installed, press Enter and select the Configure LTSP option. This starts the *ltspcfg* utility and begins LTSP configuration. *ltspcfg* first checks and summarizes the status of all the services that LTSP requires on your server. Press Enter to continue, and you'll see two options: S to summarize the status of required services of your LTSP server, and C to actually configure them. Figure 2-10 shows the summary screen.

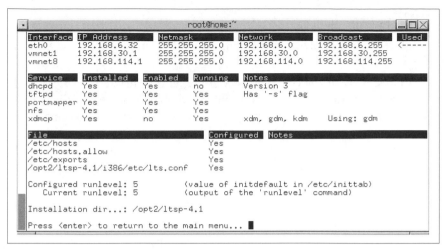

Figure 2-10. The ltspcfg utility's Summary screen

Selecting C displays the screen shown in Figure 2-11, which lists the various aspects of the LTSP server that have to be configured for the terminal server.

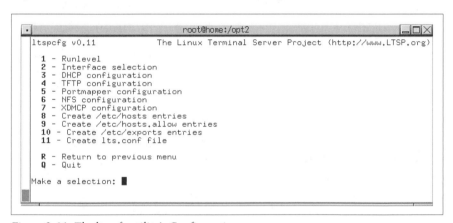

Figure 2-11. The ltspcfg utility's Configuration screen

An LTSP server must provide or have access to the following services in order to function correctly:

DHCP

Assigns the client's IP address and specifies values such as the location of the kernel that the client must download and boot, the path of the NFS root filesystem used by the client's kernel, and so on. The DHCP server doesn't need to be running on the LTSP server, but it must be configured correctly wherever it is running to provide the information required by LTSP clients.

NFS

Enables the client to access the root filesystem exported by the LTSP server, use swapfiles that live on the LTSP server over NFS, and so on.

TFTP

Enables the client to download the kernel that it will boot. The TFTP server does not need to be running on the LTSP server, but it must be configured correctly wherever it is running to provide the bootable kernel image required by LTSP clients.

XDMCP

Enables users to log in on the client system and establish an X Window System connection to the LTSP server.

> I find it easier to run all the services required by LTSP clients on the LTSP server, to simplify administrative tasks such as updating the kernel boot image or changing DHCP parameters. The overhead of maintaining special DHCP and TFTP servers on the LTSP server is usually less than that of making updates on multiple systems. However, as discussed in the list above, only NFS and XDMCP must actually be running on the LTSP server.

We're all sysadmins here, so rather than walking through each step and listing each keypress, I'll just highlight the services that you have to activate and the types of values that you need to enter:

Runlevel

Set the runlevel at which your LTSP server starts. The LTSP server typically needs to be running at runlevel 5 to enable graphical logins via XDMCP, though the runlevel associated with graphical logins differs across Linux distributions. You can also use runlevel 3 (or whatever your nongraphical, multi-user runlevel is) and manually start the X Window System after each login, but that's less fun.

Interface selection

Identify the Ethernet interface over which the LTSP server accepts connections. This information is used in setting up the DHCP and NFS services. Some sites use multiple network interface cards (NICs) in their LTSP servers and attach all LTSP clients to a specialized subnet on a dedicated interface to improve performance and minimize the chance of DHCP collisions.

DHCP configuration

Add entries to the DHCP configuration file (*/etc/dhcpd.conf*) that your LTSP clients require when they get Ethernet addresses from your DHCP server, and make sure that the DHCP server is started by default at the previously specified runlevel. If the DHCP configuration file doesn't already exist, the *ltspcfg* utility creates a template configuration file. You must subsequently edit this to reflect your local domain, network configuration, and so on. Here are some examples of the key entries in the DHCP configuration file for LTSP:

```
option routers              192.168.6.32;
option domain-name-servers  192.168.6.32;
option domain-name          "vonhagen.org";
option root-path            "192.168.6.32:/opt2/ltsp-4.1/i386";
subnet 192.168.6.0 netmask 255.255.255.0 {
    use-host-decl-names  on;
    option log-servers   192.168.6.32;
    range 192.168.6.100 192.168.6.120;
    filename             "/lts/vmlinuz-2.4.26-ltsp-2";
}
```

"Quick and Easy DHCP Setup" [Hack #20] has more detailed information about setting up DHCP and all the entries in the */etc/dhcpd.conf* file.

 If you need to provide specific settings for distinct LTSP clients, you can uniquely identify clients by their MAC addresses and provide client-specific configuration information in your DHCP configuration file.

TFTP configuration
Make sure the TFTP server is enabled in */etc/xinetd.d/tftp* and the directory where it stores files exists.

Portmapper configuration
Make sure the portmapper, required to map ports to Remote Procedure Call (RPC) services, is running on the LTSP server so that NFS (and, optionally, NIS) services will work correctly.

NFS configuration
Configure the LTSP server to start NFS at boot time if it doesn't already do so.

XDMCP configuration
Determine which of the available X display managers (*gdm*, *kdm*, or *xdm*) are installed on the LTSP server, and identify the one that is currently used in runlevel 5. This option also adds entries to the configuration file used by that display manager so that it will accept connection requests from remote LTSP clients.

Create /etc/hosts entries
Create entries in the LTSP server's */etc/hosts* for the range of IP addresses used by LTSP clients. Most RPC-based services, such as NFS, need to be able to map an IP address to a hostname and back again. If you are using DNS, you can also add these entries to your DNS server.

Create /etc/hosts.allow entries

> Add entries to the */etc/hosts.allow* file for the NFS portmapper and TFTP services required by LTSP clients. The */etc/hosts.allow* file is used by *xinetd*'s TCP wrappers to enable access from specified hosts or subnets.

Create /etc/exports entries

> Add entries to the */etc/exports* file used by NFS to identify directories to export, the hosts that can mount them, and how to mount and access those directories. The entries added by the *ltspcfg* program identify the NFS-mounted root filesystem used during the LTSP client boot process and the NFS directory that contains swapfiles for LTSP clients.

Create the lts.conf file

> Create a default Linux Terminal Server configuration file in *etc/lts.conf*, relative to the root of your NFS-mounted root filesystem (in other words, relative to the directory named in the root-path directive in your */etc/dhcp.conf* file). This file provides initial values that a client uses for local configuration and to connect to the LTSP server, and it enables you to provide client-specific settings when necessary. You may have to modify this file to reflect differences between systems such as graphics resolutions or PS/2, serial, and USB mice. See the LTSP documentation for more information about its possible contents.

At this point, you should reboot your LTSP server and verify that all the mandatory services have started automatically (DHCP, *portmapper*, NFS, and an X display manager) and that other mandatory services such as TFTP are enabled. Almost there!

Preparing LTSP Client Boot Media

Once the LTSP server is configured, the next step is to figure out how you want to boot your clients. There are a variety of ways of booting LTSP clients:

- Via the Pre-boot Execution Environment (PXE), if supported by your Ethernet card. PXE is limited to booting files that are smaller than 32K (which doesn't include the Linux kernel), so you'll have to configure it to load a network bootstrap program (NBP) first, which then loads the kernel. Some network cards or motherboards with onboard networking require the use of specialized PXE bootloaders. LTSP Versions 4.0 and greater provide a PXE bootstrap program known as *pxelinux.0*. For more information about using *pxelinux.0*, see *http://www.ltsp.org/ README.pxe*. Another open source PXE bootstrap program often used with LTSP is *bpbatch*. You can get additional information about *bpbatch* from its web site (*http://www.bpbatch.org*) or from *http://www.ltsp.org/ contrib/bpbatch.txt*.

- Via Etherboot or Netboot, two open source Linux projects for creating boot ROMs that you can plug into any network card that supports a boot ROM.

- Via floppy disk, by creating an Etherboot image customized for your network card that you write to a floppy and boot from.

Of these, the most common and easiest to start with is booting from floppy. You simply write the customized Etherboot image to a floppy and then ensure that the client system is configured to boot from its floppy disk drive first. The client boots the image on the floppy, which initializes your client's network interface, then sends out a DHCP request and uses the boot-file and root-path images to download the kernel and boot using the specified root filesystem.

Creating an Etherboot image customized for your client's network card would be completely outside the scope of this hack if it weren't for the amazing ROM-O-Matic web site (*http://www.rom-o-matic.net*)—simply identify your network card, and the web site will generate a boot image for you and download it to your system. It doesn't get much easier than that!

To create the right ROM image, you need to know the exact PCI ID of your network card. If you're not sure which card you have, the easiest thing to do is to boot your client using a rescue disk [Hack #90] or other bootable CD (the Knoppix Live CD included with *Knoppix Hacks*, also from O'Reilly, is a personal favorite). After logging in, you can run the lspci command to identify your Ethernet card and then run the lspci -n command to display the PCI identifiers (two four-digit, colon-separated numbers) for your card. You can then match these against the versions of your card listed on the ROM-O-Matic site, click Get ROM, and save the ROM image to your system. You can then write it to a floppy disk using a command like the following (as root):

```
# cat ROM-filename > /dev/fd0
```

You're now seconds away from turning an old PC into a useful X terminal.

Booting an LTSP Client

Before booting your LTSP client, make sure that all the services required by the LTSP server are running on the server, and that the client is configured to boot from its floppy disk first.

Drumroll, please! Insert the floppy disk in the client's floppy drive and power on the system. After the generic POST messages, you should see a message about loading the ROM image, followed by some Ethernet configuration information and the message "(N)etwork Boot or (Q)uit." Press N, and your system will download and boot the Linux kernel from your LTSP server. After the standard Linux boot messages, you will see a screen that displays the login dialog shown in Figure 2-12.

Figure 2-12. An LTSP client's GDM login dialog

Congratulations—your doorstop is now a useful X terminal!

Once you have an LTSP server configured and set up, the only thing you have to do to create additional client systems is to generate ROM images for the appropriate Ethernet cards, put each on a floppy, and boot the new client with an appropriate boot floppy. This is especially easy if you tend to buy your PCs in batches or from a single vendor—chances are that many of them will have the same Ethernet cards and can use the same boot floppies.

See Also

- *https://www.ltsp.org*
- "Quick and Easy DHCP Setup" [Hack #20]
- "Rescue Me!" [Hack #90]
- *http://www.rom-o-matic.net*
- *Knoppix Hacks*, by Kyle Rankin (O'Reilly)

HACK #15 Run Windows over the Network

Stop deploying Windows systems and software for people who only need occasional access to a few applications.

Regardless of how you feel about Microsoft, you can't escape the Windows operating system and the applications that require it. Even companies that live on Linux for development and testing still need to provide developers with access to Windows systems so that they can share various types of documents with management in formats that management can understand. This quickly gets expensive, and it's generally a hassle for the system administrators who have to deploy and manage these machines, set up the Windows shares de jour on each computer or in user profiles, install the right software packages, and so on.

Many companies take a first stab at saving money by putting two computers under many desks, and sharing a monitor, keyboard, and mouse between them using a KVM switch. That's fine, except that your company pays for the extra systems, Windows licenses, and KVM switches and has to deal with the administrative and security hassles inherent in deploying two desktops per user. As an alternative, some companies use the open source WINE project or its commercial variant Crossover Office (which is a great package, by the way), to run Windows applications natively on Linux machines.

If you need to give users occasional access to Windows-only applications but want to minimize costs and administrative hassles, a good solution is to install Windows Terminal Services on a reasonably beefy Windows system and purchase a pool of Client Access Licenses that are assigned to the users who need to be able to use the applications. Remote clients can then attach to the Terminal Services server and run virtual Windows sessions in windows on their desktops. Install the software that people need to use on the Terminal Services server or in shares defined in your user profiles, and any remote users connected to the server will be able to run the software they need. Luckily, access to Windows Terminal Services doesn't even require a Windows system anymore—Linux users, including those working in an LTSP environment [Hack #14] can easily access Windows Terminal servers using *rdesktop*, an open source software package that speaks the Remote Desktop Protocol (RDP) used by Windows Terminal Services. This hack shows you how it works.

Opening Your Connection

Because *rdesktop* is a graphical application, you must execute it from a Linux system that is running the X Window System. This hack discusses options that are found only in more recent versions of *rdesktop*, which was at Version 1.4.0 when this book was written. Though it's found on many Linux distributions, you can always get the latest and greatest version of *rdesktop* from the sites listed at the end of this hack.

The most minimal command line that you can use to connect to a system running Windows Terminal Services is rdesktop *host*, where *host* is the name or IP address of the system running Windows Terminal Services. Once connected, a window displaying the standard Windows login screen appears on your Linux desktop, as shown in Figure 2-13.

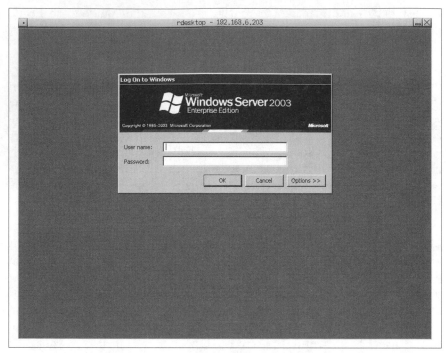

Figure 2-13. The Windows Terminal Services login screen in rdesktop

After you log in and specify the domain that you want to log into (if necessary), your *rdesktop* window will display the standard Windows desktop, as
shown in Figure 2-14.

> If you centralize Windows services by running Terminal Ser-
> vices on your domain controller, make sure the users who
> want to connect to it have the "Log on Locally" user right or
> belong to a group with that right. Otherwise, users will
> receive the message "The local policy of this system does not
> permit you to log on interactively" and be unable to connect.

Like most programs, *rdesktop* provides a number of options that can simplify access to Windows Terminal Services. Though they're all on the
manpage, I'll go through my favorites here:

-d   The domain to which you want to authenticate.

-f   Full-screen mode. This displays the desktop in a decorationless window
     that takes over your desktop. You can toggle decorations (and therefore
     window controls) by pressing Ctrl-Alt-Enter.

-p   Your password in the remote domain.

-u   The name of the user that you want to log in as.

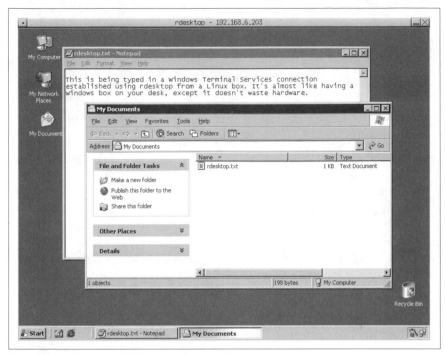

Figure 2-14. A successful Windows Terminal Services login in rdesktop

Mapping Local Devices to Your Remote Session

If the system running Windows Terminal Services is running Microsoft Windows XP, Windows Server 2003, or any newer version of Windows, one especially cool option not listed in the previous section is the -r option, which lets you directly map resources on your Linux system to your Windows Terminal Services connection. This is useful when you want to map a local print queue to a virtual printer in your Windows Terminal session or access a local drive in your Terminal session (using -r printer:*local-queue-name* and -r disk:*share-name=/device/path*, respectively). For example, to attach *PRN1* to a local print queue named *Silentwriter*, you would add -r printer:Silentwriter to your command-line options when executing the rdesktop command. Figure 2-15 shows how your local print queue shows up in a generic Windows print dialog.

To map your local CD-ROM drive to a share called *cdrom*, you could add -r disk:cdrom=/dev/cdrom to the rdesktop command line. If you still use floppies, you could map your local floppy drive to a share called *floppy* by adding -r disk:floppy=/dev/fd0 to your rdesktop command line. The name that you specify as the share must be eight characters or less.

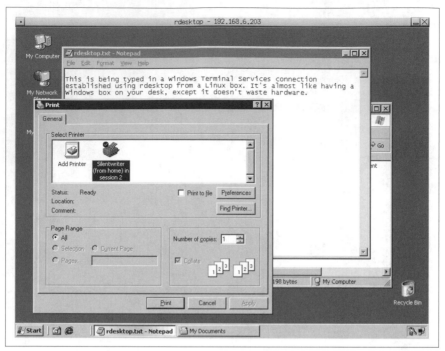

Figure 2-15. A print queue mapped by rdesktop

See Also

- man rdesktop
- *rdesktop* home page: *http://www.rdesktop.org*
- *rdesktop* project at Sourceforge: *http://sourceforge.net/projects/rdesktop/*

HACK #16 ## Secure, Lightweight X Connections with FreeNX

The standard X Window System is very network-intensive. FreeNX compresses and optimizes X communications and is ideally suited for slow connections such as dialups.

FreeNX is a free, GPL implementation of NoMachine's NX Server (*http://www.nomachine.com*). NoMachine has developed a compression technology that substantially reduces the size of X Window System communications and adds other performance improvements through caching and general protocol optimization. NoMachine provides several informative white papers about their technology and its performance at *http://www.nomachine.com/documentation.php*. If you're already a VNC fan, NX is definitely worth a look, for performance reasons as well as for the fact that it inherently uses SSH for secure communications between client and server.

The free and commercial versions of the NX server differ in terms of capabilities (and, of course, cost). FreeNX provides all of the core capabilities of the commercial NX server for remote connection, but it does not currently include the SMB and printing (CUPS) support provided by the commercial NX server. At the moment, commercial server licenses for NoMachine's personal edition cost around 55 euros, which is cheap. They also offer small business and enterprise licenses, which you may be interested in if you want to have product support, get updates, and get SMB and CUPS support now, rather than waiting for them to appear and mature in FreeNX. Personally, though I use FreeNX, I bought a server license because it seemed like the right thing to do. I use the free NoMachine client everywhere, and I also feel that the NoMachine folks deserve my support for having come up with a great technology and released it as open source.

This hack explains how to install and configure the open source versions of NoMachine's NX server, the FreeNX package, and the free commercial NX client from NoMachine.

Installing the FreeNX Server

The FreeNX server consists of two packages: the *nx* package, which consists of binaries and libraries compiled from the open source packages from NoMachine; and the *freenx* package, which is a set of client scripts that invoke the NX binaries in the right ways. Depending on the Linux distribution that your server is running, you can obtain these packages from different locations:

Debian
> By adding deb `http://debian.tu-bs.de/knoppix/nx/slh-debian/ ./` to your */etc/apt/sources.list* file

Fedora
> From *http://fedoranews.org/contributors/rick_stout/freenx/*

Gentoo
> From the Gentoo forums at *http://forums.gentoo.org/viewtopic-p-1469066-highlight-nxssh.html#1469066*

Knoppix
> From *http://debian.tu-bs.de/knoppix/nx/* (overlays for the standard NoMachine server overlays)

Red Hat 9
> From *http://apt.physik.fu-berlin.de/redhat/9/en/i386/RPMS.at-bleeding/* or by adding the appropriate entries to your *apt* or *yum* configuration files, as explained at *http://atrpms.net/install.html*

SUSE 9.2

> On the distribution DVD/CDs or from *ftp://ftp.suse.com/pub/suse/i386/ supplementary/X/NX*

Ubuntu

> By adding deb http://kanotix.com/files/debian/ ./ to your */etc/apt/ sources.list* file

If you're using a distribution that isn't listed in the previous section, or you have a policy of installing nothing on your server without having the source code, you can build the GPL version of the NoMachine NX server from scratch in several ways: retrieve the source code from *http://www.nomachine.com/ download/snapshot/nxsources* using wget -r and then follow the instructions at *http://fedoranews.org/contributors/rick_stout/freenx/freenx.txt*, or download the source RPM from one of the distributions listed above (SUSE's SRPM for the open source NX server is at *ftp://ftp.suse.com/pub/suse/i386/supplementary/X/ NX/NX-1.4.0-12.1.nosrc.rpm*), install it using rpm or extract its contents into a tarball using alien, and then follow the instructions in the *nx.spec* file to see how to build it yourself. I prefer the latter approach, since the source includes any mandatory patches to build the official RPMs for SUSE, which is my desktop/server distribution of choice.

As good open source citizens, NoMachine provides a document about building the open source portions of the NX products in the Documentation center at *http://www.nomachine.com/documentation/pdf/building-components.pdf*.

If you manually downloaded RPMs, install them in the standard fashion, as in the following example (from a Red Hat 9 system):

```
# rpm -Uvvh nx-1.4.0-4.1.rh9.at.i386.rpm
# rpm -Uvvh freenx-0.3.1-0.1.rh9.at.noarch.rpm
```

Next, use the *nxsetup* application to do the initial configuration of your NX server by specifying the --install option, as shown below:

```
# /usr/bin/nxsetup --install
Setting up /etc/nxserver ...done
Setting up /var/lib/nxserver/db ...done
Setting up /var/log/nxserver.log ...done
Setting up known_hosts and authorized_keys2 ...done
Setting up permissions ...done
Ok, nxserver is ready.
PAM authentication enabled:
    All users will be able to login with their normal passwords.
    PAM authentication will be done through SSH.
    Please ensure that SSHD on localhost accepts password authentication.
    You can change this behaviour in the file.
Have Fun!
```

This step creates the *nx* user in the server's */etc/passwd* file and sets up the files, directories, and keys used by FreeNX.

Next, add any users that you want to be able to use the NX server to its user database and set their passwords, as in the following example:

```
# nxserver --adduser wvh
NX> 100 NXSERVER - Version 1.4.0-03 OS (GPL)
NX> 1000 NXNODE - Version 1.4.0-03 OS (GPL)
NX> 716 Public key added to /home/wvh/.ssh/authorized_keys2
NX> 1001 Bye.
NX> 999 Bye
# nxserver --passwd wvh
NX> 100 NXSERVER - Version 1.4.0-03 OS (GPL)
New password:
Password changed.
NX> 999 Bye
```

Now you're ready to install and configure the NX client on any systems from which you want to access the FreeNX server.

Installing the NX Client

NoMachine's free NX clients for various Linux distributions, various flavors of Microsoft Windows, Apple's Mac OS X, and even Sun's Solaris are available from *http://www.nomachine.com/download.php*. The name of the NoMachine client binary is, surprisingly enough, *nxclient*. Though a free NX client for the KDE environment (called *knx*) is actively under development, the NoMachine NX clients are nicely done, work fine, and are free. You'll have to put up with seeing NoMachine's logo each time you start one up, but that's a small price to pay—and it's a cool logo!

> SUSE fans can get the *knx* client from the DVDs/CDs or from *ftp://ftp.suse.com/pub/suse/i386/supplementary/X/NX/*. You can subscribe to a mailing list about the *knx* client and FreeNX in general at *https://mail.kde.org/mailman/listinfo/freenx-knx*.

If you've downloaded the RPM for the NoMachine NX client, you can install it using a standard RPM invocation such as:

```
# rpm -Uvvh rh9-nxclient-1.4.0-91.i386.rpm
```

Note that the version of the file that you've downloaded, and therefore its name, may have changed by the time you read this.

After downloading and installing the client on a desktop system, you'll need to copy the FreeNX server's key to your client installation. This key is located in the file */var/lib/nxserver/home/.ssh/client.id_dsa.key* on a Linux

FreeNX server, and it should be copied to the file */usr/NX/share/client.id_ dsa.key* on any Linux system where you've installed the NoMachine client. You must also make this file readable by mere mortals, so chmod it to 644. Windows client users should copy this file to the directory *C:\Program Files\ NX Client for Windows\share*.

Configuring and Starting Your NX Client

NX client and server applications are installed in */usr/bin*, which is probably already in your path, so no path munging is required to start an NX client. NoMachine's NX client enables you to create configuration files that specify parameters with which the *nxclient* application can be invoked. To create a configuration file, execute the following command:

```
$ nxclient --wizard
```

A friendly but content-free dialog displays. Click Next, and the dialog shown in Figure 2-16 displays. Enter a logical name for the connection in the Session text box, and specify the hostname or IP address of the NX server in the Host text box. You can then modify the slider settings to specify the type of network/Internet connection you're using, so that the NX client will select appropriate compression and optimization settings for your connection speed.

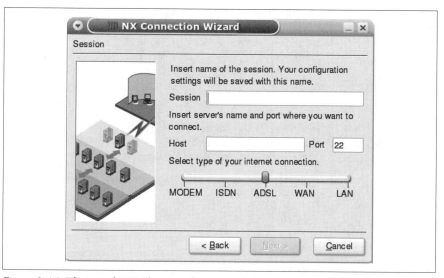

Figure 2-16. The initial NX Client configuration dialog

When you click Next, the dialog shown in Figure 2-17 displays. For standard X connections to a remote Linux or Unix server, leave the system type set to Unix, and click the KDE drop-down to select the type of desktop that you'd like the NX server to start for you. Next, click the Available Area drop-down and select the size of the remote desktop that you'd like to create. I tend to select 1024×768 because that's always smaller than the size of my desktop machine's monitor. Using the default Available Area setting is a better choice if you're using the NX client on a laptop that may or may not be connected to an external monitor.

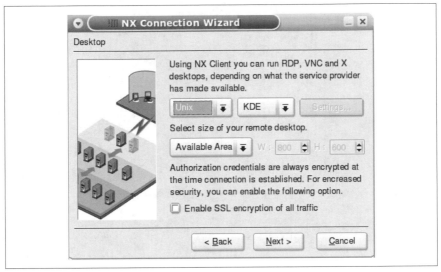

Figure 2-17. Specifying NX Client protocols and size

This dialog also enables you to provide an additional level of security by enabling SSL encryption. This encrypts all traffic between the client and the server, including your initial password exchange.

 The settings you specify when configuring a NoMachine client are saved in text configuration files in the ~/.nx/config directory, with the name of your NX client and a .conf extension. You can subsequently edit these with a text editor if you decide to modify the existing settings quickly.

When you click Next, a final dialog displays that enables you to create a desktop shortcut or open the Advanced Configuration dialog, shown in Figure 2-18. The tabs in this dialog enable you to further optimize connections between your client and the FreeNX server, customize the paths to various files on your system, and so on.

Once you've created a configuration, the standard NX Client dialog displays. Enter your password for the NX server, and the fun begins. The NX client authenticates to the remote NX server, negotiates connection parameters, and

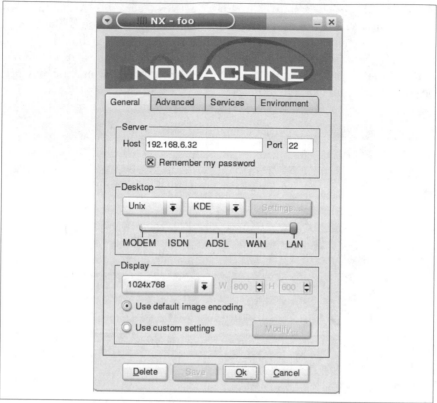

Figure 2-18. The optional NX Client Advanced configuration dialog

then displays a window in which a remote desktop session starts. You also get to see the NoMachine logo for a few seconds, which reminds you who should be thanked for this way-cool technology! Figure 2-19 shows a remote Linux desktop connection to a Red Hat 9 system running the GNOME desktop

To terminate your NX client session, simply close the window as you would any other application. Like VNC connections, NX client connections can be suspended rather than simply terminated, so you'll see a dialog that asks if you want to suspend the session, terminate the session, or cancel the termination request. If you select Suspend, your existing connection to the remote NX server will be renewed the next time you start NX Client with the current configuration.

See Also

- *http://www.nomachine.com*
- *http://openfacts.berlios.de/index-en.phtml?title=FreeNX_FAQ*

- *http://openfacts.berlios.de/index-en.phtml?title=FreeNX_distro_integration*
- "Secure VNC Connections with FreeNX" **[Hack #17]**
- "Secure Windows Terminal Connections with FreeNX" **[Hack #18]**

Figure 2-19. A remote FreeNX desktop shown in nxclient

HACK #17 Secure VNC Connections with FreeNX

FreeNX isn't just for the X Window System—it can also provide secure VNC connections.

If "Secure, Lightweight X Connections with FreeNX" **[Hack #16]** got you excited about the performance and possibilities of the FreeNX server for displaying X Window System desktops over slow connections, just wait—there's more! FreeNX also supports translating the protocols used by VNC into X Window System protocols that it can then exchange with a standard NX client. If you install an NX client (such as NoMachine's excellent *nxclient*) on your desktop system, you can use a single application to both communicate with remote X Window sessions on your NX server and also proxy through to any VNC server that you can access from the NX server. The VNC server does not have to be running on the same system as the NX server—the NX server just needs to be able to contact it over the network.

Communications between the VNC server and the NX server are not encrypted, but communications between your NX client and the NX server are. This can be especially useful if you are working remotely and want to access a VNC server inside your company's network, but you need any communication taking place over the public Internet to be secure. Your corporate firewall already supports SSH, so you don't even need to open any other ports to support VNC.

Creating an NX Client Configuration for VNC

The previous hack explained how to obtain and install NoMachine's excellent NX client. To create a configuration for accessing VNC through your NX client, click the Unix drop-down shown in Figure 2-17, and select VNC. The dialog shown in Figure 2-20 will display.

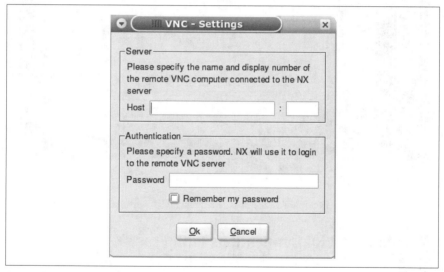

Figure 2-20. VNC configuration in NX Client

In this dialog, specify the hostname or IP address of the system on which your VNC server is running, and the port on which it is running. By default, the port will be 5900 plus the number of the display that the VNC server is using. For example, if the VNC server was running on *display:1* on the remote system, you would enter 5901 as the port number.

Next, specify the password for the remote VNC server, and check the "Remember my password" checkbox if you want to make this a permanent part of your configuration. Click OK to close this dialog, proceed with your standard NX client configuration and save your NX/VNC configuration.

When you start *nxclient* with that configuration, you'll see a screen like the one shown in Figure 2-21—congratulations, you're securely connected!

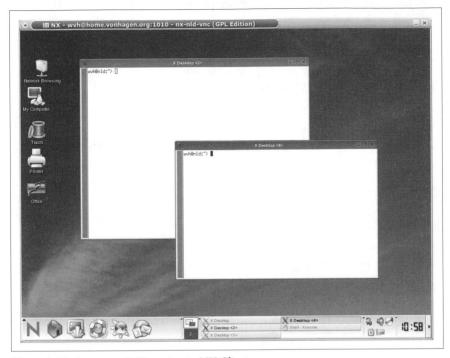

Figure 2-21. A remote VNC session in NX Client

See Also

- *http://www.nomachine.com*
- "Secure, Lightweight X Connections with FreeNX" **[Hack #16]**
- "Secure Windows Terminal Connections with FreeNX" **[Hack #18]**

H A C K
#18

Secure Windows Terminal Connections with FreeNX

FreeNX isn't just for the X Window System and VNC—it can also provide secure Windows Terminal Services connections.

If "Secure, Lightweight X Connections with FreeNX" **[Hack #16]** and "Secure VNC Connections with FreeNX" **[Hack #17]** got you excited about the performance and possibilities of the FreeNX server for displaying X Window System and VNC desktops over slow connections, get ready because FreeNX has even more tricks up its sleeve. FreeNX also supports translating the Remote Desktop Protocol (RDP) used by Windows Terminal Services into X Window System protocols that it can then exchange with a standard NX client. If you install an NX client system (such as NoMachine's excellent *nxclient*) on your desktop, you can use a single application to communicate with remote X Window sessions on your NX server, proxy through to any VNC server you can access from the NX server or proxy through to any Windows Terminal server you can access from the NX server. Like the VNC server, the Windows Terminal server does not have to be running on the same system as the NX server—which is just as well, because the NX server used by both FreeNX and NoMachine's NX runs only on Unix and Linux boxes!

Like VNC through FreeNX, communications between the Windows Terminal server and the NX server are not encrypted, but communications between your NX client and the NX server are. This can be especially useful if you are working remotely and want to access a Windows Terminal server inside your company's network, but you need any communication taking place over the public Internet to be secure. Your corporate firewall already supports SSH, so you don't even need to open any other ports to support the Windows Terminal server.

Creating an NX Client Configuration for a Windows Terminal Server

"Secure VNC Connections with FreeNX" [Hack #17] explained how to obtain and install NoMachine's excellent NX client. To create a configuration for accessing a Windows Terminal server through your NX client, click the Unix drop-down shown in previously in Figure 2-17, and select RDP. The dialog shown in Figure 2-22 will display.

In this dialog, specify the hostname or IP address of your Windows Terminal server, whether you want to use existing credentials to auto-login or see the standard Windows login screen, and whether you want to run a specific application or the standard Windows desktop.

Click OK to close this dialog, proceed with your standard NX client configuration, and save your NX/Windows Terminal configuration. When you start *nxclient* with that configuration, you'll see a screen like the one shown in Figure 2-23. Congratulations—you're securely connected!

See Also

- *http://www.nomachine.com*
- "Secure, Lightweight X Connections with FreeNX" [Hack #16]
- "Secure VNC Connections with FreeNX" [Hack #17]

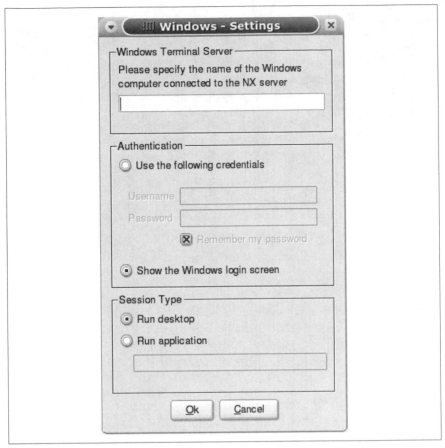

Figure 2-22. Windows Terminal configuration in NX Client

 Remote Administration with Webmin

Webmin provides secure access to logfiles, system statistics, and many
common administration tasks, all from your favorite web browser.

Administering a system can be a tough job. With user accounts to create,
services to configure, logs to check, and all the other duties system administrators face, it can become quite a load. Thankfully, there's some software
out there that can help make life easier for the weary sysadmin. One of these
pieces of software is called *Webmin*. Webmin allows you to control a large
portion of the functionality of your server from an easy-to-use web interface. Most major services are covered, including Apache, BIND, SSH, LDAP,
Samba, WU-FTP, Sendmail, MySQL, and many others.

Figure 2-23. A Windows Terminal server connection in nxclient

Installation

Installation of Webmin couldn't be easier. If you're running an RPM-based distribution such as SUSE or Fedora Core, simply grab the latest version from the Webmin home page at *http://www.webmin.com*. Install Webmin with the following command, where *version-number* is the version that you downloaded:

```
# rpm –install Webmin-version-number.rpm
```

If you're using a non-RPM-based distribution such as Debian or Slackware, you can install from source. Simply download the latest tarball from *http://www.webmin.com* and unpack it to your system as usual. Navigate into the newly created Webmin directory, and execute the following command as root:

```
# ./setup.sh /usr/local/Webmin
```

This will start the setup process for Webmin. The script will ask you for a number of options. For most of these questions, the default answers should suffice. However, there are a few answers that should be changed for security reasons. For instance, it is widely known that the default port for Webmin is 10000, so when the script asks you what port to run it on, pick something original—just make sure that you pick something above port 1024, because port numbers lower than that are typically reserved for system services. I typically use port 5555. Changing the default port helps protect against automated tools probing Webmin and discovering your Webmin login by checking its default port.

Also, choose a default username other than *admin* and definitely specify a password. If you don't, the password will be left blank and anyone who wants to log in will be able to do so. You should also make sure that you choose to use SSL for encryption. The setup script will only ask you this if you have the SSL libraries for Perl installed, so make sure they're loaded before you begin. Without them, all the information transmitted back and forth between you and Webmin will be transmitted in clear text, including passwords and other valuable system information.

The final question the script will ask you is if you want Webmin running at boot time. This is largely a matter of personal preference. I tend to say no and simply SSH in and start Webmin whenever I need it, which allows it to stay off the radar when it's not in use; however, your mileage may vary and you should use your own judgment here. If you'll be using it in a trusted environment or don't mind the limited risk of leaving it on all the time, answer yes, and the script will configure Webmin to start automatically.

Configure Away!

That's it! You now have a fully functional Webmin interface running on your server. You can access it by logging into *https://localhost:5555*, where *5555* is the port you specified during the setup. If you installed via rpm, the default port of 10000 was used. Log in with the username and password you specified earlier—you should see something similar to Figure 2-24—and have a look around.

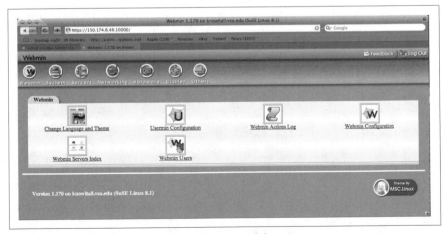

Figure 2-24. The default Webmin interface in a web browser

As you can see, the Webmin interface has several sections, including System, Networking, Servers, Hardware, and Cluster. Each of these tabs contains options related to its title. If you'd like to change the IP address of your server, for instance, select Networking, then Interfaces. Click on the name of the interface you want to change, and enter your new IP address. You can add new users, manage your logfiles, configure DNS and Apache, and perform a whole host of other administrative functions with the same ease we've just demonstrated.

The Servers tab is another area where Webmin shines, and this is where the true capabilities of Webmin can be seen. Under the Servers tab, you can see the full list of applications that Webmin supports by default. We've already mentioned quite a few, but let's take a moment to explore Webmin's capabilities. Clicking the Apache icon will show you many of the options that are available to you. For this example, let's suppose we want to add a virtual host to Apache. Normally, this would require manually editing *httpd.conf*, followed by a restart of the Apache service. With Webmin, we can do all this with a few simple clicks. The bottom of the configure page for Apache has the options for creating a virtual server—all you have to do is fill in the blanks and click Create Now. Everything will be done for you, including restarting Apache to pick up the new virtual server from the configuration file, without ever having to fire up *emacs* or *vi*.

As you can see, Webmin provides numerous options and capabilities. Webmin even makes it easy for developers to write their own modules to use with it, allowing its capabilities to be expanded and extended by the community. Webmin can be a lifesaver when you need to install or work with complicated tools such as Sendmail or DNS in a hurry. It also simplifies managing clustered or high-availability servers. No matter how you look at it, there's no denying the usefulness of such a versatile administration tool.

See Also

- *http://www.webmin.com*

—Brian Warshawsky

System Services
Hacks 20–28

The term *client/server* has been used and abused for so long that it isn't all that exciting any more—unless, of course, you're one of many busy sysadmins who need to provide certain core capabilities to their zillion-user communities. In this case, the idea of setting up centralized servers to satisfy the requirements of many clients isn't just a buzzword; it's an efficient use of your time and system resources, and it simplifies administering those services in the future. This chapter provides hacks that discuss setting up centralized services for allocating IP addresses to new clients via the Dynamic Host Configuration Protocol (DHCP), integrating these newly assigned IP addresses with an existing Domain Name Service (DNS), synchronizing the clocks on all of your systems via the Network Time Protocol (NTP), and even sharing a consistent set of X Window System fonts throughout your organization so that all your users can do their status reports using the same version of Computer Modern Ransom Note Oblique.

Another focus of this chapter is on centralizing print services and systems throughout the organization for which you're responsible. The mechanisms used to print files on different types of systems have traditionally been specific to the operating systems that they use. This was okay when each user had a printer chained to his system with a parallel umbilical cord, or when organizations used only one operating system to get their work done. However, this type of tunnel vision is completely unworkable in today's networked, heterogeneous computing environments. Luckily, unified printing solutions are now available, thanks largely to Michael Sweet and the other folks at Easy Software Products. Their creation of the Common Unix Printing System (CUPS), which might better be described as the Completely Universal Printing System, provided a powerful, centralized printing system that works everywhere. CUPS can handle and manage print jobs from modern operating systems such as Linux, Microsoft Windows, and Mac OS X to old-school Unix boxes. All you have to know is what to tweak where, why to tweak it, and how to do so. This chapter provides hacks that give you all that information and more.

HACK
#20

Quick and Easy DHCP Setup

Take control of DHCP services to better integrate with other tools in your environment.

There are lots of places where clients are running Linux-based services infrastructures in SOHO environments. I do this myself at home. When you're in a smaller environment, there are lots of black-box appliances and all-in-one software packages that will take care of automatically assigning IP addresses to all the hosts on your network. Some will even let your DNS server know about dynamically assigned addresses, which is great. However, as the environment grows and more services and machines are added, this can get to be somewhat cumbersome.

The first time I realized that I might not want my wireless router giving out IP addresses was when I got a visit from a friend of mine who has a wireless laptop (which happened to be in his truck). While we were talking, he wanted to show me a web site, but he couldn't remember what it was called. He had it bookmarked on the laptop, so I told him to go get it, and I'd put his MAC address into my wireless router's "OK" table. Problem was, I had forgotten the password to my router. I had set it up months ago, and none of my formula-derived passwords were working. He wound up saying never mind, and I was really disappointed in that piece of my infrastructure.

After thinking more about that scenario, I realized I shouldn't even need to touch a black-box appliance to allow a guest to get an IP address in my environment. If I just ran a normal DHCP server on my Linux box, I could let the wireless router do what it's supposed to do (route wireless traffic), and leave the rest to my Linux server, which is good at doing most other things (heck, if I had wireless PCI cards, it could route the wireless traffic as well!).

Another benefit to using your own DHCP server is that you can add in DHCP options that may not be supported by the appliance. For example, my wireless router will not deliver the IP addresses of NTP servers or NIS servers to my clients, and it won't tell my PXE-booted clients a filename to go grab from a DHCP server. In fact, it doesn't even support a "next-server" directive to use for NFS kickstarts of my Red Hat machines. DHCP really can open up a lot of doors to making a SOHO environment less about maintaining technology and more about getting business done!

Of course, before I could do any of these really cool things, I had to set up my own DHCP server. I've only ever used the Internet Systems Consortium's DHCP server, which is the one that comes with just about all Linux distributions, so that's what I decided to go with. It's also the one I've maintained in much larger production environments, so I know for sure it's up to whatever task I can throw at it in a SOHO setting.

Installing a DHCP Server

The first step in this hack is to get the DHCP daemon, *dhcpd*, installed on your system. On Red Hat Enterprise Linux systems, the *up2date* utility can be used to install the server and any dependencies, with the following command:

```
# up2date -i dhcp
```

On Fedora systems, use *yum* to do the same thing:

```
# yum install dhcp
```

On Debian systems, use the *apt-get* utility:

```
# apt-get install dhcp
```

 Debian stable, at the time of writing, provides a somewhat older version of the DHCP daemon, which does not contain support for dynamic DNS updates. Nor does it supply a BIND DNS server that is capable of accepting such updates. If you need this capability, it is suggested that you use the DHCP server in the unstable Debian branch or build from source.

For those building from source, you can grab a source tarball from the ISC web site at *http://www.isc.org/index.pl?/sw/dhcp/*. To build, the old magic three-command incantation still works:

```
$ ./configure
$ make
# make install
```

Configuring Simple DHCP Services

DHCP is not difficult to configure. We'll start with simple requirements, and leave more hardcore stuff to the next hack. The configuration file for this service is */etc/dhcpd.conf*. The first few lines of this file set up global parameters that apply to all hosts served by this DHCP server:

```
option domain-name "linuxlaboratory.org";
option subnet-mask 255.255.255.0;
deny unknown-clients;
option domain-name-servers 192.168.198.50;
default-lease-time 600;
max-lease-time 7200;
```

The first line assigns a domain name to our environment, which is fairly arbitrary in a small environment that's not supporting a registered Internet domain. The subnet-mask option ensures that everyone has the same subnet mask on your network. This may not be the case at your site, in which case you can specify this parameter in different places in the config file to get the desired effect.

The deny unknown-clients option keeps the server from providing IP addresses to hosts that are not specified in the configuration file. The default, for some reason, is to allow this activity.

I have but a single host right now in my budding DMZ: my domain name server, which all of my internal hosts use. Rather than configuring its address manually on each host (and having to manually update it if a change is made), I just deliver its address to the clients via DHCP, using the domain-name-servers directive.

Finally, the lease times are set up such that the default-lease-time is 600 seconds (10 minutes) and the maximum time a host can go without renewing a lease is 7,200 seconds (2 hours).

Unlike the first section, the next section of the file is not global, but is specific to a subnet. It is befittingly called a "subnet statement," and you can have as many of these as you have subnets (or more, but hopefully you see that that would hardly make sense). Here's an entry for my internal network's subnet:

```
subnet 192.168.42.0 netmask 255.255.255.0 {
   range 192.168.42.85 192.168.42.99;
   option broadcast-address 192.168.42.255;
   option routers 192.168.42.1;
}
```

Every subnet statement is required to have a netmask specified, regardless of what's in the global section of the config file. Inside the braces, the first thing you see is that I've set things up so that hosts that are to receive dynamic addresses on this subnet can receive only IP node numbers between 85 and 99. This allows me to have 15 dynamically assigned hosts on my network—a good-sized pool for now.

Next, I specify the broadcast-address for the domain, which is the address for "all hosts" on the subnet. And finally, I always specify a router for each subnet, because every subnet must have its own gateway address. I suppose I could've made this a global option in this case, since all of my internal hosts are on the same subnet, but if I then added a subnet (which I will when I break wireless hosts out to their own subnet), I'd have to make changes to different parts of the configuration instead of just adding a new subnet statement.

We're not done yet, though! You still need to tell the DHCP server about the hosts on your network. This can be a bit of drudgery, as it requires you to know or find out the MAC addresses of all the hosts on your network. When DHCP clients start up, they broadcast to request DHCP service, and you only want your DHCP server to respond to those hosts whose MAC addresses are listed in the configuration file. This beats by a mile the old default wireless gateway configuration of handing out addresses to the entire neighborhood! Here's a simple, yet fairly typical, host entry in *dhcpd.conf*:

```
host gala {
   hardware ethernet 00:30:65:0f:d8:52;
   fixed-address 192.168.42.58;
}
```

The host *gala* happens to be my Apple G4. The two pieces of information I've provided are the Ethernet address of the machine and a `fixed-address`, which is optional but ensures that *gala* will always get the exact same IP address every time it renews its lease.

Why the heck would I do that? Doesn't it defeat the "Dynamic" part of DHCP? Well, in some ways, maybe it does, but there are various reasons why you might do this. First, if you don't use DNS, you're likely still using */etc/hosts* to resolve other hosts on the network. It would be nice not to have to change these files on each host because a host's IP address has been changed. Forgetting to do so would be especially bad if that host was, say, the file server where all your important data lives. Likewise, if it's your desktop IP address that's changed and you don't update the hosts file, the file server won't resolve your hostname correctly and could export your data to someone else!

Even if you are running a DNS server, you still might want DHCP to assign fixed addresses. For example, you may not be able to use dynamic DNS updates for one reason or another. It also helps with troubleshooting: if a host can get different IP addresses at any given time, IP addresses that are not resolved to hostnames in your logs or *tcpdump* output become meaningless until and unless you track down which host had which address at the time specified in the logs.

That said, it's completely optional, and you certainly aren't forced to assign fixed addresses to your hosts. You can mix and match as well—for example, when I add my buddy's laptop to my new DHCP configuration, I don't care what IP address he gets, because he's not going to use any of my in-house services; he's just going to have Internet access. Here's the entry for his laptop:

```
host appio-wireless {
        hardware ethernet 00:90:4B:6D:97:59;
}

host appio-wired {
        hardware ethernet 00:90:3D:93:AD:3E;
}
```

Now he'll get a randomly assigned address, which of course will be from the 15-address pool specified in my earlier subnet statement. Notice that I added separate entries for his wired and wireless interfaces. You can enter as many "one-liner" entries like this as you want—those entries represent the simplest form of "host" entry. Keep in mind one important tip, though, which is to remember not to assign fixed addresses that overlap with the pool you've configured in your subnet statement. For example, if I had configured host *gala* with a fixed address of 192.168.42.88, the server would fail to start at all! It's a basic, common-sense effect when you stop to think about it, but I've actually tripped up on that more than once. Save yourself!

Fire It Up!

Now, start up the DHCP service by running /etc/init.d/dhcp start on your Debian system, or service dhcpd start on Red Hat/Fedora machines. Once you configure your hosts to actually use DHCP instead of statically assigned addresses, restart their network services, and they should be assigned addresses from your shiny new server!

See Also

- "Integrate DHCP and DNS with Dynamic DNS Updates" [Hack #21]

HACK #21 Integrate DHCP and DNS with Dynamic DNS Updates

Assign dynamic hostnames and IP addresses, and update your DNS server to reflect changes with no administrative intervention or scripted hacks.

If any two services are begging to be integrated, it's BIND and DHCP. Dynamically assigning IP addresses with DHCP isn't so useful if it makes your DNS zone information obsolete! Imagine if all of your configured printers got dynamically assigned IP addresses from your DHCP server. The next time your default printer got a new IP address from the DHCP server, addressing that host by name could return an unexpected result from DNS, because they're not in sync. Where your print job winds up could be anybody's guess.

With older versions of the ISC DHCP server and BIND, this problem was solved in one of two ways. First, you could just tell your DHCP server to statically assign addresses to your hosts [Hack #20]. This is still a useful solution to the problem, especially if the DHCP server delivers information besides an IP address, such as which NTP servers and NIS servers to use. The second option is to grab a tool (or script one yourself) to perform DNS updates.

In more recent versions of DHCP and BIND, both services support a mechanism for performing dynamic DNS updates (defined in RFC 2136), whereby an authorized user can add and delete records from forward and reverse zone files. Recent versions of DHCP also support a more flexible mechanism for deriving a dynamic hostname from an expression, which can include data sent from the client in the DHCP request.

Add these together, and you have the ability to, for example, maintain a dynamic address pool that also assigns hostnames dynamically and then updates the DNS server to reflect the changes. The alternative to dynamic hostnames is to have the DHCP server use the hostname supplied by the client, but depending on the environment, this may not be desirable. In situations where there are frequent visitors from random places, hostname overlapping can cause DNS updates to fail. Also, it's not always safe to assume that a client will supply a valid hostname (or *any* hostname, for that matter).

Let's go over how to get DHCP and BIND to work together to perform dynamic DNS updates.

The very first step that needs to be performed is the generation of a key that the two services will use to communicate with each other. The DHCP server uses this key to sign update requests sent to the DNS server, and the DNS server uses it to verify the signed requests from the DHCP server. BIND 9 comes with a utility to generate this key, called *dnssec-keygen*. You need to make three decisions about how to run the key-generation command. The first is the name of the key, the second is the number of bits used in the key's encryption, and the third is what form the name of the key will take.

Let's have a look at a key generated to represent the host that's allowed to perform the updates. We'll make it 512 bytes long, and we'll name the key using the fully qualified domain name (FQDN) of the host. Here's the command:

```
# dnssec-keygen -a HMAC-MD5 -b 512 -n HOST apollo.linuxlaboratory.org.
```

This generates a TSIG key and places it in a file in the current directory. The file is named *K<keyname>+157+<uniqueid>.private*. The contents of this file will be something similar to this:

```
Private-key-format: v1.2
Algorithm: 157 (HMAC_MD5)
Key: y3v81k9O9z6c62KgPNlik8P6QZIEB3yb/Blw/
XE8QN46RLeC4XkptJiRA56roCcCEGSAdCJb5kmM2/S7MBrmRQ==
```

The important part here is the long value after the Key keyword. Once you have this value copied to the proper places in your configuration files, you can get rid of the key files themselves.

Configuring the BIND 9 Name Server

The next step is to configure BIND to allow updates from the DHCP server, using the key you just generated. We do this step before configuring DHCP to avoid lots of log entries indicating failed update attempts from the DHCP server during the lag time between completing the configuration of both services.

The BIND server's *named.conf* file will need to have its zone blocks altered to contain an `update-policy` block, which lets the server know which keys can update what records in which zones. First, we need to tell the server about all the keys we want it to know about. In our simple setup we only have one, but some environments may have one key for each host that might be allowed to alter its own records. Here's a simple block that we can add near the top of the *named.conf* file to inform the server of our key:

```
key apollo.linuxlaboratory.org. {
    algorithm hmac-md5;
    secret "y3v81k9O9z6c62KgPNlik8P6QZIEB3yb/Blw/
XE8QN46RLeC4XkptJiRA56roCcCEGSAdCJb5kmM2/S7MBrmRQ==";
};
```

Next, we need to reference this key in our `update-policy` substatements in each zone for which the key is valid. Here's a typical zone that has been altered to accept updates using this key:

```
zone "linuxlaboratory.org" in {
    type master;
    file "db.linuxlaboratory.org";

    update-policy {
        grant apollo.linuxlaboratory.org. subdomain linuxlaboratory.org.
ANY;
    };

};
```

Here, our update policy says to allow updates signed with the key `apollo.linuxlaboratory.org.`, as long as the update is affecting an entry that is a subdomain of `linuxlaboratory.org.`. Note that the `subdomain` keyword includes the hostname. Also, we allow this key to update any record type, by including the keyword `ANY` on the end. This doesn't really mean literally *any* record type, though: it'll never update, for example, your SOA records! If you want to be explicit, you can list the record types (for example, `A PTR` would allow updates only to those record types).

For completeness, here's the reverse zone block, altered with a similar `update-policy` statement:

```
zone "42.168.192.in-addr.arpa" in {
    type master;
    file "db.192.168.42";
```

```
    update-policy {
        grant apollo.linuxlaboratory.org. subdomain 42.168.192.in-addr.arpa
ANY;
    };

};
```

Both zones allow updates to any record type of any host in the zone. This effectively makes our DHCP server the "sole master" host for performing updates.

Configuring the ISC DHCP Server

Now let's move on to configuring our DHCP server. In our example environment, we have a lot of hosts grabbing static IP addresses from our DHCP server. We'll also set aside a range to be assigned to visitors, who will also be assigned dynamic hostnames. This information will be sent to the DNS server, and the requests will be signed with the same key we used in the BIND configuration.

To get the configuration right, we'll need to add a few extra settings to the global section of the file to tell the server to do dynamic updates. We'll then define the key to use a block very similar to the one we put in our *named. conf* file. Here's the first part of our newly updated *dhcpd.conf* file:

```
ddns-update-style interim;
deny client-updates;
authoritative;
option domain-name "linuxlaboratory.org";
option domain-name-servers 192.168.42.3;

option subnet-mask 255.255.255.0;
default-lease-time 600;
max-lease-time 7200;

key apollo.protocolostomy.pvt. {
    algorithm hmac-md5;
    secret "y3v81k9O9z6c62KgPNlik8P6QZIEB3yb/Blw/
XE8QN46RLeC4XkptJiRA56roCcCEGSAdCJb5kmM2/S7MBrmRQ==";
}
```

The first two settings relate directly to our goal. `ddns-update-style` is set to the only value that allows us to perform DNS updates in newer versions of BIND. There used to be an `ad-hoc` value that was valid here, which represented a different mechanism for performing updates, but in newer versions this value is ignored and will not work. The other valid value here is `none`, which is used to explicitly state that the server will not perform updates. You must specify a value for the `ddns-update-style` setting on Red Hat–based distributions.

The next setting (deny client-updates;) tells the server to deny any requests that clients may send to update their own information. We've set this explicitly because we'll be assigning dynamic hostnames. If we do not set this, the server will try to use the hostname supplied by the client, which can cause problems in some environments.

The next new part of this file is the block that defines the key to use to sign updates before shipping them over to the DNS server. It is almost identical to the DNS server configuration file, and it performs the exact same function.

Once these settings are in place, the next thing to do is define which zones our DHCP server will attempt to update, on which servers, and using which keys. Here are the zone blocks in our *dhcpd.conf* file that we'll need to get things working:

```
zone linuxlaboratory.org. {
    primary 127.0.0.1;
    key apollo.linuxlaboratory.org.;
}

zone 42.168.192.in-addr.arpa. {
    primary 127.0.0.1;
    key apollo.linuxlaboratory.org.;
}
```

These, of course, must be valid zones on the DNS server listed as primary in each block. In our case, the DNS server is on the local host, so the updates are performed over the local loopback interface and are signed with the key we created earlier.

The last step is to set up dynamic hostnames for visitors, who will get IP addresses from a predefined range. Here's a configuration block to take care of that:

```
subnet 192.168.42.0 netmask 255.255.255.0 {
    range 192.168.42.85 192.168.42.99;
    option broadcast-address 192.168.42.255;
    option routers 192.168.42.1;
    ddns-hostname = concat ("dhcp-", binary-to-ascii (10, 8, "-", leased-
address));
}
```

Visitors on our subnet are assigned addresses between node numbers 85 and 99, inclusive. The hostname the DHCP server will send to the DNS server is defined using the ddns-hostname option. The value that results from the expression, for the host that is leased the address 192.168.42.99, will be "dhcp-192-168-42-99.linuxlaboratory.org". The first argument to concat is a static string. The second is the binary-to-ascii function. The arguments to that function, in order, are the base to use (10 is simple, familiar, decimal numbers), the width of each value (8 bits), the separator to place after each

8-bit value (a dash), and the value to act upon, which in this case is a variable defined by the server. There are many wild schemes for assigning hostnames, but this one has served me well and is very simple.

Starting the Services and Troubleshooting

Restart the *named* server, and then restart the *dhcpd* server. Both should start without error—if you run into one, it's likely to be a forgotten comma or a misplaced curly brace or parenthesis. If they both start without errors you'll at least know that your configuration is syntactically correct, so let's move on to some other things you might see in the logs.

One of the most common issues revolves around the key and how it is generated and used. You might see messages like these:

```
Sep  3 13:06:11 apollo dhcpd: DHCPDISCOVER from 00:e0:b8:5c:46:c6 via eth0
Sep  3 13:06:12 apollo dhcpd: DHCPOFFER on 192.168.42.99 to 00:e0:b8:5c:46:
c6 (moocow) via eth0
Sep  3 13:06:12 apollo named[13005]: client 127.0.0.1#32880: request has
invalid signature: TSIG DDNS_UPD: tsig verify failure (BADKEY)
Sep  3 13:06:12 apollo dhcpd: Unable to add forward map from moocow.
linuxlaboratory.org to 192.168.42.99: bad DNS key
```

More than one issue can cause these messages. For example, you might simply have mistyped the key. Make sure you have quoted strings where you need them, both in the key's value and in the name of the key. Use the examples above to guide you, as they're taken from a known working configuration. If that doesn't work, consult the manpages for the configuration files themselves to make sure you got it right.

Another reason you might get these messages is because either you used an invalid name when generating the key, or you generated the wrong key type. For example, if you ran the dnssec-keygen command with -n USER and then named the key after the *host* allowed to perform the update, the key won't work to validate either a user *or* a host. You'll also be in hot water if you generated the key with -n HOST but didn't name the key after the host. Generating the key using the method we used in this example will get you rolling in no time.

Most other issues are caused by pretty blatant configuration typos or permissions issues. For example, when BIND accepts an update from the DHCP server, it doesn't rewrite its zone files immediately. It generally updates them once an hour, and in the interim, it keeps the data in a journal file. If the journal file doesn't exist, the user that *named* is running as needs to have permission to write to the directory where the journal files will live.

When all is well, the logs generated by a successful setup will look similar to this:

```
Sep  3 15:07:55 apollo dhcpd: DHCPDISCOVER from 00:0c:f1:d6:3f:32 via eth0
Sep  3 15:07:55 apollo dhcpd: DHCPOFFER on 192.168.42.98 to 00:0c:f1:d6:3f:
32 (livid) via eth0
Sep  3 15:07:55 apollo named[14931]: client 127.0.0.1#32907: updating zone
'linuxlaboratory.org/IN': adding an RR at 'dhcp-192-168-42-98.
linuxlaboratory.org' A
Sep  3 15:07:55 apollo named[14931]: client 127.0.0.1#32907: updating zone
'linuxlaboratory.org/IN': adding an RR at 'dhcp-192-168-42-98.
linuxlaboratory.org' TXT
Sep  3 15:07:55 apollo named[14931]: zone linuxlaboratory.org/IN: sending
notifies (serial 8)
Sep  3 15:07:55 apollo dhcpd: Added new forward map from dhcp-192-168-42-98.
linuxlaboratory.org to 192.168.42.98
Sep  3 15:07:55 apollo named[14931]: client 127.0.0.1#32907: updating zone
'42.168.192.in-addr.arpa/IN': deleting rrset at '98.42.168.192.in-addr.arpa'
PTR
Sep  3 15:07:55 apollo named[14931]: client 127.0.0.1#32907: updating zone
'42.168.192.in-addr.arpa/IN': adding an RR at '98.42.168.192.in-addr.arpa'
PTR
Sep  3 15:07:55 apollo named[14931]: zone 42.168.192.in-addr.arpa/IN:
sending notifies (serial 6)
Sep  3 15:07:55 apollo named[14931]: client 192.168.42.3#32903: received
notify for zone 'linuxlaboratory.org'
Sep  3 15:07:55 apollo dhcpd: added reverse map from 98.42.168.192.in-addr.
arpa. to dhcp-192-168-42-98.linuxlaboratory.org
Sep  3 15:07:55 apollo dhcpd: DHCPREQUEST for 192.168.42.98 (192.168.42.3)
from 00:0c:f1:d6:3f:32 (livid) via eth0
Sep  3 15:07:55 apollo dhcpd: DHCPACK on 192.168.42.98 to 00:0c:f1:d6:3f:32
(livid) via eth0
```

See Also

- "Quick and Easy DHCP Setup" [Hack #20]

HACK #22 Synchronize Your Watches!

A simple NTP service that saves you hours of headaches can be set up in minutes.

The Network Time Protocol (NTP) is a service that seeks to synchronize the clocks of all its clients. An NTP daemon runs on a server, synchronizes its local system's clock with a public NTP server, and then serves as a time host so clients on the local network, including desktop PCs, can synchronize their clocks.

The number one reason to do this applies to environments of all sizes, and that reason is to enable you to easily correlate data in the logfiles on your systems. (It's also a convenient way to ensure that your coworkers meet you for lunch at the right time.) Even if you have centralized logging, there may be applications that only log locally, and any localized audit daemons, *sar* configurations, and login records kept in *utmp* and *wtmp* data files need to be kept in sync so that your troubleshooting or postmortem investigations don't begin with a list of hosts and their time offsets from the log server. You should also know that a central log host running Linux and running the *syslogd* daemon records a timestamp in the logfiles that corresponds to the time that the message was received, according to its local time, so that it can at least keep some semblance of order in its own logs.

Further encouragement to use an NTP service for your hosts will come from anyone who has ever had to maintain NFS servers and clients in an environment that does not synchronize time across the hosts. This can cause major issues with NFS, resulting in inexplicable "stale file handle" messages and mysterious make command errors stating that some required file has a "modification time in the future."

Now that you're convinced that having an NTP service is the right thing to do, let's move on to configuring a simple NTP server, and configuring your clients to use it.

First, you should make sure that you have the *ntpd* package installed. SUSE, Fedora, Red Hat, Mandrake, Debian, and all Debian variants that I've seen (including Ubuntu and Linspire) include *ntpd*. Red Hat–based systems even include it for minimal server installations. The configuration file for the server daemon is */etc/ntpd.conf*, so let's start there by having a look at a bare-bones configuration:

```
## Default rules for all connections
restrict default nomodify notrap noquery

## Allow full access to the local host
restrict 127.0.0.1

## Our client subnet
restrict 192.168.42.0 mask 255.255.255.0 nomodify notrap

# Our timeservers
server ntp.cs.princeton.edu
server clock.linuxshell.net
server ntp0.cornell.edu
```

OK, this is enough to get us started. The first line is a list of configuration keywords. The first two, restrict and default, define this line as the default access rule for all connections. The next three disallow remote hosts to modify the local server's configuration (nomodify), deny special *ntpdq* trap messages (notrap), and deny *ntpdq/ntpdc* queries to this server (noquery). Note that the noquery option is specific to queries regarding the status of the server itself, not the time: time queries are unaffected by that option.

All those restrictions may seem to make setting up the server pretty useless, but just remember it's a default rule that will be overridden by rules further down in the file.

The next line of the file, restrict 127.0.0.1, allows full access to the local host—and no, that's not a typo on my part. If you've never studied the *ntpd.conf* file, it looks weird to see a line starting with restrict that ultimately gives full access to the target of the rule. However, the way that the server reads the file is that it matches up incoming connections with all of the restrict statements, in the order they appear in the file. The keyword restrict is followed by a hostname, IP address, or the keyword default, followed by whatever restrictive flags you deem necessary. The absence of these flags means there are no restrictions, which is why the above line gives full access to the local host!

The next uncommented line gives access to our local subnet (192.168.42.0), so that users on this subnet can use this machine as their time server but cannot perform actions of any kind on the service itself.

The next three (uncommented) lines in the file are the servers that the local NTP server will trust for purposes of synchronizing the local clock. There are thousands of publicly available time servers worldwide, so consult one of the many lists online, find a few that are geographically close to you, and use them. You should be able to find a list by browsing the ISC web site, which maintains information about time server lists at *http://ntp.isc.org/bin/view/ Servers/WebHome*. Do not put IP addresses in for the servers! As sites evolve, inevitably they incur some alterations in how networking works, how IP blocks are subnetted, and the like. An IP address change at Cornell University isn't something you should be concerned with, and you won't have to be if you use hostnames instead of IP addresses, because sites generally take care to make sure that packets bound for *ntp0.cornell.edu* get there regardless of the IP address of that server at the time.

Hey! My Servers Are Gone!

It happens. Maybe you've lost connectivity to the outside world. Maybe you picked three NTP servers that are at the same site (a bad idea) and they're all down. Regardless, you have clients to serve, and you need to tell them something. Enter the magical "fudge" statement:

```
server   127.127.1.0
fudge    127.127.1.0 stratum 10
```

Here, we enter the IP address of the local system's clock in the server line and then "fudge" its priority to stratum 10. All time servers are automatically assigned strata values based on their distance from the time source. Many of the public time servers are stratum 2 or 3 time servers. That means that the only way our local NTP daemon is ever going to use a stratum 10 time server is if it's the only one available. Most Linux distributions, and many other Unix variants, supply you with a default *ntp.conf* file that has this bit of configuration wisdom already uncommented. It's safe to leave it uncommented, and doing so will mean that you don't have to worry about NTP if you lose outside connectivity or if you don't catch a hiccup in time server availability right away.

See Also

- Very detailed NTP documentation by the creator of NTP, David Mills: *http://www.eecis.udel.edu/~mills/ntp/html/index.html*

HACK
#23

Centralize X Window System Font Resources

Setting up a central X Window System font server simplifies font distribution and reduces clutter and resource use on X-based desktop systems.

The X Window System is the underpinning of most of the graphical desktops and window managers used on Linux and Unix systems today. While alternatives are under development and many people complain about the CPU impact of the X Window System's constant polling for keyboard and mouse events, it's hard to argue with success—the X Window System already works and is therefore used almost everywhere. Also, the demands it puts on modern systems with beefy processors are much less significant than they were on old workstations or systems running at 300 MHz. As an inherently network-aware client/server graphics system, X has a lot going for it in terms of usability and portability, as well as ubiquity, since it's available and supported on almost every system with graphical capabilities. Still, there are some aspects of X that can be optimized—specifically, its font handling. This hack explores how you can set up a central font server to offload local font requirements to a central resource, saving CPU cycles, disk space on your desktop systems, and administrative headaches by ensuring that the same fonts are deployed on all desktop systems that might need them.

Billions and Billions of Fonts...

Obtaining and managing the fonts used by graphical applications has always been a problem, regardless of the type of system that you're using, and it certainly isn't limited to the X Window System. I can (painfully) remember choking older Windows and Mac OS boxes by installing too many fonts. Somewhat worse than the problem of loading and supporting zillions of fonts were aesthetic problems caused by people's zealous overuse of them. I can remember getting resumes from prospective employees that looked like they'd been blasted with a shotgun loaded with different fonts and wingdings. Such is life—if you build it, they will abuse it. However, sysadmins are the wrong people to enforce aesthetics. Our job is typically to provide users with the resources they think they need and to do so in a manageable, easily administered fashion.

Today's X Window System deployments on Linux boxes typically come from either Xfree86.org or X.org. The latter is more prevalent and is probably "the X Window System of the future" (which some may view as an oxymoron, but that's another topic). Both of these X Window System implementations come with a variety of fonts located in subdirectories of *usr/X11R6/lib/X11/fonts*. Each of these subdirectories can contain many different font families as well as individual fonts. The default X.org configuration on the SUSE system where I'm writing this provides 30 subdirectories of fonts, and running the `fc-list` command shows that there are 652 separate fonts available on the system. In comparison, my Fedora Core 4 systems (where I've installed everything, since disk space is cheaper than my time) have 185 fonts installed. The SUSE boxes devote around 100 MB of disk space to font storage, while the FC4 system uses a mere 50 MB. These values would be much higher if I'd installed all of the fonts that are available for different languages. The number reported by the `fc-list` command is also independent of any fonts that individual users may have installed locally in their ~/.fonts directories. Yikes!

Discrepancies between the number of fonts delivered with various Linux distributions and X Window System implementations make it desirable to share fonts between systems. Disk space is as cheap as dirt nowadays (certainly cheaper than potting soil), but making the same huge collections of wonderful fonts available to everyone's X Window System applications is certainly logistically attractive. In addition to the default sets of fonts provided with Linux distributions, some Linux applications that may not be part of default system installs come with their own sets of fonts.

Luckily, I'm not the first person to have wished for a centralized mechanism for delivering fonts to X Window Systems across the college or enterprise. For quite a while, most X Window System implementations have come with a font server known as *xfs* (X Font Server, not to be confused with the XFS journaling filesystem). A previous incarnation of a font server, *fs*, was provided with older Linux distributions, but this has since been supplanted by *xfs*. Most desktop Linux distributions use *xfs* to deliver fonts to the local system, but with a few changes to the *xfs* configuration file and a bit of organization, you can easily configure one or two centralized font servers to handle your organization's font requirements and make as many fonts as possible available to all of your X Window System desktops, window managers, and applications.

Setting Up an X Font Server

Setting up an X font server to serve fonts to your other systems is quite simple. As most modern X Window System implementations use a font server to deliver fonts to the local system, the most important step in the reconfiguration process is to open up the X font server to external TCP requests.

The configuration file that controls the behavior of the *xfs* font server is the file */etc/X11/fs/config*. (Although the font server executable has a new name, they kept its old name in the path for consistency's sake.) We'll want to modify a few things in this file, but the critical one for turning a specific X font server instance into a centralized resource is to comment out the following line by using a text editor to put a hash mark at the beginning of the line:

```
#no-listen = tcp
```

By removing the no-listen directive, this tells the X font server to begin listening to incoming TCP requests from other hosts.

Setting up more than one font server is a good idea if you're going to be configuring your desktop systems to use centralized font resources. To identify other font servers, add an entry to the *xfs* configuration file that gives the comma-separated names or IP addresses of the other font servers on your network and the ports on which they are servicing requests. As an example:

```
alternate-servers = font2.vonhagen.org:7100,font3.vonhagen.org:7100
```

This entry tells the font server that it can redirect requests to the alternate font servers *font2.vonhagen.org* and *font3.vonhagen.org* on port 7100 if it has too many connections to handle itself. The standard port on which X font servers run, which you should probably use, is 7100. You can use a different port if you'd like, as long as you're consistent both on the font server and on any clients that want to connect to it.

Next, you'll want to set the port keyword in the *xfs* configuration file to the integer value of the port on which the X font server will be listening for incoming requests. Again, port 7100 is the standard and should thus be used unless you have some reason to use another port.

> On some Gentoo Linux distributions, the X font server port is set by the XFS_PORT directive in the */etc/conf.d/xfs* configuration file. If you are using Gentoo and your font server starts but you can't contact it, check this file to make sure the font server is actually following the directives that you specified in its configuration file.

Next, determine the appropriate limits for the number of clients that can connect to the font server and how the font server should behave when that limit is reached. This is done by a combination of the client-limit and clone-self settings in the *xfs* configuration file. The client-limit setting requires an integer value that determines the maximum number of clients that a specific font server will support before it refuses service to incoming requests. The clone-self setting requires a Boolean value and determines how the font server behaves when this limit is reached. If clone-self is on (true), the font server will start a new instance of itself when it reaches the maximum number of clients specified. If clone-self is off (false), the font server will attempt to contact any other servers identified in the alternate-servers entry, in order, until one can be contacted successfully. In environments with multiple centralized font servers that service large numbers of desktops, I'd suggest always having clone-self set to false, and starting out with a client-limit of 100. Once you see how well this performs, you can raise or lower this limit to best balance response time from the font server (affected by both system load and network bandwidth) with reasonable utilization of all of your font servers.

As the final step in creating your X font server's configuration file, you'll need to add each directory that contains X fonts to the comma-separated value for the catalogue statement. The next section explains how to copy font files from remote systems to the X font server system and create appropriate entries for them in the font server configuration file.

Copying Fonts to a Font Server

The next step in configuring your font server is to actually populate it with all of the fonts that you want it to deliver to your X Window System clients. The easiest way to do this is to examine the X Window System configuration files on each of your types of systems to see where they are currently getting fonts. This is specified in one or more FontPath statements in the Files section of the X Window System configuration file, which is either */etc/X11/xorg.conf* (for X Window servers from X.org) or */etc/X11/XF86Config-4* or */etc/X11/XF86Config* (for X Window servers from XFree86.org). If the Files section contains a single, uncommented statement such as the following, that system is using itself as a local font server:

```
FontPath    "unix/:7100"
```

For each FontPath entry that points to an actual directory on the system you're examining, first check if the same directory (with the same contents) exists on the system where you'll be running your enterprise-wide X font server. If not, you'll need to copy the contents of that directory to the X font server system, creating the directory if necessary. Once any necessary directories have been cloned to the X font server system, make sure that those same directories are being identified in the catalogue statement in the X font server's configuration file. For example, the following are some sample statements from an X font server configuration file that refers to a local font directory:

```
FontPath    "/usr/X11R6/lib/X11/fonts/misc:unscaled"
FontPath    "/usr/X11R6/lib/X11/fonts/local"
FontPath    "/usr/X11R6/lib/X11/fonts/75dpi:unscaled"
FontPath    "/usr/X11R6/lib/X11/fonts/misc/sgi:unscaled"
```

After copying font directories to the machine that will be running the X font server, you will then have to update the X font server's configuration file, */etc/X11/fs/config*, to have equivalent statements. Each FontPath statement in the X server's configuration file translates into one of the comma-separated values associated with the catalogue keyword in the X font server's configuration file. Thus, an equivalent statement to the previous example would be the following:

```
catalogue = /usr/X11R6/lib/X11/fonts/misc:unscaled,
            /usr/X11R6/lib/X11/fonts/75dpi:unscaled,
            /usr/X11R6/lib/X11/fonts/100dpi:unscaled,
            /usr/X11R6/lib/X11/fonts/misc/sgi:unscaled
```

 The last entry in the catalogue statement must not be followed by a comma.

If you copy fonts into an existing font directory on the machine that will be running the X font server, you should su to root or use the sudo command to re-run the mkfontdir command so that all the fonts in that directory can be identified and delivered by the X font server.

Starting or Restarting the X Font Server

Almost there! Before restarting the X font server to pick up the new settings and start offering fonts to any X clients that happen by, check the *xfs* startup script located in */etc/init.d/xfs* to make sure that it doesn't explicitly specify a different port than the one on which your font server expects to listen. For example, suppose that your startup script contained a statement like the following:

```
daemon --check xfs xfs -port -1 -daemon -droppriv -user xfs
```

You would want to modify this statement to the following:

```
daemon --check xfs xfs -port 7100 -daemon -droppriv -user xfs
```

Some startup scripts use a variable to hold the port number. If this is the case in your font server startup scripts, make sure that the variable identifies port 7100 as the port on which to run the server.

You're now officially ready to go! To restart (or start) your X font server, simply execute the following command:

```
# /etc/init.d/xfs restart
```

If the font server isn't already running, the *stop* portion of the restart will fail, but the *start* portion will start your X font server with all your new options.

Make sure you add the X font server startup fairly early on in your various runlevels, especially if you start your machine in graphical mode. If the X font server isn't available when you try to start the X Window System itself, and no local fonts are available, X will fail to start.

Updating Desktop Systems to Use an X Font Server

While there's a bit of work involved in setting up your X font server and making sure it offers all the fonts your clients will need, switching a desktop system to use a remote X font server is easy. As mentioned previously, many modern desktop Linux distributions already use a local font server (i.e., a font server that is running on the same host as the X server) to deliver fonts. Switching these systems to use a remote X font server is extremely easy.

The key to where your X server gets its fonts is the Files section of its configuration file. As stated previously, if the Files section contains a single, uncommented statement such as the following, that system is using itself as a local font server:

```
FontPath    "unix/:7100"
```

To switch this system to using the remote font server, change this line to something like the following:

```
FontPath    "tcp/fontserver1.vonhagen.org:7100"
```

You should then restart the X server on your desktop system to ensure that it can contact the X font server and retrieve the fonts that it needs. If the system cannot contact the font server, starting X will fail, and you should follow some of the tips in the troubleshooting section of this hack. Otherwise, you're done!

Though I'm a fan of centralizing X resources such as fonts to make everyone's lives easier, I use a somewhat paranoid X server configuration file that provides some fallback in case a font server or the network goes down. For example, the FontPath entries in the *xorg.conf* files for machines on my home office network are the following:

```
FontPath    "tcp/fontserver1.vonhagen.org:7100"
FontPath    "tcp/fontserver2.vonhagen.org:7100"
FontPath    "/usr/X11R6/lib/X11/fonts/75dpi:unscaled"
FontPath    "/usr/X11R6/lib/X11/fonts/misc:unscaled"
FontPath    "/usr/X11R6/lib/X11/fonts/local"
```

This tells my X servers to try two local font servers first and then fall back to a minimized collection of local fonts if the font servers don't work for some reason. The font servers are just *CNAMEs* in my DNS server, so I can easily move them to different hosts as my computing environment evolves. The fallback entries cover those rare cases when I just want to start a single machine.

Troubleshooting

If an X server can't contact your font server and that is the only font resource and you haven't provided any local fallback fonts, the X server will not start and will terminate with a message about not being able to contact the font server. Luckily, both Linux and the X Window System include some helpful commands to enable you to diagnose the problem.

First, on the font server, make sure that the font server is actually running by using the ps command, as in the following example:

```
$ ps -ef | grep xfs
root     13841 31053  0 04:39 pts/13   00:00:00 xfs
wvh      13848 31053  0 04:39 pts/13   00:00:00 grep -i xfs
```

Next, check that you can contact it successfully by retrieving a list of the fonts that it provides. You can do this using the fslsfonts command, as in the following example:

```
$ fslsfonts -server fontserver1:7100
```

This should display a long list of available fonts. If it doesn't, make sure that the font server is actually listening on the correct port, using a command like the following:

```
$ netstat -an | grep 7100
tcp        0      0 0.0.0.0:7100          0.0.0.0:*              LISTEN
tcp        0      0 :::7100               :::*                   LISTEN
unix  2    [ ACC ]    STREAM     LISTENING     862009    /tmp/.font-unix/
fs7100
```

If you don't see this information and you can't contact the X font server using fslsfonts, make sure that you commented out the no-listen = tcp entry in your font server's configuration file.

If you see messages like the following when you start your X font server, some of the directories specified in its configuration file either don't exist or don't contain valid fonts:

```
xfs notice: ignoring font path element /usr/X11R6/lib/X11/fonts/Speedo
(unreadable)
xfs notice: ignoring font path element /usr/X11R6/lib/X11/fonts/CID
(unreadable)
xfs notice: ignoring font path element /usr/X11R6/lib/X11/fonts/local
(unreadable)
```

These messages are nonfatal, but you should clean up your font server's configuration file so that no other sysadmin is confused about whether these directories were supposed to contain fonts that have somehow gotten "lost."

Finally, double-check that you have the right font server settings in your X server's startup file. You can use the fallback approach suggested in the previous section to start the X font server using a small collection of local fonts until you resolve your connectivity problems. While you're working on them, you can use the `fslsfonts` and `xset fp` (set font path for the X Window System) commands to, respectively, test connectivity to the font server and add it to your current X session for testing purposes. The `xset fp` command enables you to add a font server to the list of font sources that X applications search (known as a *font path*), using a command like the following:

```
$ xset +fp tcp/fontserver1:7100
```

You may need to cause the X server to re-probe its font sources by using the `xset fp rehash` command. While testing, you can also remove elements from your X font path using a command like the following:

```
$ xset -fp tcp/fontserver1:7100
```

You can determine the current settings for your X font path (along with other settings) by executing the `xset -q` command, which provides a variety of information about your working X Window System environment.

Summary

The X Window System is a great thing for Linux and Unix users, but the number of available (or required) fonts can quickly escalate, especially in internationalized (I18N) environments. Some X Window System applications, such as Wolfram Research's Mathematica, also take advantage of many custom fonts in order to display results as nicely as possible. (Wolfram's docs even identify a font server that they export over the Internet for this purpose.)

Centralizing resources such as fonts that are used by many of the machines in your computing environment can save local disk space and, more importantly, provide a single location where you can easily install custom fonts that multiple users may require. Be careful, though—central resources simplify administration, but they can also provide single points of failure unless you architect your installation correctly.

The disk space required to install most fonts locally is no big deal (or expense) nowadays. However, centralizing custom fonts is always a good idea. Installing custom fonts locally isn't really a problem until you upgrade or replace the machine on which they live, at which point you may forget that the machine had custom fonts installed. Once bitten, twice shy! An X font server is easy preventative medicine for this sort of problem.

See Also

- man xset
- man xfs
- man fslsfonts
- *http://www.x.org*
- *http://www.xfree86.org*

Create a CUPS Print Server

Let printers announce themselves and create a flexible, modern printing environment by setting up CUPS.

Today's printers are typically high-quality laser or inkjet printers, often capable of color printing and near-photographic quality. The original Unix printing system, known as *lpd* (Line Printer Daemon) was designed to queue and print jobs that were intended for huge, text-only line printers. As more sophisticated printers were developed that were capable of higher-quality printouts (such as the original x9700, Canon-CX, and Imagen-300 laser printers), the original *lpd* print system continued to be used, but it required that the jobs you were printing be preprocessed so that they contained the special commands the printer used internally to produce higher-quality printouts. This quickly became tedious, because it meant that users had to know which printers they wanted to print to and required use of the appropriate preformatting commands. Eventually, the *lpd* system was updated and a similar printing system known as *lp* was developed. *lp* encapsulated the knowledge about the formats required by specific printers, implementing the necessary preformatting commands into filters (also known as *print drivers*) that automatically formatted files as required by the target printers.

The evolution of multiple printing systems for Unix systems was not without pitfalls: it led to incompatibilities between the different print systems, required recompilation of the filters for specific printers for multiple Unix systems (if you could get the source code at all), and so on. Eventually, a company known as Easy Software Products began developing a more generalized printing system for Unix, Linux, and other Unix-like systems, called the Common Unix Printing System (CUPS). The original version of CUPS used the standard networked LDP protocol, but it quickly switched to using a new standard, the Internet Printing Protocol (IPP), which non-Unix/Linux systems such as Windows can use to print to CUPS printers. Easy Software Products also had the foresight to make the CUPS source code freely available under the GPL so that it could be compiled for multiple operating systems and thus become a true, cross-system standard popularized by zillions of users and sysadmins. This strategy has worked—today, CUPS is used by every major Linux distribution and most other Unix-like systems.

Almost every Linux system provides its own administrative tool for print system and printer configuration: SUSE provides *YaST*; Red Hat and Fedora Core distributions use *printconf-gui*; and so on. Printer configuration would therefore still be a sysadmin nightmare if not for the fact that the CUPS print daemon provides a built-in administrative tool that is easily accessed through any web browser via port 631. This provides a standard interface for CUPS configuration (though you're still welcome to use your Linux distribution's administrative printer configuration tools, if you insist). This hack focuses on the standard CUPS interface and web-based configuration.

Defining a New Printer in CUPS

To define a new printer on any Linux system using the CUPS administrative interface, you must first make sure that the CUPS daemon, *cupsd*, is running on your system. You can do this using the ps command, as shown in the following example:

```
$ ps alxww | grep cupsd
5    4 6923    1  16   0 24540 1452 - Ss   ?      0:00 /usr/sbin/cupsd
0 1000 13304 31053 17   0   536  112 - R+  pts/13 0:00 grep -i cupsd
```

If it isn't shown in the process listing, you can start it as the root user or via sudo, as in the following example:

```
# /etc/init.d/cups start
```

You should see an OK message once the system starts the CUPS daemon. Next, open your favorite web browser and connect to the network address *http://127.0.0.1:631*. The odd port number comes from its roots as an IPP print server (the default port for IPP is 631). The screen shown in Figure 3-1 will display.

When you see this screen, click the Do Administration Tasks link. An authentication dialog will display, into which you enter the name and password of a user who is authorized to do printer configuration on your system.

> The users who can administer printers and the print subsystem differ across multiple Linux distributions. On SUSE Linux systems, you must add authorized users to the CUPS authentication file using the lppasswd command (for example, lppasswd -a wvh would add the user *wvh* and prompt you twice for a password for printer administration by that user). On Red Hat, Fedora Core, and many other Linux distributions, you can simply enter the root user's login and password.

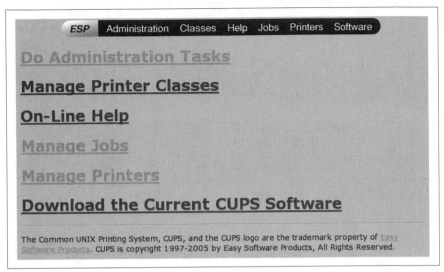

Figure 3-1. The web-based CUPS administrative interface

Once you successfully enter an authorized user's name and password, the screen shown in Figure 3-2 will display.

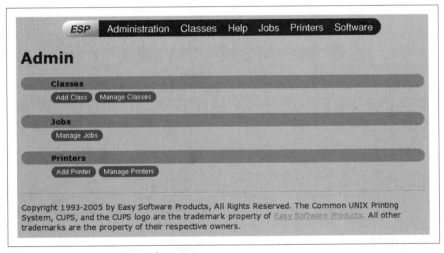

Figure 3-2. The main CUPS admin screen

Click Add Printer to display the screen shown in Figure 3-3, where you can begin configuring your printer. (You can also get to this screen by selecting the Printers item from any CUPS page header and clicking the Add Printer button, but I think of this as an administrative action and therefore usually get there from the Admin page.) This hack focuses on configuring a local (physically attached) printer. "Configure Linux Connections to Remote CUPS Printers" [Hack #25] provides information on configuring a remote printer is provided in.

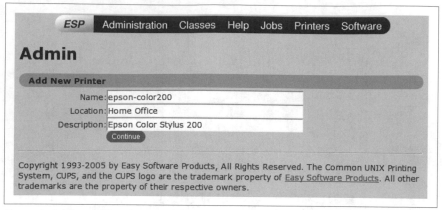

Figure 3-3. The initial printer definition screen

Enter a memorable short name for the printer in the Name field (most commonly without spaces), enter a summary of the printer's location in the Location field, and enter a short description of the printer in the Description field. The latter two are simply text strings, but putting meaningful values in these fields will help you remember which printer is which if your print server supports multiple printers. Click Continue to proceed. The screen shown in Figure 3-4 will display.

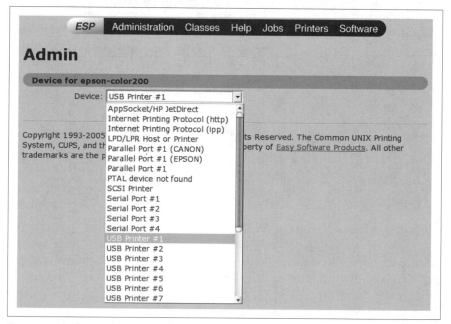

Figure 3-4. Selecting how your printer is attached

Select the device to which your printer is attached from the drop-down list shown in Figure 3-4. As you can see, some Linux distributions auto-identify the printers attached to various ports when they perform hardware detection (this example screen was captured on a SUSE Linux system). After selecting the interface to which your printer is attached, click Continue. The screen shown in Figure 3-5 will display.

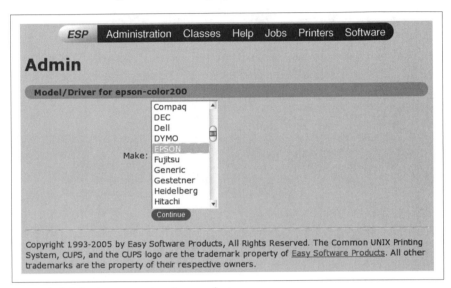

Figure 3-5. Selecting your printer's manufacturer

Select the manufacturer of your printer from the drop-down list in Figure 3-5. If the manufacturer of your printer isn't explicitly listed, your printer probably emulates a printer from some other manufacturer. (Printers that emulate various Hewlett-Packard printers are quite common. Any printer that supports PCL—HP's Printer Control Language—can emulate some sort of HP printer.)

> You'll note that many print drivers provide two printing options: *gimp-print* and *foomatic*. *gimp-print* is a print plug-in for the GNU Image Manipulation Program (GIMP) graphics package that includes many custom print drivers, while *foomatic* is a database-driven interface to another set of print drivers. I generally select whichever is marked as Recommended. If neither is recommended, it's usually best to start with *gimp-print* drivers, because *gimp-print* can also access *foomatic* drivers, but *foomatic* can't access the *gimp-print* drivers. Most Linux distributions preinstall these packages when you install CUPS, but you may have to install them separately on distributions whose goal is minimizing disk usage.

Click Continue to proceed. A screen like the one shown in Figure 3-6 will display, listing all of the printers that are available from the selected manufacturer.

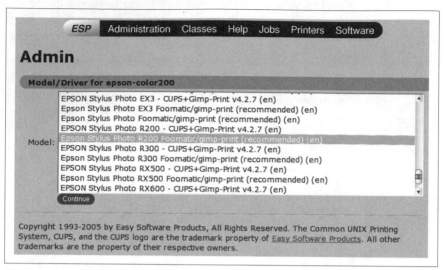

Figure 3-6. Selecting a specific print driver

Select your printer (or an equivalent) from this list. It's important to select your printer exactly if possible, to best take advantage of the printer's capabilities. Click Continue to proceed. You'll see a summary screen telling you that the printer has been set up, which includes creating the right print queues and configuration entries that are used internally by CUPS.

Testing CUPS Printing

Once you've set up a new printer, the first thing you'll want to do is test printing to it, not just to ensure that it is correctly configured in terms of ports and drivers, but also to check the default quality level for the printer. To do this, click the Printers entry in the heading of any CUPS administrative web page. A screen like the one shown in Figure 3-7 will display.

Click the Print Test Page button. You should see your printer's activity light come on, and the printer should begin to print a CUPS test page. If the activity light doesn't come on, click the Jobs entry in the web page to display a page showing the status of the test print job. If this page shows that the job has completed, your printer is not configured correctly. The most common problems are that the printer isn't connected to the port that you selected in Figure 3-4, or that you've selected the wrong print driver. You can review and modify your current settings by clicking the Modify Printer button on the Printers page, which walks you through the steps described in the previous section using your current settings as defaults.

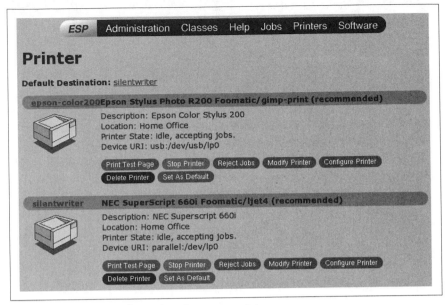

Figure 3-7. Summary information about your printer

Fine-Tuning Printer Configuration in CUPS

After you've successfully configured a printer and printed a test page, you may want to fine-tune your printer's print capabilities. To do this, click the Printers entry in the heading of any CUPS administrative web page, and click the Configure button. A screen like the one shown in Figure 3-8 will display. The contents of this page will depend on the capabilities of your printer and the driver that you selected, but they will enable you to do things like fine-tune color settings (in the Adjustment section), select a higher default printing resolution (using the General section's Printout Mode setting), and so on.

Enabling Remote Printing on the CUPS Server

Depending how CUPS is preconfigured on your Linux distribution, you may need to add your remote hosts (or your entire network) to the list of acceptable locations in the CUPS daemon's configuration file, */etc/cups/cupsd.conf*. The list of valid locations for incoming print jobs is stored inside the <Location />... </Location> stanza. On most systems, this looks like the following:

```
<Location />
  Order Deny,Allow
  Deny From All
  Allow From 127.0.0.1
</Location>
```

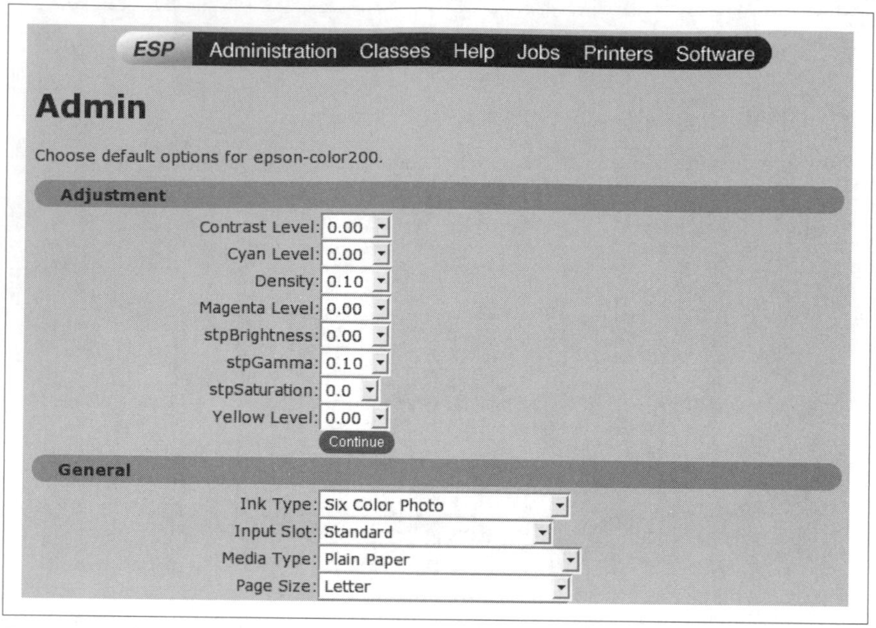

Figure 3-8. The printer-specific configuration screen

This configuration file entry supports printing to the CUPS server from the host on which the print server is running. To change the entry so that all hosts on the local network can print, add a line so the stanza now looks like this:

```
<Location />
  Order Deny,Allow
  Deny From All
  Allow From 127.0.0.1
  Allow From 192.168.6.*
</Location>
```

This stanza now enables printing from the local host and from all printers on the specified subnet (in this case, 192.168.6).

Troubleshooting CUPS Printing

CUPS print servers maintain three logfiles (stored in the directory /var/log/cups) that provide some information about attempts to access or use them:

access_log

> Records attempts to access the CUPS print server. Can be useful in determining why print jobs are rejected or discarded.

error_log

> Records all errors encountered or produced by the CUPS print server. Can be equally useful in determining why print jobs are rejected or discarded.

page_log
>Keeps track of every page printed by a specified printer, including the host from which the print job was received, the name of the printer being used, and so on.

Of these, the *access_log* and *error_log* files are the most useful for diagnostic purposes. Examining the end of these files after attempting to print but not receiving any output usually shows meaningful error messages. For example, if you forgot to update the MIME files and are trying to print to a CUPS printer from Windows, you may see messages like the following:

```
E [05/Sep/2005:17:55:49 -0400] get_job_attrs: job #0 doesn't exist!
E [05/Sep/2005:17:55:49 -0400] print_job: Unsupported format 'application/
                              octet-stream'!
I [05/Sep/2005:17:55:49 -0400] Hint: Do you have the raw file printing rules
                              enabled?
```

It doesn't get much more helpful than this in terms of identifying the problem and suggesting a fix.

The *page_log* file can be useful for cost diagnosis. A number of open source applications are available to parse and summarize the information in this file, helping you get some idea of your printing costs. Useful applications that do this sort of thing are *PrintAnalyze* and *phpPrintAnalyzer*, both of which are available from the CUPS web site at *http://www.cups.org/links.php*. Another useful script along the same lines is *cartridge_usage.pl*, a Perl script that requires that you keep a separate logfile for each new cartridge but does a great job of identifying the number of pages that each cartridge will print. This script is available at *http://www.ime.usp.br/~feferraz/en/cartusage.html*.

Summary

CUPS provides a central system for printing to modern printers on Linux and many other operating systems. Its combination of support for standards, consistency across platforms, and a common, web-based administrative interface makes it a powerful, usable package. As we'll see in the next few hacks, it's easy to configure printing to CUPS print servers from remote Linux, Windows, and Macintosh systems.

See Also

- *http://www.cups.org/documentation.php*
- "Configure Linux Connections to Remote CUPS Printers" [Hack #25]
- "Integrate Windows Printing with CUPS" [Hack #26]
- "Centralize Macintosh Printing with CUPS" [Hack #27]
- "Define a Secure CUPS Printer" [Hack #28]

Configure Linux Connections to Remote CUPS Printers

Quickly set up connections to remote printers using the CUPS web-based interface.

It would be nice if each user had her own printer, so we could all avoid the inherent bottlenecks caused when some thoughtless user prints a 100-page manual or a bunch of high-resolution vacation photos to one of your school's or company's central printers. Unfortunately, the purchase and maintenance costs of high-volume printers can be quite high, so most schools and businesses concentrate resources on one or two good ones and configure all their desktop systems to send print jobs to those printers. Luckily, the web-based administrative interface provided by CUPS makes it quite simple to configure and test connections to remote CUPS printers on Linux systems. Here's how.

Defining a Remote Printer in CUPS

The basic procedure for defining the remote printer is almost identical to that for creating the CUPS print server [Hack #24], so I won't insult your intelligence by duplicating screenshots and instructions here. Instead, I'll just focus on the two screens that are different and that really matter: the Device screen, where you specify how to connect to the printer; and a new Device URL screen, where you specify the Universal Resource Locator (URL) that uniquely identifies the remote printer.

After authenticating and beginning the process of adding a printer, you'll need to specify the protocol with which your client system will communicate with the remote printer. This is done on the Device screen, shown in Figure 3-9. Instead of selecting a physical connection, you'll usually select the Internet Printing Protocol (IPP). IPP is a modern protocol for communicating with printers from many different types of operating systems, and it is therefore the right choice in most modern, mixed-system environments.

Once you've selected IPP, click Continue to proceed to another Device screen, shown in Figure 3-10. This screen enables you to specify the URL of the remote printer so that the local system knows where to find the correct printer.

As shown in Figure 3-10, the URL of remote CUPS printer is in the form *ipp:// address-or-name/printers/printer-name*, where *address-or-name* is the IP address or name of the host to which the printer is physically attached, and *printer-name* is the name of that printer on the remote host. The URL shown in this figure reflects the print server that I defined in "Create a CUPS Print Server" [Hack #24], which is named *epson-color200* and is running on the host 192.168.6.64.

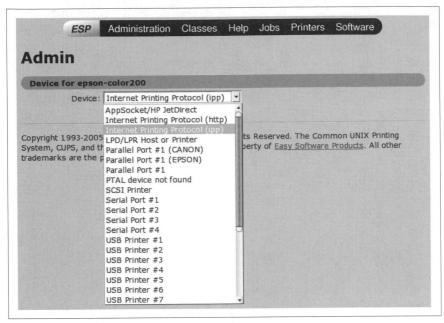

Figure 3-9. Specifying IPP as your remote printing protocol

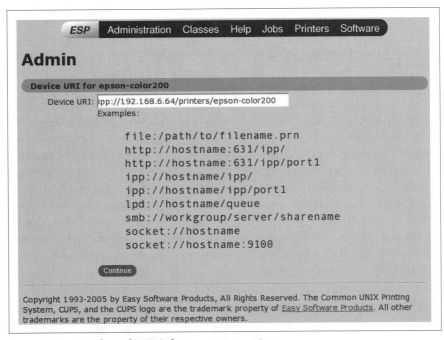

Figure 3-10. Specifying the URL for your remote printer

Once you've specified the URL for the remote printer, proceed through the rest of the printer configuration screens [Hack #24]. You'll probably also want to print a test page to ensure that you can connect to the remote printer and verify that you selected the correct print driver to format output for the remote printer.

Summary

Configuring print access from any Linux system to a remote CUPS printer is quite easy, as you can see from the simple case explained in this hack. If you need to restrict access to this printer, you can manually modify the CUPS configuration file (*/etc/cups/cupsd.conf*) on the print server, as explained in "Define a Secure CUPS Printer" [Hack #28].

Using CUPS as the printing and queuing mechanism for your school or enterprise is the perfect solution—it gives you a powerful, consistent printing utility with a consistent administrative interface that is independent of different Linux distributions, thanks to its web-oriented focus.

See Also

- *http://www.cups.org/documentation.php*
- "Create a CUPS Print Server" [Hack #24]

HACK #26 Integrate Windows Printing with CUPS

CUPS is not just a great solution for Linux and Unix printing—it can also easily handle your Windows printing needs.

As we all know, it's important to be able to play nicely with Windows systems in today's academic and business environments. This may be philosophically unattractive to many of us, but it's a reality. While printing from Windows systems to Linux print servers is often done using Samba (leveraging the standard SMB/CIFS networking protocols), you may not want to set up Samba on every desktop for which you're responsible. Luckily, Microsoft's quest for proprietary standards hasn't eliminated their support for remote printing using other standard protocols, such as HTTP, which CUPS is happy to support. This hack explains how to configure Windows systems to print to remote CUPS print servers using the standard HTTP protocol.

Configuring Printing from Windows 2000/XP Systems

It's really quite easy to configure a Windows 2000 or XP system to print to a remote CUPS printer. First, select the standard "Add printer" icon from the *Printers* folder in the Control Panel. Specify that you want to create a remote printer, and enter a URL of the following form: *http://name-or-address:631/ printers/printer-name* (as shown in Figure 3-11, which shows the Windows 2000 printer configuration dialog).

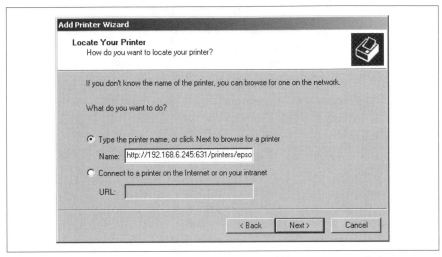

Figure 3-11. Specifying a URL in the Windows 2000 Add Remote Printer dialog

Continuing with the example used in the previous CUPS-related hacks in this book, I've entered the URL *http://192.168.6.245:631/printers/epson-color200*. Figure 3-12 shows the equivalent dialog under Windows XP.

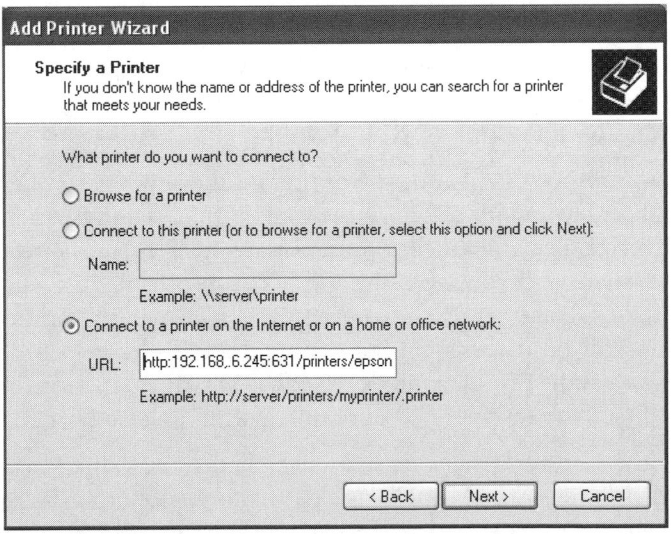

Figure 3-12. Specifying a URL in the Windows XP Add Remote Printer dialog

> Some combinations of Windows systems and CUPS versions require that you specify a hostname rather than an IP address in a printer URL. If your remote print server has a fixed IP address, the easiest way to do this is to create an entry in the Windows hosts file that maps the IP address to a hostname. This is the file *C:\WINNT\system32\drivers\etc\ hosts* on Windows 2000 systems, and the file *C:\WINDOWS\ system32\drivers\etc\hosts* on Windows XP systems. For example, adding an entry like 192.168.6.245 printserv to this file would enable me to specify the URL *http://printserv: 631/printers/epson-color200* for the remote printer.

Click Next to proceed with configuring the remote printer connection. Because you are connecting to a remote printer, you may see a dialog like the one shown in Figure 3-13. This dialog demonstrates that the Windows system is able to contact the remote print server, since the warning message displays the name of the print driver as known to the remote print server. To satisfy Windows, you can either choose an installed print driver from the subsequent dialog or locate the print driver on the Web or on the CD that accompanied your printer purchase.

Figure 3-13. Windows 2000 Print Driver Request dialog

Server-Side Configuration for HTTP Printing

Once you've finished configuring the printer on the Windows system, you'll need to make a few modifications to the CUPS printer configuration files on your print server. Because the files you print are being preformatted on your Windows system, and you are using the HTTP protocol, you will need to configure the CUPS server on the Linux system to which the printer is connected. You will need to modify two configuration files to tell the CUPS server how to handle raw data files received via HTTP, configuring it to send those files directly to the specified print queue with no local formatting.

First, edit the file */etc/cups/mime.types*, which defines valid Multipurpose Internet Mail Extensions (MIME) formats that are supported by the CUPS server. MIME defines a variety of formats that one might encounter on the Internet (such as in a web browser or in HTTP communications) and defines how MIME-aware applications should handle them. To enable printing via HTTP, remove the hash mark (#) at the beginning of the following line:

```
#application/octet-stream
```

Without the leading comment character (the hash mark), this entry tells the CUPS print server that raw data streams are an acceptable input format. Next, edit the file */etc/cups/mime.convs*, which defines the types of conversions that the CUPS server should perform on various MIME input formats. To enable printing via HTTP, remove the hash mark at the beginning of the following line:

```
#application/octet-stream    application/vnd.cups-raw    0
```

As with the change to the */etc/cups/mime.types* file, removing the comment character from the beginning of this line tells the CUPS server to handle input files in *application/octet-stream* format by passing them to a CUPS application that simply inserts them into a print queue without doing any local formatting.

Troubleshooting Windows Printing to CUPS Servers

The most common cause of being unable to print to a CUPS print server is that the printer is not configured to accept print jobs from your host's IP address. For more information about this, see the section "Enabling Remote Printing on the CUPS Server" in "Create a CUPS Print Server" **[Hack #24]**. If you're sure that this is not the problem, check the CUPS logfiles. The CUPS print servers maintain three logfiles that can provide a variety of information about attempts to access or use them: *access_log*, *error_log*, and *page_log*. Of these, the *access_log* and *error_log* files are the most useful for diagnostic purposes. Examining the end of these files after attempting to print but not receiving any output usually shows meaningful error messages. For example, if you forgot to update the MIME files and are trying to print to a CUPS printer from Windows, you may see messages like the following:

```
E [05/Sep/2005:17:55:49 -0400] get_job_attrs: job #0 doesn't exist!
E [05/Sep/2005:17:55:49 -0400] print_job: Unsupported format 'application/
                              octet-stream'!
I [05/Sep/2005:17:55:49 -0400] Hint: Do you have the raw file printing rules
                              enabled?
```

These messages should help you identify the problem and suggest a fix.

See Also

- *http://www.cups.org/documentation.php*
- "Create a CUPS Print Server" **[Hack #24]**
- "Share Files Across Platforms Using Samba" **[Hack #60]**

Centralize Macintosh Printing with CUPS

#27   Mac OS X makes CUPS printers readily available from Macintosh systems.

Now that the Mac OS is actually a Unix system with graphical gravy, it's much easier to get to the underpinnings of the operating system when necessary. Also, because much of the software that actually powers Mac OS X is now familiar open source software, it's easier than ever to reapply your existing Linux/Unix knowledge to working with Mac OS X. Integrating Mac OS X printing with a CUPS server running on a remote Linux system is one of the best examples of this, because Mac OS X actually uses CUPS as the core of its printing subsystem. This hack explains how to use the familiar CUPS web interface to quickly and easily set up your Mac OS X systems to print to centralized CUPS print servers running on Linux systems. If you're still running a version of the Mac OS earlier than Mac OS X, this hack isn't for you unless you upgrade.

Configuring Access to a Remote CUPS Server

As well as supporting CUPS, Mac OS X also includes its own printer configuration tool, the Printer Setup Utility. The versions of the Printer Setup Utility provided with Mac OS X 10.4 and above can locate remote CUPS printers automatically, because CUPS supports the standard Internet Printing Protocol (IPP). However, just in case you can't find your printer using IPP, this hack explains the details of configuring a printer using our old friend, the web-based CUPS administrative interface. The procedure discussed in this section works fine with Versions 10.2 and later of Mac OS X.

Thanks to the fact that Mac OS X uses CUPS, the basic procedure of defining a remote printer on Mac OS X is almost identical to that of configuring remote printing on Linux systems. It is therefore also almost identical to that for creating a CUPS print server [Hack #24]. As in "Configure Linux Connections to Remote CUPS Printers" [Hack #25], I'll focus on the two screens that are different and that really matter: the Device screen, where you specify how to connect to the printer; and a new Device URL screen, where you specify the Universal Resource Locator (URL) that uniquely identifies the remote printer.

After authenticating (using the login and password of any user with administrative privileges) and beginning the process of adding a printer, you'll need to specify the protocol with which your OS X system will communicate with the remote printer. This is done on the Device screen, shown in Figure 3-14. Instead of selecting a physical connection, you'll usually select the "Internet Printing Protocol (http)" entry to specify that you want to use IPP with the HTTP protocol as its transport mechanism.

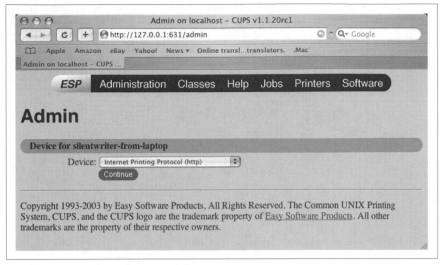

Figure 3-14. Specifying the protocol for remote printing

Once you've selected IPP over HTTP, click Continue to proceed to another Device screen, shown in Figure 3-15. This screen enables you to specify the URL of the remote printer so that the local system knows where to find the correct printer.

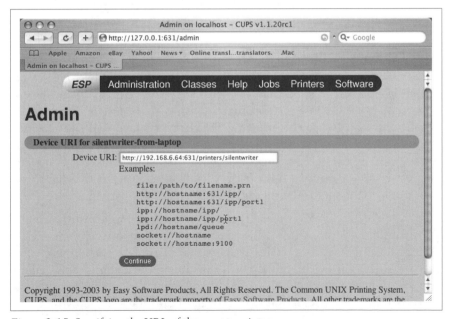

Figure 3-15. Specifying the URL of the remote printer

As shown in Figure 3-15, the URL of the remote CUPS printer is in the form *http://address-or-name/printers/printer-name*, where *address-or-name* is the IP address or name of the host to which the printer is physically attached, and *printer-name* is the name of that printer on the remote host. The URL shown in this figure reflects a different print server than was used previously; it's named *silentwriter* and is running on the host 192.168.6.64.

> If Windows printers are available in your environment or you are running Samba on one of your systems and you prefer to print using Windows SMB protocols, you can select "Windows Printer via SAMBA" as the printing protocol that you want to use and enter a URL of the form *smb://username: passwd@hostname/printers/printer-name*. If you're using a version of Mac OS X earlier than 10.4, you'll also have to verify that */usr/libexec/cups/backend/smb* is a symbolic link to */usr/ bin/smbspool* and, if not, create that link.

Once you've specified the URL for the remote printer, proceed through the rest of the printer configuration screens [Hack #24]. You'll probably also want to print a test page to ensure that you can connect to the remote printer and verify that you selected the correct print driver to format output for the remote printer. You can do that after making sure you've tweaked your server's configuration to handle HTTP print jobs correctly, as described in the next section.

Server-Side Configuration for HTTP Printing

Once you've finished configuring the printer on the Mac OS X system, you'll need to make a few modifications to the CUPS printer configuration files on your print server. Because the files that you print are being preformatted on your OS X system and you are using the HTTP protocol, you will need to configure the CUPS server on the Linux system to which the printer is connected. You will need to modify two configuration files to tell the CUPS server how to handle raw data files received via HTTP, configuring it to simply send those files directly to the specified print queue with no local formatting.

First, edit the file */etc/cups/mime.types*, which defines valid Multipurpose Internet Mail Extensions (MIME) formats that are supported by the CUPS server. MIME defines a variety of formats that one might encounter on the Internet (such as in a web browser or in HTTP communications) and defines how MIME-aware applications should handle them. To enable printing via HTTP, remove the hash mark (#) at the beginning of the following line:

```
#application/octet-stream
```

Without the leading comment character (the hash mark), this entry tells the CUPS print server that raw data streams are an acceptable input format. Next, edit the file */etc/cups/mime.convs*, which defines the types of conversions that the CUPS server should perform on various MIME input formats. To enable printing via HTTP, remove the hash mark at the beginning of the following line:

```
#application/octet-stream       application/vnd.cups-raw       0
```

As with the change to the */etc/cups/mime.types* file, removing the comment character from the beginning of this line tells the CUPS server to handle input files in *application/octet-stream* format by passing them to a CUPS application that simply inserts them into a print queue without doing any local formatting.

You will need to restart the CUPS print server to make sure that it picks up these changes. The startup script for your CUPS server is called *cups* and is typically located in */etc/init.d*. To restart the CUPS print server, execute the following command (or one appropriate for your distribution):

```
# /etc/init.d/cups restart
```

Testing Printing from Mac OS X to Your CUPS Server

At this point, you're ready to try a test print job. In your web browser, select the Printers button in the CUPS page header. Click the Print Test Page button and verify that a test page prints correctly on the remote printer. If so, congratulations! If not, check the Jobs status page in your web browser by clicking Jobs in the CUPS page header. If you've made a syntax error in your URL, you'll see a message saying "Unable to connect to IPP host: Invalid Argument." Correct the URL, abort the current test page, and retry printing a test page. If you don't see any error messages but the print job claims to have completed, see the next section for some debugging tips.

Once you've successfully printed a page from your OS X system, you'll notice that the printer that you defined using the CUPS web interface is also now visible in the Printer Setup Utility. Magic!

Troubleshooting Mac OS X Printing to CUPS Servers

The most common cause of being unable to print to a CUPS print server is that the printer is not configured to accept print jobs from your host's IP address [Hack #24].

If you're sure that this is not the problem, check the CUPS logfiles. CUPS print servers maintain three logfiles that can provide a variety of information about attempts to access or use them: *access_log*, *error_log*, and *page_log*. Of these, the *access_log* and *error_log* files are the most useful for diagnostic purposes. Examining the end of these files after attempting to print but not receiving any output usually shows meaningful error messages. For example, if you forgot to update the MIME files and are trying to print to a CUPS printer from Mac OS X, you may see messages like the following:

```
E [05/Sep/2005:17:55:49 -0400] get_job_attrs: job #0 doesn't exist!
E [05/Sep/2005:17:55:49 -0400] print_job: Unsupported format 'application/
                              octet-stream'!
I [05/Sep/2005:17:55:49 -0400] Hint: Do you have the raw file printing rules
                              enabled?
```

Talk about useful error messages! Double-check the changes you made to the CUPS MIME configuration files, restart the CUPS daemon, and try printing again.

See Also

- *http://www.cups.org/documentation.php*
- "Create a CUPS Print Server" [Hack #24]
- "Configure Linux Connections to Remote CUPS Printers" [Hack #25]

HACK #28 Define a Secure CUPS Printer

Integrated support for various authentication mechanisms makes it easy to limit access to specific printers with CUPS.

The other CUPS hacks in this chapter have focused on its most excellent web-based administrative interface and how the interface simplifies and standardizes printer setup, regardless of the type of CUPS client you're configuring. However, like most Unix/Linux programs, you can also administer the CUPS server by directly manipulating its configuration file, */etc/cups/cupsd.conf*. While this may seem somewhat intimidating at first blush, the format of this file is actually quite simple and is conceptually evocative of an Apache configuration file (which we've all probably had to modify at one time or another). A few simple changes to this file can quickly add a new layer of security to your CUPS printing environment.

Many sysadmins are paranoid today, and for good reason. Securing your existing systems by eliminating unnecessary services is just plain smart [Hack #63]. Similarly, there may be cases where you want to restrict access to certain printers. There are many security and cost reasons for limiting access to specific printers to certain users or certain IP addresses, whether it's because of who "owns" the printer (such as your CEO or department head) or because the printer uses platinum toner to print on gold sheets (and is therefore the wrong place for freshmen to print their CS101 homework). Here's how to do just that with your favorite text editor (which should be *emacs*) and a few minutes of your spare time.

> You will have to restart the CUPS server after making any changes to the CUPS configuration file, as discussed in this (or any other) hack. The startup script for your CUPS server is called *cups* and is typically located in */etc/init.d*. To restart the CUPS print server after saving your changes to its configuration file, execute the following command (or one appropriate for your distribution):
>
> ```
> # /etc/init.d/cups restart
> ```

Enabling Remote Printing on a CUPS Server

Depending 'on how CUPS is preconfigured on your Linux distribution, you may need to add your remote hosts (or your entire network) to the list of acceptable locations in the CUPS daemon's configuration file, */etc/cups/cupsd. conf*, so they can print on the printer in the first place. The list of valid locations for incoming print jobs is stored inside a `<Location />...</Location>` stanza in the CUPS configuration file. The default CUPS configuration file contains a single `Location` stanza, which applies to all printers that the CUPS server knows about. On most systems, this looks like the following:

```
<Location />
  Order Deny,Allow
  Deny From All
  Allow From 127.0.0.1
</Location>
```

This configuration file entry supports printing to the CUPS server only from the host on which the print server is running. Many CUPS printer configuration files use the `@LOCAL` macro to tell CUPS that any host that has a non-point-to-point connection to the print server can print to the printer. This generally includes hosts on the local network and typically looks like the following:

```
<Location />
  Order Deny,Allow
  Deny From All
  Allow From 127.0.0.1
  Allow from @LOCAL
</Location>
```

If you are having problems printing to a specific printer from other hosts on your network, check the */etc/cups/cupsd.conf* file to ensure that the `Location` stanza includes an `@LOCAL` entry.

If you want to explicitly configure the CUPS server so that only hosts on a specific local network can print to the printer, remove the @LOCAL entry and add a line for the local subnet, so that the stanza now looks something like the following:

```
<Location />
  Order Deny,Allow
  Deny From All
  Allow From 127.0.0.1
  Allow From 192.168.6.*
</Location>
```

This stanza now enables printing from the local host and from all printers on the specified subnet (in this case, 192.168.6), as well as the host to which the printer is physically connected.

Restricting Printer Access to Specific IP Addresses

The most straightforward way to create a secure printer is to put the printer in a secure location and physically restrict access to it. If you don't have a secure location available, you can also restrict printing to a particular printer so that only hosts with specific IP addresses can print to it. To do this, you simply create a new Location stanza in */etc/cups/cupsd.conf* for that printer and use the Allow/Deny approach introduced in the previous section to identify any IP addresses that you want to be able to print to the printer. For example, a Location stanza that restricts access to the printer *silentwriter* such that only the host to which the printer is actually attached and the host with the IP address 192.168.6.101 can print to it would be the following:

```
<Location /printers/silentwriter>
  Order Deny,Allow
  Deny From All
  Allow From 127.0.0.1
  Allow From 192.168.6.101
</Location>
```

Restricting Printer Access to Specific Users

Restricting access to a specific printer based on the IP address of the host that you want to allow to print to it is useful, but those pesky users often tend to move around from host to host. An alternative to restricting access by IP address is to require authentication in order to print to a specified printer. You can do this by using users' standard Linux passwords, but I find it most useful to require a separate password for printer access. Using standard Linux passwords causes the print server to invoke the PAM modules for CUPS (defined in */etc/pam.d/cups*), which often differ from Linux distribution to Linux distribution. (PAMs were discussed in "Customize Authentication with PAMs" [Hack #4]) Also, since most people using Linux systems have Linux passwords, that approach doesn't really limit access to any significant extent. Using a separate password for printer access is quite standard across all CUPS-oriented Linux distributions.

You can define a CUPS access password using the lppasswd command. To add a new user to the CUPS password file (stored in *etc/cups/passwd.md5* by default), execute the following command as root or via sudo:

```
# lppasswd -a username
```

You'll be prompted twice for the specified user's password. Once a user has a CUPS password, you can add this level of authentication to a specific printer by creating a new Location stanza for that printer (or updating an existing one), as in the following example:

```
<Location /printers/silentwriter>
  Order Deny,Allow
  Deny From All
  Allow From 127.0.0.1
  Allow From 192.168.6.*
  AuthType Digest
</Location>
```

This lets anyone from the 192.168.6 subnet who has a valid CUPS password entry print to the *silentwriter* printer. Users will be prompted for this password whenever they try to send print jobs to the specified printer, as in the following example:

```
$ lpr /etc/printcap
Password for wvh on localhost?
```

> Some applications, such as Microsoft Windows applications running under WINE, open connections to your default printer when they start up. If you start them in the background, these programs will appear to hang because they are prompting you for a printer password in the background, but you're not seeing the prompt. If you use CUPS passwords and a specific application seems to hang, try starting it in the foreground (i.e., without a trailing ampersand) to see if it's actually prompting you for additional information.

Summary

Beyond the simple authentication and IP address entries discussed in this hack, CUPS provides many other mechanisms for authentication, such as printer classes and alternatives to digest authentication that are outside the scope of this hack and really deserve a book of their own. As a matter of fact, there is one: Michael Sweet's book on CUPS is complete and easy to read (and as the original author of CUPS, he should know all about it). Excellent, complete, and readable documentation is also available from the CUPS web site (*http://www.cups.org/documentation.php*).

See Also

- *http://www.cups.org/documentation.php*
- *CUPS: Common UNIX Printing System*, by Michael Sweet (SAMS)
- "Create a CUPS Print Server" **[Hack #24]**

Cool Sysadmin Tools and Tips

Hacks 29–45

Behind the calm, collected exterior of the seasoned system administrator is a mad scientist who lives and breathes only to be the first to discover the next esoteric hack that will provide information, or a way to act on it, that was previously unknown to all but a very small contingent of tireless caffeine-swigging hackers.

The reason for this unquenchable thirst goes beyond bragging rights to something more practical than you might imagine: efficiency. If there's a way to do something better, faster, or in a way that doesn't require any human intervention, the system administrator will be on constant lookout for a way to implement that solution.

In this chapter, we're going to take a look at some tools and techniques that we hope are new to most readers, and that will greatly enhance your productivity. Whether it's a desktop shortcut for connecting to your hosts, a way to run commands on multiple hosts at the same time, or a way to type fewer commands at the command line or fewer characters in Vim, we'll show you the tools and techniques that will enable you to cross the border from system serf to Bitmaster General in no time.

Technical prowess is great, but "soft skills" such as communicating with people and multitasking count for more and more in today's competitive job market. For that reason, we'll also have a look at hacking the softer side of system administration, covering areas ranging from time management to *talking* to management!

HACK #29 Execute Commands Simultaneously on Multiple Servers

Run the same command at the same time on multiple systems, simplifying administrative tasks and reducing synchronization problems.

If you have multiple servers with similar or identical configurations (such as nodes in a cluster), it's often difficult to make sure the contents and configuration of those servers are identical. It's even more difficult when you need to make configuration modifications from the command line, knowing you'll have to execute the exact same command on a large number of systems (better get coffee first). You could try writing a script to perform the task automatically, but sometimes scripting is overkill for the work to be done. Fortunately, there's another way to execute commands on multiple hosts simultaneously.

A great solution for this problem is an excellent tool called *multixterm*, which enables you to simultaneously open *xterm*s to any number of systems, type your commands in a single central window and have the commands executed in each of the *xterm* windows you've started. Sound appealing? Type once, execute many—it sounds like a new pipelining instruction set.

multixterm is available from *http://expect.nist.gov/example/multixterm.man.html*, and it requires *expect* and *tk*. The most common way to run *multixterm* is with a command like the following:

```
$ multixterm -xc "ssh %n" host1 host2
```

This command will open *ssh* connections to *host1* and *host2* (Figure 4-1). Anything typed in the area labeled "stdin window" (which is usually gray or green, depending on your color scheme) will be sent to both windows, as shown in the figure.

As you can see from the sample command, the –xc option stands for execute command, and it must be followed by the command that you want to execute on each host, enclosed in double quotation marks. If the specified command includes a wildcard such as %n, each hostname that follows the command will be substituted into the command in turn when it is executed. Thus, in our example, the commands ssh host1 and ssh host2 were both executed by *multixterm*, each within its own *xterm* window.

See Also

- man multixterm
- "Enable Quick telnet/SSH Connections from the Desktop" [Hack #41]
- "Disconnect Your Console Without Ending Your Session" [Hack #34]

—Lance Tost

Figure 4-1. Multiple xterms and a multixterm control window

 ### HACK #30 Collaborate Safely with a Secured Wiki

Get out of the business of coding, supporting, debugging, and maintaining project collaboration sites by using a tool that allows users to create their own sites.

If you're a busy webmaster trying to perform systems work, the last thing you need is yet another user coming to you with a request to build and host another web site or to install yet another content management solution. Instead, promote a Wiki solution that can be up and running in seconds, ready for the user to create and edit content with no further help needed from you.

Wikis evolved around the idea that content can be editable by anyone who happens upon the site and sees a mistake or has something to add. Webmasters and system administrators alike were wary of this concept, which sounded like an idea just waiting to be completely abused by spammers, digivandals, and the like. If you last looked at Wiki solutions when the buzzword was fresh off the front page of Slashdot and wrote them off as unmanageable or as security issues waiting to happen (like I did), I urge you to have another look.

MediaWiki is the powerhouse Wiki application that runs the *http:// wikipedia.com* web site. Since Wikipedia runs the most visible Wiki site in the world and prides itself on being a resource for the people by the people, what better endorsement do you need for a Wiki application?

Wikis need not be unsecured free-for-alls. Nowadays, you can configure MediaWiki to authenticate to your internal LDAP server, completely disallow anonymous edits, and greatly restrict the damage that can be done to your Wiki site. In addition, MediaWiki makes it very easy both to track changes to the pages of their sites, and to revert to older copies of the pages.

So why use a Wiki if you're just going to lock it down? Wikis make wonderful content management solutions, for one fundamental reason: they make absolutely no assumptions about the purpose of your site. Many of the LAMP-based, open source content management solutions are built around the concept of a news distribution site *first*—extensions to do everything else, from blogging to forums and weather to file repositories, are added later, often by members of the respective user communities. If you're not planning to run a news site, you wind up having to find some hack to make your content management site act the way you want. If you use extensions to make your site work, you can't just upgrade right away and assume everything will still function correctly.

I've used dozens of open source content management solutions and, depending on your needs, you'll probably find many of them to be adequate. But if you support users in academia, R&D, or internal departments, each project group may have different needs. A simple framework that puts the power to structure and format the content in the hands of the content creators and users is a powerful tool, and the ability to restrict access and edits in a number of ways will give both you and your users peace of mind. If they want a "wide open" site, and you allow for that, that's no problem. But if you have other security requirements, chances are that with MediaWiki you can implement them easily.

MediaWiki allows you to authenticate to a backend LDAP server or database connection, and there are patches available to rely on other authentication methods available in your environment. In addition, you can opt to restrict access such that only registered and logged-in users can edit pages, create a more open site where anyone can edit pages, or disable registration altogether to create a site for internal staff documentation.

Installing MediaWiki

Another nice benefit of MediaWiki is that it's a breeze to install. It does require PHP, and its creators strongly suggest using MySQL as the backend database. Depending on the features you want to use (for example, image thumbnailing or LDAP authentication), you may need PHP to be compiled against specific libraries, but the requirements to run a simple site are pretty slim.

If you're hosting your own site (i.e., you have root privileges), installation takes, quite literally, seconds. All you do is untar the distribution into the document root of your web server, and go to the site! MediaWiki knows if it's your first visit, and prompts you to perform an installation. Once you supply the MySQL administrator password, MediaWiki will create a new user, a new database, and all the necessary tables, which is 90% of the installation process.

If you're running MediaWiki on a hosted remote server, however, you're not likely to have a root password or an administrative password for MySQL. In this case, you'll want to create the MediaWiki database first, and then point the installation at this database to create its tables. Unfortunately, I can't tell you how to do this, as every hosting service will provide different tools to assist you.

Once the installation has been performed successfully, you'll be presented with a link to visit your new site.

Configuring MediaWiki

Installing it was easy, but how do you lock this thing down? There's about a metric ton of documentation available on how to do this, but I'll summarize some of the features that are of primary importance to administrators.

First and foremost is site access. Many sites haven't deployed Wikis because they're under the illusion that they can't be secured. Not so!

With Version 1.4 of MediaWiki, it's possible to use the configuration file and/or a few SQL statements to change the functions available to different types of users. Version 1.5, on the other hand, has quite a robust collection of potential roles that users can play, implemented via user groups. We'll work with Version 1.5 here, because it'll likely be in its final form by the time this goes to press.

I'm working with 1.5rc4, which can be managed largely in a browser. There are separate pages for adding, deleting, and blocking users. There is also a page for changing the groups to which users belong, which will affect the rights they have when they visit your site. In addition, there are plug-ins available to help you correlate users with all the known IP addresses used by them and perform other functions not available in the main distribution.

However, there isn't yet an interface for changing the rights for a group, or adding/deleting groups. For those tasks, you'll need to have shell access to the web server, or you'll need to create a local copy of the *LocalSettings.php* file, edit it, and copy it back into place to make the changes take effect. The file is simple to edit, and the documentation for making the changes is more than adequate, but I'll go over examples of one or two quick changes you might want to make.

If you just want to change the group a user is associated with, you can log in as an administrative user and go to the Special Pages link. At the bottom of the screen you'll see Restricted special pages that are listed only when the admin is logged in. This section contains the link to the user rights management page, which is currently just an interface to change the group memberships of specific users.

If you want to create a group, you'll need to edit *LocalSettings.php* and set up the rights available to the group. To see how the default groups are set up, check the documentation or open up the *includes/DefaultSettings.php* file in your install directory. Here are the lines you would add to *LocalSettings.php* to add a group called *newgroup* with permission to read and edit but not to delete:

```
$wgGroupPermissions['newgroup']['edit'] = true;
$wgGroupPermissions['newgroup']['read'] = true;
$wgGroupPermissions['newgroup']['delete']= false;
```

As you can see, there's no explicit "create group" function. Assigning rights to a nonexistent group, as I've done here, will cause the group to be created, and it will be listed as an available group the next time you go to the user rights page.

Keep in mind that there are global settings as well, for the *all* group (represented in the configuration as *). Here are a few default settings for that group from the *DefaultSettings.php* file:

```
$wgGroupPermissions['*'    ]['createaccount']   = true;
$wgGroupPermissions['*'    ]['read']            = true;
$wgGroupPermissions['*'    ]['edit']            = true;
```

If you want to override these settings, just place similar lines in the *LocalSettings.php* file, setting the appropriate permissions to true or false as desired. The *LocalSettings.php* file overrides any corresponding settings that may be found in the *DefaultSettings.php* file.

This model gives you the flexibility to, for example, disable anonymous users from creating accounts at all or allow them only to read, and to require users to log in to edit anything. There are also additional rights you can give users to make them quasi-administrators, allowing them to create accounts for other users, delete files, and roll back bad edits.

Getting Started: Data Structure

Once user access is out of the way, probably the most important decisions you'll make in running your Wiki have to do with how the content on your site will be structured and how your content best maps to the organizational elements available to you in MediaWiki. There are many useful tools you can use, and all of them are fairly generic—again making no assumptions about the purpose of the site.

There are many ways to use the various organizational elements. If you have just one project group, they can have their own Wiki devoted to their project. However, you could potentially have several projects share a single Wiki by providing separate namespaces on the site. A *namespace* is the highest-level data element provided in MediaWiki. Within the namespaces are categories, that the project maintainers themselves can use to break up their sites into various pieces that make sense for their needs.

Lest you think the pages of the site need to be completely static documents, have a look at the Templates feature of MediaWiki, which allows you to embed documents within various pages. This gives you the flexibility to, for example, make your main page nothing but a collection of various other documents placed into the main page. Maintainers of the various templated pages can then update their own content, and changes will be reflected on the main page without affecting templates created by other users.

HACK
#31
Edit Your GRUB Configuration with grubby

Save tons of typing (and typos), by using a ready-made tool for editing grub. conf.

A machine that doesn't boot doesn't work. And there are many environments in which the *grub.conf* file supplied with the distribution just doesn't cut it. Whether you're using kickstart to install a server farm, or just hacking around with new kernel builds on your web server, you can leave your scripting skills on the back burner by making use of *grubby*, a simple command-line tool that will edit your kernel definitions for you.

Here's an example of a very simple kernel definition from a *grub.conf* file on a Red Hat Enterprise Linux server:

```
title Red Hat Enterprise Linux AS (2.4.21-32.0.1.EL)
        root (hd0,0)
        kernel /vmlinuz-2.4.21-32.0.1.EL ro root=LABEL=/
        initrd /initrd-2.4.21-32.0.1.EL.img
```

This is a fairly standard stanza referred to in the GRUB documentation as an "OS definition" (owing to GRUB's ability to boot seemingly any operating system in existence). Occasionally, it becomes necessary to alter the *grub.conf* file to pass arguments to the kernel at boot time. For example, if you kickstart a server farm and later add serial console connections to the servers, the kernels will not automatically detect the console, and GRUB will not automagically add the arguments necessary to redirect output to the serial terminal device. How to do this is covered in "Use a Serial Console for Centralized Access to Your Systems" [Hack #76].

This would normally mean hand-editing the *grub.conf* file to add the arguments—unless you happen to know about *grubby*. Here's the command, run as root, that you would use to add the requisite arguments to all kernels to allow for console redirection:

```
# grubby --update-kernel=ALL --args=console=ttyS0,9600
```

The ALL keyword works with several flags and, in this case, it will add the arguments to every kernel line in the configuration file. There's also a DEFAULT keyword that will alter only the kernel line of the default kernel, as per the *grub.conf* default parameter.

grubby can also alter options to the *grub* bootloader itself. Using the following commands, you can add a new kernel to the *grub.conf* file and make it the kernel that *grub* will boot by default:

```
# grubby --add-kernel=/boot/vmlinuz-2.4.21-new --make-default
# grubby --set-default=/boot/vmlinuz-2.4.21-32.0.1.ELsmp
```

I used the --make-default flag to set the vmlinuz-2.4.21-new kernel to be the default. If you tell *grubby* to change the default kernel to one that the config file doesn't know about, it'll try to do it, fail, remove the "default" parameter from your config file entirely, and not complain about it one bit. Since I failed to put my new kernel in place, in the second command, I've reset the default kernel back to one that was defined earlier by using the -set-default parameter.

So how has this saved you any typing? Changing a default kernel is as simple as changing a single digit in the *grub.conf* file, right? Well, yes, assuming that you're doing this on a single machine. However, if you need to run a scripted update to your *grub.conf* file on all the machines you manage or you're altering *grub.conf* during an automated installation to make a customized kernel the default, I'd much rather use *grubby* than *sed, awk, vi, ed,* and/or Perl to do the work. In these cases, it does save you some typing, not to mention saving you from reinventing the wheel!

HACK #32 Give Your Tab Key a Workout

Use bash programmable completion to autocomplete much more than just filenames.

Tab completion in the *bash* shell isn't new, and I don't know how I'd live without it. Being able to type, for example, ls fo<tab><tab> and get a list of five or six files that start with "fo" can be very handy. Got a long script name you always mistype? Just type the first few letters and hit Tab twice, and *bash* will try to complete the name for you. This is a wonderful time-saver that I, for one, sorely miss when I log into other Unix machines where the default shell is *csh* and tab completion is not set up by default (causing control characters to appear on the command line instead of nice, clean, filenames).

In *bash* v2.04, "programmable" completion was introduced into the shell. This lets you add strange and wonderful bits of goodness to your *bash* initialization routines (usually found in *~/.bashrc* and *~/.bash_profile*).

> Your *bash* initialization routines are dependent on how your shell environment is set up—*bash* can use a global */etc/bashrc*, a *~/.bash_profile*, a *~/.bashrc*, a *~/.profile*, and I believe a *~/.login* file to get its initialization info.

Here's a quick example:

```
complete -f -X '!*.@(sxw|stw|sxg|sgl|doc|dot|rtf|txt|htm|html|odt|\
ott|odm)' oowriter
```

This looks pretty cryptic, but really it's quite simple. `complete` is a *bash* built-in keyword that causes the shell to try to complete the text before the cursor on the command line. The `-f` flag means we'll be looking to complete a filename. The `-X` flag specifies that what follows is a pattern to use in performing the match. Since the shell is actually parsing the entire line, it's important to always quote your pattern to make sure no shell expansion takes place, causing odd things to happen when you hit your Tab key.

The pattern itself can be broken down and looked at this way:

```
!*.@(extension)
```

The leading exclamation point, in this context, says that when performing filename completion, we'll be removing things that do not match this pattern. The string `*.@(extension)` means "anything, followed by a dot, followed by exactly one occurrence of any of the listed extensions" (here, `sxw`, `stw`, `sxg`, and so on). The `@` character is a *bash* extended globbing character that means, "match exactly one occurrence of the pattern." The `|` characters in our list of extensions are logical "or" separators. If any match, they'll be included in the file listing generated by hitting the Tab key twice.

The last word on the line (in this case, `oowriter`) specifies the command to which all the stuff on that line applies. In other words, this `complete` line won't be touched unless the command being run is `oowriter`.

You can write thousands of these lines if you want, but it would likely take you forever to think of all the things you'd want to complete, get all the regex patterns right, and then debug the whole thing to make sure only the right filenames are returned. Alternatively, you could just download a preconfigured file put together by a fine fellow named Ian MacDonald, creator of the "*bash programmable completion*" package, available at *http://www.caliban.org/bash/index.shtml#completion*. The package consists mostly of simple documentation and a file containing a very large collection of *bash* completion "cheats." A version I recently downloaded contained over 200 shortcuts!

Many of the shortcuts are very simple file completion patterns that are bound to specific applications, which is more useful than you could ever know. Being able to type tar xvzf f<tab><tab> and have only those files with a *tar.gz* extension returned is wonderful, but shortcuts that complete hostnames after the ssh command (from your *known_hosts* file) or targets in a Makefile after you type make are truly time-savers for admins who are constantly doing remote administration and building software from source.

The great thing is that the only real dependency is the *bash* shell itself: the rest of what happens is completely up to you! If you have root access on the local machine, you can create a file under */etc/profile.d* called *bash_complete.sh*, and paste in a bit of code to set up *bash* completion in a sane way. The code comes straight from the *bash* distribution's *README* file:

```
bash=${BASH_VERSION%.*}; bmajor=${bash%.*}; bminor=${bash#*.}
if [ "$PS1" ] && [ $bmajor -eq 2 ] && [ $bminor '>' 04 ] \
    && [ -f /etc/bash_completion ]; then # interactive shell
        # Source completion code
        . /etc/bash_completion
fi
unset bash bmajor bminor
```

This code does a simple check to make sure the version of *bash* you're running supports programmable completion, then checks to see if you're launching an interactive shell before sourcing the *bash* programmable completion file.

Putting this code under */etc/profile.d* or in your global */etc/bashrc* file allows all users on the machine to reap the benefits of *bash* programmable completion.

If, on the other hand, you want to use this just for yourself or upload it to your shell account at a web host, you can paste the same code from above into your own *~/.bashrc* file.

See Also

- *http://www.caliban.org/bash/index.shtml#completion*

Keep Processes Running After a Shell Exits

Process-control commands such as nohup and disown make it easy for you to start long-running processes and keep them running even after you log out.

Suppose you're running a troubleshooting or monitoring tool on your server or compiling a very large program, and the process is going to need to run for hours, days, or longer. What if you need that process to keep running even after you've logged out or if your shell session ends before you meant it to? You can make this happen with the nohup and disown commands.

When you run a shell session, all the processes you run at the command line are child processes of that shell. If you log out or your session crashes or otherwise ends unexpectedly, SIGHUP (signal to hang up) kill signals will be sent to its child processes to end them too.

You can get around this by telling the process(es) that you want kept alive to ignore SIGHUP signals. There are two ways to do this: by using the nohup ("no hangup") command to run the command in an environment where it will ignore certain termination signals or by using the *bash* shell's disown command to make a specified background job independent of the current shell.

Using nohup to Execute Commands

The nohup command provides a quick and easy mechanism for keeping a process running regardless of whether its parent process is still active. To take advantage of this capability, run your favorite command, preceded by the nohup command:

```
$ nohup command
```

This executes the specified command and keeps it running even if the parent session ends. If you don't redirect output from this process, both its output and error messages (*stdout* and *stderr*) will be sent to a file called *nohup.out* in the current directory. If this file can't be created there, it will be created in the home directory of the user that ran the command.

You can monitor what's being written to *nohup.out* using the tail command:

```
$ tail -f ~/nohup.out
```

You can also explicitly direct the output of your command to a specified file. For example, the following command line runs the specified command in the background, sends its output to a file called *my_test_output.txt* in your home directory and continues running it even if the parent session ends:

```
$ nohup command > ~/my_test_output.txt &
```

If you don't want to save the output of the specified command, you can discard it (and not create the *nohup.out* file) by redirecting output to */dev/null*, the Linux bit-bucket:

```
$ nohup command > /dev/null &
```

This runs the command or program in the background, ignores its output by sending it to */dev/null*, and continues running it even if the parent session ends.

> If you've used nohup to keep a process running after its parent exits, there is no way to reconnect to that process if you subsequently want to shoot it down. However, nohup only protects the process from the SIGHUP signal. You can still terminate it manually using the big *kill* hammer, kill -9 *PID*.

Using disown with Background Jobs

If you're using the *bash* shell, you can tell an existing process to ignore SIGHUPs by using the shell's disown built-in command:

```
$ disown -h jobnumber
```

This tells a job already running in the background to keep running when its parent process shuts down. You can find its job number using the shell's jobs command. If you use the disown built-in's -h option, the running job won't be removed from the jobs table when you disown it, but it will keep running if the current shell ends. You can still reconnect to this process using the standard bash %job-number mechanism. If you use the disown built-in with no options, the running job will be removed from the jobs table: it will still continue running after you log out, but you won't be able to reconnect to it.

You can also use the disown command to keep all current background jobs running:

```
$ disown -ar
```

This tells all running jobs to keep running even if the current shell closes.

See Also

- man bash
- man1 nohup

—Jon Fox

Disconnect Your Console Without Ending Your Session

Start a long-running job at work and connect to it from home or on the road.

Here's the setup: you're a Linux systems consultant with a busy schedule. It's 9 A.M. now, and you're already an hour into a very large database installation at one site, but you have to be at another site in about an hour. The build will never finish in time for you to thoroughly test it, create the developer databases, and set up security restrictions before you leave. What do you do?

One solution, of course, is to talk to your client and tell him you'll be back later to finish up. Another solution, however, may be to start the job in a *screen* session and log in later from wherever you happen to be to finish up. Lest you think that this will involve building yet another piece of software for your machines, take heart in knowing that *screen* is usually installed or readily available and prepackaged for whatever distribution you're running. You can also get more information on *screen*, including download information, at the GNU *screen* home page: *http://www.gnu.org/software/screen/*.

Getting started with *screen* couldn't be simpler. Just open your favorite terminal emulator and run the command, like this:

```
$ screen
```

You will be greeted with a new shell, running inside a *screen* session. You can still talk to *screen* from within the shell, much like you can talk to any console terminal application from within a shell. The key combination you use to send input to *screen* instead of to the shell running inside the *screen* session is Ctrl-A. Ctrl-A in *screen* is similar to the Escape key in *vi*—it gets the application's attention so you can tell it what to do. For example, to access a quick command reference in *screen*, press Ctrl-A followed by ?.

The output should be a list of the many commands you can feed to *screen*. If you don't get any output, you can make sure you're actually in a *screen* session by invoking *screen* with the -list flag. You should see something similar to the following:

```
$ screen -list
There is a screen on:
        28820.pts-2.willy      (Attached)
1 Socket in /tmp/screen-jonesy.
```

You can see from the output that there is a *screen* session running, to which we are currently attached. The process ID for this session is 28820, and we've been assigned to pseudo-terminal number 2. Now let's start a job that we can continue later from another location. A simple way to test the functionality is to just open a file in an editor such as Vim. Once you have the file open, press Ctrl-A followed by d, and you will be detached from the *screen* session and given back your plain old shell.

At this point, you can leave for your next appointment. Maybe at the next stop you have to do an OS installation, which leaves you with some free time while the packages are installing. Fire up your laptop, SSH to the machine where your *screen* session is running, and type screen -r to reattach to the session already in progress. If you have more than one *screen* session running, type screen -r *pid*, where *pid* is the process ID of the *screen* session to which you want to attach (discernible from the screen -list output we went over above).

Of course, trying to associate the process ID of a *screen* session with what's going on in that session can be a bit daunting, especially if you have lots of sessions running. Instead of doing that, you can name your session something meaningful when you launch it. So, when you launch *screen* for the purpose of kicking off a long-running software build, just type screen -S make, and the next time you attach to it, you can type screen -r make instead of trying to remember which process ID you need to attach to.

screen Scripting

If you manage more than a few machines, you've probably come up with some way of automating the process of connecting to some subset of your service machines at login time, or with a desktop icon, or by some other means that is more automated than manually opening up terminal windows and typing the commands to connect to each host. If you use SSH keys (**Hack #66** in the original *Linux Server Hacks*), you can create a simple shell script to automate this process for you. Here's an example shell script:

```
#!/bin/bash

screen -d -m -S svr1 -t jonesy@svr1 ssh server1.linuxlaboratory.org
screen -d -m -S svr2 -t jonesy@svr2 ssh server2.linuxlaboratory.org
screen -d -m -S svr3 -t jonesy@svr3 ssh server3.linuxlaboratory.org
```

Save this script to your *~/bin* directory, and make sure you make it executable!

What makes this script work well is calling *screen* with the -d -m flags, which tell *screen* to start the session, but not to attach to it. Note as well that I've used -S to specify a session name, so when I want to attach to, say, *svr1*, I can just type screen -r svr1. In addition, I've used the -t flag to specify a title for my shell, which will show in the titlebar of my terminal emulator to help me keep track of where I am.

Running the above script will open up SSH sessions to, in this case, *server1*, *server2*, and *server3*. It might be tempting to put this into your shell's initialization script. *Do not do this*! In environments where home directories (and therefore, shell init scripts) are shared across hosts, this can create an endless stream of looping SSH sessions.

See Also

- *http://www.gnu.org/software/screen/*
- *Linux Server Hacks*, by Rob Flickenger (O'Reilly)
- "Use script to Save Yourself Time and Train Others" [Hack #35]

Use script to Save Yourself Time and Train Others

#35 The standard script command ensures repeatability and lends itself nicely to training junior admins.

If you took computer science courses in college, you may have run into the script command before. Professors often want you to hand in the entire contents of an interactive shell session with assignments, so what students often do is simply run script as the first command of their session. That copies all IO taking place in the terminal to a file (named, by default, *typescript*). When they're done, they just type exit, and they can then turn in the *typescript* file to the professor.

script has some uses beyond the classroom as well, though. In some stricter production environments, everything that gets done to non-testing, full-production systems has to be "repeatable"—in other words, scripted, thoroughly tested, and documented to the point that someone in change management, with no training in Unix, can do it. One tool that can be used to create the documentation is script. You'll still have to script your procedure into oblivion, using the corporate coding standard, but then you can actually record a session where you invoke the tool and hand it over to the change management personnel, so they can see exactly what they need to do, in order.

One extremely cool feature of the script command is that it can output timing information to a separate file. The entire terminal session can then be replayed later using the scriptreplay command, and it will be replayed using the same timing as the original session! This is great for newer users who have a hard time remembering how to perform tasks that you don't have time to script for them.

Here's a quick session using the two commands:

```
$ script -t 2> timing
Script started, file is typescript
$ ls
Desktop        hax      hog.sh   My Computer        ostg         src
$ pwd
/home/jonesy
$ file hax
hax: empty
$ exit
exit
Script done, file is typescript
$ scriptreplay timing
$ ls
Desktop        hax      hog.sh   My Computer        ostg         src
$ pwd
/home/jonesy
$ file hax
hax: empty
$ exit
exit
```

Using the -t flag tells the script command to output all timing information to standard error, so we redirect that to a file (here, *timing*) so that we can use it later. We then call scriptreplay, feeding it the *timing* file. We don't have to tell it where the actual session output is in this case, because it looks for a file named *typescript* by default, which also happens to be the default session output file for the script command.

Note that every keystroke is recorded, so if you mess up and hit backspace to delete a few characters, that'll show up in the replay of the session! Also note that replaying a session is only guaranteed to work properly on the terminal where the original session output file was created.

If you want a more "real-time" approach to showing someone how to get things done, there's another way script can help. Create a named pipe and redirect all output to the pipe. Someone else, logged in remotely, can then cat the pipe and see what's going on while it's happening.

Here's how it works. First, create a named pipe with mkfifo:

```
$ mkfifo out
```

Then run script with the -f flag, which will flush all output to your pipe on every write. Without that flag, things won't work. The last argument to script is the file to which the output should be sent:

```
$ script -f out
```

You're now in a session that looks and acts completely normal, but someone else can log in from elsewhere and run the following command to watch the action:

```
$ cat out
```

Everything will be shown to that user as it happens. This is a little easier than remembering how to set up multi-user *screen* sessions!

See Also

- "Disconnect Your Console Without Ending Your Session" [Hack #34]

HACK #36   Install Linux Simply by Booting

Let server daemons that are already running in your environment and a simple PXE configuration make installs as easy as powering on the target hosts.

Many distributions have some form of automated installation. SUSE has AutoYaST, Debian has Fully Automated Install (FAI), Red Hat has kickstart, and the list goes on. These tools typically work by parsing a configuration file or template, using keywords to tell the installation program how the machine will be configured. Most also allow for customized scripts to be run to account for anything the automated installation template hasn't accounted for.

The end result is a huge time savings. Though an initial time investment is required to set up and debug a template and any other necessary tools, once this is done, you can use a single template file to install all machines of the same class, or quickly edit a working template file to allow for the automated installation of a "special case" target host. For example, a template for a web server can quickly be edited to take out references to Apache and replace them with, say, Sendmail.

The only downside to automated installations is that, without any supporting infrastructure in place to further automate things, you have to boot to a CD or some other media and issue a command or two to get the installation process rolling. It would really be wonderful if installing Linux were as simple as walking through the machine room (or lab, or anyplace else where there are a lot of target hosts that need installing), powering on all the new machines, and walking away. Let's have a look at how this (and more!) can be accomplished.

In my examples, I'll be using the Red Hat/Fedora kickstart mechanism for my automated installations, but other tools can accomplish similar if not identical results.

Preparatory Steps

The list of components you'll need to configure may sound slightly intimidating, but it's much easier than it looks, and once you get it to work once, automating the setup process and replicating the ease of installation is a breeze. Before you do anything, though, make sure that the hosts you want to install have network cards that support a Preboot eXecution Environment (PXE). This is a standard booting mechanism supported by firmware burned into the network card in your server. Most server-grade network cards, and even recent desktop network cards, support PXE. The way to check is generally to enter the BIOS settings and see if there's an option to enable PXE, or to carefully watch the boot messages to see if there are settings there for PXE booting. On a lot of systems, simply hitting a function key during bootup will cause the machine to boot using PXE.

Configuring DHCP. When you know for sure that your machines support PXE, you can move on to configuring your DHCP/BOOTP server. This service will respond to the PXE broadcast coming from the target node by delivering an IP address, along with the name of a boot file and the address of a host from which the boot file can be retrieved. Here's a typical entry for a target host:

```
host pxetest {
    hardware ethernet 0:b:db:95:84:d8;
    fixed-address 192.168.198.112;
    next-server 192.168.101.10;
    filename "/tftpboot/linux-install/pxelinux.0";
    option ntp-servers 192.168.198.10, 192.168.198.23;
}
```

All the lines above are perfectly predictable in many environments. Only the lines in bold type are specific to what we're trying to accomplish. Once this information is delivered to the client, it knows what filename to ask for and which server to ask for that file.

At this point, you should be able to boot the client, tell it to PXE boot, and see it get an IP address and report to you what that address is. In the event that you have a PXE implementation that tells you nothing, you can check the DHCP server logs for confirmation. A successful DHCP request and response will look something like this in the logs:

```
Aug  9 06:05:55 livid dhcpd: [ID 702911 daemon.info] DHCPDISCOVER from 00:
40:96:35:22:ff (jonesy-thinkpad) via 172.16.1.1
Aug  9 06:05:55 livid dhcpd: [ID 702911 daemon.info] DHCPOFFER on 192.168.
198.101 to 00:40:96:35:22:ff (jonesy-thinkpad) via 192.168.198.100
```

Configuring a TFTP server. Once the machine is able to get an IP address, the next thing it will try to do is get its grubby RJ45 connectors on a boot file. This will be housed on a TFTP server. On many distributions, a TFTP server is either included or readily available. Depending on your distribution, it may or may not run out of *inetd* or *xinetd*. If it is run from *xinetd*, you should be able to enable the service by editing */etc/xinetd.d/in.tftpd* and changing the disable option's value to no. Once that's done, restarting *xinetd* will enable the service. If your system runs a TFTP server via *inetd*, make sure that an entry for the TFTP daemon is present and not commented out in your */etc/inted.conf* file. If your system runs a TFTP server as a permanent daemon, you'll just have to make sure that the TFTP daemon is automatically started when you boot your system.

Next, we need to create a directory structure for our boot files, kernels, and configuration files. Here's a simple, no-frills directory hierarchy that contains the bare essentials, which I'll go over in a moment:

```
/tftpboot/
    linux-install/
        pxelinux.0
        vmlinuz
        initrd.img
        pxelinux.cfg/
            default
```

First, run this command to quickly set up the directory hierarchy described above:

```
$ mkdir -p /tftpboot/linux-install/pxelinux.cfg
```

The -p option to mkdir creates the necessary parent directories in a path, if they don't already exist. With the directories in place, it's time to get the files! The first one is the one our client is going to request: *pxelinux.0*. This file is a simple bootloader meant to enable the system to do nothing more than grab a configuration file, from which it learns which kernel and initial ramdisk image to grab in order to continue on its way. The file itself can be obtained from the *syslinux* package, which is readily available for almost any distribution on the planet. Grab it (or grab the source distribution), install or untar the package, and copy the *pxelinux.0* file over to */tftpboot/linux-install/pxelinux.0*.

Once that file is delivered to the client, the next thing the client does is look for a configuration file. It should be noted here that the *syslinux*-supplied *pxelinux.0* always looks for its config file under *pxelinux.cfg* by default. Since our DHCP server only specifies a boot file, and you could have a different configuration file for every host you PXE boot, it looks for the config file using the following formula:

1. It looks for a file named using its own MAC address, in all-uppercase hex, prefixed by the hex representation of its ARP type, with all fields separated by dashes. So, using our example target host with the MAC address 00:40:96:35:22:ff, the file would be named *01-00-40-96-35-22-FF*. The 01 in the first field is the hex representation of the Ethernet ARP type (ARP type 1).

2. Next, it looks for a file named using the all-uppercase hex representation of the client IP address. The *syslinux* project provides a binary called *gethostip* for figuring out what this is, which is much nicer than doing it in your head. Feeding my IP address to this command returns C0A8C665.

3. If neither of these files exists, the client iterates through searching for files named by lopping one character off the end of the hex representation of its IP address (*C0A8C66, C0A8C6, C0A8C, C0A8...you get the idea*).

4. If there's still nothing, the client finally looks for a file named *default*. If that's not there, it fails to proceed.

In our simple test setup, we've just put a file named *default* in place, but in larger setups, you can set up a configuration file for each class of host you need to install. So, for example, if you have 40 web servers to install and 10 database servers to install, you don't need to create 50 configuration files— just create one called *web-servers* and one called *db-servers*, and make symlinks that are unique to the target hosts, either by using *gethostip* or by appending the ARP type to the MAC address, as described above.

Whichever way you go, the configuration file needs to tell the client what kernel to boot from, along with any options to pass to the kernel as it boots. If this sounds familiar to you, it should, because it looks a lot like a LILO or GRUB configuration. Here's our *default* config file:

```
default linux

label linux
    kernel vmlinuz
    append ksdevice=eth0 load_ramdisk=1 prompt_ramdisk=0 network
    ks=nfs:myserver:/kickstart/Profiles/pxetest
```

I've added a bunch of options to our kernel. The ksdevice and ks= options are specific to Red Hat's kickstart installation mechanism; they tell the client which device to use for a network install (in the event that there is more than one present) and how and where to get the kickstart template, respectively. From reading the ks= option, we can see that the installation will be done using NFS from the host *myserver*. The kickstart template is */kickstart/Profiles/pxetest*.

The client gets nowhere, however, until it gets a kernel and ramdisk image. We've told it to use *vmlinuz* for the kernel and the default initial ramdisk image, which is always *initrd.img*. Both of these files are located in the same directory as *pxelinux.0*. The files are obtained from the distribution media that we're attempting to install. In this case, since it's Red Hat, we go to the *isolinux* directory on the boot CD and copy the kernel and ramdisk images from there over to */tftpboot/linux-install*.

Getting It Working

Your host is PXE-enabled; your DHCP server is configured to deliver the necessary information to the target host; and the TFTP server is set up to provide the host with a boot file, a configuration file, a kernel, and a ramdisk image. All that's left to do now is boot! Here's the play-by-play of what takes place, for clarity's sake:

1. You boot and press a function key to tell the machine to boot using PXE.
2. The client broadcasts for, and hopefully gets, an IP address, along with the name and location of a boot file.
3. The client contacts the TFTP server, asks for the boot file, and hopefully gets one.
4. The boot file launches and then contacts the TFTP server again for a configuration file, using the formula we discussed previously. In our case it will get the one named *default*, which tells it how to boot.
5. The client grabs the kernel and ramdisk image specified in *default* and begins the kickstart using the NFS server specified on the kernel append line.

Quick Troubleshooting

Here are some of the problems you may run into and how to tackle them:

- If you get TFTP ACCESS VIOLATION errors, these can be caused by almost anything. However, the obvious things to check are that the TFTP server can actually access the file (using a TFTP client) and that the DHCP configuration for the target host lists only a `filename` parameter specifying `pxelinux.0`, and doesn't list the BOOTP `bootfile-name` parameter.
- If you fail to get a boot file and you get a "TFTP open timeout" or some other similar timeout, check to make sure the TFTP server is allowing connections from the client host.

- If you fail to get an IP address at all, grep for the client's MAC address in the DHCP logs for clues. If you don't find it, your client's broadcast packets aren't making it to the DHCP server, in which case you should look for a firewall/ACL rule as a possible cause of the issue.

- If you can't seem to get the kickstart configuration file, make sure you have permissions to mount the NFS source, make sure you're asking for the right file, and check for typos!

- If everything fails and you can test with another identical box or another *vmlinuz*, do it, because you might be running into a flaky driver or a flaky card. For example, the first *vmlinuz* I used in testing had a flaky b44 network driver, and I couldn't get the kickstart file. The only change I made was to replace *vmlinuz*, and all was well.

H A C K #37 Turn Your Laptop into a Makeshift Console

Use minicom and a cable (or two, if your laptop doesn't have a serial port) to connect to the console port of any server.

There are many situations in which the ability to connect to the serial console port of a server can be a real lifesaver. In my day-to-day work, I sometimes do this for convenience, so I can type commands on a server's console while at the same time viewing some documentation that is inevitably available only in PDF format (something I can't do from a dumb terminal). It's also helpful if you're performing tasks on a machine that is not yet hooked up to any other kind of console or if you're on a client site and want to get started right away without having to learn the intricacies of the client's particular console server solution.

Introducing minicom

How is this possible? There's an age-old solution that's provided as a binary package by just about every Linux distribution, and it's called *minicom*. If you need to build from source, you can download it at *http://alioth.debian.org/ projects/minicom/*. *minicom* can do a multitude of great things, but what I use it for is to provide a console interface to a server over a serial connection, using a null modem cable (otherwise known as a crossover serial cable).

Actually, that's a big, fat lie. My laptop, as it turns out, doesn't have a serial port! I didn't even look to confirm that it had one when I ordered it, but I've found that many newer laptops don't come with one. If you're in the same boat, fear not! Available at online shops everywhere, for your serial connection pleasure, are USB-to-serial adapters. Just plug this thing into a USB port, then connect one end of the null modem cable to the adapter and the other end to the server's serial port, and you're in business.

With hardware concerns taken care of, you can move on to configuring *minicom*. A default configuration directory is usually provided on Debian systems in */etc/minicom*. On Red Hat systems, the configuration files are usually kept under */etc* and do not have their own directory. Customizing the configuration is generally done by running this command as root:

```
# minicom -s
```

This opens a text-based interface where you can make the necessary option changes. The configuration gets saved to a file called *minirc.dfl* by default, but you can use the "Save setup as" menu option to give the configuration a different name. You might want to do that in order to provide several configuration files to meet different needs—the profile used at startup time can be passed to *minicom* as a lone argument.

For example, if I run `minicom -s`, and I already have a default profile stored in *minicom.dfl*, I can, for instance, change the baud rate from the default 9,600 to 115,200 and then save this as a profile named *fast*. The file created by this procedure will be named *minicom.fast*, but when I start up I just call the profile name, not the filename, like this:

```
$ minicom fast
```

Of course, this assumes that a regular user has access to that profile. There is a user access file, named *minicom.users*, that determines which users can get to which profiles. On both Debian and Red Hat systems, all users have access to all profiles by default.

A slightly simpler way to get a working configuration is to steal it. Here is a barebones configuration for *minicom*. Though it's very simple, it's really the only one I've ever needed:

```
# Machine-generated file - use "minicom -s" to change parameters.
pu port             /dev/ttyUSB0
pu baudrate         9600
pu bits             8
pu parity           N
pu stopbits         1
pu minit
pu mreset
pu mconnect
pu mhangup
```

I included here the options stored to the file by default, even though they're not used. The unused settings are specific to situations in which *minicom* needs to perform dialups using a modem. Note in this config file that the serial device I'm using (the local device through which *minicom* will communicate) is */dev/ttyUSB0*. This device is created and assigned by a Linux kernel module called *usbserial*. If you're using a USB-to-serial adapter and there's no indication that it's being detected and assigned to a device by the kernel, check to make sure that you have this module. Almost every distribution these days provides the *ubserial* module and dynamically loads it when needed, but if you build your own kernels, make sure you don't skip over this module! In your Linux kernel configuration file, the option `CONFIG_USB_SERIAL` should be set to y or m. It should not be commented out.

The next setting is the `baudrate`, which has to be the same on both the client and the server. In this case, I've picked 9,600, not because I want to have a turtle-slow terminal, but because that's the speed configured on the servers to which I usually connect. It's plenty fast enough for most things that don't involve tailing massive logfiles that are updated multiple times per second.

The next three settings dictate how the client will be sending its data to the server. In this case, a single character will be eight bits long, followed by no parity bit and one stop bit. This setting (referred to as "8N1") is by far the most common setting for asynchronous serial communication. These settings are so standard that I've never had to change them in my *minicom.conf* file—in fact, the only setting I do change is the baud rate.

Testing It

Once you have your configuration in place, connect your null modem or USB-to-serial adapter to your laptop and connect the other end to the serial console port on the server. If you're doing this for the first time, the serial console port on the server is a 15-pin male connection that looks a lot like the male version of a standard VGA port. It's also likely to be the only place you can plug in a null modem cable! If there are two of them, generally the one on the top (in a vertical configuration) or on the left (in a horizontal configuration) will be *ttyS0* on the server, and the other will be *ttyS1*.

After you've physically connected the laptop to the server, the next thing to do is fire up a terminal application and launch *minicom*:

```
$ minicom
```

This command will launch *minicom* with its default configuration. Note that on many systems, launching the application alone doesn't do much: you have to hit Enter once or twice to get a login prompt returned to you.

Troubleshooting

I've rarely had trouble using *minicom* in this way, especially when the server end is using *agetty* to provide its of the communication, because *agetty* is pretty forgiving and can adjust for things like seven-bit characters and other unusual settings. In the event that you have no output or your output looks garbled, check to make sure that the baud rate on the client matches the baud rate on the server. Also make sure that you are, in fact, connected to the correct serial port! On the server, try typing the following to get a quick rundown of the server settings:

```
$ grep agetty /etc/inittab
co:2345:respawn:/sbin/agetty ttyS0 9600 vt100-nav
$
```

This output shows that *agetty* is in fact running on *ttyS0* at 9600 baud. The vt100-nav option on the end is put there by the Fedora installation program, which sets up your *inittab* entry by default if something is connected to the console port during installation. The vt100-nav option sets the TERM environment variable. If you leave this setting off, most Linux machines will just set this to vt100 by default, which is generally fine. If you want, you can tell *minicom* to use an alternate terminal type on the client end with the -t flag.

If you're having trouble launching *minicom*, make sure you don't have restrictions in place in the configuration file regarding who is allowed to use the default profile.

Usable Documentation for the Inherently Lazy

HACK #38

Web-based documentation is great, but it's not very accessible from the command line. However, manpages can be with you always.

I know very few administrators who are big fans of creating and maintaining documentation. It's just not fun. Not only that, but there's nothing heroic about doing it. Fellow administrators aren't going to pat you on the back and congratulate you on your wicked cool documentation. What's more, it's tough to see how end users get any benefit when you document stuff that's used only by administrators, and if you're an administrator writing documentation, it's likely that everyone in your group already knows the stuff you're documenting!

Well, this is one way to look at it. However, the fact is that turnover exists, and so does growth. It's possible that new admins will come on board due to growth or turnover in your group, and they'll have to be taught about all of the customized tools, scripts, processes, procedures, and hacks that are specific to your site. This learning process is also a part of any new admin's enculturation into the group, and it should be made as easy as possible for everyone's benefit, including your own.

In my travels, I've found that the last thing system administrators want to do is write documentation. The only thing that might fall below writing documentation on their lists of things they're dying to do is writing web-based documentation. I've tried to introduce in-browser WYSIWYG HTML editors, but they won't have it. Unix administrators are quite happy using Unix tools to do their work. "Give me Vim or give me death!"

Another thing administrators typically don't want to do is learn how to use tools like LaTeX, SGML, or *groff* to create formal documentation. They're happiest with plain text that is easily typed and easily understood by anyone who comes across the raw file. Well, I've found a tool that enables administrators to create manpages from simple text files, and it's cool. It's called *txt2man*.

Of course, it comes with a manpage, which is more than enough documentation to use the tool effectively. It's a simple shell script that you pass your text file to, along with any options you want to pass for a more polished end result, and it spits out a perfectly usable manpage. Here's how it works.

I have a script called *cleangroup* that I wrote to help clean up after people who have departed from our department (see "Clean Up NIS After Users Depart" **[Hack #77]**). It goes through our NIS map and gets rid of any references made to users who no longer exist in the NIS password map. It's a useful script, but because I created it myself there's really no reason that our two new full-time administrators would know it exists or what it does. So I created a new manpage directory, and I started working on my manpages for all the tools written locally that new admins would need to know about. Here is the actual text I typed to create the manpage:

```
NAME
    cleangroup - remove users from any groups if the account doesn't exist
SYNOPSIS
    /usr/local/adm/bin/cleangroup groupfile
DESCRIPTION
    cleangroup is a perl script used to check each uid found in the group file
    against the YP password map. If the user doesn't exist there, the user is
    removed from the group.

    The only argument to the file is groupfile, which is required.

ENVIRONMENT
        LOGNAME        You need to be root on the YP master to run this
    script successfully.

BUGS
    Yes. Most certainly.

AUTHOR
    Brian Jones jonesy@linuxlaboratory.org
```

The headings in all caps will be familiar to anyone who has read his fair share of manpages. I saved this file as *cleangroup.txt*. Next, I ran the following command to create a manpage called *cleangroup.man*:

```
$ txt2man -t cleangroup -s 8 cleangroup.txt > cleangroup.man
```

When you open this manpage using the man command, the upper-left and -right corners will display the title and section specified on the command line with the -t and -s flags, respectively. Here's the finished output:

```
cleangroup(8)                                                    cleangroup(8)

NAME
        cleangroup-remove users from any groups if the account doesn't exist

SYNOPSIS
        /var/local/adm/bin/beta/cleangroup groupfile

DESCRIPTION
        cleangroup is a perl script used to check each uid found in the group
        file against the YP password map. If the user doesn't exist there,
        the user is removed from the group.

        The only argument to the file is groupfile, which is required.

ENVIRONMENT
        LOGNAME
                You need to be root on nexus to run this script successfully.

BUGS
        Yes. Most certainly.

AUTHOR
        Brian Jones jonesy@cs.princeton.edu
```

For anyone not enlightened as to why I chose section 8 of the manpages, you should know that the manpage sections are not completely arbitrary. Different man sections are for different classes of commands. Here's a quick overview of the section breakdown:

1   User-level commands such as ls and man

2   System calls such as gethostname and setgid

3   Library calls such as isupper and getchar

4   Special files such as *fd* and *fifo*

5   Configuration files such as *ldap.conf* and *nsswitch.conf*

6   Games and demonstrations

7   Miscellaneous

8   Commands normally run by the root user, such as MAKEDEV and pvscan

Some systems have a section 9 for kernel documentation. If you're planning on making your own manpage section, try to pick an existing one that isn't being used, or just work your manpages into one of the existing sections. Currently, man only traverses man*X* directories (where *X* is a single digit), so man42 is not a valid manpage section.

Though the resulting manpage isn't much different from the text file, it has the advantage that you can actually use a standard utility to read it, and everyone will know what you mean when you say "check out man 8 clean-group." That's a whole lot easier than saying "go to our intranet, click on Documentation, go to Systems, then Linux/Unix, then User Accounts, and click to open the PDF."

If you think that *txt2man* can handle only the simplest of manpages, it has a handy built-in help that you can send to itself; the resulting manpage is a pretty good sample of what *txt2man* can do with just simple text. Run this command (straight from the *txt2man* manpage) to check it out:

```
$ txt2man -h 2>&1 | txt2man -T
```

This sends the help output for the command back to *txt2man*, and the -T flag will preview the output for you using *more* or whatever you've set your PAGER environment variable to. This flag is also a quick way to preview manpages you're working on to make sure all of your formatting is correct instead of having to create a manpage, open it up, realize it's hosed in some way, close it, and open it up again in your editor. Give it a try!

HACK #39 Exploit the Power of Vim

Use Vim's recording and keyboard macro features to make monotonous tasks lightning fast.

Every administrator, at some point in his career, runs into a scenario in which it's unclear whether a task can be performed more quickly using the Vim command . (a period) and one or two other keystrokes for every change, or using a script. Often, admins wind up using the . command because they figure it'll take less time than trying to figure out the perfect regex to use in a Perl, *sed*, or *awk* script.

However, if you know how to use Vim's "recording" feature, you can use on-the-fly macros to do your dirty work with a minimum of keystrokes. What's more, if you have tasks that you have to perform all the time in Vim, you can create a keyboard macros for those tasks that will be available any time you open your editor. Let's have a look!

Recording a Vim Macro

The best way to explain this is with an example. I have a file that is the result of the dumping of all the data in my LDAP directory. It consists of the LDIF entries of all the users in my environment.

One entry looks like this:

```
dn: cn=jonesy,ou=People,dc=linuxlaboratory,dc=org
objectClass: top
objectClass: person
objectClass: organizationalPerson
objectClass: inetOrgPerson
objectClass: posixAccount
objectClass: evolutionPerson
uid: jonesy
sn: Jones
cn: Brian K. Jones
userPassword: {crypt}eRnFAci.Ie2Ny
loginShell: /bin/bash
uidNumber: 3025
gidNumber: 410
homeDirectory: /u/jonesy
gecos: Brian K. Jones,STAFF
mail: jonesy@linuxlaboratory.org
roomNumber: 213
fileas: Jones, Brian K.
telephoneNumber: NONE
labeledURI: http://www.linuxlaboratory.org
businessRole: NONE
description: NONE
homePostalAddress: NONE
birthDate: 20030101
givenName: Brian
displayName: Brian K. Jones
homePhone: 000-000-0000
st: NJ
l: Princeton
c: US
title: NONE
o: Linuxlaboratory.org
ou: Systems Group
```

There are roughly 1,000 entries in the file. What I need to do, for every user, is tag the end of every labeledURI line with a value of *~username*. This will reflect a change in our environment in which every user has some web space accessible in her home directory, which is found on the Web using the URL *http://www.linuxlibrary.org/~username*. Some entries have more lines than others, so there's not a whole heckuva lot of consistency or predictability to make my job easy. You could probably write some really ugly shell script or Perl script to do this, but you don't actually even have to leave the cozy confines of Vim to get it done. First, let's record a macro. Step 1 is to type (in command mode) q*n*, where *n* is a register label. Valid register labels are the values 0–9 and a–z. Once you do that, you're recording, and Vim will store in register *n* every single keystroke you enter, so type carefully! Typing q again will stop the recording.

Here are the keystrokes I used, including my keystrokes to start and stop recording:

```
qz
/uid:<Enter>
ww
yw
/labeledURI<Enter>
A
/~
<Esc>
p
q
```

The first line starts the recording and indicates that my keystrokes will be stored in register z. Next, I search for the string uid: (/uid:), move two words to the right (ww), and yank (Vim-ese for copy) that word (yw). Now I have the username, which I need to paste on the end of the URL that's already in the file. To accomplish this, I do a search for the labeledURI attribute (/labeledRUI), indicate that I am going to append to the end of the current line (A), type a /~ (because those characters need to be there and aren't part of the user's ID), and then hit Esc to enter command mode and immediately hit p to paste the copied username. Finally, I hit q to stop recording.

Now I have a nice string of keystrokes stored in register z, which I can view by typing the following command:

```
:register z
"z   /uid: ^Mwwyw/labeledURI: ^MA/~^[p
```

If you can see past the control characters (^M is Enter and ^[is Escape), you'll see that everything I typed is there. Now I can call up this string of keystrokes any time I want by typing (again, in command mode) @z. It so happens that there are 935 entries in the file I'm working on (I used wc -l on the file to get a count), one of which has been edited already, so if I just place my cursor on the line underneath the last edit I performed and type 934@z, that will make the changes I need to every entry in the file. Sadly, I have not found a way to have the macro run to the end of the file without specifying a number.

Creating Vim Shortcut Keys

I happen to really like the concept of WYSIWYG HTML editors. I like the idea of not having to be concerned with tag syntax. To that extent, these editors represent a decent abstraction layer, enabling me to concentrate more on content than form. They also do away with the need to remember the tags for things such as greater than and less than characters and non-breaking spaces, which is wonderful.

Unfortunately, none of these shiny tools allows me to use Vim keystrokes to move around within a file. I'm not even asking for search and replace or any of the fancy register stuff that Vim offers—just the simple ability to move around with the h, j, k, and l keys, and maybe a few other conveniences. It took me a long time to figure out that I don't need to compromise anymore! I can have the full power of Vim and use it to create an environment where the formatting, while not completely invisible, is really a no-brain-required activity.

Here's a perfect example of one way I use Vim keyboard shortcuts every day. I have to write some of my documentation at work in HTML. Any time my document contains a command that has to be run, I enclose that command in <code></code> tags. This happens a lot, as the documentation I write at work is for an audience of sysadmins like me. The other two most common tags I use are the <p></p> paragraph tags and the <h2></h2> tags, which mark off the sections in the documentation. Here's a line I've entered in my ~/.vimrc file so that entering code tags is as simple as hitting F12 on my keyboard.

```
imap <F12> <code> </code> <Esc>2F>a
```

The keyword imap designates this mapping as being active only in insert mode. I did this on purpose, because I'm always already in insert mode when I realize I need the tags. Next is the key I'm mapping to, which is, in this case, F12. After that are the actual tags as they will be inserted. Had I stopped there, hitting F12 in insert mode would put in my tags and leave my cursor to the right of them. Because I'm too lazy to move my cursor manually to place it between the tags, I put more keystrokes on the end of my mapping. First, I enter command mode using the Esc key. The 2F> bit says to search from where the cursor is backward to the second occurrence of >, and then the a places the cursor, back in insert mode, after the > character. I never even realize I ever left insert mode—it's completely seamless!

HACK #40 Move Your PHP Web Scripting Skills to the Command Line

PHP is so easy, it's made web coders out of three-year-olds. Now, move that skill to the CLI!

These days, it's rare to find a person who works with computers of any kind for a living who has not gotten hooked on PHP. The barrier to entry for coding PHP for the Web is a bit lower than coding Perl CGI scripts, if only because you don't have to compile PHP scripts in order to run them. I got hooked on PHP early on, but I no longer code much for the Web. What I have discovered, however, is that PHP is a very handy tool for creating command-line scripts, and even one-liners on the command line.

Go to the PHP.net function reference (*http://www.php.net/manual/en/funcref.php*) and check out what PHP has to offer, and you'll soon find that lots of PHP features of PHP are perfect for command-line programming. PHP has built-in functions for interfacing with *syslog*, creating daemons, and utilizing streams and sockets. It even has a suite of POSIX functions such as getpwuid and getpid.

For this hack, I'll be using PHP5 as supplied in the Fedora Core 4 distribution. PHP is readily available in binary format for SUSE, Debian, Red Hat, Fedora, Mandrake, and other popular distributions. Some distros have not yet made the move to PHP5, but they'll likely get there sooner rather than later.

Obviously, the actual code I use in this hack will be of limited use to you. The idea is really to make you think outside the box, using skills you already have, coding in PHP and applying it to something unconventional like system administration.

The Code

Let's have a look at some code. This first script is really simple; it's a simplified version of a script I use to avoid having to use the standard *ldapsearch* tool with a whole bunch of flags. For example, if I want to search a particular server in another department for users with the last name Jones and get back the distinguished name (dn) attribute for each of these users, here's what I have to type:

```
$ ldapsearch -x -h ldap.linuxlaboratory.org -b"dc=linuxlaboratory,dc=org" '
(sn=Jones)' dn
```

Yucky. It's even worse if you have to do this type of search often. I suppose you could write a shell script, but I found that PHP was perfectly capable of handling the task without relying on the *ldapsearch* tool being on the system at all. In addition, PHP's universality is a big plus—everyone in my group has seen PHP before, but some of them code in *tcsh*, which is different enough from *ksh* or *bash* to be confusing. Don't forget that the code you write today will become someone else's problem if a catastrophic bug pops up while you're on a ship somewhere sipping margaritas, far from a cell phone tower. Anyway, here's my script, which I call *dapsearch*:

```
#!/usr/bin/php

<?php

$conn=ldap_connect("ldap.linuxlaboratory.org")
  or die("Connect failed\n");

$bind = ldap_bind($conn)
  or die("Bind failed\n");
```

```
$answer = ldap_search($conn, "dc=linuxlaboratory,dc=org", "($argv[1])");
$output = ldap_get_entries($conn, $answer);

for ($i=0; $i < count($output); $i++) {
        if(!isset($output[$i])) break;
        echo $output[$i]["dn"]."\n";
}
echo $output["count"]." entries returned\n";
?>
```

There are a couple of things to note in the code above. On the first line is your everyday "shebang" line, which contains the path to the binary that will run the code, just like in any other shell or Perl script. If you're coding on your desktop machine for later deployment on a machine you don't control, you might replace that line with one that looks like this:

```
#!/usr/bin/env php
```

This does away with any assumption that the PHP binary is in a particular directory by doing a standard PATH search for it, which can be more reliable.

In addition, you'll notice that the <?php and ?> tags are there in the shell script, just like they are in web scripts. This can be useful in cases where you have static text that you'd like output to the screen, because you can put that text outside the tags instead of using echo statements. Just close the tag, write your text, then open a new set of tags, and the parser will output your text, then start parsing PHP code when the tags open again.

Also, you can see I've simplified things a bit by hard-coding the attribute to be returned (the dn attribute), as well as the server to which I'm connecting. This script can easily be altered to allow for that information to be passed in on the command line as well. Everything you pass on the command line will be in the argv array.

Running the Code

Save the above script to a file called *dapsearch*, make it executable, and then run it, passing along the attribute for which you want to search. In my earlier *ldapsearch* command, I wanted the distinguished name attributes of all users with the last name "Jones." Here's the (greatly shortened) command I run nowadays to get that information:

```
$ dapsearch sn=Jones
```

This calls the script and passes along the search filter, which you'll see referenced in the code as $argv[1]. This might look odd to Perl coders who are used to referencing a lone argument as either @_, $_, or $argv[0]. In PHP, $argv[0] returns the command being run, rather than the first argument handed to it on the command line.

Speaking of the argv array, you can run into errors while using this feature if your installation of PHP doesn't enable the argv and argc arrays by default. If this is the case, the change is a simple one: just open up your *php.ini* file (the configuration file for the PHP parser itself) and set register_argc_argv to on.

HACK #41 Enable Quick telnet/SSH Connections from the Desktop

Desktop launchers and a simple shell script make a great combo for quick telnet and SSH connections to remote systems.

Many of us work with a large number of servers and often have to log in and out of them. Using KDE or GNOME's Application Launcher applet and a simple shell script, you can create desktop shortcuts that enabled you to quickly connect to any host using a variety of protocols.

To do this, create a script called *connect*, make it executable, and put it in a directory that is located in your PATH. This script should look like the following:

```
#!/bin/bash

progname=`basename $0`

type="single"

if [ "$progname" = "connect" ] ; then
        proto=$1
        fqdn=$2
        shift
        shift
elif [ "$progname" = "ctelnet" ]; then
        proto="telnet"
        fqdn=$1
        shift
elif [ "$progname" = "cssh" ]; then
        proto="ssh"
        fqdn=$1
        shift
elif [ "$progname" = "mtelnet" ]; then
        proto="telnet"
        fqdn=$1
        hosts=$*
        type="multi"
elif [ "$progname" = "mssh" ]; then
        proto="ssh"
        fqdn=$1
        hosts=$*
        type="multi"
fi
```

```
args=$*

#
# Uncomment the xterm command and comment out the following if/else/fi
clause
# if you just want to use xterms everywhere
#
# xterm +mb -sb -si -T "${proto}::${fqdn}" -n ${host} -bg black -fg yellow -
e ${proto} ${fqdn} ${args}
#
# Change Konsole to gnome-console and specify correct options if KDE is not
installed
#
if [ "$type" != "multi" ]; then
        konsole -T "${proto}::${fqdn}" --nomenubar --notoolbar ${extraargs}
-e ${proto} ${fqdn} ${args}
else
        multixterm -xc "$proto %n" $hosts
fi
```

After creating this script and making it executable, create symbolic links to this script called *cssh*, *ctelnet*, *mssh*, and *mtelnet* in that same directory. As you can see from the script, the protocol and commands that it uses are based on the way in which the script was called.

To use this script when you are using KDE, right-click on the desktop and select Create New → File → Link to Application. This displays a dialog like the one shown in Figure 4-2. Enter the name of the script that you want to execute and the host that you want to connect to, and save the link.

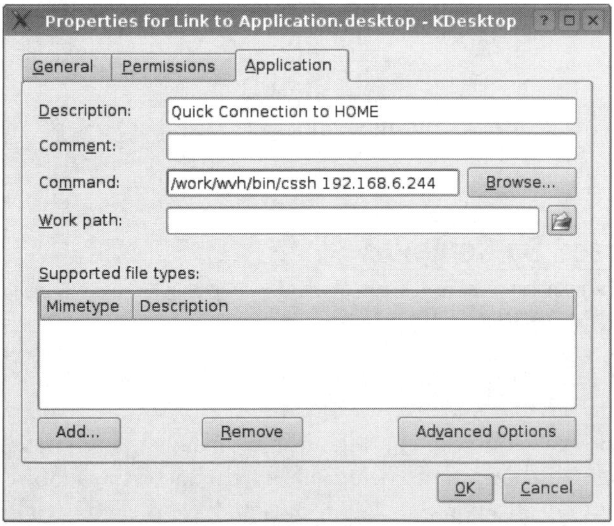

Figure 4-2. Creating a desktop launcher in KDE

To use this script when you are using GNOME, right-click on the desktop and select Create Launcher. This displays a dialog like the one shown in Figure 4-3. Enter the name of the script that you want to execute and the host that you want to connect to, and save the link.

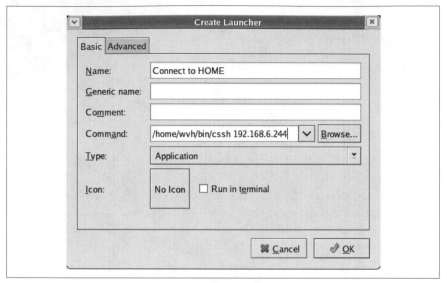

Figure 4-3. Creating a desktop launcher in GNOME

Using either of these methods, you quickly create desktop shortcuts that allow you to initiate a connection to a remote system by clicking on the link on your desktop—no fuss, no muss!

See Also

- "Execute Commands Simultaneously on Multiple Servers" [Hack #29]

—*Lance Tost*

HACK
#42

Speed Up Compiles

While compiling, make full use of all of your computers with a distributed compiling daemon

Many other distribution users make fun of the Gentoo fanboys, because Gentoo users have to spend a lot of time compiling all of their code. And even though these compiles can take hours or days to complete, Gentooists still tout their distribution as being one of the fastest available. Because of their constant need to compile, Gentoo users have picked up a few tricks on making the process go faster, including using *distcc* to create a cluster of computers for compiling. *distcc* is a distributed compiling daemon that allows you to combine the processing power of other Linux computers on your network to compile code. It is very simple to set up and use, and it should produce identical results to a completely local compile. Having three machines with similar speeds should make compiling 2.6 times faster. The *distcc* home page at *http://distcc.samaba.org* has testimonials concerning real user's experiences using the program. Using this hack, you can get *distcc* to work with any Linux distribution, which will make compiling KDE and GNOME from scratch quick and easy.

> *distcc* does not require the machines in your compile farm to have shared filesystems, synchronized clocks, or even the same libraries and headers. However, it is a good idea to make sure you are on the same major version number of the compiler itself.

Before getting started with *distcc*, first you must know how to perform a parallel make when building code. To perform a parallel make, use the -j option in your make command:

```
dbrick@rivendell:$ make -j3; make -j3 modules
```

This will spawn three child processes that will make maximum use of your processor power by ensuring that there is always something in the queue to be compiled. A general rule of thumb for how many parallel makes to perform is to double the number of processors and then add one. So a single processor system will have -j3 and a dual processor system -j5. When you start using *distcc*, you should base the -j value on the total number of processors in your compiling farm. If you have eight processors available, then use -j17.

Using distcc

You can obtain the latest version of *distcc* from *http://distcc.samba.org/download.html*. Just download the archive, uncompress it, and run the standard build commands:

```
dbrick@rivendell:$ tar -jxvf distcc-2.18.3.tar.bz2
dbrick@rivendell:$ cd distcc-2.18.3
dbrick@rivendell:$ ./configure && make && sudo make install
```

You must install the program on each machine you want included in your compile farm. On each of the compiling machines, you need to start the *distccd* daemon:

```
root@bree:# distccd -daemon -N15
root@moria:# distccd -daemon -N15
```

These daemons will listen on TCP port 3632 for instructions and code from the local machine (the one which you are actually compiling software for). The -N value sets a niceness level so the distributed compiles won't interfere too much with local operations. Read the *distccd* manpage for further options.

On the client side, you need to tell *distcc* which computers to use for distributed compiles. You can do this by creating an environment variable:

```
dbrick@rivendell:$ export DISTCC_HOSTS='localhost bree moria'
```

Specify localhost to make sure your local machine is included in the compiles. If your local machine is exceptionally slow, or if you have a lot of processors to distribute the load to, you should consider not including it at all. You can use machine IP addresses in place of names. If you don't want to set an environment variable, then create a *distcc* hosts file in your home directory to contain the values:

```
dbrick@rivendell:$ mkdir ~/.distcc
dbrick@rivendell:$ echo "localhost bree moria" > ~/.distcc/hosts
```

To run a distributed compile, simply pass a CC=distcc option to the make command:

```
dbrick@rivendell:$ make -j7 CC=distcc
```

It's that simple to distribute your compiles. Read the manpages for *distcc* and *distccd* to learn more about the program, including how to limit the number of parallel makes a particular computer in your farm will perform.

Distribute Compiles to Windows Machines

Though some clever people have come up with very interesting ways to distribute compiles to a Windows machine using Cygwin, there is an easier way to perform the same task using a live CD distribution known as distccKnoppix, which you can download from *http://opendoorsoftware.com/cgi/http.pl?p=distccKNOPPIX*. Be sure to download the version that has the same major version number of gcc as your local machine.

To use distccKnoppix, simply boot the computer using the CD, note it's IP address, and then enter that in your *distcc* hosts file or environment variable as instructed earlier. Happy compiling!

—*David Brickner*

Avoid Common Junior Mistakes
HACK #43
Get over the junior admin hump and land in guru territory.

No matter how "senior" you become, and no matter how omnipotent you feel in your current role, you will eventually make mistakes. Some of them may be quite large. Some will wipe entire weekends right off the calendar. However, the key to success in administering servers is to mitigate risk, have an exit plan, and try to make sure that the damage caused by potential mistakes is limited. Here are some common mistakes to avoid on your road to senior-level guru status.

Don't Take the root Name in Vain

Try really hard to forget about root. Here's a quick comparisonof the usage of root by a seasoned vet versus by a junior administrator.

Solid, experienced administrators will occasionally forget that they need to be root to perform some function. Of course they know they need to be root as soon as they see their terminal filling with errors, but running su - root occasionally slips their mind. No big deal. They switch to root, they run the command, and they exit the root shell. If they need to run only a single command, such as a make install, they probably just run it like this:

```
$ su -c 'make install'
```

This will prompt you for the root password and, if the password is correct, will run the command and dump you back to your lowly user shell.

A junior-level admin, on the other hand, is likely to have five terminals open on the same box, all logged in as root. Junior admins don't consider keeping a terminal that isn't logged in as root open on a production machine, because "you need root to do anything anyway." This is horribly bad form, and it can lead to some really horrid results. Don't become root if you don't have to be root!

Building software is a good example. After you download a source package, unzip it in a place you have access to as a user. Then, as a normal user, run your ./configure and make commands. If you're installing the package to your ~/bin directory, you can run make install as yourself. You only need root access if the program will be installed into directories to which only root has write access, such as /usr/local.

My mind was blown one day when I was introduced to an entirely new meaning of "taking the root name in vain." It doesn't just apply to running commands as root unnecessarily. It also applies to becoming root specifically to grant unprivileged access to things that should only be accessible by root!

I was logged into a client's machine (as a normal user, of course), poking around because the user had reported seeing some odd log messages. One of my favorite commands for tracking down issues like this is `ls -lahrt /etc`, which does a long listing of everything in the directory, reverse sorted by modification time. In this case, the last thing listed (and hence, the last thing modified) was `/etc/shadow`. Not too odd if someone had added a user to the local machine recently, but it so happened that this company used NIS+, and the permissions had been changed on the file!

I called the number they'd told me to call if I found anything, and a junior administrator admitted that he had done that himself because he was writing a script that needed to access that file. Ugh.

Don't Get Too Comfortable

Junior admins tend to get really into customizing their environments. They like to show off all the cool things they've recently learned, so they have custom window manager setups, custom logging setups, custom email configurations, custom tunneling scripts to do work from their home machines, and, of course, custom shells and shell initializations.

That last one can cause a bit of headache. If you have a million aliases set up on your local machine and some other set of machines that mount your home directory (thereby making your shell initialization accessible), things will probably work out for that set of machines. More likely, however, is that you're working in a mixed environment with Linux and some other Unix variant. Furthermore, the powers that be may have standard aliases and system-wide shell profiles that were there long before you were.

At the very least, if you modify the shell you have to test that everything you're doing works as expected on all the platforms you administer. Better is just to keep a relatively bare-bones administrative shell. Sure, set the proper environment variables, create three or four aliases, and certainly customize the command prompt if you like, but don't fly off into the wild blue yonder sourcing all kinds of *bash* completion commands, printing the system load to your terminal window, and using shell functions to create your shell prompt. Why not?

Well, because you can't assume that the same version of your shell is running everywhere, or that the shell was built with the same options across multiple versions of multiple platforms! Furthermore, you might not always be logging in from your desktop. Ever see what happens if you mistakenly set up your initialization file to print stuff to your terminal's titlebar without checking where you're coming from? The first time you log in from a dumb terminal, you'll realize it wasn't the best of ideas. Your prompt can wind up being longer than the screen!

Just as versions and build options for your shell can vary across machines, so too can "standard" commands—drastically! Running chown -R has wildly different effects on Solaris than it does on Linux machines, for example. Solaris will follow symbolic links and keep on truckin', happily skipping about your directory hierarchy and recursively changing ownership of files in places you forgot existed. This doesn't happen under Linux. To get Linux to behave the same way, you need to use the -H flag explicitly. There are lots of commands that exhibit different behavior on different operating systems, so be on your toes!

Also, test your shell scripts across platforms to make sure that the commands you call from within the scripts act as expected in any environments they may wind up in.

Don't Perform Production Commands "Off the Cuff"

Many environments have strict rules about how software gets installed, how new machines are built and pushed into production, and so on. However, there are also thousands of sites that don't enforce any such rules, which quite frankly can be a bit scary.

Not having the funds to come up with a proper testing and development environment is one thing. Having a blatant disregard for the availability of production services is quite another. When performing software installations, configuration changes, mass data migrations, and the like, do yourself a huge favor (actually, a couple of favors):

Script the procedure!
    Script it and include checks to make sure that everything in the script runs without making any assumptions. Check to make sure each step has succeeded before moving on.

Script a backout procedure.
    If you've moved all the data, changed the configuration, added a user for an application to run as, and installed the application, and something blows up, you really will *not* want to spend another 40 minutes cleaning things up so that you can get things back to normal. In addition, if things blow up in production, you could panic, causing you to misjudge, mistype, and possibly make things worse. Script it!

The process of scripting these procedures also forces you to think about the consequences of what you're doing, which can have surprising results. I once got a quarter of the way through a script before realizing that there was an unmet dependency that nobody had considered. This realization saved us a lot of time and some cleanup as well.

Ask Questions

The best tip any administrator can give is to be conscious of your own ignorance. Don't assume you know every conceivable side effect of everything you're doing. Ask. If the senior admin looks at you like you're an idiot, let him. Better to be thought an idiot for asking than proven an idiot by not asking!

Get Linux Past the Gatekeeper
HACK #44

What not to do when trying to get Linux into your server room.

Let's face it: you can't make use of *Linux Server Hacks* (Volume One or Two) unless you have a Linux server to hack! I have learned from mistakes made by both myself and others that common community ideals are meaningless in a corporate boardroom, and that they can be placed in a more tie-friendly context when presented to decision-makers. If you use Linux at home and are itching to get it into your machine room, here are some common mistakes to avoid in navigating the political side of Linux adoption in your environment.

Don't Talk Money

If you approach the powers that be and lead with a line about how Linux is free (as in beer), you're likely doing yourself a disservice, for multiple reasons. First, if you point an IT manager at the Debian web site (home of what's arguably the only "totally free in all ways" Linux distribution) and tell him to click around because this will be his new server operating system, he's going to ask you where the support link is. When you show him an online forum, he's going to think you are completely out in left field.

Linux IRC channels, mailing lists, and forums have given me better support for all technology, commercial or not, than the vendors themselves. However, without spending money on vendor support, your IT manager will likely feel that your company has no leverage with the vendor and no contractual support commitment from anyone. There is no accountability, no feel-good engineer in vendor swag to help with migrations, and no "throat to choke" if something goes wrong.

To be fair, you can't blame him much for thinking this—he's just trying to keep his job. What do you think would happen if some catastrophic incident occurred and he was called into a meeting with all the top brass and, when commanded to report status, he said "I've posted the problem to the *linuxgoofball.org* forums, so I'll keep checking back there. In the meantime, I've also sent email to a mailing list that one of the geeks in back said was pretty good for support..."? He'd be fired immediately!

IT departments are willing to spend money for software that can get the job done. They are also willing to spend money for branded, certified vendor support. This is not wasted money. To the extent that a platform is only one part of a larger technology deployment, the money spent on the software and on support is their investment in the success of that deployment. If it costs less for the right reasons (fewer man hours required to maintain, greater efficiency), that's great. But "free" is not necessary, expected, or even necessarily good.

It is also not Linux's greatest strength, so leading with "no money down" is also doing an injustice to the people who create and maintain it. The cost of Linux did many things that helped it get where it is today, not the least of which was to lower the barrier of entry for new users to learn how to use a Unix-like environment. It also lowered the barrier of entry for developers, who were able to grow the technological foundation of Linux and port already trusted applications such as Sendmail and Apache to the platform, making it a viable platform that companies were willing to adopt in some small way. Leading with the monetary argument implies that that's the best thing about Linux, throwing all of its other strengths out the window.

Don't Talk About Linux in a Vacuum

It's useless (at best) to talk about running Linux in your shop without talking about it in the context of a solution that, when compared to the current solution, would be more useful or efficient.

To get Linux accepted as a viable platform, you have to start somewhere. It could be a new technology deployment, or it could be a replacement for an existing service. To understand the best way to get Linux in the door, it's important to understand all of the aspects of your environment. Just because you know that management is highly displeased with the current office-wide instant messaging solution doesn't mean that Jabber is definitely the solution for them. Whining to your boss that you should just move to Jabber and everything would be great isn't going to get you anywhere, because you've offered no facts about Jabber that make your boss consider it an idea with any merit whatsoever. It also paints you in a bad light, because making blanket statements like that implies that you think you know all there is to know about an office-wide IM solution.

Are you ready for the tough questions? Have you even thought about what they might be? Do you know the details of the current solution? Do you know what might be involved in migrating to another solution? *Any* other solution? Do you know enough about Jabber to take the reins or are you going to be sitting at a console with a Jabber book open to page 4 when your boss walks in to see how your big, high-profile, all-users-affected project is going?

"Linux is better" isn't a credible statement. "A Linux file-sharing solution can work better at the department level because it can serve all of the platforms we support" is better. But what you want to aim for is something like "I've seen deployments of this service on the Linux platform serve 1,500 users on 3 client platforms with relatively low administrative overhead, whereas we now serve 300 clients on only 1 platform, and we have to reboot twice a week. Meanwhile, we have to maintain a completely separate server to provide the same services to other client platforms." The first part of this statement is something you might hear in a newbie Linux forum. The last part inspires confidence and hits on something that IT managers care about—server consolidation.

When talking to decision makers about Linux as a new technology or replacement service, it's important to understand where they perceive value in their current solution. If they deployed the current IM solution because it was inexpensive to get a site license and it worked with existing client software without crazy routing and firewall changes, be ready. Can existing client software at your site talk to a Jabber server? Is there infrastructure in place to push out software to all of your clients?

It's really simple to say that Linux rocks. It's considerably more difficult to stand it next to an existing solution and justify the migration cost to a manager whose concerns are cost recovery, ROI, FTEs, and man-hours.

Don't Pitch Linux for Something It's Not Well Suited For

Linux is well suited to performing an enormous variety of tasks that are currently performed using lower-quality, higher-cost, proprietary software packages (too many to name—see the rest of this book for hints). There's no reason to pitch it for tasks it *can't* handle, as this will only leave a bad taste in the mouths of those whose first taste of Linux is a complete and utter failure.

What Linux is suitable for is 100% site-dependent. If you have a large staff of mobile, non-technical salespeople with laptops who use VPN connections from wireless hotspot sites around the globe, and you have a few old ladies manning the phones in the office all day, the desktop might not be the place for Linux to shine.

On the other hand, if you have an operator on a switchboard built in the 1920s, and the lifeblood of the business is phone communication, a Linux-based Asterisk PBX solution might be useful and much appreciated!

The point is, choose your battles. Even in Unix environments, there will be resistance to Linux, because some brands of Unix have been doing jobs for decades that some cowboy now wants Linux to perform. In some cases, there is absolutely no reason to switch.

Sybase databases have run really well on Sun servers for decades. Sybase released a usable version of their flagship product for Linux only about a year ago. This is not an area you want to approach for a migration (new deployments may or may not be another story). On the other hand, some features of the Linux *syslog* daemon might make it a little nicer than Solaris as a central log host. Some software projects readily tell you that they build, develop, and test on Linux. Linux is the reference Unix implementation in some shops, so use that leverage to help justify a move in that direction. Do your homework and pick your battles!

Don't Be Impatient

Personally, I'd rather have a deployment be nearly flawless than have it done yesterday. Both would be wonderful, but if history is any indication, that's asking too much.

Don't bite off more than you can chew. Let Linux grow on your clients, your boss, and your users. Get a mail server up and running. Get SpamAssassin, *procmail*, and a webmail portal set up on an Apache server. Then maintain it, optimize it, and secure it. If you do all this, Linux will build its own track record in your environment. Create a mailing list server. Build an LDAP-based white pages directory that users can point their email applications at to get user information. If you play your cards right, a year from now people will begin to realize that relatively few resources have been devoted to running these services, and that, generally, they "just work." When they're ready to move on to larger things, whom do you think they'll turn to? The guy who wanted to replace an old lady's typewriter with a dual-headed Linux desktop?

Think again. They'll be calling you.

HACK #45   Prioritize Your Work

Perhaps no one in the company needs to learn good time management more than system administrators, but they are sometimes the last people to attempt to organize their work lives.

Like most system administrators, you probably find it next to impossible to keep up with the demands of your job while putting in just 40 hours a week. You find yourself working evenings and weekends just to keep up. Sometimes this is fun, as you get to work with new technologies—and let's face it, most sysadmins like computers and often work on them even in their free time. However, working 60-hour weeks, month after month, is not a good situation to be in. You'll never develop the social life you crave, and you won't be doing your company a service if you're grouchy all the time because of lack of sleep or time away. But the work keeps coming, and you just don't see how you'll ever be able to cram it all into a standard work week...which is why you need this hack about task prioritization. I know, it's not really a hack about Linux servers, but it is a hack about being a sysadmin, which means it should speak directly to everyone reading this book.

Prioritizing Tasks

Managing your tasks won't only ensure you get everything done in a timely manner. It will also help you make better predictions as to when work can be done and, more importantly, it will make your customers happier because you'll do a better job of meeting *their* expectations about when their requests will be met. The next few sections discuss the methods you can use to order your tasks.

Doing tasks in list order. One method for ordering your tasks is to not spend time doing it. Make the decision simple and just start at the top of the task list and work your way down, doing each item in order. In the time you might have spent fretting about where to start, chances are you'll have completed a couple of smaller items. In addition, because the first items on the list are usually tasks you couldn't complete the previous day, you'll often be working on the oldest items first.

Doing your to-do items in the order they appear is a great way to avoid procrastination. To quote the Nike advertisements, "Just do it."

If your list is short enough that you can get through all the items in one day, this scheme makes even more sense—if it doesn't matter if a task gets done early in the day or late in the day, who cares in what order it's completed? Of course, that's not often the case...

Prioritizing based on customer expectations. Here's a little secret I picked up from Ralph Loura when he was my boss at Bell Labs. If you have a list of tasks, doing them in any order takes (approximately) the same amount of time. However, if you do them in an order that is based on customer expectations, your customers will perceive you as working faster. Same amount of work for you, better perception from your customers. Pretty cool, huh?

So what are your customer expectations? Sure, all customers would love all requests to be completed immediately, but in reality they do have some conception that things take time. User expectations may be unrealistic, and they're certainly often based on misunderstandings of the technology, but they still exist.

We can place user expectations into a few broad categories:

Some requests should be handled quickly.
Examples include requests to reset a password, allocate an IP address, and delete a protected file. One thing these requests have in common is that they often involve minor tasks that hold up larger tasks. Imagine the frustration a user experiences when she can't do anything until a password is reset, but you take hours to get it done.

"Hurry up and wait" tasks should be gotten out of the way early.
Tasks that are precursors to other tasks are expected to happen quickly. For example, ordering a small hardware item usually involves a lot of work to push the order through purchasing, then a long wait for the item to arrive. After that, the item can be installed. If the wait is going to be two weeks, there is an expectation that the ordering will happen quickly so that the two-week wait won't stretch into three weeks.

Some requests take a long time.
Examples include installing a new PC, creating a service from scratch, or anything that requires a purchasing process. Even if the vendor offers overnight shipping, people accept that overnight is not "right now."

All other work stops to fix an outage.
The final category is outages. Not only is there an expectation that during an outage all other work will stop to resolve the issue, but there is an expectation that the entire team will work on the project. Customers generally do not know that there is a division of labor within a sysadmin team.

Now that we understand our customers' expectations better, how can we put this knowledge to good use? Let's suppose we had the tasks shown in Figure 4-4 on our to-do list.

Task	Description	Expectation	Actual work	Time completed
T1	Reset password	1 minute	10 minutes	9:10 a.m.
T2	Create new user account	Next day	20 minutes	9:30 a.m.
T3	Install new server	Next day	4 hours (+1 for lunch)	2:30 p.m.
T4	Add new CGI area to web server	1 hour	30 minutes	3:00 p.m.
T5	Order a software package	1 hour	1 hour	4:00 p.m.
T6	Debug minor NetNews error	10 minutes	25 minutes	4:25 p.m.
T7	Allocate IP address	2 minutes	5 minutes	4:30 p.m.

Figure 4-4. Tasks that aren't prioritized by customer expectations

If we did the tasks in the order listed, completing everything on the day it was requested in six and a half hours of solid work (plus an hour for lunch), we could be pretty satisfied with our performance. Good for us.

However, we have not done a good job of meeting our customers' perceptions of how long things should have taken. The person that made request "T7" had to wait all day for something that he perceived should have taken two minutes. If I was that customer, I would be pretty upset. For the lack of an IP address, the installation of a new piece of lab equipment was delayed all day.

(Actually, what's more likely to happen is that the frustrated, impatient customer wouldn't wait all day. He'd ping IP addresses until he found one that wasn't in use at that moment and "temporarily borrow" that address. If this were your unlucky day, the address selected would conflict with something and cause an outage, which could ruin your entire day. But I digress....)

Let's reorder the tasks based on customer perceptions of how long things should take. Tasks that are perceived to take little time or to be urgent will be batched up and done early in the day. Other tasks will happen later. Figure 4-5 shows the reordered tasks.

Task	Description	Expectation	Actual work	Time completed
T1	Reset password	1 minute	10 minutes	9:10 a.m.
T7	Allocate IP address	2 minutes	5 minutes	9:15 a.m.
T5	Order a software package	1 hour	1 hour	10:15 a.m.
T4	Add new CGI area to web server	1 hour	30 minutes	10:45 a.m.
T2	Create new user account	Next day	20 minutes	11:05 a.m.
T3	Install new server	Next day	4 hours (+1 for lunch)	4:05 p.m.
T6	Debug minor NetNews error	10 minutes	25 minutes	4:30 p.m.

Figure 4-5. Tasks ordered based on customer expectations

We begin the day by doing the two tasks (T1 and T7) that customers expect to happen quickly and that will hold up other, larger, projects. We succeed in meeting the perceived amount of time that these tasks should take, and everyone's happy.

Prioritizing Projects

The previous section described ways to prioritize individual tasks. Now I'll present some useful techniques for prioritizing projects.

Prioritization for impact. Let's say that you and your fellow sysadmins brain-stormed 20 great projects to do next year. However, you only have the budget and manpower to accomplish a few of them. Which projects should you pick?

It's tempting to pick the easy projects and do them first. You know how to do them, and there isn't much controversy surrounding them, so at least you'll know that they'll be completed.

It's also very tempting to pick out the fun projects, or the politically safe projects, or the projects that are the obvious next steps based on past projects.

Ignore those temptations, and find the projects that will have the biggest positive impact on your organization's goals. It's actually better to do one big project that will have a large positive impact than many easy projects that are superficial—I've seen it many times. Also, an entire team working on one goal works better than everyone having a different project, because we work better when we work together.

Here's another way to look at it. All projects can fit into one of the four categories listed in Figure 4-6.

	Easy (small effort)	Difficult (big effort)
Big positive impact	A	B
Superficial impact	C	D

Figure 4-6. Project impact versus effort

Doing category A projects first seems like the obvious course. An easy project that will have a big impact is rare, and when such projects magically appear in front of us, doing them always looks like the right choice. (Warning: Be careful, because their A status may be a mirage!)

It's also obvious to avoid category D projects. A project that is difficult and won't change much shouldn't be attempted.

However, most projects are either in category B or C, and it's human nature to be drawn to the easy C projects. We can fill our year with easy projects, list many accomplishments, and come away looking very good. However, highly successful companies train management to reward workers who take on category B projects—the difficult but necessary ones.

If you think about it in terms of Return on Investment (ROI), it makes sense. You're going to spend a certain amount of money this year. Do you spend it on many small projects, each of which will not have a big impact? No, you look at what will have the biggest positive impact and put all your investment into that effort.

It's important to make sure that these "big-impact" projects are aligned with your company's goals—important for the company and important for you too. You will be more highly valued that way.

Prioritizing requests from your boss. If your boss asks you to do something, and it's a quick task (not a major project), do it right away. For example, if your boss asks you to find out approximately how many PCs are running the old version of Windows, get back to her with a decent estimate in a few minutes.

It helps to understand the big picture. Usually, such requests are made because your boss is putting together a much larger plan or budget (perhaps a cost estimate for bringing all PCs up to the latest release of Windows), and you can hold up her entire day by not getting back to her quickly with an answer.

Why does this matter? Well, your boss decides what happens at your next salary review. Do I need to say more? Maybe I do. Your boss will have a fixed amount of money to dole out for all raises. If she gives more to Moe, Larry is going to get less. When your boss is looking at the list of people on the team, do you want her to look at your name and think "he sure did get me an estimate of the number of out-of-date Windows PCs quickly. Gosh, he always gets me the things I need quickly." Or do you want your boss to be thinking "you know, the entire budget was held up for a day because I was waiting for that statistic." Or worse yet "all the times I looked foolish in front of my boss because I was late, it was because I was waiting for [insert your name here] to get me a piece of information. So-and-so isn't getting a good raise this year." Keeping the boss happy is always a good idea!

Summary

Managing your priorities ensures that you meet your customers' expectations and get the work with the biggest impact done in a timely manner. However, prioritization is just one part of a time-management solution. Though you can go to general time-management books for more ideas, I humbly suggest a reading of my book, *Time Management for System Administrators* (O'Reilly).

—*Tom Limoncelli*

Storage Management and Backups
Hacks 46–55

One of the core responsibilities of any computer system is to provide enough storage space to enable users to get their work done. Storage requirements depend largely on the types of files your users work with, which may range in size from the 100–200 KB that many word processing documents use to the megabytes of disk space consumed by music and image files. Add the gigabytes of old email that most people have lying around, and you can see that today's users require more disk space than ever before.

The obvious solution to increasing storage requirements is to add more disks and disk controllers. However, simply adding filesystems to your machine can result in an administrative nightmare of symbolic links that reflect the migration paths of certain directories as they move from disk to disk in search of lebensraum. This chapter opens with a hack that helps you address increasing storage requirements in a cool, calm, organized fashion by using logical volumes. This storage management technique makes it easy to add disk space to existing filesystems without having to move anything anywhere.

Once you've added new disk space in one fashion or another, backing up today's large drives can pose a problem, so we've included hacks to help you back up and clone modern systems without needing a stack of mag tapes or tape cartridges that reaches to the moon. This chapter also includes a hack that explains how to combine RAID with logical volumes to increase system reliability in general. You can't eliminate backups, but you can easily minimize the need for restores.

This chapter will also discuss how to help your users use disk space intelligently by sharing central collections of files whenever possible, preventing disk space bloat because all 500 of your users have their own copies of every file that their team has ever worked on. And because huge directories and filesystems often make it more difficult to find the specific file you're looking for, we've added a hack about how to take advantage of Linux extended attributes to tag files with metadata that makes them easier to locate. This chapter ends with a hack that discusses Linux quotas, which provide an excellent mechanism to identify the biggest users of disk space on your systems and even enable you to set limits on per-user or per-group disk consumption. An ounce of protection is worth a pound of cure—or, in this case, a few hundred gigabytes, the cost of new disks, and the associated administrative overhead.

Create Flexible Storage with LVM

HACK
#46   "User disk requirements expand to consume all available space" is a fundamental rule of system administration. Prepare for this in advance using Logical Volume Management (LVM).

When managing computer systems, a classic problem is the research project or business unit gone haywire, whose storage requirements far exceed their current allocation (and perhaps any amount of storage that's currently available on the systems they're using). Good examples of this sort of thing are simulation and image analysis projects, or my research into backing up my entire CD collection on disk. *Logical volumes*, which are filesystems that appear to be single physical volumes but are actually assembled from space that has been allocated on multiple physical partitions, are an elegant solution to this problem. The size of a logical volume can exceed the size of any of the physical storage devices on your system, but it cannot exceed the sum of all of their sizes.

Traditional solutions to storage management have their limitations. Imposing quotas [Hack #55], can prevent users from hogging more than their fair share of disk resources, helping your users share their resources equitably. Similarly, paying scrupulous attention to detail in cleaning out old user accounts can maximize the amount of space available to the active users on your system. However, neither of these approaches solves the actual problem, which is the "fixed-size" aspect of disk storage. Logical volumes solve this problem in a truly elegant fashion by making it easy to add new disk storage to the volumes on which existing directories are located. Without logical volumes, you could still add new disk storage to the system by formatting new disks and partitions and mounting them at various locations in the existing filesystem, but your system would quickly become an unmanageable administrative nightmare of mount points and symbolic links pointing all over the place.

Linux has had two implementations of logical volumes, aptly known as LVM and LVM2. LVM2, which is backward compatible with logical volumes created with LVM, is the version that is provided by default with 2.6-based systems. This hack focuses on LVM2, although newer LVM technologies—such as the Enterprise Volume Management System (EVMS), which was originally developed by IBM and is now an active SourceForge project (*http://sourceforge.net/ projects/evms*)—are actively under development.

Logical Volume Buzzwords

When using logical volumes, the pool of storage space from which specific volumes are created is known as a *volume group*. Volume groups are created by first formatting specific physical devices or partitions as *physical volumes*, using the pvcreate command, and then creating the volume group on some number of physical volumes using the vgcreate command. When the volume group is created, it divides the physical volumes of which it is composed into *physical extents*, which are the actual allocation units within a volume group. The size of each physical extent associated with a specific volume group can be set from 8 KB to 512 MB in powers of 2 when the volume group is created, with a default size of 4 MB.

> Nowadays, all of the individual commands related to physical and logical volumes are implemented by one central binary called *lvm*. Most Linux distributions install symbolic links to this binary with the names of the traditional, individual commands for physical and logical volume management. The hacks in this chapter use the names of the specific commands, but you can also always execute them by prefacing them with the lvm command. For example, if your distribution doesn't install the symlinks, you could execute the pvcreate command by executing lvm pvcreate.

When you create a volume group, a directory with the same name as that volume group is created in your system's */dev* directory, and a character-special device file called *group* is created in that directory. As you create logical volumes from that volume group, the block-special files associated with each of them are also created in this directory.

Once you've created a volume group, you can use the lvcreate command to create logical volumes from the accumulation of storage associated with that volume group. Physical extents from the volume group are allocated to logical volumes by mapping them through *logical extents*, which have a one-to-one correspondence to specific physical extents but provide yet another level of abstraction between physical and logical storage space. Using logical extents reduces the impact of certain administrative operations, such as moving the physical extents on a specific physical volume to another physical volume if you suspect (or, even worse, know) that the disk on which a specific physical volume is located is going bad.

Once you have created a logical volume, you can create your favorite type of filesystem on it using the mkfs command, specifying the type of filesystem by using the -t type option. You can then modify your *etc/fstab* file to mount the new logical volume wherever you want, and you're in business. The rest of the hack shows you how to perform the actions I've just described.

Allocating Physical Volumes

You can use either existing partitions or complete disks as storage for logical volumes. As the first step in your LVM odyssey, you must use the pvcreate command to create physical volumes on those partitions or disks in order to identify them to the system as storage that you can assign to a volume group and subsequently use in a logical volume. There are several ways to allocate an entire disk for use with LVM2:

- Make sure the disk does not contain a partition table and create a single physical volume on the disk.

- Create a single partition on the disk and create a physical volume on that partition.

- Create multiple partitions on your disk and create physical volumes on each.

Each of these has advantages and disadvantages, but I prefer the third as a general rule. The first two approaches don't localize disk problems, meaning that sector failures on the disk can kick the entire physical volume out of your volume group and therefore quite possibly prevent recovery or repair. You can minimize the hassle inherent in this situation by combining RAID and LVM [Hack #47], but you can minimize headaches and lost data in the first place (without using RAID) by manually partitioning the disk and allocating each of those smaller partitions as physical volumes. To do this, use the fdisk command to create reasonably sized, manageable partitions that are clearly identified as Linux LVM storage, and then use the pvcreate command to create physical volumes on each, as in the following example:

```
# fdisk /dev/hdb

The number of cylinders for this disk is set to 30401.
There is nothing wrong with that, but this is larger than 1024,
and could in certain setups cause problems with:
```

1) software that runs at boot time (e.g., old versions of LILO)
2) booting and partitioning software from other OSs
   (e.g., DOS FDISK, OS/2 FDISK)

Command (m for help): **p**

Disk /dev/hdb: 250.0 GB, 250059350016 bytes
255 heads, 63 sectors/track, 30401 cylinders
Units = cylinders of 16065 * 512 = 8225280 bytes

   Device Boot   Start   End   Blocks   Id System

Command (m for help): **n**
Command action
   e   extended
   p   primary partition (1-4)
p
Partition number (1-4): **1**
First cylinder (1-30401, default 1):
Using default value 1
Last cylinder or +size or +sizeM or +sizeK (1-30401, default 30401):
Using default value 30401

Command (m for help): **t**
Selected partition 1
Hex code (type L to list codes): **8e**
Changed system type of partition 1 to 8e (Linux LVM)

Command (m for help): **p**

Disk /dev/hdb: 250.0 GB, 250059350016 bytes
255 heads, 63 sectors/track, 30401 cylinders
Units = cylinders of 16065 * 512 = 8225280 bytes

   Device Boot   Start   End   Blocks   Id System
/dev/hdb1   1   30401   244196001   8e Linux LVM

Command (m for help): **w**
The partition table has been altered!

Calling ioctl( ) to re-read partition table.
Syncing disks.
#

In some older versions of LVM, pvcreate will complain if it finds a partition table on a disk that you are allocating as a single physical volume. If this is the case with the version of LVM that you are using, you'll need to allocate the entire disk as a physical volume. To do this, make sure you wipe any existing partition table (using dd if=/dev/zero of=/dev/*DISK* bs=512 count=1, where *DISK* is the base name of the disk, such as */dev/hda*, */dev/sda*, and so on—whatever is appropriate for your system).

With most modern versions of LVM2, this is not the case—disks can have existing partition tables and still be allocated in their entirety for use with LVM. Any partitions that you create on a disk for use as a physical volume should have their types set to Linux Logical Volume (0x8e) when you use *fdisk* (or any equivalent utility) to partition the disk. Always be kind to your fellow sysadmins. You won't necessarily always work for the same company, and you should always follow the sysadmin's golden rule: leave behind understandable systems, as you would have other sysadmins leave behind understandable systems for you.

In the preceding example and throughout this hack, I'm creating a single partition on a disk and using it as a physical volume. This is to keep the sample output from fdisk shorter than the rest of the book. In actual practice, as explained previously, I suggest creating smaller partitions of a more manageable size—40 GB or so—and using them as physical volumes. It doesn't matter to LVM whether they're primary or extended partitions on your disk drive. Using smaller partitions helps localize disk problems that you may encounter down the road.

After creating partitions you want to use as physical volumes, use the pvcreate command to allocate them for use as physical volumes, as in this example:

```
# pvcreate /dev/hdb1
  Physical volume "/dev/hdb1" successfully created
```

You can then confirm the status and size of your new physical volume by using the pvdisplay command:

```
# pvdisplay
  --- NEW Physical volume ---
  PV Name               /dev/hdb1
  VG Name
  PV Size               232.88 GB
  Allocatable           NO
  PE Size (KByte)       0
  Total PE              0
  Free PE               0
  Allocated PE          0
  PV UUID               hy8hck-B5lp-TLZf-hyD4-U9Mu-EFn8-wob9Km
```

Assigning Physical Volumes to Volume Groups

Once you've created one or more physical volumes, you need to add them to a specific volume group so that they can be allocated for use in a logical volume. Adding a physical volume to a volume group is done with the vgcreate command, as in the following example:

```
# vgcreate data /dev/hdb1
  Volume group "data" successfully created
```

If you have multiple physical volumes to add to your volume group, simply specify them after the first physical volume. You can then confirm the status of your new volume group by using the vgdisplay command:

```
# vgdisplay data
  --- Volume group ---
  VG Name               data
  System ID
  Format                lvm2
  Metadata Areas        1
  Metadata Sequence No  1
  VG Access             read/write
  VG Status             resizable
  MAX LV                0
  Cur LV                0
  Open LV               0
  Max PV                0
  Cur PV                1
  Act PV                1
  VG Size               232.88 GB
  PE Size               4.00 MB
  Total PE              59618
  Alloc PE / Size       0 / 0
  Free  PE / Size       59618 / 232.88 GB
  VG UUID               SeYOpJ-QOEj-AQbT-FriO-tai6-5oED-7ujb1F
```

Creating a Logical Volume from a Volume Group

As mentioned previously, creating a physical volume divides the allocated space in that volume into physical extents. Unlike traditional inode-based storage, filesystems that use logical volumes track free space by preallocated units of space known as *extents*. Extents are physically linear series of blocks that can be read one after the other, minimizing disk head movement.

When you create a logical volume, you must specify its size. If you're only creating a single logical volume, you probably want to create it using all of the available space in the volume group where you create it.

The number of free extents is listed as the Free PE entry in the output of the pvdisplay command for each partition in the volume group (in this case, only the disk /dev/hdb1):

```
# pvdisplay /dev/hdb1
--- Physical volume ---
PV Name               /dev/hdb1
VG Name               data
PV Size               232.88 GB / not usable 0
Allocatable           yes
PE Size (KByte)       4096
Total PE              59618
Free PE               59618
Allocated PE          0
PV UUID               9OBPOt-OZeQ-2Zbl-DCmh-iEJu-p8Je-SLm1Gg

# pvdisplay /dev/hdb1 | grep "Free PE"
Free PE               59618
```

You could also infer this value by looking at the volume group itself, but the output there requires a little more thought:

```
# vgdisplay data
--- Volume group ---
VG Name               data
System ID
Format                lvm2
Metadata Areas        1
Metadata Sequence No  2
VG Access             read/write
VG Status             resizable
MAX LV                0
Cur LV                1
Open LV               0
Max PV                0
Cur PV                1
Act PV                1
VG Size               232.88 GB
PE Size               4.00 MB
Total PE              59618
Alloc PE / Size       59618 / 232.88 GB
Free  PE / Size       0 / 0
VG UUID               SeYOpJ-QOEj-AQbT-Fri0-tai6-5oED-7ujb1F
```

This output shows that a total of 59,618 physical extents have been allocated to this volume group, but it also shows them all as being in use. They're considered to be in use because they are allocated to the volume group—this doesn't reflect whether they actually contain data, are mounted anywhere, and so on.

Your next step is to use the lvcreate command to create logical volumes within the volume group you just defined, using as much of the volume as you want to allocate to the new logical volume. To create a logical volume called *music* that uses all the space available in the *data* volume group, for example, you would execute the following command:

```
# lvcreate -l 59618 data -n music
  Logical volume "music" created
```

You can then use the lvdisplay command to get information about the logical volume you just created:

```
# lvdisplay
  --- Logical volume ---
  LV Name                /dev/data/music
  VG Name                data
  LV UUID                yVO6uh-BshS-IqiK-GeIi-A3vm-Tsjg-TOkCT7
  LV Write Access        read/write
  LV Status              available
  # open                 0
  LV Size                232.88 GB
  Current LE             59618
  Segments               1
  Allocation             inherit
  Read ahead sectors     0
  Block device           253:0
```

As you can see from this output, the actual access point for the new logical volume *music* is the directory */dev/data/music*, which was created when the volume was created by the lvcreate command.

When you create a logical volume, the logical volume system also creates an appropriate entry in the directory */dev/mapper* that maps the logical volume to the physical volume from which it was created, as in the following example:

```
# ls /dev/mapper
control  data-music
```

Now that we've created the logical volume, let's see how the output from pvdisplay changes to reflect this allocation:

```
# pvdisplay /dev/hdb1
  --- Physical volume ---
  PV Name                /dev/hdb1
  VG Name                data
  PV Size                232.88 GB / not usable 0
  Allocatable            yes (but full)
  PE Size (KByte)        4096
  Total PE               59618
  Free PE                0
  Allocated PE           59618
  PV UUID                9OBPOt-OZeQ-2Zbl-DCmh-iEJu-p8Je-SLm1Gg
```

This output now shows that there are no free physical extents on the physical volume, because all of them have been allocated to the logical volume that we created from the volume group with which this physical volume is associated.

Now that we've created a logical volume, we have to put a filesystem on it in order to actually use it on our Linux box. You do this using the mkfs command that's appropriate for the type of filesystem you want to create. I'm a big XFS fan, so I'd use the following command to create an XFS filesystem on the new logical volume and mount it at */mnt/music* on my system:

```
# mkfs -t xfs /dev/data/music
meta-data=/dev/data/music       isize=256    agcount=16, agsize=3815552 blks
         =                       sectsz=512
data     =                       bsize=4096   blocks=61048832, imaxpct=25
         =                       sunit=0      swidth=0 blks, unwritten=1
naming   =version 2             bsize=4096
log      =internal log          bsize=4096   blocks=29809, version=1
         =                       sectsz=512   sunit-0 blks
realtime =none                   extsz=65536  blocks=0, rtextents=0
#
# mount -t xfs /dev/data/music /mnt/music
```

Doing a standard disk free listing on my system shows that the new volume is mounted and available:

```
Filesystem           1K-blocks       Used Available Use% Mounted on
/dev/sda1            10490040     3763676   6726364  36% /
tmpfs                  511956          44    511912   1% /dev/shm
/dev/sda3              257012       43096    213916  17% /boot
/dev/sda8           160010472   127411776  32598696  80% /home
/dev/sda5             4200824      986308   3214516  24% /tmp
/dev/sda6            31462264     5795132  25667132  19% /usr
/dev/sda7            31454268    15228908  16225360  49% /usr/local
/dev/hda1           241263968   196779092  32229292  86% /opt2
/dev/mapper/data-music
                    244076092         272 244075820   1% /mnt/music
```

Note that mounting the logical volume */dev/data/music* actually mounted the control device for that logical volume, which is */dev/mapper/data-music*. This enables the logical volume system to better track allocations, especially in the case where a logical volume is composed of physical volumes that reside on physically distinct disks (which isn't the case in this simple example, but almost certainly will be in a production environment).

To make sure that your new logical volume is automatically mounted each time you boot your system, add the following entry to your */etc/fstab* file:

```
/dev/data/music  /mnt/music     xfs     defaults,noatime   0 0
```

You'll note that I specified the noatime option in the */etc/fstab* mount options for my logical volume, which tells the filesystem not to update inodes each time the files or directories associated with them are accessed. This eliminates what I consider frivolous updates to the logical volume (I don't really care when a file was accessed last) and therefore reduces some of the wear and tear on my drives.

That's it—now that I have all this new space, it's time for me to go back up some more of my music collection…but that's outside the scope of this hack.

Suggestions

One general suggestion that I've found useful is to keep / and /boot on physical partitions, and use *ext3* for those filesystems. The recovery tools for *ext2*/*ext3* filesystems are time-tested and sysadmin-approved. If you can at least easily boot your system in single-user mode, you have a much better chance of recovering your logical volumes using established tools.

Also, always use multiple partitions on your systems. Resist the urge to simplify things by creating a single huge logical volume as / and putting everything in there. This makes complete system backups huge and provides a single point of failure. The time you save during installation will be spent tearing your hair out later if disk problems take your system to its knees. A recovery disk and a lost weekend are no substitutes for proper initial planning.

See Also

- "Combine LVM and Software RAID" [Hack #47]
- The EVMS Project: *http://sourceforge.net/projects/evms*
- LVM HOWTO: *http://www.tldp.org/HOWTO/LVM-HOWTO/*

HACK #47 Combine LVM and Software RAID

Combining the flexibility of LVM with the redundancy of RAID is the right thing for critical file servers.

RAID (Redundant Array of Inexpensive Disks or Redundant Array of Independent Disks, depending on who you ask) is a hardware and/or software mechanism used to improve the performance and maintainability of large amounts of disk storage through some extremely clever mechanisms. As the name suggests, RAID makes a large number of smaller disks (referred to as a *RAID array*) appear to be one or more large disks as far as the operating system is concerned. RAID was also designed to provide both performance and protection against the failure of any single disk in your system, which it does by providing its own internal volume management interface.

RAID is provided by specialized disk controller hardware, by system-level software, or by some combination of both. The support for software RAID under Linux is known as the *multiple device* (*md*) interface. Hardware RAID has performance advantages over software RAID, but it can be a problem in enterprise environments because hardware RAID implementations are almost always specific to the hardware controller you are using. While most newer hardware RAID controllers from a given manufacturer are compatible with their previous offerings, there's never any real guarantee of this, and product lines do occasionally change. I prefer to use the software RAID support provided by Linux, for a number of reasons:

- It's completely independent of the disk controllers you're using.

- It provides the same interface and customization mechanisms across all Linux distributions.

- Performance is actually quite good.

- It can be combined with Linux Logical Volume Management (LVM) to provide a powerful, flexible mechanism for storage expansion and management.

Hardware RAID arrays usually enable you to remove and replace failed drives without shutting down your system. This is known as *hot swapping*, because you can swap out drives while the system is running (i.e., "hot"). Hot swapping is supported by software RAID, but whether or not it's possible depends on the drive hardware you're using. If you're using removable or external FireWire, SCSI, or USB drives with software RAID (though most USB drives are too slow for this purpose), you can remove and replace failed drives on these interfaces without shutting down your system.

Mirroring and Redundancy

To support the removal and replacement of drives without anyone but you noticing, RAID provides services such as *mirroring*, which is the ability to support multiple volumes that are exact, real-time copies of each other. If a mirrored drive (or a drive that is part of a mirrored volume) fails or is taken offline for any other reason, the RAID system automatically begins using the failed drive's mirror, and no one notices its absence (except for the sysadmins who have to scurry for a replacement).

As protection against single-device failures, most RAID levels support the use of spare disks in addition to mirroring. Mirroring protects you when a single device in a RAID array fails, but at this point, you are immediately vulnerable to the failure of any other device that holds data for which no mirror is currently available. RAID's use of spare disks is designed to immediately reduce this vulnerability. In the event of a device failure, the RAID subsystem immediately allocates one of the spare disks and begins creating a new mirror there for you. When using spare disks in conjunction with mirroring, you really only have a non-mirrored disk array for the amount of time it takes to clone the mirror to the spare disk. However, as explained in the next section, the automatic use of spare disks is supported only for specific RAID levels.

RAID is *not* a replacement for doing backups. RAID ensures that your systems can continue functioning and that users and applications can have uninterrupted access to mirrored data in the event of device failure. However, the simultaneous failure of multiple devices in a RAID array can still take your system down and make the data that was stored on those devices unavailable. If your primary storage fails, only systems of which you have done backups (from which data can therefore be restored onto your new disks) can be guaranteed to come back up.

Overview of RAID Levels

The different capabilities provided by hardware and software RAID are grouped into what are known as different RAID *levels*. The following list describes the most common of these (for information about other RAID levels or more detailed information about the ones listed here, grab a book on RAID and some stimulants to keep you awake):

RAID-0

Often called *stripe mode*, volumes are created in parallel across all of the devices that are part of the RAID array, allocating storage from each in order to provide as many opportunities for parallel reads and writes as possible. This RAID level is strictly for performance and does not provide any redundancy in the event of a hardware failure.

RAID-1

Usually known as *mirroring*, volumes are created on single devices and exact copies (mirrors) of those volumes are maintained in order to provide protection from the failure of a single disk through redundancy. For this reason, you cannot create a RAID-1 volume that is larger than the smallest device that makes up a part of the RAID array. However, as explained in this hack, you can combine Linux LVM with RAID-1 to overcome this limitation.

RAID-4

RAID-4 is a fairly uncommon RAID level that requires three or more devices in the RAID array. One of the drives is used to store parity information that can be used to reconstruct the data on a failed drive in the array. Unfortunately, storing this parity information on a single drive exposes this drive as a potential single point of failure.

RAID-5

One of the most popular RAID levels, RAID-5 requires three or more devices in the RAID array and enables you to support mirroring through parity information without restricting the parity information to a single

device. Parity information is distributed across all of the devices in the
RAID array, removing the bottleneck and potential single point of failure in RAID-4.

RAID-10

A high-performance modern RAID option, RAID-10 provides mirrored
stripes, which essentially gives you a RAID-1 array composed of two
RAID-0 arrays. The use of striping offsets the potential performance
degradation of mirroring and doesn't require calculating or maintaining
parity information anywhere.

In addition to these RAID levels, Linux software RAID also supports *linear
mode*, which is the ability to concatenate two devices and treat them as a single large device. This is rarely used any more because it provides no redundancy and is functionally identical to the capabilities provided by LVM.

Combining Software RAID and LVM

Now we come to the conceptual meat of this hack. Native RAID devices
cannot be partitioned. Therefore, unless you go to a hardware RAID solution, the software RAID modes that enable you to concatenate drives and
create large volumes don't provide the redundancy that RAID is intended to
provide. Many of the hardware RAID solutions available on motherboards
export RAID devices only as single volumes, due to the absence of onboard
volume management software. RAID array vendors get around this by selling RAID arrays that have built-in software (which is often Linux-based)
that supports partitioning using an internal LVM package. However, you
can do this yourself by layering Linux LVM over the RAID disks in your systems—in other words, by using software RAID drives as physical volumes
that you then allocate and export to your system as logical volumes. Voilà!
Combining RAID and LVM gives you flexible volume management with the
warm fuzzy feeling of redundancy provided by RAID levels such as 1, 5, and
10. It just doesn't get much better than that.

Creating RAID Devices

RAID devices are created by first defining them in the file */etc/raidtab* and
then using the mkraid command to actually create the RAID devices specified in the configuration file.

For example, the following */etc/raidtab* file defines a linear RAID array composed of the physical devices */dev/hda6* and */dev/hdb5*:

```
raiddev /dev/md0
        raid-level              linear
        nr-raid-disks           2
```

```
        chunk-size              32
        persistent-superblock   1
        device                  /dev/hda6
        raid-disk               0
        device                  /dev/hdb5
        raid-disk               1
```

Executing the mkraid command to create the device */dev/md0* would produce output like the following:

```
# mkraid /dev/md0
handling MD device /dev/md0
analyzing super-block
disk 0: /dev/hda6, 10241406kB, raid superblock at 10241280kB
disk 1: /dev/hdb5, 12056751kB, raid superblock at 12056640kB
```

If you are recycling drives that you have previously used for some other purpose on your system, the mkraid command may complain about finding
existing filesystems on the disks that you are allocating to your new RAID
device. Double-check that you have specified the right disks in your */etc/
raidtab* file, and then use the mkraid command's -f option to force it to use
the drives, regardless.

At this point, you can create your favorite type of filesystem on the device
/dev/md0 by using the mkfs command and specifying the type of filesystem
by using the appropriate -t *type* option. After creating your filesystem,
you can then update the */etc/fstab* file to mount the new volume wherever
you want, and you're in business.

A linear RAID array is RAID at its most primitive, and isn't really useful now
that Linux provides mature logical volume support. The */etc/raidtab* configuration file for a RAID-1 (mirroring) RAID array that mirrors the single-par-
tition disk */dev/hdb1* using the single partition */dev/hde1* would look
something like the following:

```
raiddev /dev/md0
        raid-level          1
        nr-raid-disks       2
        nr-spare-disks      0
        chunk-size          4
        persistent-superblock 1
        device              /dev/hdb1
        raid-disk           0
        device              /dev/hde1
        raid-disk           1
```

Other RAID levels are created by using the same configuration file but specifying other mandatory parameters, such as a third disk for RAID levels 4 and
5, and so on. See the references at the end of this hack for pointers to more
detailed information about creating and using devices at other RAID levels.

An important thing to consider when creating mirrored RAID devices is the amount of load they will put on your system's device controllers. When creating mirrored RAID devices, you should always try to put the drive and its mirror on separate controllers so that no single drive controller is overwhelmed by disk update commands.

Combining RAID and LVM

As mentioned earlier, RAID devices can't be partitioned. This generally means that you have to use RAID devices in their entirety, as a single filesystem, or that you have to use many small disks and create a RAID configuration file that is Machiavellian in its complexity. A better alternative to both of these (and the point of this hack) is that you can combine the strengths of Linux software RAID and Linux LVM to get the best of both worlds: the safety and redundancy of RAID with the flexibility of LVM. It's important to create logical volumes on top of RAID storage and not the reverse, though—even software RAID is best targeted directly at the underlying hardware, and trying to (for example) mirror logical devices would stress your system and slow performance as both the RAID and LVM levels competed to try to figure out what should be mirrored where.

Combining RAID and LVM is quite straightforward. Instead of creating a filesystem directly on top of /dev/md0, you define /dev/md0 as a physical volume that can be associated with a volume group [Hack #46]. You then create whatever logical volumes you need within that volume group, format them as described earlier in this hack, and mount and use them however you like on your system.

If you decide to use Linux software RAID and LVM and support for these is not compiled into your kernel, you must remember to update any initial RAM disks that you use to include the RAID and LVM kernel modules. I generally use a standard *ext2/ext3* partition for /boot on my systems, which is where the kernel and initial RAM disks live. This avoids bootstrapping problems, such as when the system needs information from a logical volume or RAID device but has not yet loaded the kernel modules necessary to get that information.

To expand your storage after creating this sort of setup, you physically add additional new devices to your system, define the new RAID device in /etc/raidtab (as /dev/md1, etc.), and run the mkraid command followed by the name of the new device to have your system create and recognize it as a RAID volume. You then create a new physical volume on the resulting device, add that to your existing volume group, and then either create new logical volumes in that volume group or use the lvextend command to increase the size of your existing volumes. Here's a sample sequence of commands to do all of this (using the mirrored */etc/raidtab* from the previous section):

```
# mkraid /dev/md0
# pvcreate /dev/md0
# vgcreate data /dev/md0
# vgdisplay data | grep "Total PE"
  Total PE              59618
# lvcreate -n music -l 59618 data
  Logical volume "music" created
# mkfs -t xfs /dev/data/music
meta-data=/dev/mapper/data-music isize=256    agcount=16, agsize=3815552 blks
         =                       sectsz=512
data     =                       bsize=4096    blocks=61048832, imaxpct=25
         =                       sunit=0       swidth=0 blks, unwritten=1
naming   =version 2              bsize=4096
log      =internal log           bsize=4096    blocks=29809, version=1
         =                       sectsz=512    sunit=0 blks
realtime =none                   extsz=65536   blocks=0, rtextents=0
# mount /dev/mapper/data-music /mnt/music
```

These commands create a mirrored RAID volume called */dev/md0* using the storage on */dev/hdb1* and */dev/hde1* (which live on different controllers), allocate the space on */dev/md0* as a physical volume, create a volume group called *data* using this physical volume, and then create a logical volume called *music* that uses all of the storage available in this volume group. The last two commands then create an XFS filesystem on the logical volume and mount that filesystem on */mnt/music* so that it's available for use. To make sure that your new logical volume is automatically mounted each time you boot your system, you'd then add the following entry to your */etc/fstab* file:

```
/dev/data/music  /mnt/music    xfs    defaults,noatime    0 0
```

> Specifying the noatime option in the */etc./fstab* mount options for my logical volume tells the filesystem not to update inodes each time the files or directories associated with them are accessed.

Until the Linux LVM system supports mirroring, combining software RAID and LVM will give you the reliability and redundancy of RAID with the flexibility and power of LVM. Combining software RAID and LVM on Linux is conceptually elegant and can help you create a more robust, flexible, and reliable system environment. Though RAID levels that support mirroring require multiple disks and thus "waste" some potential disk storage by devoting it to mirroring rather than actual, live storage, you'll be glad that you used them if any of your disks ever fail.

See Also

- Linux software RAID HOWTO: *http://unthought.net/Software-RAID. HOWTO/Software-RAID.HOWTO.html*

- "Create Flexible Storage with LVM" [Hack #46]

HACK #48 Create a Copy-on-Write Snapshot of an LVM Volume

Logical volumes don't just provide a great way to supply flexible storage— they can also provide a great way to preserve files that have changed recently, simplifying restores and reducing restore requests.

A snapshot is a copy of a logical volume that reflects the contents of that logical volume when the snapshot was created. With a *copy-on-write snapshot*, each time a file changes in the original volume, the contents of the original file (as of the time that the snapshot was made) are preserved in the snapshot volume. In other words, the complete contents of the original file are copied to the snapshot volume when you write changes to the file in the original volume. Implementing a copy-on-write volume to track changed files is like having a built-in backup mechanism, because it provides you with a point-in-time copy of the filesystem that is contained on your logical volume. This copy of your filesystem can then be used for retrieving files that have accidentally been deleted or modified. For system administrators, copy-on-write snapshots can be particularly useful in preserving the original copies of system configuration files (just in case you ever make a mistake). However, their real beauty is in preserving copies of volumes containing users' home directories. I've found that taking a nightly snapshot of the logical volume that contains the users' home directories and automatically mounting it enables most users to satisfy their own restore requests by simply retrieving the original copies of lost or incorrectly modified files from the snapshot. This makes them happier and also lightens my workload. Not a bad combination!

This hack explains how to create a snapshot of an existing volume and mount it, and provides some examples of how the snapshot preserves your original files when they are modified in the parent volume.

Kernel Support for Snapshots

Snapshots of logical volumes are created and maintained with the help of the *dm_snapshot* filesystem driver. This is built as a loadable kernel module on most modern Linux distributions. If you cannot find this module or snapshots simply do not work on your system, cd to your kernel source directory (typically */usr/src/linux*) and check your kernel configuration file to make sure this module is either built in or available as a kernel module, as in the following example:

```
$ cd /usr/src/linux
$ grep -i DM-SNAPSHOT .config
CONFIG_SM_SNAPSHOT=m
```

In this case, the *dm-snapshot* driver is available as a loadable kernel module. If the value of the CONFIG_DM_SNAPSHOT configuration variable is n, this option is not available in your kernel. You will have to rebuild your kernel with this driver built in (a value of y) or as a loadable kernel module (a value of m) in order to take advantage of logical volume snapshots as discussed in this hack.

> Even if the *dm_snapshot* module is available on your system, you may need to manually load it using the standard modprobe command, as in the following example:
>
> ```
> # modprobe dm_snapshot
> ```

Creating a Snapshot

This section explains how to create a snapshot of an existing filesystem. The filesystem that you are taking a snapshot of must reside on a logical volume, as shown by the presence of the device mapper directory in the following example:

```
# df -Ph /test
Filesystem              Size  Used Avail Use% Mounted on
/dev/mapper/testvg-testvol 485M   18M  442M   4% /test
```

Next we'll use the dd command to create a few sample files in the test volume for use in testing later in this hack:

```
# dd if=/dev/zero of=/test/5M bs=1048576 count=5
5+0 records in
5+0 records out
# dd if=/dev/zero of=/test/10M bs=1048576 count=10
10+0 records in
10+0 records out
```

To create a snapshot of the *testvol* volume, execute a command like the following:

```
# lvcreate -s -L 100M -n testsnap /dev/testvg/testvol
  Logical volume "testsnap" created
```

In this example, I allocated 100 MB for the snapshot. This means that we can make 100 MB in changes to the original volume before the snapshot is full. Snapshots eventually fill up because they are preserving old data, and there is no way to purge the files that it has preserved because it is a snapshot of another volume, not an original logical volume itself. Once a snapshot is 100% used, it becomes useless—you must remove it and create a new snapshot.

To confirm that the snapshot was created correctly, use the lvs command to display logical volume status information:

```
# lvs
LV        VG     Attr   LSize   Origin  Snap% Move Copy%
testsnap  testvg swi-a- 100.00M testvol  0.02
testvol   testvg owi-ao 500.00M
```

Mounting a Snapshot

Having a snapshot of a logical volume is fairly useless unless you enable people to access it. To mount the sample *testsnap* snapshot, use a standard mount command such as the following:

```
# mount /dev/testvg/testsnap /testsnap
# df -Ph /test*
Filesystem                  Size  Used Avail Use% Mounted on
/dev/mapper/testvg-testvol  485M   18M  442M   4% /test
/dev/mapper/testvg-testsnap 485M   18M  442M   4% /testsnap
```

> Note that a snapshot volume always lives in the same volume group as the logical volume of which it is a copy.

Just to be sure, you can use the ls command to verify that both the snapshot and the original volume are available:

```
# ls -l /test
total 15436
-rw-r--r--  1 root root 10485760 Apr 21 23:48 10M
-rw-r--r--  1 root root  5242880 Apr 21 23:48 5M
drwx------  2 root root    12288 Apr 21 23:15 lost+found

# ls -l /testsnap/
total 15436
-rw-r--r--  1 root root 10485760 Apr 21 23:48 10M
-rw-r--r--  1 root root  5242880 Apr 21 23:48 5M
drwx------  2 root root    12288 Apr 21 23:15 lost+found
```

Now, create a 50-MB file in the */test* filesystem and examine what happens to the */testsnap* filesystem and the snapshot usage (using our favorite lvs command):

```
# dd if=/dev/zero of=/test/50M bs=1048576 count=50
50+0 records in
50+0 records out
# df -Ph /test*
Filesystem                  Size  Used Avail Use% Mounted on
/dev/mapper/testvg-testvol  485M   68M  392M  15% /test
/dev/mapper/testvg-testsnap 485M   18M  442M   4% /testsnap
# ls -l /test
total 66838
```

```
-rw-r--r--  1 root root 10485760 Apr 21 23:48 10M
-rw-r--r--  1 root root 52428800 Apr 22 00:09 50M
-rw-r--r--  1 root root  5242880 Apr 21 23:48 5M
drwx------  2 root root    12288 Apr 21 23:15 lost+found
# ls -l /testsnap/
total 15436
-rw-r--r--  1 root root 10485760 Apr 21 23:48 10M
-rw-r--r--  1 root root  5242880 Apr 21 23:48 5M
drwx------  2 root root    12288 Apr 21 23:15 lost+found
# lvs
   LV       VG     Attr   LSize   Origin  Snap%  Move Copy%
   testsnap testvg swi-ao 100.00M testvol 50.43
   testvol  testvg owi-ao 500.00M
```

Notice that the 50-MB file does not immediately show up in /testsnap, but some of the snapshot space has been used up (50.43%).

Next, simulate a user accidentally removing a file by removing /test/10M and examine the results:

```
# rm /test/10M
rm: remove regular file `/test/10M'? y
# df -Ph /test*
Filesystem                   Size  Used Avail Use% Mounted on
/dev/mapper/testvg-testvol   485M   58M  402M  13% /test
/dev/mapper/testvg-testsnap  485M   18M  442M   4% /testsnap
```

Note that disk space utilization in your snapshot increased slightly:

```
# lvs
   LV       VG     Attr   LSize   Origin  Snap%  Move Copy%
   testsnap testvg swi-ao 100.00M testvol 50.44
   testvol  testvg owi-ao 500.00M
```

> When using the lvs command after significant file opera-
> tions, you may need to wait a few minutes for the data that
> lvs uses to be updated.

If you now need to recover the file 10M, you can get it back by simply copying it out of the snapshot (to somewhere safe). Say goodbye to most of your restore headaches!

Remember, once the snapshot is 100% full, its contents can no longer be relied upon, because no new files can be written to it and it is therefore no longer useful for tracking recent updates to its parent volume. You should monitor the size of your snapshots and recreate them as needed. I find that recreating them once a week and remounting them keeps them up to date and also usually prevents "snapshot overflow."

See Also

- Snapshot section of the LVM HWOTO: *http://www.tldp.org/HOWTO/ LVM-HOWTO/snapshots_backup.html*
- "Create Flexible Storage with LVM" [Hack #46]
- "Combine LVM and Software RAID" [Hack #47]

—Lance Tost

HACK #49 Clone Systems Quickly and Easily

Once you've customized and fine-tuned a sample machine, you can quickly and easily deploy other systems based on its configuration by simply cloning it.

Now that Linux is in widespread use, many businesses that don't want to roll their own Linux systems simply deploy out-of-the-box systems based on supported distributions from sources such as SUSE, Mandriva, Turbo Linux, and Red Hat. Businesses that need a wider array of system or application software than these distributions provide often spend significant effort adding this software to their server and desktop systems, fine-tuning system configuration files, setting up networking, disabling unnecessary services, and setting up their corporate distributed authentication mechanisms. All of this takes a fair amount of time to get "just right"—it also takes time to replicate on multiple systems and can be a pain to recreate if this becomes necessary. You do have backups, don't you?

To speed up deploying multiple essentially identical systems, the classic Unix approach that I used to take in the "bad old days" was to purchase large numbers of disks that were the same size, use the Unix *dd* utility to clone system disks containing my tricked out systems to new disks, and then deploy the cloned disks in each new system of the specified type. This still works, but the downside of this approach is that the *dd* utility copies every block on a disk, regardless of whether it's actually in use or not. This process can take hours, even for relatively small disks, and seems interminable when cloning today's larger (200-GB and up) drives.

Thanks to the thousands of clever people in the open source community, faster and more modern solutions to this classic problem are now readily available for Linux. The best known are Ghost for Linux (a.k.a. *g4l*, *http://sourceforge.net/ projects/g4l/*), which takes its name from the commercial *Ghost* software package from Symantec (formerly Norton) for Windows systems, and *partimage*, the popular GNU Partition Image application (*http://www.partimage.org*). Both of these are open source software packages that are designed to create compressed images of partitions on your systems and make it easy for you to restore these partition images on different drives. The Ghost for Linux software is largely targeted for use on bootable system disks and provides built-in support for transferring the compressed filesystem or disk images that it creates to central servers using FTP. It is therefore extremely useful when you need to boot and back up a system that won't boot on its own. This hack focuses on *partimage* because it is easier to build, deploy, and use as an application on a system that is currently running. Of course, you have to have enough local disk space to store the compressed filesystem images, but that's easy enough to dig up nowadays. Like Ghost for Linux, you can't use *partimage* to create an image of a filesystem that is currently mounted, because a mounted filesystem may change while the image is being created, which would be "a bad thing."

 The ability to create small, easily redeployed partition images is growing in popularity thanks to virtual machine software such as Xen, where each virtual machine requires its own root filesystem. Though many people use a loopback filesystem for this, those consume memory on both the host and client. *partimage* makes it easy to clone existing partitions that have been customized for use with Xen, which is something you can easily do while your system is running if you have already prepared a Xen root filesystem on its own partition.

partimage easily creates optimal, compressed images of almost any type of filesystem that you'd find on a Linux system (and even many that you would not). It supports *ext2fs/ext3fs*, FAT16/32, HFS, HPFS, JFS, NTFS, ReiserFS, UFS, and XFS partitions, though its support for both HFS (the older Mac OS filesystem) and NTFS (the Windows filesystem de jour) is still experimental.

Building partimage

partimage is easy enough to build, but it has a fair number of dependencies. To build *partimage*, you must build or already have installed the following libraries:

liblzo
> Used for fast compression. Available from *http://www.oberhumer.com/opensource/lzo*.

libmcrypt
> An encryption library required for newer versions of *partimage*. Available from *http://mcrypt.hellug.gr/lib/index.html*.

libnewt
> A text-oriented, semi-graphical interface. Available from *http://www.partimage.org/deps/newt-0.50.tar.gz*.

libslang

An internationalization package used by *newt*. Available from *http://www.s-lang.org*.

libssl

A Secure Sockets Layer library required for newer versions of *partimage*. Available from *http://www.openssl.org*. Must be built in shared mode after configuring it using the following `configure` command:

```
# ./configure --prefix=/usr -shared
```

libz

Used for *gzip* compression. Available from *http://www.zlib.org*.

libbz2

Necessary for *bzip2* compression. Available at *http://sources.redhat.com/bzip2*.

Once you've built and installed any missing libraries, you can configure and compile *partimage* using the standard commands for building most modern open source software:

```
# ./configure && make install
```

The fun begins once the build and installation is complete. The final product of the `make` command is two applications: *partimage*, which is the application that you run on a system to create an image of an existing partition; and *partimaged*, which is a daemon that you can run on a system in order to be able to save partition images to it over the network, much like the built-in FTP support provided by Ghost for Linux.

At the time that this book was written, the latest version of *partimage* was 0.6.4, which was not 64-bit clean and could not be compiled successfully on any of my 64-bit systems. If you need to run *partimage* on a 64-bit system and no newer version is available by the time that you read this (or if you're just in a hurry), you can always download precompiled static binaries for your Linux system. Precompiled static binaries are available from the *partimage* download page listed at the end of this hack.

Cloning Partitions Using partimage

Using *partimage* to create a copy of an existing unmounted partition is easy. Because *partimage* needs raw access to partitions, you must execute the partimage command as root or via sudo. As shown in Figure 5-1, the initial *partimage* screen enables you to select the partition of which you want to create an image, the full pathname to which you want to save the partition image, and the operation that you want to perform (in this case, saving a partition into a file). To move to the next screen, press F5 or use the Tab key to select the Next button and press Enter.

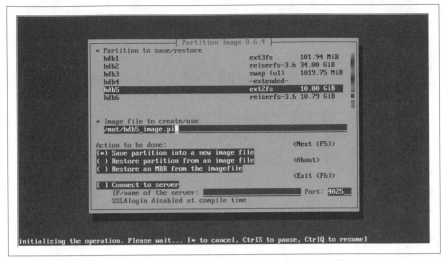

Figure 5-1. Selecting a partition to image and specifying the output file

The second *partimage* backup screen, shown in Figure 5-2, enables you to specify the compression mechanism that you want to use in the image file. Here you can specify that you want to check the consistency of the partition that you are imaging before creating the partition image file, which is always a good idea since you don't want to clone an inconsistent filesystem. You can also optionally specify that you want to add a descriptive comment to the file, which is often a good idea if you are going to be saving and working with a large number of partition image files. You can also specify what *partimage* should do after the image file has been created: wait for input, quit automatically, halt the machine, and so on. (The latter is probably only useful if you've booted from a rescue disk containing *partimage* in order to image one of the system partitions on your primary hard drive.) Press F5 to proceed to the next screen.

> Note that the existing type of the partition in */dev/hdb6* is ReiserFS. The existing type of the target partition and the size of the partition that was backed up do not matter (as long as the target partition can hold the uncompressed contents of the partition image file). When restoring a partition image, the partition that is being populated with its contents is automatically created using the same type of filesystem as was used in the filesystem contained in the image file, but using all available space on the target partition.

If you specified that you wanted to check the consistency of the filesystem before imaging it, *partimage* checks the filesystem and displays a summary

Clone Systems Quickly and Easily

```
┌──────────────────┤ save partition to image file ├──────────────────┐
│ Compression level                                                   │
│ ( ) None (very fast + very big file)                                │
│ (*) Gzip (.gz: medium speed + small image file)                     │
│ ( ) Bzip2 (.bz2: very slow + very small image file)                 │
│                                                                     │
│ Options                         If finished successfully:           │
│ [X] Check partition before saving      (*) Wait                     │
│ [X] Enter description                   ( ) Halt                     │
│ [ ] Overwrite without prompt            ( ) Reboot                   │
│                                         ( ) Quit                     │
│ Image split mode                        ( ) Last                    │
│ (*) Automatic split (when no space left)                            │
│ ( ) Into files whose size is:............ 2037     MiB              │
│ [ ] Wait after each volume change                                   │
│                                                                     │
│    ◄Continue (F5)►        ◄Exit (F6)►          ◄Main window (F7)►   │
└─────────────────────────────────────────────────────────────────────┘
 initializing the operation. Please wait... [* to cancel, CtrlS to pause, CtrlQ to resume]
```

Figure 5-2. Specifying compression methods and other options

screen that you can close after reviewing it by pressing Enter. *partimage* then proceeds to create an image file of the specified partition, as shown in Figure 5-3, displaying a summary screen when the image has been successfully created. If you specified Wait (i.e., wait for input—the default) as the action to perform after creating the image file, you will have to press Enter to close the summary screen and exit *partimage*.

```
┌──────────────────┤ save partition to image file ├──────────────────┐
│ Partition to save:...........dev/hdb5                               │
│ Size of the Partition:.......10.00 GiB = 10742183424 bytes          │
│ Current image file:..........mnt/hdb5_image.pi.000                  │
│ Image file size:.............8.16 MiB                               │
│ Available space for image:...10.73 GiB = 11518062592 bytes          │
│ Detected file system:........ext2fs                                 │
│ Compression level:...........gzip                                   │
│                                                                     │
│                                                                     │
│ Time elapsed:................9sec                                   │
│ Estimated time remaining:....7m:47sec                               │
│ Speed:.......................352.97 MiB/min                         │
│ Data copied:.................52.95 MiB / 2.74 GiB                   │
│                                                                     │
│ ─────────────────────────────1%───────────────────────  1 %        │
└─────────────────────────────────────────────────────────────────────┘
 copying used data blocks [* to cancel, CtrlS to pause, CtrlQ to resume]
```

Figure 5-3. Creating the partition image file

Restoring Partitions Using partimage

Using *partimage* to restore a partition image to an existing partition is even simpler than creating the image in the first place. The initial *partimage* restore screen, shown in Figure 5-4, is the same as that shown in Figure 5-1. It enables you to identify the partition to which you want to restore the partition image, the name of the image file that you want to restore from, and the action that you want to perform (in this case, restoring a partition from a file). To move to the next screen, press F5 or use the Tab key to select the Next button and press Enter.

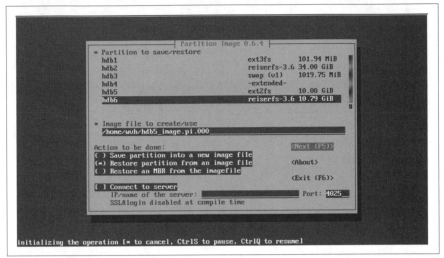

Figure 5-4. Selecting a partition to restore to and the partition image file

The second *partimage* restore screen, shown in Figure 5-5, enables you to run a consistency check by performing a dry run of restoring from the image file and also enables you to zero out unused blocks on the target filesystem when it is created. As with the image-creation process, you can also specify what *partimage* should do after the image file has been restored: wait for input, quit automatically, halt or reboot the machine, and so on. Press F5 to proceed to the next screen.

partimage then proceeds to restore the partition image file to the specified partition, as shown in Figure 5-6, displaying a summary screen by default when the image has been successfully restored. If you specified Wait (i.e., wait for input—the default) as the action to perform after creating the image file, you will have to press Enter to close the summary screen and exit *partimage*.

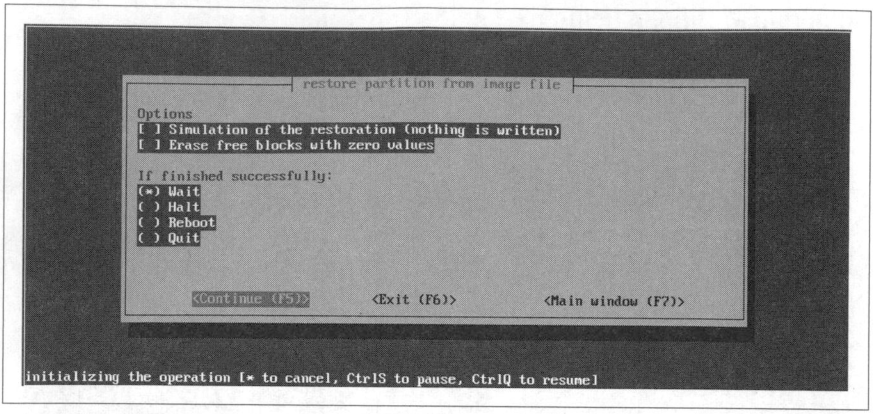

Figure 5-5. Specifying restore options and completion behavior

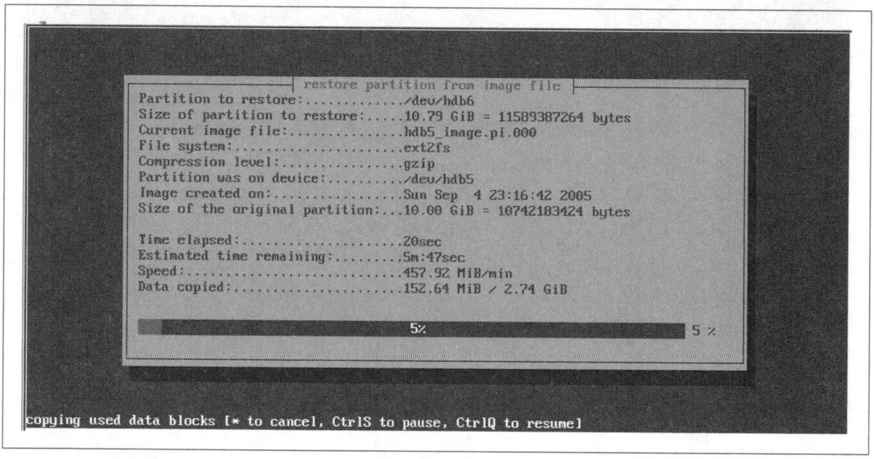

Figure 5-6. Restoring the partition image

Summary

Creating partition image files of customized, optimized, and fine-tuned desktop and server partitions provides a quick and easy way of cloning those systems to new hardware. You can always clone partitions containing applications, such as */opt*, */var*, */usr*, and */usr/local*. (Your actual partition scheme is, of course, up to you.) If your new systems have the same devices as the system on which the image file was created, you can even easily copy pre-configured system partitions such as */boot* and */ itself. Either way, applications such as *partimage* can save you lots of time in configuring additional hardware by enabling you to reuse your existing customizations as many times as you want to.

See Also

- "Make Disk-to-Disk Backups for Large Drives" [Hack #50]
- Ghost for Linux home page: *http://sourceforge.net/projects/g4l/*
- Ghost for Linux download page: *ftp://fedoragcc.dyndns.org*
- *partimage* home page: *http://www.partimage.org*
- *partimage* download page: *http://www.partimage.org/download.en.html*
- System Rescue CD home page: *http://www.sysresccd.org*

Make Disk-to-Disk Backups for Large Drives

Today's hard drives are large enough that you could spend the rest of your life backing them up to tape. Putting drive trays in your servers and using removable drives as a backup destination provides a modern solution.

Some of us are old, and therefore remember when magnetic tape was the de facto backup medium for any computer system. Disk drives were small, and tapes were comparatively large. Nowadays, the reverse is generally true—disk drives are huge, and few tapes can hold more than a fraction of a drive's capacity. But these facts shouldn't be used as an excuse to skip doing backups! Backups are still necessary, and they may be more critical today than ever, given that the failure of a single drive can easily cause you to lose multiple partitions and hundreds of gigabytes of data.

Luckily, dynamic device buses such as USB and FireWire (a.k.a. IEEE 1094) and adaptors for inexpensive ATA drives to these connection technologies provide inexpensive ways of making any media removable without disassembling your system. Large, removable, rewritable media can truly simplify life for you (and your operators, if you're lucky enough to have some). A clever combination of removable media and a good backup strategy will make it easy for you to adapt disk drives to your systems to create large, fast, removable media devices that can solve your backup woes and also get you home in time for dinner (today's dinner, even). If you're fortunate enough to work somewhere that can buy the latest, partial terabyte backup tape technology, I'm proud to know you. This hack is for the rest of us.

Convenient Removable Media Technologies for Backups

Depending on the type of interfaces available on your servers, an easy way to roll your own removable media is to purchase external drive cases that provide USB or FireWire interfaces, but in which you can insert today's largest IDE or SATA disk drives. Because both USB and FireWire support dynamic device detection, you can simply attach a new external drive to your server and power it up, and the system will assign it a device identifier. If you don't know every possible device on your system, you can always check the tail of your system's logfile, */var/log/messages*, to determine the name of the device associated with the drive you've just attached. Depending on how your system is configured, you may also need to insert modules such as *uhci_hcd*, *ehci_hcd*, and *usb_storage* in order to get your system to recognize new USB storage devices, or *ohci1394* for FireWire devices.

> This presumes that the default USB and FireWire controller modules (*usbcore* and *sbp2*, respectively) are already being loaded by your kernel (as well as the SCSI emulation module, *scsi_mod*, if you need it), and that what you really need is support for recognizing hot-plug storage devices.

Empty external drive cases with USB and/or FireWire interfaces start at around $35 on eBay or from your local computer vendor, but can run much higher if you decide you want a case that holds multiple drives. I was a Boy Scout eons ago and have been a sysadmin for a long time, and I like to "be prepared." I therefore further hedge my external drive options by putting drive trays in the external cases, so that I can quickly and easily swap drives in and out of the external cases without having to look for a screwdriver in a time of crisis.

Figure 5-7 shows a sample drive tray. Drive trays come with a small rack that you mount in a standard drive bay and a drive tray into which you insert your hard drive. This combination makes it easy to swap hard drives in and out of the external drive case without opening it. I also put drive racks in the standard drive bays in my servers so that I can quickly add or replace drives as needed.

> If you decide to use USB as the underpinnings of a removable media approach to backups, make sure that the USB ports on your servers support USB 2.0. USB 1.x is convenient and fine for printing, connecting a keyboard or mouse, and so on, when speed is really not a factor. However, it's painfully slow when transferring large amounts of data, which is the best-case scenario for new backups and the worst-case scenario for all others.

Figure 5-7. A removable drive rack with drive tray inserted

Choosing the Right Backup Command

Once you have a mechanism for attaching removable storage devices to your system and have a few large drives ready, it's important to think through the mechanism that you'll use for backups. Most traditional Unix backups are done using specialized backup and restore commands called dump and restore, but these commands take advantage of built-in knowledge about filesystem internals and therefore aren't portable across all of the different filesystems available for Linux. (A version of these commands for *ext2/ext3* filesystems is available at *http://dump.sourceforge.net.*) Another shortcoming of the traditional dump/restore commands for Unix/Linux is that they reflect their origins in the days of mag tapes by creating output data in their own formats in single output files (or, traditionally, a stream written to tape). This is also true of more generic archiving commands that are also often used for backups, such as tar, cpio, and pax.

If you're using logical volumes, "Create a Copy-on-Write Snapshot of an LVM Volume" [Hack #48] explained how to create a copy-on-write snapshot of a volume that automatically picks up a copy of any file that's modified on its parent volume. That's fine for providing a mechanism that enables people to recover copies of files that they've just deleted, which satisfies the majority of restore requests. However, copy-on-write volumes don't satisfy the most basic tenet of backups—*thou shalt not store backups on-site*. (There are exceptions, such as if you're using a sophisticated distributed filesystem such as AFS or OpenAFS, but that's a special case that we'll ignore here.) The removable storage approach satisfies the off-site backup rule as long as you actually take the backup drives elsewhere.

So I can use the same backup scripts and commands regardless of the type of Linux filesystem that I'm backing up, I prefer to use file- and directory-level commands such as cp rather than filesystem-level commands. This is easy to do when doing disk-to-disk backups, because the backup medium is actually a disk that contains a filesystem that I mount before starting the backup. After mounting the drive, I use a script that invokes cp to keep the backup drive synchronized with the contents of the filesystem that I'm backing up, using a cp command such as the following:

```
# cp –dpRux /home /mnt/home-backup
```

As you can see from this example, the script creates mount points for the backup filesystems that indicate their purpose, which makes it easier for other sysadmins to know why a specific drive is mounted on any given system. I use names that append the string *–backup* to the name of the filesystem that I'm backing up—therefore, */mnt/home-backup* is used as a mount point for the backup filesystem for the filesystem mounted as */home*. You're welcome to choose your own naming convention, but this seems intuitive to me. The cp options that I use have the following implications:

d   Don't dereference symbolic links (i.e., copy them as symbolic links rather than copying what they point to).

p   Preserve modes and ownership of the original files in the copies.

R   Recursively copy the specified directory.

u   Copy files only when the original file is newer than an existing copy, or if no copy exists.

v   Display information about each file that is copied.

x   Don't follow mount points to other filesystems.

The Code

The actual script that I use to do these sorts of backups is the following (feel free to use or modify it if you'd like):

```bash
#!/bin/bash
#
# wvh's simple backup script using cp
#

if [ $# != 2 ] ; then
    echo "  Usage: cp_backup partition backup-device"
    echo "  Example: cp_backup /home /dev/sda1"
    exit
fi

VERBOSE="no"
STDOPTS="-dpRux"
LOGFILE="/var/log/backup/simple.log"

TARGETBASE=`echo $1 | sed -e 's;^\/;;' -e 's;\/;-;g'`
FULLTARGET="/mnt/"$TARGETBASE"-backup"
DATE=`date`
export BACKUPTASK="$1 to $2"

trap cleanup 1 2 3 6

cleanup()
{
  echo "  Uh-oh, caught signal: tidying up..." | tee -a $LOGFILE
  DATE=`date`
  umount $FULLTARGET
  echo "Aborted simple backups of $BACKUPTASK $DATE" | tee -a $LOGFILE
  exit 1
}

if [ ! -d /var/log/backup ] ; then
    mkdir -p /var/log/backup
fi

echo "Starting simple backups of $BACKUPTASK at $DATE" | tee -a $LOGFILE

if [ ! -d $FULLTARGET ] ; then
    echo "  Creating mountpoint $FULLTARGET" | tee -a $LOGFILE
    mkdir -p $FULLTARGET
fi

MOUNTED=`df | grep $FULLTARGET`

if [ "x$MOUNTED" != "x" ] ; then
    echo "  Something is already mounted at $FULLTARGET - exiting" | tee -a
$LOGFILE
    exit
fi
```

```
mount $2 $FULLTARGET

if [ x$? != "x0" ] ; then
    echo "  Mount of backup volume $2 failed - exiting" | tee -a $LOGFILE
    exit
fi


#
# This block keeps copies of important system files on all backup volumes
# in a special directory called .123_admin. They're small, it's only slow
# once, and I'm paranoid.
#
if [ ! -d $FULLTARGET"/.123_admin" ] ; then
    mkdir -p $FULLTARGET"/.123_admin/conf"
fi
echo "  Backing up system files to $FULLTARGET/.123_admin" | tee -a $LOGFILE
cd /etc
cp -u passwd group shadow $FULLTARGET"/.123_admin"
if [ -d sysconfig ] ; then
    cp -uR sysconfig $FULLTARGET"/.123_admin"
fi
find . -name "*.conf" -print | while read file ; do
    cp -u $file $FULLTARGET"/.123_admin/conf"
done


#
# Now we actually do the cp backups
#
DATE=`date`
echo "  Starting actual backup of $BACKUPTASK at $DATE" | tee -a $LOGFILE
cd $1

if [ x$VERBOSE != "xno" ] ; then
    cp $STDOPTS"v" . $FULLTARGET
else
    cp $STDOPTS . $FULLTARGET
fi

umount $FULLTARGET

DATE=`date`
echo "Completed simple backups of $BACKUPTASK at $DATE" | tee -a $LOGFILE
```

You'll note that I don't log each file that's being backed up, though that
would be easy to do if running the script in verbose mode by using the tee
command to clone the cp command's output to the logfile. The traditional
Unix/Linux dump and restore commands use the file */etc/dumpdates* to figure out which full and incremental backups to use in order to restore a specific file or filesystem, but this isn't necessary in this case because we're
copying the updated files from the specified partition to a full backup of that
partition, not just doing an incremental backup in traditional Unix/Linux
terms.

Running the Code

If you're following along at home, you can use this script by entering it in your favorite text editor, saving it to a file called *cp_backup* in */usr/local/bin*, making it executable (chmod 755 /usr/local/bin/cp_backup), and then executing it (after making sure that you've mounted a spare disk as a backup target, and that the spare disk is the same size as or larger than the filesystem that you want to back up). For example, to back up the partition mounted as */mnt/music* on my system (which contains 100% legally purchased music in digital form) to a 250-GB disk containing the single partition */dev/sda1*, I would use the following command:

```
# /usr/local/bin/cp_backup /mnt/music /dev/sda1
```

You can even automate these sorts of backups by adding an entry that executes them to root's *crontab* file. As the root user or via sudo, execute the crontab -e command and append a line like the following to the end of the file:

```
0 2 * * *        $/usr/local/bin/cp_backup /mnt/music /dev/sda1
```

This will run the *cp_backup* script to back up */mnt/music* to */dev/sda1* every night at 2 A.M.

Choosing What to Back Up

The previous sections explained why disk-to-disk backups are the smartest choice for low-cost backups of today's huge disk drives, and advocated file- and directory-level commands as an easy backup mechanism that is independent of the actual format of the filesystem that houses the data you're backing up. Keeping a large number of spare drives around can be costly, though, so I try to minimize the number of filesystems that I back up. The traditional Unix/Linux dump command does this through entries in the */etc/fstab* file that identify whether the filesystem should be backed up or not—if the entry in the next-to-last column in */etc/fstab* is non-zero, the filesystem will be backed up. My general rule is to only back up filesystems that contain user data. Standard Linux filesystems such as */* and */usr* can easily be recreated from the distribution media or from partition images [Hack #49]. Since the backup script I use keeps copies of system configuration files, I'm not that worried about preserving system configuration information.

Summary and Tips

This hack provides an overview of doing modern backups and a script that I use to do them on most of the systems I deploy. To use this approach, the target devices that you're backing up to have to have at least as much space as the filesystem that you're backing up, and you'll have to preen or wipe the daily backup devices every so often (generally after a full backup) in order to minimize the number of copies of files and directories that have been deleted from the live filesystem but still exist on the backup drives. If your systems use logical volumes that span multiple disks, you'll have to use equivalent, multi-disk backup devices, but they can often be simpler, cheaper devices than those that house your live data. For example, if you're backing up filesystems that live on a RAID array, you don't have to have a RAID backup device—you can get away with sets of drives that are large enough to hold the data itself, not its mirrors or checksum disks.

HACK #51 Free Up Disk Space Now

Moving large files to another partition isn't always an option, especially if running services are holding them open. Here are a few tips for truncating large files in emergency situations.

Server consolidation takes planning, and it usually means adjusting the way you set up your OS installations. Running multiple services on a single OS image means not only increased network traffic to the same hardware, but increased disk usage for logfiles.

What's more is that administrators' thirst for more data about the services they run has resulted in a tendency for logging to be more verbose these days than it was in the past, partially because the tools for analyzing the data are getting better.

However, someday you'll inevitably be faced with a situation where you're receiving pages from some form of service monitoring agent telling you that your web server has stopped responding to requests. When you log in, you immediately type df -h to see if what you suspect is true, and it is—your verbose logging has just bitten you by filling up the partition, leaving your web server unable to write to its logfiles, and it has subsequently stopped serving pages and become useless. What to do?

There are several commands you can use to deal with this. If the service is completely dead, you could actually move the file to another partition, or simply run rm -f *logfile* if you know that the data is not particularly useful. If the service is still running, however, and needs its logfile to be available in order to do anything useful, truncation may be the way to go. Some admins have a watchdog script that polls for large files created by noncritical services and truncates them before they get out of control, without having to restart the service. A command that might appear in a script to do this (which can also be issued at a command line) is:

```
$ cat /dev/null > filename
```

Obviously, you should run this command as root if the file you are truncating requires elevated privileges. Why use */dev/null*? You could also use the following command:

```
$ cat > filename
```

This is certainly a little shorter, but the downfall here is that it doesn't exit by itself—you need to terminate it manually. On the command line, that means typing Ctrl-C to exit.

While these commands definitely work, I'd like to show you what I believe to be the shortest file truncation command known to *bash*. It goes a little something like this:

```
$ > filename
```

The above command has no dependency on anything except for the redirection operator >. Essentially, you are redirecting what's on the left of the operator (which is to say, nothing) into the file in question. What makes this perfectly elegant is that it exits all by itself and leaves behind a file of zero bytes in length. What more could an admin ask for?

Technically, understanding what has happened above involves knowing how redirection in the shell works. In the *bash* shell, if the redirection operator is pointing to the right (i.e., >), what is being directed is the standard output of whatever is on the left. Since we've specified no command on the lefthand side, the standard output is nothing, and our redirection operator happily overwrites our large file, replacing the contents with...nothing.

HACK #52 Share Files Using Linux Groups

Traditional Unix/Linux groups have always made it easy to share files among users.

Though this is more of a basic system capability than a hack, creating files that other users can both read and write can be done in various ways. The easiest way to do this is to make all files and directories readable and writable by all users, which is the security equivalent of putting a sign on your computer reading, "Please screw this up." No sysadmin in his right mind would do this, and most would also want to protect their users against accidentally setting themselves up for a catastrophe by doing so.

This hack provides an overview of how to use Linux protections to create directories that can be protected at the group level, but in which all members of that group will be able to read and write files. This doesn't involve any special scripts or software packages, but provides a simple refresher that will help you help your users get their work done as efficiently as possible—and with as few phone calls or pages to you as possible.

Linux Protections 101

Basic Linux protection modes, inherited from Unix, provide the ability to protect files and directories at three basic levels:

- Owner-specific permissions that control what the person who owns a file can do
- Group-specific permissions that control what other members of the group that owns a file or directory can do
- One more set of permissions that control what anyone else on the system can do

These permissions are reflected in the leftmost entry in the long listing of any file or directory, as in the following example:

```
$ ls -al /home/top-secret
total 8
drwxrwx---  2 ts    top-secret   80 2005-07-04 16:02 .
drwxr-xr-x  8 root  root        184 2005-07-04 15:57 ..
-rw-r--r--  1 wvh   top-secret 5386 2005-07-04 16:02 wmd_overview.sxw
```

This listing shows three sets of Unix permissions: those for the directory in which the command was executed (.), those for that directory's parent directory (..), and those for a file in that directory (*wmd_overview.sxw*). The permissions for the directory show that it is owned by the user *ts* and the group *top-secret*, and that the directory can only be read, written to, or searched by the user *ts* or anyone in the *top-secret* group. The permissions entry for the *wmd_overview.sxw* file say that the file can be read or written to by its owner (*wvh*) and by any member of the *top-secret* group. In practice, this seems pretty straightforward—anyone in the *top-secret* group who needs to modify the *wmd_overview.sxw* file can just open it, make their changes, and save the file. Because only the user *ts* user and people in the *top-secret* group have access to the directory in the first place, it seems like a natural place for members of the group to create files that they can share with other group members.

Setting the umask to Create Sharable Files

The ownership and permissions on files that a user creates are controlled by three things: the user's user ID when creating the file, the group to which she belongs, and her default protection file settings, known as her *umask*. The umask is a numeric value that is subtracted from the permissions used when creating or saving files or directories.

In the previous example, assume that the users *wvh* and *juser* are both members of the *top-secret* group. The user *juser* creates a file called *juser_comments.txt* in the */home/top-secret* directory, but its protections are set to -rw-r--r--.

This means that no other user in the *top-secret* group can modify this file unless *juser* changes the permissions so that the file is also writable by group members, which can be done with either of the following commands:

```
$ chmod 660 juser_comments.txt
$ chmod g+w,o-r juser_comments.txt
```

You find out a user's default umask setting by issuing the umask command, which is a built-in command in most Linux shells. By default, most users' umasks are set to 0022 so that newly created files are writable only by their owners, as in the example in the previous paragraph.

Setting the user's umask to 0002 may seem like an easy way to ensure that files are created with permissions that enable other group members to modify them. This turns off the world-writable bit for the file, but leaves the group-writable bit set. However, there are two problems with this approach:

- It affects every file that the user creates, including files that are typically kept private, such as the user's mailbox.
- It applies only to the group to which the user belonged at the time the file was created.

If you want to use a group-writable umask setting everywhere, the first of these issues is usually solved by turning off the executable and read permissions for group members and standard users on your home directory. (In Unix/Linux permissions, the executable bit on a directory determines whether the directory is searchable.) This means that while the files being created there are writable by group members, group members can't view the directory or locate the files in the first place.

If you don't want to globally set your umask to create files that are group-writable, another common approach is to define an alias for file creation (in your shell's startup file, such as *~/.bashrc*) that automatically sets file permissions appropriately, as in the following example:

```
alias newfile=`(umask 0002 ; touch $1)`
```

This command forks a sub-shell, sets the umask within that shell, and then creates the file and exits the sub-shell. You can do the same sort of thing without forking a sub-shell by manually changing the file permissions within an alias:

```
alias newfile=`touch $1; chmod 660 $1`
```

Any of these solutions works fine if the group that you want to be able to share files with is the group that you initially belong to when you log in, known as your *login group*.

Linux enables users to belong to multiple groups at the same time, in order to let people work on multiple projects that are protected at the group level. For the purposes of creating files, Linux users function as members of a single group at any given time, and they can change the group that is in effect via the newgrp command. However, as explained in the next section, you can also set Linux directory protections to control the group that owns files created in a particular directory.

Using Directory Permissions to Set Group Membership

Directory permissions in Linux have a different impact on the group ownership of files created in a directory than they do in other Unix-like operating systems. On BSD-based systems, for example, files created in a directory are always created with the group ownership of the group that owns the directory. On Linux systems, files created in a directory retain the group membership of the user that was in effect at the time the file was created.

However, you can easily force group membership under Linux by taking advantage of a special permission mode, known as the *s-bit*. Unix systems have traditionally used this bit to enable users to run applications that require specific user or group privileges, but when set on a directory, the s-bit causes any files created in that directory to be created with the group membership of the directory itself. The s-bit on a directory is set using the command chmod g+s *filename*. If the s-bit is set on a specific directory, the x in the group permissions for that directory is replaced with an s.

The following is an example of group ownership after the s-bit has been set on the same */home/top-secret* directory (note the s in the executable bit of the group settings):

```
# chmod g+s /home/top-secret
# ls -al
total 8
drwxrws---  2 ts    top-secret   80 2005-07-04 16:02 .
drwxr-xr-x  8 root  root        184 2005-07-04 15:57 ..
-rw-r--r--  1 wvh   top-secret 5386 2005-07-04 16:02 wmd_overview.sxw
```

At this point, creating any file in this directory gives it the same group ownership as the directory, as in the following example:

```
$ touch testfile.txt
$ ls -al
total 8
drwxrws---  2 ts    top-secret  112 2005-07-04 16:06 .
drwxr-xr-x  8 root  root        184 2005-07-04 15:57 ..
-rw-r--r--  1 wvh   top-secret    0 2005-07-04 16:06 testfile.txt
-rw-rw-r--  1 wvh   top-secret 5386 2005-07-04 16:02 wmd_overview.sxw
```

Because of the umask settings discussed earlier, this file was created with a mode that made it both user- and group-writable, which is exactly what you want.

As you can see, Unix groups provide a useful and flexible mechanism for enabling users to share access to selected files and directories. They work in the same way on every modern Unix system, and thus provide a portable and standard protection mechanism.

See Also

- "Refine Permissions with ACLs" **[Hack #53]**

Refine Permissions with ACLs

#53
Access control lists bring granular permissions control to your files and directories.

Standard Unix/Linux file permissions are fine if you have a relatively small number of users with limited requirements for sharing and working on the same files. ("Share Files Using Linux Groups" **[Hack #52]** explained the classic approaches to enabling multiple users to work on the same files.) However, using groups to control shared access requires the intervention of a system administrator and can result in incredibly huge and complex */etc/group* files. This makes it difficult to set the group memberships for any new accounts correctly and requires frequent sysadmin intervention as users leave or move between projects. ACLs, which are supported in most modern Linux distributions, eliminate this hassle by providing a fine-grained set of permissions that users can impose on their own directories, going far beyond the permissions and protections provided by standard Linux groups.

Simply put, an ACL is a list of Linux users and/or groups and the access rights that they have to a specific file or directory. ACLs enable you to define totally granular permissions such as "only the users *wvh* and *alex* can write this file, but the user *juser* can at least read it" without requiring that you create any special-purpose Linux groups.

ACLs as implemented on Linux systems today are defined by the draft Portable Operating System Interface (POSIX) standard 1003.1e, draft 17, from the Institute of Electrical and Electronics Engineers (IEEE). This is not an official standard, but it is publicly available and has become the foundation for ACL implementations for modern operating systems such as Linux. (See the end of this hack for pointers to this document on the Web.)

Installing and Activating ACL Support

To use ACLs to enhance the granularity of permissions on your system, you must have several things in place:

- Your kernel must be compiled with both enhanced attribute and ACL support for the type(s) of filesystem(s) that you are using.

- Your filesystem(s) must be mounted with extended attribute and ACL support enabled [Hack #54].

- You must install the user-space ACL utilities (*chacl*, *getfacl*, and *setfacl*) in order to examine and set ACLs.

Kernel ACL support. Most modern Linux distributions provide support for ACLs in the default kernels that they deliver. If you have access to the configuration file used to build your kernel, you can use the *grep* utility to check to make sure that the POSIX_ACL configuration variable associated with the types of filesystems that you are using is set to y, as in the following example:

```
$ grep POSIX_ACL /boot/config-2.6.8-24.16-default
EXT2_FS_POSIX_ACL=y
EXT3_FS_POSIX_ACL=y
REISERFS_FS_POSIX_ACL=y
JFS_POSIX_ACL=y
XFS_POSIX_ACL=y
```

If the POSIX_ACL value associated with any of the types of filesystems you are using is set to n, you will have to enable it, save the updated kernel configuration, and recompile your kernel in order to use ACLs. To enable the appropriate POSIX_ACL value, you will also have to enable extended attributes for that filesystem. Extended attributes must be separately enabled for each type of filesystem you are using (with the exception of the XFS journaling filesystem, which inherently supports them). The kernel configuration options that enable them are located on the File Systems pane in your favorite kernel configuration editor (make xconfig, make menuconfig, and so on). See "Make Files Easier to Find with Extended Attributes" [Hack #54] for more information about enabling and using extended attributes.

fstab ACL support. Once you are running a kernel with support for POSIX ACLs, you will also need to make sure that the filesystems in which you want to use ACLs are mounted with ACL support enabled. Check your */etc/fstab* file to verify this. Filesystems mounted with ACL support will have the acl keyword in the mount options portions of their entries in the file. In the following example, the *reiserfs* filesystem on */dev/sda6* is mounted with ACL support, while the *ext3* filesystem on */dev/hda1* is not:

```
/dev/sda6    /usr    reiserfs    noatime,acl,user_xattr 1 2
/dev/hda1    /opt2   ext3        defaults               0 0
```

If your kernel supports ACLs, you can edit this file to enable ACL support when you initially mount a filesystem by adding the acl keyword to the mount options for that filesystem, as in the following example:

```
/dev/hda1   /opt2   ext3      defaults,acl        0 0
```

After updating this file, you can enable ACL support in currently mounted filesystems without rebooting by executing a command like the following, which would remount the example *ext3* filesystem */dev/hda1*, activating ACL support:

```
# mount -o remount,acl /dev/hda1
```

User-space ACL support. The last step in using ACLs on your system is to make sure that the user-space applications that enable you to display and set ACLs are present. If your system uses a package management system, you can query that system's database to see if the *acl* package and its associated library, *libacl*, are installed. The following is an example query on a system that uses RPM:

```
# rpm -qa | grep acl
acl-2.2.25-2
libacl-2.2.25-2
```

You can also look for the utilities themselves, using the which command:

```
# which getfacl
/usr/bin/getfacl
# which setfacl
/usr/bin/setfacl
# which chacl
/usr/bin/chacl
```

If the *acl* package is not installed and the binaries are not present on your system, you can find the source code or binary packages for your system by following links from *http://acl.bestbits.at*. You'll need to install these packages before continuing.

Overview of Linux ACLs and Utilities

Linux supports two basic types of ACLs:

- ACLs used to control access to specific files and directories
- Per-directory ACLs (known as *mask* ACLs), which define the default ACLs that will be assigned to any files created within that directory

Conversationally and in print, ACLs are represented in a standard format consisting of three colon-separated fields:

- The first field of an ACL entry is the entry type, which can be one of the following: *user* (u), *group* (g), *other* (o), or *mask* (m).

- The second field of an ACL entry is a username, numeric UID, group name, or numeric GID, depending on the value of the first field. If this field is empty, the ACL refers to the user or group that owns the file or directory. *mask* and *other* ACLs must have an empty second field.

- The third field lists the access permissions for the ACL. These are represented in two forms:

  - A standard Unix-like permissions string or "rwx" (read, write, and execute permissions, where execute permissions on directories indicate the ability to search those directories). Each letter may be replaced by a dash (-), indicating that no access of that type is permitted. These three permissions must appear in this order.

  - A relative symbolic form that is preceded by a plus sign (+) or a caret symbol (^), much like the symbolic permissions that are designed for use with the chmod command by people who are octally challenged. In this ACL representation, the + or ^ symbols are followed by single r, w, or x permission characters, indicating that these permissions should be added to the current set for a file or directory (+) or removed from the current set (^) for a given file or directory.

When listed or stored in files, different ACL entries are separated by white space or new lines. Everything after a # character to the end of a line is considered a comment and is ignored.

The Linux *acl* package provides the following three utilities for ACL creation, modification, and examination:

chacl
> Lets you change, examine, or remove *user*, *group*, *mask*, or *other* ACLs on files or directories

getfacl
> Lets you examine file ACLs for files and directories

setfacl
> Lets you set file and directory ACLs

Displaying Current ACLs

As an example of using ACLs, let's use a directory with the following contents and permissions:

```
$ ls -al
total 49
drwxr-xr-x    2 wvh users    80 2005-07-04 13:59 .
drwxr-xr-x  106 wvh users  5288 2005-07-04 14:47 ..
-rw-r-----    1 wvh users 44032 2005-07-04 13:58 resume.xml
```

The default ACL for this directory is the following:

```
$ getfacl .
# file: .
# owner: wvh
# group: users
user::rwx
group::r-x
other::r-x
```

The default ACL for the file *resume.xml* is the following:

```
$ getfacl resume.xml
# file: resume.xml
# owner: wvh
# group: users
user::rw-
group::r--
other::---
```

The default ACL for a file in a directory for which a default ACL has not been set reflects the default Unix permissions associated with the user that created the file. The default Unix permissions for a file are based on the setting of the umask environment variable **[Hack #52]**.

Setting ACLs

There are three common ways to change the ACL of a file or directory:

- By setting it explicitly using the setfacl command, which overwrites any existing ACL settings
- By using the setfacl command with the -m (modify) option to modify an existing ACL
- By using the chacl command to modify an existing ACL

For the examples in this hack, I'll use the chacl command to change ACLs, since this doesn't overwrite the existing ACL. It also provides a bit more information about how ACLs really work than the shorthand version of the setfacl command.

For example, to add the user *alex* as someone who can read the file *resume.xml*, I would use a chacl (change ACL) command like the following:

```
$ chacl u::rw-,g::r--,o::---,u:alex:r--,m::rw- resume.xml
```

No, that isn't static from a bad modem or Internet connection (though it probably is a command in the old TECO editor)—that's the way ACLs look in real life. As mentioned previously, ACLs consist of three colon-separated fields that represent the permissions of the user (the owner of the file), group (the group ownership of the file), and others. When changing an ACL with the chacl command, you need to first specify the ACL of the file and then append the changes that you want to make to that ACL. The u::rw-,g::r-- ,o::--- portion of the ACL in this example is the existing ACL of the file; the u:alex:r--,m::rw- portion specifies the new user that I want to add to the ACL for that file and the effective rights mask to be used when adding that user. The effective rights mask is the union of all of the existing user, group, and other permissions for a file or directory. You must specify a mask when adding a random user to the ACL for a file.

Using the getfacl command to retrieve the ACL for my resume shows that the user *alex* has indeed been added to the list of people who have access to the file:

```
$ getfacl resume.xml
# file: resume.xml
# owner: wvh
# group: wvh
user::rwx
group::r--
other::---
user:alex:r--
mask::rw-
```

> Though the content is the same, the format of the output of the *getfacl* command depends on the version of the ACL suite that is being used on your Linux system.

Using the ls -al command shows that the visible, standard Unix file and directory permissions haven't changed:

```
$ ls -al
total 49
drwxr-xr-x    2 wvh users    80 2005-07-04 13:59 .
drwxr-xr-x  106 wvh users  5288 2005-07-04 14:47 ..
-rw-r-----    1 wvh users 44032 2005-07-04 13:58 resume.xml
```

You can verify that the user *alex* now has access to the file by asking him to attempt to read the file. (If you know his password, you can check this yourself by su'ing to that user or by connecting to your machine over the network, logging in as *alex*, and examining the file using a text editor or a command such as more or cat.)

Even more interesting and useful than just giving specific individuals read access to files is the ability to give specific users the ability to write to specific files. For example, to add the user *alex* as someone who can both read and write to the file *resume.xml*, I would use a chacl command like the following:

```
$ chacl u::rw-,g::r--,o::---,u:alex:rw-,m::rw- resume.xml
```

Using the getfacl command shows that the user *alex* now has both read and write access to the file:

```
$ getfacl resume.xml
# file: resume.xml
# owner: wvh
# group: users
user::rw-
group::rw-
other::---
user:alex:rw-
mask::rw-
```

As before, you can verify that the user *alex* now has both read and write access to the file by asking him to attempt to read and write to the file. (If you know the test user's password, you can check this yourself by connecting to your machine over the network, logging in as that user, and editing and saving the file using a text editor.)

I'm a big fan of ACLs, primarily because they give knowledgeable users total control over who can access their files and directories. ACLs remove one of the main administrative complaints about Unix systems: the need for root access to set up granular permissions. As a fringe benefit, they also silence one more argument for using systems such as Windows 2000/2003/XP.

See Also

- "Share Files Using Linux Groups" **[Hack #52]**
- "Make Files Easier to Find with Extended Attributes" **[Hack #54]**
- POSIX.1e draft specification: *http://wt.xpilot.org/publications/posix.1e*
- POSIX ACLs on Linux: *http://www.suse.de/~agruen/acl/linux-acls/online*

Make Files Easier to Find with Extended Attributes

Define file- and directory-specific metadata to make it easier to find critical data.

Most projects and users organize their files by taking advantage of the inherently hierarchical nature of the Linux filesystem. Conceptually related items are given meaningful names and stored in hierarchical directories with equally memorable or evocative names. But unfortunately, file and directory names and structures that were memorable at the time of creation are not always equally memorable a month or two later, when you're desperately looking for a specific file.

Extended attributes are name/value pairs that you can associate with any file or directory in a Linux filesystem. These are a special type of *metadata*, which is the term for data about data, such as modification and access times, user and group ownership, protections, and so on. Extended attributes can be associated with any object in a Linux filesystem that has an inode. The names of extended attributes can be up to 256 bytes long, are usually standard ASCII text, and (like standard Linux strings) are terminated by the first NULL byte. The value of an attribute can be up to 64 KB of arbitrary data in any format.

Extended attributes are often used for system purposes, by tagging files with metadata about who can access them, and under what circumstances. This hack discusses how extended attributes can be extremely useful for any user or system administrator who wants to tag important files and directories with information that makes them easier to find, work with, track modifications to, and so on.

Getting and Installing Extended Attribute Support

Extended attributes are currently supported by all major Linux filesystems for desktop and server use, including *ext2*, *ext3*, *reiserfs*, JFS, and XFS. They are not currently supported in NFS filesystems, even if they are being set and used in the actual filesystem being exported via NFS—the code that transfers file data and metadata across the network does not currently understand extended attributes.

Like the ACLs [Hack #53], using extended attributes also requires that your kernel supports them, that the filesystems in which you want to use them are mounted with extended attribute support, and that the user-space utilities for displaying and setting the values of different extended attributes (*attr*, *getfattr*, and *setfattr*) are compiled and installed on your system.

The JFS and XFS filesystems automatically support extended attributes in the 2.6 Linux kernel. If you are using an earlier version of the kernel, see *http://acl.bestbits.at* for links to any patches needed to add extended attribute support to the kernel you are using.

Configuring your kernel for extended attributes. Most modern Linux distributions provide support for extended attributes in the default kernels that they deliver. If you have access to the configuration file used to build your kernel, you can use the *grep* utility to check that the FS_XATTR configuration variable associated with your *ext2*, *ext3*, or *reiserfs* filesystem is set to y, as in the following example:

```
$ grep FS_XATTR /boot/config-2.6.8-24.16-default
CONFIG_EXT2_FS_XATTR=y
CONFIG_EXT3_FS_XATTR=y
CONFIG_REISERFS_FS_XATTR=y
```

If the FS_XATTR value associated with the type of filesystem you are using is set to n, you will have to enable that configuration variable, save the updated kernel configuration, and recompile your kernel in order to use extended attributes. Extended attributes must be separately enabled for each type of filesystem you are using (with the exception of the XFS journaling filesystem, which inherently supports them). The kernel configuration options that enable them are located on the File Systems pane in your favorite kernel configuration editor (make xconfig, make menuconfig, and so on).

Configuring fstab for extended attributes. Once you are running a kernel with support for extended attributes, you will need to make sure that the filesystems in which you want to use extended attributes are mounted with extended attribute support enabled. Check your */etc/fstab* file to verify this. Filesystems mounted with extended attribute support will have the user_xattr keyword in the mount options portions of their entries in the file. In the following example, the *reiserfs* filesystem on */dev/sda6* is mounted with extended attribute support, while the *ext3* filesystem on */dev/hda1* is not:

```
/dev/sda6   /usr    reiserfs   noatime,user_xattr  1 2
/dev/hda1   /opt2   ext3       defaults            0 0
```

If your kernel supports extended attributes, you can edit this file to enable extended attribute support when you initially mount a filesystem by adding the user_xattr keyword to that filesystem's mount options, as in the following example:

```
/dev/hda1   /opt2   ext3       defaults,user_xattr 0 0
```

After updating this file, you can enable extended attribute support in currently mounted filesystems without rebooting by executing a command like the following, which would enable extended attribute support in the example *ext3* filesystem */dev/hda1*:

```
# mount -o remount,user_xattr /dev/hda1
```

Installing user-space applications for extended attributes. The last step in using extended attributes on your system is to make sure that the user-space applications that enable you to display and set attributes are present. The Linux *attr* package provides the following three utilities for extended creation, modification, and examination:

attr

   Lets you set, get, or remove an extended attribute on any filesystem object(s) represented by an inode (files, directories, symbolic links, and so on)

getfattr

   Lets you examine extended attributes for any filesystem object(s)

setacl

   Lets you set extended attributes for any filesystem object(s)

If your system uses a package management system, you can query that system's database to see if the *attr* package and its associated library, *libattr*, are installed. The following is an example query on a system that uses RPM:

```
# rpm -qa | grep attr
libattr-2.4.16-2
attr-2.4.16-2
```

You can also look for the utilities themselves, using the which command:

```
# which attr
/usr/bin/attr
# which getfattr
/usr/bin/getfattr
# which setfattr
/usr/bin/setfattr
```

If the *attr* package is not installed and the binaries are not present on your system, you can find the source code or binary packages for your system by following links from *http://acl.bestbits.at*. You must install this package before continuing with the rest of this hack.

Displaying Extended Attributes and Their Values

Both the attr and getfattr commands enable you to display the name and value of a specific extended attribute on a given file or files. To look for the value of the extended attribute backup for the file *hack_attrs.txt*, I could use either of the following commands:

```
$ attr -g backup hack_attrs.txt
Attribute "backup" had a 3 byte value for hack_attrs.txt:
yes
```

```
$ getfattr -n user.backup hack_attrs.txt
# file: hack_attrs.txt
user.backup="yes"
```

As you'd expect, querying the attributes of a file that does not have any returns nothing.

> Note that these two commands require slightly different attribute syntax, which is confusing at best. User-defined extended attributes in the *ext2*, *ext3*, JFS, and *reiserfs* filesystems are always prepended with the string "user". The attr command is an older command for retrieving extended attributes and is primarily intended for use with extended attributes in the XFS journaling filesystem; therefore, it follows slightly different (older) syntax conventions. As a general rule, you should always use the getfattr command to accurately query extended attributes across different filesystems.

It is sometimes useful to query all of the extended attributes on a specific file, which you can do with the getfattr command's -d option:

```
$ getfattr -d hack_attrs.txt
# file: hack_attrs.txt
user.backup="yes"
user.status="In progress"
```

If you are only interested in seeing the value of an extended attribute without any additional explanation, you can use the getfattr command's --only-values option, as in the following example:

```
$ getfattr -n user.backup --only-values hack_attrs.txt
yes$
```

Note that the output of this command does not have a newline appended, so any scripts from which you invoke this command must take into account the fact that its output will appear to include the *bash* prompt of the user who executed the script (here, a $).

Setting Extended Attributes

System capabilities such as SELinux make internal use of extended attributes. These attributes are not viewable or settable by normal users. However, normal users can take advantage of extended attributes to provide convenient meta-information about the files that they are working on, simplifying search-ing and eliminating the "now what was I working on?" problem.

Setting extended attribute values can be done with either the attr or setfattr commands. The following are examples of setting the user.status attribute to the value "In progress" using each of these commands:

```
$ attr -s status -V "In Progress" hack_attrs.txt
Attribute "status" set to a 11 byte value for hack_attrs.txt:
In Progress

$ setfattr -n status -v "In progress" hack_attrs.txt
setfattr: hack_attrs.txt: Operation not supported

$ setfattr -n user.status -v "In progress" hack_attrs.txt
```

As you'll note from the second of these examples, the setfattr command explicitly requires that you identify the attribute you are setting as being a user-defined extended attribute. Attempting to set an attribute in any other attribute namespace, or to create a namespace, results in the "Operation not supported" error shown in this example. The third example command shows the correct syntax for setting a user-defined extended attribute with setfattr.

Removing Extended Attributes

The ability to set user-defined extended attributes isn't completely useful for associating user-defined metadata unless you can also remove existing attributes. You can do this with both the attr and setfattr commands, though the setfattr command is recommended because its syntax is consis-tent with the values returned by the getfattr command. For example, you can remove the user.status attribute from the file *hack_attrs.txt* using either of the following commands:

```
$ attr -r status hack_attrs.txt
$ setfattr -x user.status hack_attrs.txt
```

Searching Using Extended Attributes

Extended attributes are inherently interesting, but the proof of their value is in using them cleverly. On my systems, I use a shell script called *find_by_attr* to query extended attributes and display a list of files that contain a specific extended attribute. The script is the following:

```
#!/bin/bash
#
# Simple script to find files by attribute and value
#   - Bill von Hagen (wvh)
#
```

```
if [ $# -lt 3 ] ; then
    echo "Usage: find_by_attr attribute value files..."
    exit -1
fi

attr=$1
val=$2

shift 2

#
# Set IFS to TAB to allow files with space in their names
#
IFS='   '

for file in $* ; do
    result=`getfattr -d "$file" | grep $attr | \
            sed -e "s;user\.$attr=;;" -e "s;$attr=;;" -e 's;";;g'`
    if [ x$result = x$val ] ; then
        echo $file
    fi

done
```

Using the getfattr command's -d option to dump all file/directory attributes and then searching the output for the attribute specified as the first argument with a value of the second argument may seem like overkill, but I did this to eliminate error messages from files on which the specified attribute has not been set.

You can invoke this script either from the command line, by specifying explicit filenames, or as the target of a find command, as in the following example:

```
$ find . -exec find_by_attr backup yes {} \; 2>/tmp/find_by_attr.$$.err
```

Note that you'll want to redirect standard error to a temporary file (as shown here) or to */dev/null* in order to eliminate any noise from filenames that can't be resolved, such as bad symlinks and the like.

I use this script in combination with the user.backup extended attribute that I used in the previous command examples to identify critical files that I back up daily. This makes it easy for me to use the script as input to a backup command to save an archive of the files that I am actively working on.

Extended attributes are powerful tools that are immediately useful to users and system administrators. They serve as the foundation for Linux desktop search tools such as the GNOME project's *Beagle* tool, and they provide an infinitely flexible way of passing information to other programs, identifying specific files to multiple users, and accomplishing many other tasks. Once you become familiar with using extended attributes, you'll find yourself using them in more and varied ways. As SUSE says, "Have a lot of fun!"

Prevent Disk Hogs with Quotas

Wasting disk space can cost you resources and bloat backup times and storage requirements. Setting up disk quotas provides a quick solution.

Every network has one of those users who's the quintessential digital pack-rat, storing files and emails for years and years, regardless of their content or relative unimportance. With the growing popularity of digital media files that can range from 3 MB to 3 GB in size, these users can fill a disk to capacity in very little time. To prevent these types of users from crashing your server, consider implementing disk quotas to keep them in line.

Setting Up Disk Quotas

There are a few steps to setting up quotas, but it's a relatively simple process. After setting up quotas, you'll either have to reboot your system or manually unmount and remount any partitions to which you've added quotas. Adding and configuring disk quotas is best done while the system is in single-user mode or otherwise down for maintenance.

Let's first explore the basic concepts of disk quotas, which are soft and hard limits. The *soft limit* is the maximum number of disk blocks or inodes that the user can use. Once this number is exceeded, the user is warned and allowed to continue for a specified grace period. Once that grace period expires, the user may no longer allocate any additional blocks or inodes (depending on how you have the quota configured).

Hard limits are indeed hard. A hard limit may never be exceeded, and once it's reached the user will automatically be barred from using further disk space.

Installing the Quota Software

Your system may or may not already have the software for implementing and managing disk quotas installed. It is usually located in */sbin* or */usr/sbin*, depending on your Linux distribution. To check, su to root and use the which command to determine if the *quotacheck* package is installed, as in the following example:

```
# which quotacheck
/sbin/quotacheck
```

If you get a response from the which command (as shown above), you have the quota software installed and can proceed to the next step. If you don't already have it, the latest version can be found at *http://www.sourceforge.net/ projects/linuxquota*. The software installs with the typical commands:

```
# ./configure, make, make install
```

Alternatively, if you're using a package- or RPM-based distribution, you can install the quota software via your package manager. For instance, with Ubuntu or Debian you can simply issue the following command:

```
$ sudo apt-get install quota
```

This will install and configure the software for you. SUSE users can use *YaST* to accomplish the same thing. These days, many distributions come with quota enabled by default, though, so most likely you won't have to worry about it.

Entering Single-User Mode

To configure your partitions to work with quotas, you'll need to bring the system into single-user mode. If this is not possible for you, at the very least you'll want to make sure that no one is logged in when you start this process, and that the system will remain in a quiet state [Hack #3]. To bring the system down to single-user mode, physically log into the console and issue the following command:

```
# init 1
```

This will bring the system into single-user mode, thereby disabling all network services (such as *ssh* and *ftp*).

Editing /etc/fstab

Navigate to the */etc* directory. Fire up *vi* (or your favorite text editor) and edit the file */etc/fstab*. The contents of an */etc/fstab* file from a typical one-disk system might look something like the following:

```
LABEL=/           /          ext3    defaults          1 1
LABEL=/boot       /boot      ext3    defaults          1 2
none              /dev/pts   devpts  gid=5,mode=620    0 0
none              /dev/shm   tmpfs   defaults          0 0
LABEL=/data       /data      ext3    defaults          1 3
none              /proc      proc    defaults          0 0
none              /sys       sysfs   defaults          0 0
LABEL=SWAP-hda2   swap       swap    defaults          0 0
```

The only change that you need to make to this file is to add the usrquota option next to the partitions on which you wish to enable disk quotas. Once you've done that, you're done editing the *fstab* file—simply save it and exit your text editor to commit your changes to the file.

Next, you'll need to remount your filesystems so that your changes to the filesystem mount options will take effect. If, for example, you want to remount the */data* partition, you can do this by simply issuing the following command:

```
# mount -o remount /data
```

Once the partition is remounted, you're ready to revert back into your original runlevel. To do so, issue the command `init 5` or `init 3`, depending on what your original runlevel was.

Initializing the Quota Configuration Files

You'll then need to create two files in the root of each partition to which you've just added quotas. These two files are named *aquota.user* for user-based disk quotas and *aquota.group* for group-based quotas. You can create both of these files using the touch command. Make sure you change the access permissions with the command chmod 600. This will help prevent your disk quotas from being circumvented.

Once you've created these files, you'll need to import your user and group data into the quota files that you just created in each filesystem. This might take a long time if you had to do it by hand, but thankfully there's an automated utility to do it for you:

```
# quotacheck -vguam
```

The options tell the quotacheck command to be verbose (v), to check group (g) and user (u) quotas on all (a) filesystems on which quotas have been enabled, and not to try to mount (m) the filesystem as read-only in order to do the check.

The first time you use the quotacheck command, it might return an error telling you that it can't save the quota settings. This is normal and can safely be ignored.

Configuring Your Quotas

Now that you've created and initialized the files, you may now edit the quota information. This can be accomplished with the edquota command. This command offers several options that are of interest to us. The three most prominent are -u, -g, and -t. Using any of these options launches your default text editor to edit the relevant configuration files. The -u flag allows you to edit the quotas on a per-user basis, while the -g flag acts on a per-group basis (the -t option will be explained in just a bit). Both of these configuration files are largely the same, so we'll just look at the user file here:

```
$ sudo edquota -u jdouble
Disk quotas for user jdouble (uid 1001):
  Filesystem    blocks     soft     hard    inodes  soft  hard
  /dev/hda1     100000    200000   250000   127     0     0
```

As you can see, there are two main ways in which you may limit users: via the total number of blocks they can utilize, or via the total number of inodes (i.e., the total number of files the user may have on the partition). I tend to use blocks when allocating disk space, but you may of course do as you see fit. While assigning quotas, keep in mind that 1,000 blocks equals 1 MB. In the example above, you can see that the user *jdouble* is currently using 100 MB of space and has a soft limit of 200 MB and a hard limit of 250 MB. The listing under inodes tells us that *jdouble* has 127 files on the filesystem */dev/hda1*. You might also note that as the hard and soft limits after the inodes listing are set to zero, there is no quota for the total number of files the user can have.

The edquota -t command allows you to configure grace periods for your users. Grace periods are periods of time during which users are allowed to temporarily violate their disk quotas while they receive warnings regarding their disk utilization. Once the grace period has ended, the user may no longer violate her quota, and the soft-limit quota is enforced. You'll see something like this when you run this command:

```
# edquota -t
Grace period before enforcing soft limits for users:
Time units may be: days, hours, minutes, or seconds
   Filesystem              Block grace period     Inode grace period
   /dev/hda1                   3days                    99days
```

Be sure to set something reasonable here so that your users have at least a few minutes to free up some space if they accidentally overrun their quotas.

Even with quotas enabled, you'll probably be interested to know which of your users are utilizing the most disk space. Thankfully, there's a built-in feature to handle that as well. The repquota command, which takes a directory or filesystem as an argument, will give you a brief report of your users' total disk utilization, as well as their configured hard and soft limits.

```
# repquota /
*** Report for user quotas on device /dev/hda1
Block grace time: 3days; Inode grace time: 99days
                       Block limits              File limits
User           used    soft    hard  grace   used  soft  hard  grace
----------------------------------------------------------------------
root       -- 20932272     0       0          73865    0     0
daemon     --       44     0       0              4    0     0
man        --      396     0       0             21    0     0
news       --        4     0       0              1    0     0
postfix    --       88     0       0             45    0     0
jdouble    --   100000 200000  250000            127    0     0
klog       --        8     0       0              3    0     0
kida       --     2800     0       0            181    0     0
cupsys     --       72     0       0             11    0     0
fetchmail  --        4     0       0              1    0     0
hal        --        8     0       0              2    0     0
```

Through this report, you can see the disk utilization of every user on the system, including our test case *jdouble*. Any user with the default 0 under the hard or soft column is not subject to disk quotas.

By using the report feature within a cron job, you can be updated on disk utilization as often as you'd like. I have this information emailed to me every weekday morning so that I can keep track of my users and hunt down those pesky disk hogs. To do this, I added the following entry to root's *crontab* file using the crontab -e command as root:

```
0 5 * * *    repquota -a
```

This tells the cron processes to check all filesystems on which quotas are enabled at 5 A.M. every day and to mail the output of the repquota command to root. Configuring disk quotas can be a lifesaver if you run a heavily used, multi-user server and can be made even more powerful if you take advantage of the group features of disk quotas. The Linux quota system's group mechanism provides a way of creating different levels of users, from those that may only need 10 MB of space all the way up to those who want (and actually need) gigabytes of space.

See Also

- man edquota
- man repquota
- man quota
- man quotacheck
- man quotactl

—*Brian Warshawsky*

## CHAPTER SIX

Standardizing, Sharing, and Synchronizing Resources

Hacks 56–62

Once you finally get over the hump of setting up centralized access to various resources in your environment, you won't know how you lived without it. Maintaining resources in a central location for use by the masses saves endless numbers of trips to peoples' offices, and it can save you money because you'll only have to back up a central file server instead of its individual clients.

This chapter will delve into various methods of file sharing, each applicable in different circumstances. For web farms, an NFS server can store the web pages, making backups and repurposing a breeze. For end user file access, Samba can provide cross-platform, authenticated file sharing. For web-based collaboration, have a look at WebDAV.

HACK #56   Centralize Resources Using NFS

Make recovering from disaster—and preparing for it—simpler by centralizing shared resources and service configuration.

A key goal of all system administrators is to maximize the availability of the services they maintain. With an unlimited budget you could create a scenario where there are two or three "hot standby" machines for every one machine in production, waiting to seamlessly take over in the event of a problem. But who has an unlimited budget?

Standalone machines that store their own local copies of configuration and data can be nice, if you have lots of them, and you have load balancers, and you have a good cloning mechanism so you don't spend all your time making sure all of your mail servers (for example) are identical. Oh yeah, and when you make a configuration change to one, you'll need a system to push it out to the other clones. This could take quite a bit of time and/or money to get right—and this doesn't even touch on the expense of putting backup software on every single machine on your network. I'm sure there are some smaller sites using standard Unix and Linux utilities for backup and nothing else, but the majority of sites are using commercial products, and they're not cheap!

Wouldn't it be nice if a test box could be repurposed in a matter of minutes to take over for a server with a failed drive? Wouldn't it be great if you only needed to back up from a couple of file servers instead of every single service machine? NFS, the Network File System, can get you to this place, and this hack will show you how.

Admins new to Linux, particularly those coming from Microsoft products, may not be familiar with NFS, the file-sharing protocol used in traditional Unix shops. What's great about NFS is that it allows you to store configuration files and data in a centralized location and transparently access that location from multiple machines, which treat the remote share as a local filesystem.

Let's say you have five Apache web servers, all on separate hardware. One is the main web presence for your company, one is a backup, and the other three perform other functions, such as hosting user home pages, an intranet site, and a trouble-ticket system. They're all configured to be standalone machines right now, but you want to set things up so that the machine that's currently just a hot standby to the main web server can serve as a standby for pretty much any web server.

To do this, we'll create an NFS server with mountable partitions that provide the configuration information, as well as the content, to the web servers. The first step is to configure the NFS server.

Configuring the NFS Server

To configure the NFS server, you must first create a directory hierarchy to hold Apache configurations for all of your different web servers, since it's hubris to assume they're all configured identically. There are numerous ways to organize the hierarchy. You could try to emulate the native filesystem as closely as possible, using symlinks to get it all perfect. You could also create a tree for each web server to hold its configuration, so that when you add another web server you can just add another directory on the NFS server for its configuration. I've found the latter method to be a bit less taxing on the brain.

The first thing to do on the NFS server is to create the space where this information will live. Let's say your servers are numbered *web1* through *web5*. Here's an example of what the directory structure might look like:

```
/servconf
    mail/
    common/
    web/
```

```
web1/
    conf/
        httpd.conf
        access.conf
        modules.conf
    conf.d/
        php4.conf
web2/
    conf/
        httpd.conf
        access.conf
        modules.conf
    conf.d/
        php4.conf
        python.conf
        mod_auth_mysql.conf
```

This sample hierarchy illustrates a few interesting points. First, notice the directories *mail/* and *common/*. As these show, the configuration tree doesn't need to be limited to a single service. In fact, it doesn't actually have to be service-specific at all! For example, the *common/* tree can hold configuration files for things like global shell initialization files that you want to be constant on all production service machines (you want this, believe me) and the OpenSSH server configuration file, which ensures that the *ssh* daemon acts the same way on each machine.

That last sentence brings up another potential benefit of centralized configuration: if you want to make global changes to something like the *ssh* daemon, you can make the changes in one place instead of many, since all of the *ssh* daemons will be looking at the centralized configuration file. Once a change is made, the daemons will need to be restarted or sent a SIGHUP to pick up the change. "Execute Commands Simultaneously on Multiple Servers" [Hack #29]) shows a method that will alow you to do this on multiple servers quickly.

All of this is wonderful, and some sites can actually use a hierarchy like this to have a single NFS server provide configuration to all the services in their department or business. However, it's important to recognize that, depending on how robust your NFS deployment is, you could be setting yourself up with the world's largest single point of failure. It's one thing to provide configuration to all your web servers, in which case a failure of the NFS server affects the web servers. It's quite another to use a single NFS server to provide configuration data to every production service across the board. In this case, if there's a problem with the file server, you're pretty much dead in the water, all owing to a glitch in a single machine! It would be smart to either invest in technologies that ensure the availability of the NFS service, or break up the NFS servers to lessen the impact of a failure of any one server.

Now it's time to export our configuration tree. It's important to note that some NFS daemons are somewhat "all or nothing" in the sense that they cannot export a subdirectory of an already exported directory. The exception to that rule is if the subdirectory is actually living on a separate physical device on the NFS server. For safety's sake, I've made it a rule never to do this anyway, in the event that changes in the future cause the subdirectory to share a device with its parent. Note that the same rule applies to exporting a subdirectory and then trying to export a parent directory separately.

Some implementations of the *nfsd* server do allow subdirectory exports, but for the sake of simplicity I avoid this, because it has implications as to the rules applied to a particular exported directory and can make debugging quite nightmarish.

Let's see how this works. Using the above "best practices," you cannot export the whole */servconf* tree in our example to one server, and then export *mail/* separately to the mail servers. You *can* export each of the directories under */servconf* separately if */servconf* itself is not exported, but that would make it slightly more work to repurpose a server, because you'd have to make sure permissions were in place to allow the mount of the new configuration tree, and you'd have to make sure the */etc/fstab* file on the NFS client was updated—otherwise, a reboot would cause bad things to happen.

It's easier just to export the entire */servconf* tree to a well-defined subset of the machines, so that */etc/fstab* never has to be changed and permissions are not an issue from the NFS server side of the equation. That's what we'll do here. The file that tells the NFS server who can mount what is almost always */etc/exports*. After all this discussion, here's the single line we need to accomplish the goal of allowing our web servers to mount the */servconf* directory:

```
/servconf    192.168.198.0/24(ro,root_squash) @trusted(rw,no_root_squash)
```

The network specified above is a DMZ where my service machines live. Two important things to note here are the options applied to the export. The ro option ensures that changes cannot be made to the configuration of a given machine by logging into the machine itself. This is for the sake of heightened security, to help guarantee that a compromised machine can't be used to change the configuration files of all the other machines. Also to that end, I've explicitly added the root_squash option. This is a default in some NFS implementations, but I always state it explicitly in case that default ever changes (this is generally good practice for all applications, by the way). This option maps UID 0 on the client to *nobody* on the server, so even root on the client machine cannot make changes to files anywhere under the mount point.

The second group of hosts I'm exporting this mount point to are those listed in an NIS netgroup named *trusted*. This netgroup consists of two machines that are locked down and isolated such that only administrators can get access to them. I've given those hosts read/write (rw) access, which allows administrators to make changes to configuration files from machines other than the NFS server itself. I've also specified the no_root_squash option here, so that admins can use these machines even to change configuration files on the central server owned by root.

For the Apache web server example, we can create a very similar hierarchy on our NFS server to store content served up by the servers, and export it in the exact same way we did for the configuration. However, keep in mind that many web sites assume they can write in the directories they own, so you'll need to make sure that you either export a writable directory for these applications to use, or export the content tree with read/write privileges.

Configuring the NFS Clients

Getting NFS clients working is usually a breeze. You'll need to decide where you want the local Apache daemon to find its configuration and content, create the mount points for any trees you'll need to mount, and then edit the */etc/fstab* file to make sure that the directory is always mounted at boot time.

Generally, I tend to create the local mount points under the root directory, mainly for the sake of consistency. No matter what server I'm logged in to, I know I can always run ls -1 / and see all of the mount points on that server. This is simpler than having to remember what services are running on the machine, then hunting around the filesystem to check that the mount points are all there. Putting them under / means that if I run the mount command to see what is mounted, and something is missing, I can run one command to make sure the mount point exists, which is usually the first step in trouble-shooting an NFS-related issue.

I also attempt to name the mount point the same as the exported directory on the server. This makes debugging a bit simpler, because I don't have to remember that the mount point named *webstuff* on the client is actually *servconf* on the server. So, we create a mount point on the NFS client like this:

```
# mkdir /servconf
```

Then we add a line like the following to our */etc/fstab* file:

```
mynfs:/servconf    /servconf        nfs    ro,intr,nfsvers=3,proto=tcp 0 0
```

Now we're assured that the tree will be mounted at boot time. The other important factor to consider is that the tree is mounted *before* the service that needs the files living there is started. It *should* be safe to assume that this will just work, but if you're trying to debug services that seem to be ignoring configuration directives, or that fail to start at all, you'll want to double check, just in case!

Configuring the Service

We've now mounted our web server configuration data to all of our web servers. Let's assume for now that you've done the same with the content. What we've essentially accomplished is a way to have one hot spare machine, which also mounts all of this information, that can take over for any failed web server in the blink of an eye. Two ways to get it to work are to use symlinks or to edit the service's initialization script.

To use the symlink method, you consult the initialization script for the service. In the case of Apache, the script will most likely be */etc/init.d/apache* or */etc/init.d/httpd*. This script, like almost all service initialization scripts, will tell you where the daemon will look for its configuration file(s). In my case, it looks under */etc/apache*. The next thing to do is to move this directory out of the way and make a symlink to the directory that will take its place. This is done with commands like the following:

```
# mv /etc/apache /etc/apache.DIST
# ln -s /servconf/web/web1 /etc/apache
```

Now when the service starts up, it will use whichever configuration files are pointed to by the symlink. The critical thing to make sure of here is that the files under the mount point conform to what the initialization script expects. For example, if the initialization script for Apache in this case was looking for */etc/apache/config/httpd.conf*, it would fail to start at all, because the */etc/apache* directory is now a symlink to a mount point that has put the file under a sub-directory called *conf/*, not *config/*. These little "gotchas" are generally few, and are worked out early in the testing phase of any such deployment.

Now, if we want to make our hot spare look like *web3* instead of *web1*, we can simply remove the symlink we had in place, create a new symlink to point to *web3*'s configuration directory, and restart the service. Note that if all of the web servers mount the content in the same way under the same mount points, you don't have to change any symlinks for content, since the configuration file in Apache's case tells the daemon where to find the content, not the initialization script! Here are the commands to change the personality of our hot spare to *web3*:

```
# rm /etc/apache; ln -s /servconf/web/web3 /etc/apache
# /etc/init.d/apache restart
```

The commands used to restart Apache can vary depending on the platform. You might run the *apachectl* program directly, or you might use the service command available on some Linux distributions.

A Final Consideration

You can't assume that you're completely out of the woods just because a server looks and acts like the one it replaces. In the case of Apache, you'll also want to make sure that your hot spare is actually reachable by clients without them having to change any of their bookmarks. This might involve taking down the failed web server and assigning its IP address to the hot spare or making the DNS record for the failed web server point to the hot spare.

Automount NFS Home Directories with autofs

#57

Let users log in from any machine and be in familiar territory.

If you administer an environment that supports large numbers of users who occasionally need access to any one of a wide array of hosts on your network, you might find it a bit tiring having to answer support calls every time your users try to log into a machine only to find that their home directories are nowhere to be found. Sure, you could run over and edit the */etc/fstab* file to NFS-mount the remote home directories and fix things using that machine's NFS client, but there are a couple of downsides to handling things in this way.

First, your */etc/fstab* file will eventually grow quite large as you add more and more mounts. Second, if a user leaves your department, you'll be left with the choice of either dealing with failed mount requests in your logfiles (assuming you removed the user's home directory at the time of departure) or running around and editing files on all of the machines that have the entry causing the error. Which machines have the offending entry? Well, you'll just have to look, won't you? This is not a position you want to find yourself in if you maintain large labs, clusters, and testing or development environments.

One thought might be to mount a directory from an NFS server that holds the */etc/fstab* file. This is asking for trouble, since this file is in charge of handling not only NFS mounts, but the mounts of your local devices (read: hard drives). In the end, you're sure to find that centralizing this file on an NFS share is impossible, since the local machine needs to mount the hard drives before it can do anything with the network, including mounting NFS shares.

A good solution is one that allows you to mount NFS shares without using */etc/fstab*. Ideally, it could also mount shares dynamically, as they are requested, so that when they're not in use there aren't all of these unused directories hanging around and messing up your ls -l output. In a perfect world, we could central-ize the mount configuration file and allow it to be used by all machines that need the service, so that when a user leaves, we just delete the mount from one configuration file and go on our merry way.

Happily, you can do just this with the Linux *autofs* daemon. The *autofs* dae-mon lives in the kernel and reads its configuration from "maps," which can be stored in local files, centralized NFS-mounted files, or directory services such as NIS or LDAP. Of course, there has to be a master configuration file to tell *autofs* where to find its mounting information. That file is almost always stored in */etc/auto.master*. Let's have a look at a simple example con-figuration file:

```
/.autofs   file:/etc/auto.direct    --timeout 300
/mnt       file:/etc/auto.mnt       --timeout 60
/u         yp:homedirs              --timeout 300
```

The main purpose of this file is to let the daemon know where to create its mount points on the local system (detailed in the first column of the file), and then where to find the mounts that should live under each mount point (detailed in the second column). The rest of each line consists of mount options. In this case, the only option is a timeout, in seconds. If the mount is idle for that many seconds, it will be unmounted.

In our example configuration, starting the *autofs* service will create three mount points. */u* is one of them, and that's where we're going to put our home directories. The data for that mount point comes from the *homedirs* map on our NIS server. Running ypcat homedirs shows us the following line:

```
hdserv:/vol/home:users
```

The server that houses all of the home directories is called *hdserv*. When the automounter starts up, it will read the entry in *auto.master*, contact the NIS server, ask for the *homedirs* map, get the above information back, and then contact *hdserv* and ask to mount */vol/home/users*. (The colon in the file path above is an NIS-specific requirement. Everything under the directory named after the colon will be mounted.) If things complete successfully, everything that lives under */vol/home/users* on the server will now appear under */u* on the client.

Of course, we don't have to use NIS to store our mount maps—we can store them in an LDAP directory or in a plain-text file on an NFS share. Let's explore this latter option, for those who aren't working with a directory ser-vice or don't want to use their directory service for automount maps.

The first thing we'll need to alter is our *auto.master* file, which currently thinks that everything under */u* is mounted according to NIS information.

Instead, we'll now tell it to look in a file, by replacing the original /u line with this one:

```
/u          file:/usr/local/etc/auto.home     --timeout 300
```

This tells the automounter that the file */usr/local/etc/auto.home* is the authoritative source for information regarding all things mounted under the local /u directory.

In the file on my system are the following lines:

```
jonesy    -rw hdserv:/vol/home/users/&
matt      -rw hdserv:/vol/home/usrs/&
```

What?! One line for every single user in my environment?! Well, no. I'm doing this to prove a point. In order to hack the automounter, we have to know what these fields mean.

The first field is called a *key*. The key in the first line is *jonesy*. Since this is a map for things to be found under /u, this first line's key specifies that this entry defines how to mount */u/jonesy* on the local machine.

The second field is a list of mount options, which are pretty self-explanatory. We want all users to be able to mount their directories with read/write access (-rw).

The third field is the location field, which specifies the server from which the automounter should request the mount. In this case, our first entry says that */u/jonesy* will be mounted from the server *hdserv*. The path on the server that will be requested is */vol/home/users/&*. The ampersand is a wildcard that will be replaced in the outgoing mount request with the key. Since our key in the first line is *jonesy*, the location field will be transformed to a request for *hdserv:/vol/home/users/jonesy*.

Now for the big shortcut. There's an extra wildcard you can use in the key field, which allows you to shorten the configuration for every user's home directory to a single line that looks like this:

```
*     -rw hdserv:/vol/home/users/&
```

The * means, for all intents and purposes, "anything." Since we already know the ampersand takes the value of the key, we can now see that, in English, this line is really saying "Whichever directory a user requests under /u, that is the key, so replace the ampersand with the key value and mount that directory from the server."

This is wonderful for two reasons. First, my configuration file is a single line. Second, as user home directories are added and removed from the system, I don't have to edit this configuration file at all. If a user requests a directory that doesn't exist, he'll get back an error. If a new directory is created on the file server, this configuration line already allows it to be mounted.

Keep Filesystems Handy, but Out of Your Way

Use the amd automounter, and some handy defaults, to maintain mounted resources without doing without your own local resources.

The *amd* automounter isn't the most ubiquitous production service I've ever seen, but it can certainly be a valuable tool for administrators in the setup of their own desktop machines. Why? Because it gives you the power to be able to easily and conveniently access any NFS share in your environment, and the default settings for *amd* put all of them under their own directory, out of the way, without you having to do much more than simply start the service.

Here's an example of how useful this can be. I work in an environment in which the */usr/local* directories on our production machines are mounted from a central NFS server. This is great, because if we need to build software for our servers that isn't supplied by the distribution vendor, we can just build it from source in that tree, and all of the servers can access it as soon as it's built. However, occasionally we receive support tickets saying that something is acting strangely or isn't working. Most times, the issue is environmental: the user is getting at the wrong binary because */usr/local* is not in her PATH, or something simple like that. Sometimes, though, the problem is ours, and we need to troubleshoot it.

The most convenient way to do that is just to mount the shared */usr/local* to our desktops and use it in place of our own. For me, however, this is suboptimal, because I like to use my system's */usr/local* to test new software. So I need another way to mount the shared */usr/local* without conflicting with my own */usr/local*. This is where *amd* comes in, as it allows me to get at all of the shares I need, on the fly, without interfering with my local setup.

Here's an example of how this works. I know that the server that serves up the */usr/local* partition is named *fs*, and I know that the file mounted as */usr/local* on the clients is actually called */linux/local* on the server. With a properly configured *amd*, I just run the following command to mount the shared directory:

```
$ cd /net/fs/linux/local
```

There I am, ready to test whatever needs to be tested, having done next to no configuration whatsoever!

The funny thing is, I've run into lots of administrators who don't use *amd* and didn't know that it performed this particular function. This is because the *amd* mount configuration is a little bit cryptic. To understand it, let's take a look at how *amd* is configured. Soon you'll be mounting remote shares with ease.

amd Configuration in a Nutshell

The main *amd* configuration file is almost always */etc/amd.conf*. This file sets up default behaviors for the daemon and defines other configuration files that are authoritative for each configured mount point. Here's a quick look at a totally untouched configuration file, as supplied with the Fedora Core 4 *am-utils* package, which supplies the *amd* automounter:

```
[ global ]
normalize_hostnames =     no
print_pid =               yes
pid_file =                /var/run/amd.pid
restart_mounts =          yes
auto_dir =                /.automount
#log_file =               /var/log/amd
log_file =                syslog
log_options =             all
#debug_options =          all
plock =                   no
selectors_on_default =    yes
print_version =           no
# set map_type to "nis" for NIS maps, or comment it out to search for all
# types
map_type =                file
search_path =             /etc
browsable_dirs =          yes
show_statfs_entries =     no
fully_qualified_hosts =   no
cache_duration =          300

# DEFINE AN AMD MOUNT POINT
[ /net ]
map_name =                amd.net
map_type =                file
```

The options in the [global] section specify behaviors of the daemon itself and rarely need changing. You'll notice that search_path is set to /etc, which means it will look for mount maps under the */etc* directory. You'll also see that auto_dir is set to /.automount. This is where *amd* will mount the directories you request. Since *amd* cannot perform mounts "in-place," directly under the mount point you define, it actually performs all mounts under the auto_dir directory, and then returns a symlink to that directory in response to the incoming mount requests. We'll explore that more after we look at the configuration for the [/net] mount point.

From looking at the above configuration file, we can tell that the file that tells *amd* how to mount things under */net* is *amd.net*. Since the search_path option in the [global] section is set to /etc, it'll really be looking for */etc/amd.net* at startup time. Here are the contents of that file:

```
/defaults fs:=${autodir}/${rhost}/root/${rfs};opts:=nosuid,nodev
*   rhost:=${key};type:=host;rfs:=/
```

Eyes glazing over? Well, then let's translate this into English. The first entry is /defaults, which is there to define the symlink that gets returned in response to requests for directories under [/net] in *amd.conf*. Here's a quick tour of the variables being used here:

- ${autodir} gets its value from the auto_dir setting in *amd.conf*, which in this case will be /.automount.

- ${rhost} is the name of the remote file server, which in our example is *fs*. It is followed closely by /root, which is really just a placeholder for / on the remote host.

- ${rfs} is the actual path under the / directory on the remote host that gets mounted.

Also note that fs: on the /defaults line specifies the local location where the remote filesystem is to be mounted. It's not the name of our remote file server.

In reality, there are a couple of other variables in play behind the scenes that help resolve the values of these variables, but this is enough to discern what's going on with our automounter. You should now be able to figure out what was really happening in our simple cd command earlier in this hack.

Because of the configuration settings in *amd.conf* and *amd.net*, when I ran the cd command earlier, I was actually requesting a mount of *fs:/linux/local* under the directory */net/fs/linux/local*. *amd*, behind my back, replaced that directory with a symlink to */.automount/fs/root/linux/local*, and that's where I really wound up. Running pwd with no options will say you're in */net/fs/linux/local*, but there's a quick way to tell where you really are, taking symlinks into account. Look at the output from these two pwd commands:

```
$ pwd
/net/fs/linux/local
$ pwd -P
/.automount/root/fs/linux/local
```

The -P option reveals your true location.

So, now that we have some clue as to how the *amd.net* /defaults entry works, we need to figure out exactly why our wonderful hack works. After all, we haven't yet told *amd* to explicitly mount anything!

Here's the entry in */etc/amd.net* that makes this functionality possible:

```
* rhost:=${key};type:=host;rfs:=/
```

The * wildcard entry says to attempt to mount any requested directory, rather than specifying one explicitly. When you request a mount, the part of the path after */net* defines the host and path to mount. If *amd* is able to perform the mount, it is served up to the user on the client host. The rfs=/ bit means that *amd* should request whatever directory is requested from the server under the root directory of that server. So, if we set `rfs=/mnt` and then request */linux/local*, the request will be for *fs:/mnt/linux/local*.

Synchronize root Environments with rsync

HACK #59

When you're managing multiple servers with local root logins, rsync provides an easy way to synchronize the root environments across your systems.

Synchronizing files between multiple computer systems is a classic problem. Say you've made some improvements to a file on one machine, and you would like to propagate it to others. What's the best way? Individual users often encounter this problem when trying to work on files on multiple computer systems, but it's even more common for system administrators who tend to use many different computer systems in the course of their daily activities.

rsync is a popular and well-known remote file and directory synchronization program that enables you to ensure that specified files and directories are identical on multiple systems. Some files that you may want to include for synchronization are:

- *.profile*
- *.bash_profile*
- *.bashrc*
- *.cshrc*
- *.login*
- *.logout*

Choose one server as your *source* server (referred to as *srchost* in the examples in this hack). This is the server where you will maintain the master copies of the files that you want to synchronize across multiple systems' root environments. After selecting this system, you'll add a stanza to the *rsync* configuration file (*/etc/rsyncd.conf*) containing, at a minimum, options for specifying the path to the directory that you want to synchronize (path), preventing remote clients from uploading files to the source server (read only), the user ID that you want synchronization to be performed as (uid), a list of files and directories that you want to exclude from synchronization (exclude), and the list of files that you want to synchronize (include). A sample stanza will look like this:

```
[rootenv]
    path = /
    uid = root    # default uid is nobody
    read only = yes
    exclude = * .*
```

```
include = .bashrc .bash_profile .aliases
hosts allow = 192.168.1.
hosts deny = *
```

Then add the following command to your shell's login command file (*.profile*, *.bash_profile*, *.login*, etc.) on the source host:

```
rsync -qa rsync://srchost/rootenv /
```

Next, you'll need to manually synchronize the files for the first time. After that, they will automatically be synchronized when your shell's login command file is executed. On each server you wish to synchronize, run this rsync command on the host as root:

```
rsync -qa rsync://srchost/rootenv /
```

For convenience, add the following alias to your *.bashrc* file, or add an equivalent statement to the command file for whatever shell you're using (*.cshrc*, *.kshrc*, etc.):

```
alias envsync='rsync -qa rsync::/srchost/rootenv / && source .bashrc'
```

By running the *envsync* alias, you can immediately sync up and source your *rc* files.

To increase security, you can use the */etc/hosts.allow* and */etc/hosts.deny* files to ensure that only specified hosts can use *rsync* on your systems **[Hack #64]**

See Also

- `man rsync`

—Lance Tost

HACK #60 Share Files Across Platforms Using Samba

Linux, Windows, and Mac OS X all speak SMB/CIFS, which makes Samba a one-stop shop for all of their resource-sharing needs.

It used to be that if you wanted to share resources in a mixed-platform environment, you needed NFS for your Unix machines, AppleTalk for your Mac crowd, and Samba or a Windows file and print server to handle the Windows users. Nowadays, all three platforms can mount file shares and use printing and other resources through SMB/CIFS, and Samba can serve them all.

Samba can be configured in a seemingly endless number of ways. It can share just files, or printer and application resources as well. You can authenticate users for some or all of the services using local files, an LDAP directory, or a Windows domain server. This makes Samba an extremely powerful, flexible tool in the fight to standardize on a single daemon to serve all of the hosts in your network.

At this point, you may be wondering why you would ever need to use Samba with a Linux client, since Linux clients can just use NFS. Well, that's true, but whether that's what you really want to do is another question. Some sites have users in engineering or development environments who maintain their own laptops and workstations. These folks have the local root password on their Linux machines. One mistyped NFS export line, or a chink in the armor of your NFS daemon's security, and you could be inadvertently allowing remote, untrusted users free rein on the shares they can access. Samba can be a great solution in cases like this, because it allows you to grant those users access to what they need without sacrificing the security of your environment.

This is possible because Samba can be (and generally is, in my experience) configured to ask for a username and password before allowing a user to mount anything. Whichever user supplies the username and password to perform the mount operation is the user whose permissions are enforced on the server. Thus, if a user becomes root on his local machine it needn't concern you, because local root access is trumped by the credentials of the user who performed the mount.

Setting Up Simple Samba Shares

Technically, the Samba service consists of two daemons, *smbd* and *nmbd*. The *smbd* daemon is the one that handles the SMB file- and print-sharing protocol. When a client requests a shared directory from the server, it's talking to *smbd*. The *nmbd* daemon is in charge of answering NetBIOS over IP name service requests. When a Windows client broadcasts to browse Windows shares on the network, *nmbd* replies to those broadcasts.

The configuration file for the Samba service is */etc/samba/smb.conf* on both Debian and Red Hat systems. If you have a tool called *swat* installed, you can use it to help you generate a working configuration without ever opening *vi*—just uncomment the *swat* line in */etc/inetd.conf* on Debian systems, or edit */etc/xinetd.d/swat* on Red Hat and other systems, changing the disable key's value to no. Once that's done, restart your *inetd* or *xinetd* service, and you should be able to get to *swat*'s graphical interface by pointing a browser at *http://localhost:901*.

Many servers are installed without *swat*, though, and for those systems editing the configuration file works just fine. Let's go over the config file for a simple setup that gives access to file and printer shares to authenticated users. The file is broken down into sections. The first section, which is always called [global], is the section that tells Samba what its "personality" should be on the network. There are a myriad of possibilities here, since

Samba can act as a primary or backup domain controller in a Windows domain, can use various printing subsystem interfaces and various authentication backends, and can provide various different services to clients.

Let's take a look at a simple [global] section:

```
[global]
    workgroup = PVT
    server string = apollo
    hosts allow = 192.168.42. 127.0.0.
    printcap name = CUPS
    load printers = yes
    printing = CUPS
    logfile = /var/log/samba/log.smbd
    max log size = 50
    security = user
    smb passwd file = /etc/samba/smbpasswd
    socket options = TCP_NODELAY SO_RCVBUF=8192 SO_SNDBUF=8192
    interfaces = eth0
    wins support = yes
    dns proxy = no
```

Much of this is self-explanatory. This excerpt is taken from a working configuration on a private SOHO network, which is evidenced by the hosts allow values. This option can take values in many different formats, and it uses the same syntax as the */etc/hosts.allow* and */etc/hosts.deny* files (see hosts_access(8) and "Allow or Deny Access by IP Address" **[Hack #64]**). Here, it allows access from the local host and any host whose IP address matches the pattern 192.168.42.*. Note that a netmask is not given or assumed—it's a pure regex match on the IP address of the connecting host. Note also that this setting can be removed from the [global] section and placed in each subsection. If it exists in the [global] section, however, it will supersede any settings in other areas of the configuration file.

In this configuration, I've opted to use CUPS as the printing mechanism. There's a CUPS server on the local machine where the Samba server lives, so Samba users will be able to see all the printers that CUPS knows about when they browse the PVT workgroup, and use them (more on this in a minute).

The server string setting determines the server name users will see when the host shows up in a Network Neighborhood listing, or in other SMB network browsing software. I generally set this to the actual hostname of the server if it's practical, so that if users need to manually request something from the Samba server, they don't try to ask to mount files from my Linux Samba server by trying to address it as "Samba Server."

The other important setting here is security. If you're happy with using the */etc/samba/smbpasswd* file for authentication, this setting is fine. There are many other ways to configure authentication, however, so you should definitely read the fine (and copious) Samba documentation to see how it can be integrated with just about any authentication backend. Samba includes native support for LDAP and PAM authentication. There are PAM modules available to sync Unix and Samba passwords, as well as to authenticate to remote SMB servers.

We're starting with a simple password file in our configuration. Included with the Samba package is a tool called *mksmbpasswd.sh*, which will add users to the password file en masse so you don't have to do it by hand. However, it cannot migrate Unix passwords to the file, because the cryptographic algorithm is a one-way hash and the Windows hash sent to Samba by the clients doesn't match.

To change the Samba password for a user, run the following command on the server:

```
# smbpasswd username
```

This will prompt you for the new password, and then ask you to confirm it by typing it again. If a user ran the command, she'd be prompted for her current Samba password first. If you want to manually add a user to the password file, you can use the -a flag, like this:

```
# smbpasswd -a username
```

This will also prompt for the password that should be assigned to the user.

Now that we have users, let's see what they have access to by looking at the sections for each share. In our configuration, users can access their home directories, all printers available through the local CUPS server, and a public share for users to dabble in. Let's look at the home directory configuration first:

```
[homes]
    comment = Home Directories
    browseable = no
    writable = yes
```

The [homes] section, like the [global] section, is recognized by the server as a "special" section. Without any more settings than these few minimal ones, Samba will, by default, take the username given during a client connection and look it up in the local password file. If it exists, and the correct password has been provided, Samba clones the [homes] section on the fly, creating a new share named after the user. Since we didn't use a path setting, the actual directory that gets served up is the home directory of the user, as supplied by the local Linux system. However, since we've set browseable = no, users will only be able to see their own home directories in the list of available shares, rather than those of every other user on the system.

Here's the printer share section:

```
[printers]
    comment = All Printers
    path = /var/spool/samba
    browseable = yes
    public = yes
    guest ok = yes
    writable = no
    printable = yes
    use client driver = yes
```

This section is also a "special" section, which works much like the [homes] special section. It clones the section to create a share for the printer being requested by the user, with the settings specified here. We've made printers browseable, so that users know which printers are available. This configuration will let any authenticated user view and print to any printer known to Samba.

Finally, here's our public space, which anyone can read or write to:

```
[tmp]
    comment = Temporary file space
    path = /tmp
    read only = no
    public = yes
```

This space will show up in a browse listing as "tmp on Apollo," and it is accessible in read/write mode by anyone authenticated to the server. This is useful in our situation, since users cannot mount and read from each other's home directories. This space can be mounted by anyone, so it provides a way for users to easily exchange files without, say, gumming up your email server.

Once your *smb.conf* file is in place, start up your *smb* service and give it a quick test. You can do this by logging into a Linux client host and using a command like this one:

```
$ smbmount '//apollo/jonesy' ~/foo/ -o username=jonesy,workgroup=PVT
```

This command will mount my home directory on *Apollo* to *~/foo/* on the local machine. I've passed along my username and the workgroup name, and the command will prompt for my password and happily perform the mount. If it doesn't, check your logfiles for clues as to what went wrong.

You can also log in to a Windows client, and see if your new Samba server shows up in your Network Neighborhood (or My Network Places under Windows XP).

If things don't go well, another command you can try is smbclient. Run the following command as a normal user:

```
$ smbclient -L apollo
```

On my test machine, the output looks like this:

```
Domain=[APOLLO] OS=[Unix] Server=[Samba 3.0.14a-2]

        Sharename       Type        Comment
        ---------       ----        -------
        tmp             Disk        Temporary file space
        IPC$            IPC         IPC Service (Samba Server)
        ADMIN$          IPC         IPC Service (Samba Server)
        MP780           Printer     MP780
        hp4m            Printer     HP LaserJet 4m
        jonesy          Disk        Home Directories
Domain=[APOLLO] OS=[Unix] Server=[Samba 3.0.14a-2]

        Server                  Comment
        ---------               -------

        Workgroup               Master
        ---------               -------
        PVT                     APOLLO
```

This list shows the services available to me from the Samba server, and I can
also use it to confirm that I'm using the correct workgroup name.

HACK #61 Quick and Dirty NAS

Combining LVM, NFS, and Samba on new file servers is a quick and easy
solution when you need more shared disk resources.

Network Attached Storage (NAS) and Storage Area Networks (SANs) aren't
making as many people rich nowadays as they did during the dot-com
boom, but they're still important concepts for any system administrator.
SANs depend on high-speed disk and network interfaces, and they're
responsible for the increasing popularity of other magic acronyms such as
iSCSI (Internet Small Computer Systems Interface) and AoE (ATA over
Ethernet), which are cool and upcoming technologies for transferring block-
oriented disk data over fast Ethernet interfaces. On the other hand, NAS is
quick and easy to set up: it just involves hanging new boxes with shared,
exported storage on your network.

"Disk use will always expand to fill all available storage" is one of the immu-
table laws of computing. It's sad that it's as true today, when you can pick
up a 400-GB disk for just over $200, as it was when I got my CS degree and
the entire department ran on some DEC-10s that together had a whopping
900 MB of storage (yes, I am old). Since then, every computing environment I've ever worked in has eventually run out of disk space. And let's face
it—adding more disks to existing machines can be a PITA (pain in the ass).
You have to take down the desktop systems, add disks, create filesystems,

mount them, copy data around, reboot, and then figure out how and where you're going to back up all the new space.

This is why NAS is so great. Need more space? Simply hang a few more storage devices off the network and give your users access to them. Many companies made gigabucks off this simple concept during the dot-com boom (more often by selling themselves than by selling hardware, but that's beside the point). The key for us in this hack is that Linux makes it easy to assemble your own NAS boxes from inexpensive PCs and add them to your network for a fraction of the cost of preassembled, nicely painted, dedicated NAS hardware. This hack is essentially a meta-hack, in which you can combine many of the tips and tricks presented throughout this book to save your organization money while increasing the control you have over how you deploy networked storage, and thus your general sysadmin comfort level. Here's how.

Selecting the Hardware

Like all hardware purchases, what you end up with is contingent on your budget. I tend to use inexpensive PCs as the basis for NAS boxes, and I'm completely comfortable with basing NAS solutions on today's reliable, high-speed EIDE drives. The speed of the disk controller(s), disks, and network interfaces is far more important than the CPU speed. This is not to say that recycling an old 300-MHz Pentium as the core of your NAS solutions is a good idea, but any reasonably modern 1.5-GHz or greater processor is more than sufficient. Most of what the box will be doing is serving data, not playing Doom. Thus, motherboards with built-in graphics are also fine for this purpose, since fast, hi-res graphics are equally unimportant in the NAS environment.

> In this hack, I'll describe minimum requirements for hardware characteristics and capabilities rather than making specific recommendations. As I often say professionally, "Anything better is better." That's not me taking the easy way out—it's me ensuring that this book won't be outdated before it actually hits the shelves.

My recipe for a reasonable NAS box is the following:

- A mini-tower case with at least three external, full-height drive bays (four is preferable) and a 500-watt or greater power supply with the best cooling fan available. If you can get a case with mounting brackets for extra cooling fans on the sides or bottom, do so, and purchase the right number of extra cooling fans. This machine is always going to be on, pushing at least four disks, so it's a good idea to get as much power and cooling as possible.

- A motherboard with integrated video hardware, at least 10/100 on-board Ethernet (10/100/1000 is preferable), and USB or FireWire support. Make sure that the motherboard supports booting from external USB (or FireWire, if available) drives, so that you won't have to waste a drive bay on a CD or DVD drive. If at all possible, on-board SATA is a great idea, since that will enable you to put the operating system and swap space on an internal disk and devote all of the drive bays to storage that will be available to users. I'll assume that you have on-board SATA in the rest of this hack.

- A 1.5-GHz or better Celeron, Pentium 4, or AMD processor compatible with your motherboard.

- 256 MB of memory.

- Five removable EIDE/ATA drive racks and trays, hot-swappable if possible. Four are for the system itself; the extra one gives you a spare tray to use when a drive inevitably fails.

- One small SATA drive (40 GB or so).

- Four identical EIDE drives, as large as you can afford. At the time I'm writing this, 300-GB drives with 16-MB buffers cost under $150. If possible, buy a fifth so that you have a spare and two others for backup purposes.

- An external CD/DVD USB or FireWire drive for installing the OS.

I can't really describe the details of assembling the hardware because I don't know exactly what configuration you'll end up purchasing, but the key idea is that you put a drive tray in each of the external bays, with one of the IDE/ATA drives in each, and put the SATA drive in an internal drive bay. This means that you'll still have to open up the box to replace the system disk if it ever fails, but it enables you to maximize the storage that this system makes available to users, which is its whole reason for being. Putting the EIDE/ATA disks in drive trays means that you can easily replace a failed drive without taking down the system if the trays are hot-swappable. Even if they're not, you can bounce a system pretty quickly if all you have to do is swap in another drive and you already have a spare tray available.

At the time I wrote this the hardware setup cost me around $1000 (exclusive of the backup hard drives) with some clever shopping, thanks to *http://www.pricewatch.com*. This got me a four-bay case; a motherboard with on-board GigE, SATA, and USB; four 300-GB drives with 16-MB buffers; hot-swappable drive racks; and a few extra cooling fans.

Installing and Configuring Linux

As I've always told everyone (regardless of whether they ask), I always install everything, regardless of which Linux distribution I'm using. I personally prefer SUSE for commercial deployments, because it's supported, you can get regular updates, and I've always found it to be an up-to-date distribution in terms of supporting the latest hardware and providing the latest kernel tweaks. Your mileage may vary. I'm still mad at Red Hat for abandoning everyone on the desktop, and I don't like GNOME (though I install it "because it's there" and because I need its libraries to run Evolution, which is my mailer of choice due to its ability to interact with Microsoft Exchange). Installing everything is easy. We're building a NAS box here, not a desktop system, so 80% of what I install will probably never be used, but I hate to find that some tool I'd like to use isn't installed.

To install the Linux distribution of your choice, attach the external CD/DVD drive to your machine and configure the BIOS to boot from it first and the SATA drive second. Put your installation media in the external CD/DVD drive and boot the system. Install Linux on the internal SATA drive. As discussed in "Reduce Restart Times with Journaling Filesystems" [Hack #70], I use ext3 for the /boot and / partitions on my systems so that I can easily repair them if anything ever goes wrong, and because every Linux distribution and rescue disk in the known universe can handle *ext2/ext3* partitions. There are simply more *ext2/ext3* tools out there than there are for any other filesystem. You don't have to partition or format the drives in the bays—we'll do that after the operating system is installed and booting.

Done installing Linux? Let's add and configure some storage.

Configuring User Storage

Determining how you want to partition and allocate your disk drives is one of the key decisions you'll need to make, because it affects both how much space your new NAS box will be able to deliver to users and how maintainable your system will be. To build a reliable NAS box, I use Linux software RAID to mirror the master on the primary IDE interface to the master on the secondary IDE interface and the slave on the primary IDE interface to the slave on the secondary IDE interface. I put them in the case in the following order (from the top down): master primary, slave primary, master secondary, and slave secondary. Having a consistent, specific order makes it easy to know which is which since the drive letter assignments will be *a*, *b*, *c*, and *d* from the top down, and also makes it easy to know in advance how to jumper any new drive that I'm swapping in without having to check.

By default, I then set up Linux software RAID and LVM so that the two drives on the primary IDE interface are in a logical volume group [Hack #47].

On systems with 300-GB disks, this gives me 600 GB of reliable, mirrored storage to provide to users. If you're less nervous than I am, you can skip the RAID step and just use LVM to deliver all 1.2 TB to your users, but backing that up will be a nightmare, and if any of the drives ever fail, you'll have 1.2 TB worth of angry, unproductive users. If you need 1.2 TB of storage, I'd strongly suggest that you spend the extra $1000 to build a second one of the boxes described in this hack. Mirroring is your friend, and it doesn't get much more stable than mirroring a pair of drives to two identical drives.

> If you experience performance problems and you need to export filesystems through both NFS and Samba, you may want to consider simply making each of the drives on the main IDE interface its own volume group, keeping the same mirroring layout, and exporting each drive as a single filesystem—one for SMB storage for your Windows users and the other for your Linux/Unix NFS users.

The next step is to decide how you want to partition the logical storage. This depends on the type of users you'll be delivering this storage to. If you need to provide storage to both Windows and Linux users, I suggest creating separate partitions for SMB and NFS users. The access patterns for the two classes of users and the different protocols used for the two types of networked filesystems are different enough that it's not a good idea to export a filesystem via NFS and have other people accessing it via SMB. With separate partitions they're still both coming to the same box, but at least the disk and operating system can cache reads and handle writes appropriately and separately for each type of filesystem.

Getting insights into the usage patterns of your users can help you decide what type of filesystem you want to use on each of the exported filesystems [Hack #70]. I'm a big *ext3* fan because so many utilities are available for correcting problems with *ext2/ext3* filesystems.

Regardless of the type of filesystem you select, you'll want to mount it using noatime to minimize file and filesystem updates due to access times. Creation time (ctime) and modification time (mtime) are important, but I've never cared much about access time and it can cause a big performance hit in a shared, networked filesystem. Here's a sample entry from */etc/fstab* that includes the noatime mount option:

```
/dev/data/music   /mnt/music   xfs   defaults,noatime   0 0
```

Similarly, since many users will share the filesystems in your system, you'll want to create the filesystem with a relatively large log. For *ext3* filesystems, the size of the journal is always at least 1,024 filesystem blocks, but larger logs can be useful for performance reasons on heavily used systems. I typically use a log of 64 MB on NAS boxes, because that seems to give the best tradeoff between caching filesystem updates and the effects of occasionally flushing the logs. If you are using *ext3*, you can also specify the journal flush/sync interval using the `commit=number-of-seconds` mount option. Higher values help performance, and anywhere between 15 and 30 seconds is a reasonable value on a heavily used NAS box (the default value is 5 seconds). Here's how you would specify this option in */etc/fstab*:

```
/dev/data/writing  /mnt/writing   ext3  defaults, cls, commit=15  0 0
```

A final consideration is how to back up all this shiny new storage. I generally let the RAID subsystem do my backups for me by shutting down the systems weekly, swapping out the mirrored drives with a spare pair, and letting the RAID system rebuild the mirrors automatically when the system comes back up. Disk backups are cheaper and less time-consuming than tape [Hack #50], and letting RAID mirror the drives for you saves you the manual copy step discussed in that hack.

Configuring System Services

Fine-tuning the services running on the soon-to-be NAS box is an important step. Turn off any services you don't need [Hack #63]. The core services you will need are an NFS server, a Samba server, a distributed authentication mechanism, and NTP. It's always a good idea to run an NTP server [Hack #22] on networked storage systems to keep the NAS box's clock in sync with the rest of your environment—otherwise, you can get some weird behavior from programs such as *make*.

You should also configure the system to boot in a non-graphical runlevel, which is usually runlevel 3 unless you're a Debian fan. I also typically install Fluxbox [Hack #73] on my NAS boxes and configure X to automatically start that rather than a desktop environment such as GNOME or KDE. Why waste cycles?

"Centralize Resources Using NFS" [Hack #56] explained setting up NFS and "Share Files Across Platforms Using Samba" [Hack #60] shows the same for Samba. If you don't have Windows users, you have my congratulations, and you don't have to worry about Samba.

The last step involved in configuring your system is to select the appropriate authentication mechanism so that you have the same users on the NAS box as you do on your desktop systems. This is completely dependent on the authentication mechanism used in your environment in general. Chapter 1 of this book discusses a variety of available authentication mechanisms and how to set them up. If you're working in an environment with heavy dependencies on Windows for infrastructure such as Exchange (shudder!), it's often best to bite the bullet and configure the NAS box to use Windows authentication. The critical point for NAS storage is that your NAS box must share the same UIDs, users, and groups as your desktop systems, or you're going to have problems with users using the new storage provided by the NAS box. One round of authentication problems is generally enough for any sysadmin to fall in love with a distributed authentication mechanism—which one you choose depends on how your computing environment has been set up in general and what types of machines it contains.

Deploying NAS Storage

The final step in building your NAS box is to actually make it available to your users. This involves creating some number of directories for the users and groups who will be accessing the new storage. For Linux users and groups who are focused on NFS, you can create top-level directories for each user and automatically mount them for your users using the NFS automounter and a similar technique to that explained in [Hack #57], wherein you automount your users' NAS directories as dedicated subdirectories somewhere in their accounts. For Windows users who are focused on Samba, you can do the same thing by setting up an [NAS] section in the Samba server configuration file on your NAS box and exporting your users' directories as a named NAS share.

Summary

Building and deploying your own NAS storage isn't really hard, and it can save you a significant amount of money over buying an off-the-shelf NAS box. Building your own NAS systems also helps you understand how they're organized, which simplifies maintenance, repairs, backups, and even the occasional but inevitable replacement of failed components. Try it—you'll like it!

See Also

- "Combine LVM and Software RAID" [Hack #47]
- "Centralize Resources Using NFS" [Hack #56]
- "Share Files Across Platforms Using Samba" [Hack #60]
- "Reduce Restart Times with Journaling Filesystems" [Hack #70]

HACK #62   Share Files and Directories over the Web

WebDAV is a powerful, platform-independent mechanism for sharing files over the Web without resorting to standard networked filesystems.

WebDAV (Web-based Distributed Authoring and Versioning) lets you edit and manage files stored on remote web servers. Many applications support direct access to WebDAV servers, including web-based editors, file-transfer clients, and more. WebDAV enables you to edit files where they live on your web server, without making you go through a standard but tedious download, edit, and upload cycle.

Because it relies on the HTTP protocol rather than a specific networked filesystem protocol, WebDAV provides yet another way to leverage the inherent platform-independence of the Web. Though many Linux applications can access WebDAV servers directly, Linux also provides a convenient mechanism for accessing WebDAV directories from the command line through the *davfs* filesystem driver. This hack will show you how to setup WebDAV support on the Apache web server, which is the most common mechanism for accessing WebDAV files and directories.

Installing and Configuring Apache's WebDAV Support

WebDAV support in Apache is made possible by the *mod_dav* module. Servers running Apache 2.x will already have *mod_dav* included in the package *apache2-common*, so you should only need to make a simple change to your Apache configuration in order to run *mod_dav*. If you compiled your own version of Apache, make sure that you compiled it with the –enable-dav option to enable and integrate WebDAV support.

> To enable WebDAV on an Apache server that is still running Apache 1.x, you must download and install the original Version 1.0 of *mod_dav*, which is stable but is no longer being actively developed. This version can be found at *http://www.webdav.org/mod_dav/*.

If WebDAV support wasn't statically linked into your version of Apache2, you'll need to load the modules that provide WebDAV support. To load the Apache2 modules for WebDAV, do the following:

```
# cd /etc/apache2/mods-enabled/
# ln -s /etc/apache2/mods-available/dav.load dav.load
# ln -s /etc/apache2/mods-available/dav_fs.load dav_fs.load
# ln -s /etc/apache2/mods-available/dav_fs.conf dav_fs.conf
```

Next, add these two commands to your *httpd.conf* file to set variables used by Apache's WebDAV support:

```
DAVLockDB /tmp/DAVLock
DAVMinTimeout 600!
```

These can be added anywhere in the top level of your *httpd.conf* file—in other words, anywhere that is not specific to the definition of a single directory or server. The `DAVLockDB` statement identifies the directory where locks should be stored. This directory must exist and should be owned by the Apache service account's user and group. The `DAVMinTimeout` variable specifies the period of time after which a lock will automatically be released.

Next, you'll need to create a WebDAV root directory. Users will have their own subdirectories beneath this one, so it's a bit like an alternative */home* directory. This directory must be readable and writable by the Apache service account. On most distributions, this user will probably be called *apache* or *www-data*. You can check this by searching for the Apache process in ps using one of the following commands:

```
# ps -ef | grep apache2
# ps -ef | grep httpd
```

A good location for the WebDAV root is at the same level as your Apache document root. Apache's document root is usually at */var/www/apache2-default* (or, on some systems, */var/www/html*). I tend to use */var/www/webdav* as a standard WebDAV root on my systems.

Create this directory and give read and write access to the Apache service account (*apache*, *www-data*, or whatever other name is used on your systems):

```
# mkdir /var/www/webdav
# chown root:www-data /var/www/webdav
# chmod 750 /var/www/webdav
```

Now that you've created your directory, you'll need to enable it for WebDAV in Apache. This is done with a simple `Dav On` directive, which can be located inside a directory definition anywhere in your Apache configuration file (*httpd.conf*):

```
<Directory /var/www/webdav>
  Dav On
</Directory>
```

Creating WebDAV Users and Directories

If you simply activate WebDAV on a directory, any user can access and modify the files in that directory through a web browser. While a complete absence of security is convenient, it is not "the right thing" in any modern computing environment. You will therefore want to apply the standard Apache techniques for specifying the authentication requirements for a given directory in order to properly protect files stored in WebDAV.

As an example, to set up simple password authentication you can use the htpasswd command to create a password file and set up an initial user, whom we'll call *joe*:

```
# mkdir /etc/apache2/passwd
# htpasswd -c /etc/apache2/passwd/htpass.dav joe
```

> The htpasswd command's -c flag creates a new password file, over-writing any previously created file (and all usernames and passwords it contains), so it should only be used the first time the password file is created.

The htpasswd command will prompt you once for *joe*'s new WebDAV password, and then again for confirmation. Once you've specified the password, you should set the permissions on your new password file so that it can't be read by standard users but is readable by any member of the Apache service account group:

```
# chown root:www-data /etc/apache2/passwd/htpass.dav
# chmod 640 /etc/apache2/passwd/htpass.dav
```

Next, the sample user *joe* will need a WebDAV directory of his own, with the right permissions set:

```
# mkdir /var/www/webdav/joe
# chown www-data:www-data /var/www/webdav/joe
# chmod 750 /var/www/webdav/joe
```

The sample user will also need to use the password file that you just created with htpasswd to authenticate access to his directory, so you'll have to update *httpd.conf* with another directive for that directory:

```
<Directory /var/www/webdav/joe/>
  require user joe
</Directory>
```

> WebDAV in Apache uses the same authorization conventions as any Apache authentication declaration. You can therefore require group membership, enable access to a single directory by multiple users by listing them, and so on. See your Apache documentation for more information.

Now just restart your Apache server, and you're done with the Apache side of things:

```
# /usr/sbin/apache2ctl restart
```

At this point, you should be able to connect to your web server and access files in */var/www/webdav/joe* as the user *joe* from any WebDAV-enabled application.

See Also

- General information about WebDAV: *http://webdav.org*
- Linux *davfs* module: *http://dav.sourceforge.net*

—Jon Fox

## CHAPTER SEVEN

Security
Hacks 63–68

We've come a long way since the 1980s, when Richard Stallman advocated using a carriage return as your password—and a long, sad trip it's been. Today's highly connected systems and the very existence of the Internet have provided exponential increases in productivity. The downside of this connectivity is that it also provides infinite opportunities for malicious intruders to crack your systems. The goals in attempting this range from curiosity to industrial espionage, but you can't tell who's who or take any chances. It's the responsibility of every system administrator to make sure that the systems that they're responsible for are secure and don't end up as worm-infested zombies or warez servers serving up bootleg software and every episode of SG-1 to P2P users everywhere.

The hacks in this chapter address system security at multiple levels. Several discuss how to set up secure systems, detect network intrusions, and lock out hosts that clearly have no business trying to access your machines. Others discuss software that enables you to record the official state of your machine's filesystems and catch changes to files that shouldn't be changing. Another hack discusses how to automatically detect well-known types of Trojan horse software that, once installed, let intruders roam unmolested by hiding their existence from standard system commands. Together, the hacks in this chapter discuss a wide spectrum of system security applications and techniques that will help you minimize or (hopefully) eliminate intrusions, but also protect you if someone does manage to crack your network or a specific box.

Increase Security by Disabling Unnecessary Services

Many network services that may be enabled by default are both unnecessary and insecure. Take the minimalist approach and enable only what you need.

Though today's systems are powerful and have gobs of memory, optimizing the processes they start by default is a good idea for two primary reasons. First, regardless of how much memory you have, why waste it by running things that you don't need or use? Secondly, and more importantly, every service you run on your system is a point of exposure, a potential cracking opportunity for the enlightened or lucky intruder or script kiddie.

There are three standard places from which system services can be started on a Linux system. The first is */etc/inittab*. The second is scripts in the */etc/rc.d/rc?. d* directories (*/etc/init.d/rc?.d* on SUSE and other more LSB-compliant Linux distributions). The third is by the Internet daemon, which is usually *inetd* or *xinetd*. This hack explores the basic Linux startup process, shows where and how services are started, and explains easy ways of disabling superfluous services to minimize the places where your systems can be attacked.

Examining /etc/inittab

Changes to */etc/inittab* itself are rarely necessary, but this file is the key to most of the startup processes on systems such as Linux that use what is known as the "Sys V init" mechanism (this startup mechanism was first implemented on AT&T's System V Unix systems). The */etc/inittab* file initiates the standard sequence of startup scripts, as described in the next section. The commands that start the initialization sequence for each runlevel are contained in the following entries from */etc/inittab*. These run the scripts in the runlevel control directory associated with each runlevel:

```
l0:0:wait:/etc/rc.d/rc 0
l1:1:wait:/etc/rc.d/rc 1
l2:2:wait:/etc/rc.d/rc 2
l3:3:wait:/etc/rc.d/rc 3
l4:4:wait:/etc/rc.d/rc 4
l5:5:wait:/etc/rc.d/rc 5
l6:6:wait:/etc/rc.d/rc 6
```

When the *init* process (the seminal process on Linux and Unix systems) encounters these entries, it runs the startup scripts in the directory associated with its target runlevel in numerical order, as discussed in the next section.

Optimizing Per-Runlevel Startup Scripts

As shown in the previous section, there are usually seven *rc?.d* directories, numbered *0* through *6* that are found in the */etc/init.d* or the */etc/rc.d* directory, depending on your Linux distribution. The numbers correspond to the Linux runlevels. A description of each runlevel, appropriate for the age and type of Linux distribution that you're using, can be found in the *init* man page. (Thanks a lot, Debian!) Common runlevels for most Linux distributions are 3 (multi-user text) and 5 (multi-user graphical).

The directory for each runlevel contains symbolic links to the actual scripts that start and stop various services, which reside in */etc/rc.d/init.d* or */etc/init.d*. Links that begin with *S* will be started when entering that runlevel, while links that begin with *K* will be stopped (or killed) when leaving that runlevel. The numbers after the *S* or *K* determine the order in which the scripts are executed, in ascending order.

The easiest way to disable a service is to remove the *S* script that is associated with it, but I tend to make a directory called *DISABLED* in each runlevel directory and move the symlinks to start and kill scripts that I don't want to run there. This enables me to see what services were previously started or terminated when entering and leaving each runlevel, should I discover that some important service is no longer functioning correctly at a specified runlevel.

Streamlining Services Run by the Internet Daemon

One of the startup scripts in the directory for each runlevel starts the Internet daemon, which is *inetd* on older Linux distributions or *xinetd* on most newer Linux distributions. The Internet daemon starts specified services in response to incoming requests and eliminates the need for your system to permanently run daemons that are accessed only infrequently. If your distribution is still using *inetd* and you want to disable specific services, edit */etc/inetd.conf* and comment out the line related to the service you wish to disable. To disable services managed by *xinetd*, cd to the directory */etc/xinetd.conf*, which is the directory that contains its service control scripts, and edit the file associated with the service you no longer want to provide. To disable a specific service, set the disabled entry in each stanza in its control file to yes. After making changes to */etc/inetd.conf* or any of the control files in */etc/xinetd.conf*, you'll need to send a HUP signal to *inetd* or *xinetd* to cause it to restart and re-read its configuration information:

```
# kill -HUP PID
```

Many Linux distributions provide tools that simplify manag-ing *rc* scripts and *xinetd* configuration. For example, Red Hat Linux provides *chkconfig*, while SUSE Linux provides this functionality within its *YaST* administration tool.

Of course, the specific services each system requires depends on what you're using it for. However, if you're setting up an out-of-the-box Linux distribu-tion, you will often want to deactivate default services such as a web server, an FTP server, a TFTP server, NFS support, and so on.

Summary

Running extra services on your systems consumes system resources and pro-vides opportunities for malicious users to attempt to compromise your sys-tems. Following the suggestions in this hack can help you increase the performance and security of the systems that you or the company you work for depend upon.

—Lance Tost

Allow or Deny Access by IP Address

Using the power of your text editor, you can quickly lock out malicious systems.

When running secure services, you'll often find that you want to allow and/ or deny access to and from certain machines. There are many different ways you can go about this. For instance, you could implement access control lists (ACLs) at the switch or router level. Alternatively, you could configure *iptables* or *ipchains* to implement your access restrictions. However, a sim-pler method of implementing access control is via the proper configuration of the */etc/hosts.allow* and */etc/hosts.deny* files. These are standard text files found in the */etc* directory on almost every Linux system. Like many config-uration files found within Linux, they can appear daunting at first glance, but with a little help, setting them up is actually quite easy.

Protecting Your Machine with hosts.allow and hosts.deny

Before we jump into writing complex network access rules, we need to spend a few moments reviewing the way the Linux access control software works. Inbound packets to *tpcd*, the Linux TCP daemon, are filtered through the rules in *hosts.allow* first, and then, if there are no matches, they are checked against the rules in *hosts.deny*. It's important to note this order, because if you have contradictory rules in each file you should be aware that the rule in *hosts.allow* will always be implemented, as the first match is found there. This ceases the filtering, and the incoming packets are never checked against *hosts.deny*. If a matching rule is not found in either file, access is granted.

In their most simple form, the lines in each of these files should conform to the following format:

```
daemon-name: hostname or ip-address
```

Here's a more recognizable example:

```
sshd: 192.168.1.55,192.168.155.56
```

If we inserted this line into *hosts.allow*, all SSH traffic between our local host and 192.168.1.55 and 192.168.1.56 would be allowed. Conversely, if we placed it in *hosts.deny*, no SSH traffic would be permitted from those two machines to the local host. This would seem to limit the usability of these files for access control—but wait, there's more!

The Linux TCP daemon provides an excellent language and syntax for configuring access control restrictions in the *hosts.allow* and *hosts.deny* files. This syntax includes pattern matching, operators, wildcards, and even shell commands to extend the capabilities. This might sound confusing at first, but we'll run through some examples that should clear things up. Continuing with our previous SSH example, let's expand the capabilities of the rule a bit:

```
#hosts.allow
sshd: .foo.bar
```

In the example above, take note of the leading dot. This tells Linux to match anything with *.foo.bar* in its hostname. In this example, both *www.foo.bar* and *mail.foo.bar* would be granted access. Alternatively, you can place a trailing dot to filter anything that matches the prefix:

```
#hosts.deny
sshd: 192.168.2.
```

This would effectively block SSH connections from every address between 192.168.2.1 and 192.168.2.255. Another way to block a subnet is to provide the full network address and subnet mask in the *xxx.xxx.xxx.xxx/mmm.mmm.mmm.mmm* format, where the *x*s represent the network address and the *m*s represent the subnet mask.

A simple example of this is the following:

```
sshd: 192.168.6.0/255.255.255.0
```

This entry is equivalent to the previous example but uses the network/subnet mask syntax.

Several other wildcards can be used to specify client addresses, but we'll focus on the two that are most useful: ALL and LOCAL. ALL is the universal wildcard. Everything will match this, and access will be granted or denied based on which file you've used it in. Being careless with this wildcard can leave you open to attacks that you would normally think you're safe from, so make sure that you mean to open up a service to the world when you use it in *hosts.allow*. LOCAL is used to specify any hostname that doesn't have a dot (.) within it. This can be used to match against any entries contained in the local */etc/hosts* file.

Configuring hosts.allow and hosts.deny for Use

Now that we've mastered all that, let's move on to a more complex setup. We'll set up a *hosts.allow* configuration that allows SSH connections from anywhere and restricts HTTP traffic to our local network and entries specifically configured in our hosts file. As intelligent sysadmins, we know that telnet shares many of the same security features as string cheese, so we'll use *hosts.deny* to deny telnet connections from everywhere as well.

First, edit *hosts.allow* to read:

```
sshd: ALL
httpd: LOCAL, 192.168.1.0/255.255.255.0
```

Next, edit *hosts.deny* to read:

```
telnet: ALL
```

As you can see, securing your machine locally isn't that hard. If you need to filter on a much more complicated scale, employing network-level ACLs or using *iptables* to create specific packet-filtering rules might be appropriate. However, for simple access control, the simplicity of *hosts.allow* and *hosts.deny* can't be beat.

One thing to keep in mind is that it is typically bad practice to perform this kind of filtering upon hostnames. If you rely on hostnames, you're also relying on name resolution. Should your network lose the ability to resolve hostnames, you could potentially leave yourself wide open to attack, or cause all your protected services to come to a screeching halt as all network traffic to them is denied. Usually, it's better to play it safe and stick to IP addresses.

Hacking the Hack

Wouldn't it be cool if we could set up a rule in our access control files that alerted us whenever an attempt was made from an unauthorized IP address? The *hosts.allow* and *hosts.deny* files provide a way to do just that! To make this work, we'll have to use the shell command option from the previously mentioned syntax. Here's an example *hosts.deny* config to get you started:

```
sshd: 192.168.2. spawn (/bin/echo illegal connection attempt from %h %a to
%d %p at 'date' >>/var/log/unauthorized.log | tee /var/log/unauthorized.log|
mail root
```

Using this command in our *hosts.deny* file will append the hostname (%h), address (%a), daemon process (%d), and PID (%p), as well as the date and time, to the file */var/log/unauthorized.log*. Traditionally, the `finger` or `safe_finger` commands are used; however, you're certainly not limited to these.

See Also

- `man tcpd`
- *http://www.die.net/doc/linux/man/man5/hosts.allow.5.html*

—*Brian Warshawsky*

Detect Network Intruders with snort

Let snort watch for network intruders and log attacks—and alert you when problems arise.

Security is a big deal in today's connected world. Every school and company of any decent size has an internal network and a web site, and they are often directly connected to the Internet. Many connected sites use dedicated firewall hardware to allow only certain types of access through certain network ports or from certain network sites, networks, and subnets. However, when you're traveling and using random Internet connections from hotels, cafes, or trade shows, you can't necessarily bank on the security that your academic or work environment traditionally provides. Your machine may actually be on the Net, and therefore a potential target for script kiddies and dedicated hackers anywhere. Similarly, if your school or business has machines that are directly on the Net with no intervening hardware, you may as well paint a big red bull's-eye on yourself.

Most Linux distributions nowadays come with built-in firewalls based on the in-kernel packet-filtering rules that are supported by the most excellent *iptables* package. However, these can be complex even to *iptables* devotees, and they can also be irritating if you need to use standard old-school transfer and connectivity protocols such as TFTP or telnet, since these are often blocked by firewall rule sets. Unfortunately, this leads many people to disable the firewall rules, which is the conceptual equivalent of dropping your pants on the Internet. You're exposed!

This hack explores the *snort* package, an open source software intrusion detection system (IDS) that monitors incoming network requests to your system, alerts you to activity that appears to be spurious, and captures an evidence trail. While there are a number of other popular open source packages that help you detect and react to network intruders, none is as powerful, flexible, and actively supported as *snort*.

Installing snort

The source code for *snort* is freely available from its home page at *http://www. snort.org*. At the time this book was written, the current version was 2.4. Because *snort* needs to be able to capture and interpret raw Ethernet packets, it requires that you have the Packet Capture library and headers (*libpcap*) installed on your system. *libpcap* is installed as a part of most modern Linux distributions, but it is also available in source form from *http://www.tcpdump.org*.

You can configure and build *snort* with the standard configuration, build, and install commands used by any software package that uses *autoconf*:

```
$ tar zxf snort-2.4.0.tar.gz
$ cd snort-2.4.0
$ ./configure
[much output removed]
$ make
[much output removed]
```

As with most open source software, installing into */usr/local* is the default. You can change this behavior by specifying a new location, using the configure command's --prefix option. To install *snort*, su to root or use sudo to install the software to the appropriate subdirectories of */usr/local* using the standard make install command:

```
# make install
```

At this point, you can begin using *snort* in various simple packet capture modes, but to take advantage of its full capabilities, you'll want to create a *snort* configuration file and install a number of default rule sets, as explained in the next section.

Configuring snort

snort is a highly customizable IDS that is driven by a combination of configuration statements and loadable rule sets. The default *snort* configuration file is the file */etc/snort.conf*, though you can use a configuration file in any location by specifying the full path to and name of the configuration file using the snort command's -c option. The *snort* source package includes a generic configuration file that is preconfigured to load many sets of rules, which are also available from the *snort* web site at *http://www.snort.org/pub-bin/downloads.cgi*.

> To get up-to-the-minute rule sets, subscribe to the latest *snort* updates from the SourceFire folks, the people who wrote, support, and update *snort*. Subscriptions are explained at *http://www.snort.org/rules/why_subscribe.html*. This is generally a good idea, especially if you're using *snort* in a business environment, but this hack focuses on using the free rule sets that are also available from the *snort* site.

It's perfectly fine to create your own configuration file, but since the template provided with the *snort* source is quite complete and shows how to take advantage of many of the capabilities of *snort*, we'll focus on adapting the template configuration file to your system.

To begin customizing *snort*, su to root and create two directories that we'll use to hold information produced by and about *snort*:

```
# mkdir -p /var/log/snort
# mkdir -p /etc/snort/rules
```

The */var/log/snort* directory is required by *snort*; this is where alerts are recorded and packet captures are archived. The */etc/snort* directory and its subdirectories are where I like to centralize *snort* configuration information and rules. You can select any location that you want, but the instructions in this hack will assume that you're putting everything in */etc/snort*.

Next, cd to */etc/snort* and copy the files *snort.conf* and *unicode.map* to the parent directory (*/etc*). The */etc* directory is the default location specified in the source code for these core *snort* configuration files. As we'll see in the rest of this hack, we'll put everything else in our own */etc/snort* directory.

Now you can bring up the file */etc/snort.conf* in your favorite text editor (which should be *emacs*, by the way), and start making changes.

First, set the value of the HOME_NET variable to the base value of your home or business network. This prevents *snort* from logging outbound and generic intermachine communication on your network unless it triggers an IDS rule.

> If the machine on which you'll be running *snort* gets its IP address via DHCP, you can set HOME_NET using the declaration var HOME_NET $eth0_ADDRESS, which sets the variable to the IP address assigned to your Ethernet interface. Note that this will require restarting *snort* if the interface goes down and comes back up while *snort* is running.

Next, set the variable EXTERNAL_NET to identify the hosts/networks from which you want to monitor traffic. To avoid logging local traffic between hosts on the network, the most convenient setting is !$HOME_NET:

```
var EXTERNAL_NET !$HOME_NET
```

> Forgetting the $ is a common mistake that will generate an error about *snort* not being able to resolve the address *HOME_NET*. Make sure you include the $ so that *snort* references the value of the $HOME_NET variable, not the string *HOME_NET*.

If your network runs various servers, the next step is to update the configuration file to identify the hosts on which they are running. This enables *snort* to focus on looking for certain types of attacks on systems that are actually running those services. *snort* provides a number of variables for various services, all of which are set to the value of the HOME_NET variable by default:

```
# List of DNS servers on your network
var DNS_SERVERS $HOME_NET
# List of SMTP servers on your network
var SMTP_SERVERS $HOME_NET
# List of web servers on your network
var HTTP_SERVERS $HOME_NET
# List of sql servers on your network
var SQL_SERVERS $HOME_NET
# List of telnet servers on your network
var TELNET_SERVERS $HOME_NET
# List of snmp servers on your network
var SNMP_SERVERS $HOME_NET
```

Next, copy the *classification.config* and *reference.config* files to */etc/snort* and set the include statements for these in *snort.conf* to point to the full path to these files:

```
include /etc/snort/classification.config
include /etc/snort/reference.config
```

Now set the value of the RULE_PATH variable in the *snort* configuration file to */etc/snort/rules* (this variable can point anywhere, of course, but I prefer to centralize as much of the *snort* configuration information in */etc/snort* as possible):

```
var RULE_PATH /etc/snort/rules
```

Finally, configure *snort*'s output plug-ins to log rule transgressions (known as *alerts*) however you'd like. By default, *snort* enables you to log alerts to the system log and various databases, and also makes it easy for you to define custom alert mechanisms. I'll focus on using the system log, since that's the most common (and generic) logging mechanism. To enable logging alerts to the system log (*/var/log/messages*), simply uncomment the following line in */etc/snort.conf*:

```
output alert_syslog: LOG_AUTH LOG_ALERT
```

Almost there! You're now ready to download and install the rules files that are referenced in your *snort* configuration file. As mentioned previously, you should seriously consider subscribing to these if you're using *snort* in an enterprise environment, both in order to support further development of *snort* and because it's simply the right thing to do. For the purposes of this hack, you can retrieve and install the free (unregistered user) rules files from *http://www.snort.org/pub-bin/downloads.cgi* by searching the page for the "unregistered user release" section and retrieving a gzipped tarball of the rules that match the version of *snort* you've built.

To install these rules, change directory to your */etc/snort* directory and su to root or use sudo to extract the contents of the tarball with a standard tar incantation:

```
$ cd /etc/snort
$ sudo tar zxvf /home/wvh/snortrules-pr-2.4.tar.gz
```

This will create */rules* and */doc* subdirectories in */etc/snort*. (Again, these rules can actually live anywhere on your system since their location is identified by the RULE_PATH variable in the *snort* configuration file. We set this variable to */etc/snort/rules* earlier.)

Starting snort

At this point, you're ready to run *snort*. Though *snort* offers a daemon mode, it's generally useful to run it in interactive mode from the command line until you're sure you've made the correct modifications to your */etc/snort.conf* file. To do this, execute the following command:

```
# snort -A full
```

You'll see a lot of output as *snort* parses your configuration file and rule sets. If you've done everything right and not made any typos, this output will conclude with the following block of output:

```
--== Initialization Complete ==--

      ,,_        -*> Snort! <*-
   o"  )~     Version 2.4.0 (Build 18) x86_64
      ''''        By Martin Roesch & The Snort Team: http://www.snort.org/team.html
               (C) Copyright 1998-2005 Sourcefire Inc., et al.
```

If you see this, all is well and *snort* is running correctly. If not, correct the problems identified by the *snort* error messages (which are usually quite good), and try the snort command again until *snort* starts correctly.

One especially common and irritating message when getting started using *snort* is the following:

```
socket: Address family not supported by protocol
```

You will see this message if your system's kernel is not configured to support the CONFIG_PACKET option, which enables applications (the packet capture library, in this case) to read directly from network interfaces. This capability can be compiled directly into the kernel, but it's more commonly built as a loadable kernel module (LKM) with the name *af_packet.ko* (*af_packet.o* if you're still running a pre-2.6 Linux kernel).

If this capability is provided as an LKM on your system, you can generally load it by executing the modprobe af_packet.ko command as root or via sudo. If modprobe doesn't work for some reason, you can load the module directly using the insmod command. The name of the appropriate */lib/modules* subdirectory where the module is located is contingent on the version of the kernel you're running, which you can determine by executing the uname -r command. For example:

```
# uname -r
2.6.11.4-21.8-default
# insmod /lib/modules/2.6.11.4-21.8-default/kernel/net/packet/af_packet.ko
Testing Snort
```

The fact that *snort* is running without complaints is all well and good, but executing correctly isn't the same thing as doing what you want it to do. It's therefore useful to actually test *snort* by triggering one of its rules. The easiest of these to trigger are the port scan rules. To test these, connect to a machine outside your network and issue the nmap command, identifying the machine on which you're running *snort* as the target, as in the following example:

```
$ nmap -P0 24.3.53.235
Starting nmap V. 2.54BETA31 ( www.insecure.org/nmap/ )
Warning:  You are not root -- using TCP pingscan rather than ICMP
Nmap run completed -- 1 IP address (0 hosts up) scanned in 60 seconds
```

You can now check */var/log/snort*, in which you should see a filenames alert with contents like the following:

```
a[**] [122:17:0] (portscan) UDP Portscan [**]
09/14-20:53:16.024463 24.3.53.235 -> 192.168.6.64
RAW TTL:0 TOS:0xC0 ID:29863 IpLen:20 DgmLen:163
```

You will also see a directory with the name *24.3.53.235*. This directory contains logs of the offending packets that triggered the alert. Congratulations! *snort* is working correctly.

If you have port forwarding active on a home or business gateway, you'll probably see a file with the IP address of the gateway instead of the IP address of the host from which you did the port scan.

Once you're satisfied that *snort* is working correctly, you'll probably want to terminate the interactive *snort* session we started earlier and restart *snort* in daemon mode, using the following command:

```
# snort -A full -D
```

This starts *snort* in the background and sends its initialization messages to */var/log/messages*. To add this command to your system's startup mechanisms, either append it to a startup script such as */etc/rc.local* or integrate it into the standard system startup process by creating a start/stop script in */etc/init.d* and adding the appropriate symbolic links to the */etc/rc.runlevel* directory that corresponds to the default runlevel for the system on which you're running *snort*.

Advanced snort

You can extend *snort* in an infinite number of ways. One of the easiest is to take advantage of more of its default capabilities by activating additional rule sets that are provided in the bundle that you downloaded but are commented out of the default *snort* configuration file template. Some of my favorites to uncomment are the following:

```
include $RULE_PATH/web-attacks.rules
include $RULE_PATH/backdoor.rules
include $RULE_PATH/shellcode.rules
include $RULE_PATH/virus.rules
```

Once you uncomment these and restart *snort*, you'll probably start to see additional *snort* alerts such as the following:

```
[**] [1:651:8] SHELLCODE x86 stealth NOOP [**]
[Classification: Executable code was detected] [Priority: 1]
09/15-04:49:32.299135 70.48.80.189:6881 -> 192.168.6.64:52757
TCP TTL:109 TOS:0x0 ID:53803 IpLen:20 DgmLen:1432 DF
***AP*** Seq: 0x1869E9D1  Ack: 0x18F60ED8  Win: 0xFFFF  TcpLen: 32
TCP Options (3) => NOP NOP TS: 719694 594700245
[Xref => http://www.whitehats.com/info/IDS291]
```

Better to know about attempted attacks than to be blissfully unaware! Of course, whether or not you want to monitor your network for these types of attacks is entirely dependent on your site's network policies—which is why they're commented out of the *snort* configuration file template. Your mileage may vary, but I find these quite useful.

Summary

snort is an extremely powerful, flexible, and configurable intrusion detection system. This hack focused on getting it up and running in a standard fashion—explaining how to create your own rules and take advantage of all of its capabilities would require its own book. Actually, a number of books on *snort* are available, as well as extensive discussions in more general networking texts such as O'Reilly's own *Network Security Hacks*, by Andrew Lockhart.

If you're interested in a simpler network-monitoring package, *PortSentry* (*http://sourceforge.net/projects/sentrytools/*) is one of the best known, though it hasn't been updated for quite a while now. However, *snort* is a much more powerful tool and is actively under development. Newer *snort* developments include the ability to actively respond to certain types of attacks by sending certain types of packages (known as *flexresp*, or flexible response) and increasing integration with dynamic notification tools on both the Linux and Windows platforms. In today's connected world, you can't really afford not to firewall your hosts and scan for clever folks that can still punch through your defenses. In the open source world, there's no better tool for the latter task than *snort*.

See Also

- "Monitor Network Traffic with MRTG" **[Hack #79]**
- *Network Security Hacks*, by Andrew Lockhart (O'Reilly)
- `man snort`
- Snort Central: *http://www.snort.org*

HACK #66 Tame Tripwire

The Tripwire program is a great intrusion-detection system, but it can also be a pain to configure. Save yourself time and trouble with these tips and tricks.

Do you ever wake up in a cold sweat at night, worrying about someone compromising your servers? Have you ever found yourself wondering if the *ls* binary that you execute on your machine is actually telling you the truth about the files in your home directory? If so, welcome to the wonderful world of system administrator paranoia. And here's a tip: you should look into the possibility of deploying an intrusion-detection system on your servers so that you can rest easy every night.

There are many different types of IDS out there. Some focus on analyzing incoming network connections, some simply monitor logs and send alerts to sleeping sysadmins, and others analyze the binaries, configuration files, and libraries on a system and notify sysadmins of any changes. Tripwire is an excellent example of the third type of IDS software. It creates a database of the characteristics of the files in your filesystem and can then monitor the integrity of every single file and directory on your server. But while such security can be massively reassuring to the paranoid sysadmin, it doesn't come without a cost. Tripwire can be a beast to set up and configure properly, and hours of tweaking may be required to tune it properly for your filesystem. However, with a little bit of help, you can have Tripwire running strong on your system without too much effort.

Installing Tripwire

Obviously, the first step is to obtain and install the software. You have two options for this. The first, and by far the easiest, is to use your package management software to install Tripwire. Alternatively, you can install from an RPM available on a third-party site. The procedure I'm going to go through is for installing Tripwire on Fedora Core 4 via the RPM available on an independent Fedora software site, but the procedure should be similar for any other RPM-based distribution.

First, download the RPM from *http://rpm.chaz6.com/?p=fedora/tripwire/ tripwire-2.3.1-18.fdr.3.1.fc4.i686.rpm*. Install it as normal from the command line:

```
# rpm -Uvh tripwire-2.3.1-18.fdr.3.1.fc2.i686.rpm
```

If you don't have any unsatisfied dependencies, the RPM will successfully load Tripwire onto your system.

Now that the application is installed, take a moment to become familiar with the configuration files that control Tripwire. There are two main files, and we'll cover each of them in detail.

Tripwire's Execution Configuration File

The file *etc/tripwire/twcfg.txt* controls the environment and manner in which Tripwire operates. It is in this file that you can specify alternate installation directories, the location of the policy and database files, where to output reports, and where to find the site and local keys so that everything can be securely signed. The following is a sample *twcfg.txt* file:

```
ROOT =/usr/sbin
POLFILE =/etc/tripwire/tw.pol
DBFILE =/var/lib/tripwire/$(HOSTNAME).twd
REPORTFILE =/var/lib/tripwire/report/$(HOSTNAME)-$(DATE).twr
SITEKEYFILE =/etc/tripwire/site.key
```

```
LOCALKEYFILE =/etc/tripwire/$(HOSTNAME)-local.key
EDITOR =/bin/vi
LATEPROMPTING =false
LOOSEDIRECTORYCHECKING =false
MAILNOVIOLATIONS =true
EMAILREPORTLEVEL =3
REPORTLEVEL =3
MAILMETHOD =SENDMAIL
SYSLOGREPORTING =false
MAILPROGRAM =/usr/sbin/sendmail -oi -t
```

Most of the directives within this file are self-explanatory; however, there are a few that can be somewhat misleading. My favorites are:

LATEPROMPTING

Controls how long Tripwire will wait before asking for a password. If this option is set to true, Tripwire will wait as long as possible before prompting the user for a password. This limits the password's time of exposure within system memory, therefore keeping it more secure.

LOOSEDIRECTORYCHECKING

Used to configure Tripwire to notice how files change within directories that are modified. If this is set to false and a file within a watched directory changes, Tripwire will notify you that both the directory and the file have changed. When set to true, it will simply notify you that the file has changed. This option is present to prevent you from becoming inundated with redundant messages within the Tripwire reports.

MAILNOVIOLATIONS

Instructs Tripwire whether or not to email you even if everything has checked out okay. When set to true, Tripwire will send you email just to let you know everything is okay. When set to false, only problem reports are sent.

EMAILREPORTLEVEL

Configures the level of detail that Tripwire should report. Experiment with this one and see how you prefer it. Alternatively, you may override this option when launching Tripwire from the command line.

MAILMETHOD

Enables you to identify how Tripwire reports are delivered via email. There are two possible values: SMTP, for using an open SMTP relay; and SENDMAIL, for using your own Sendmail server. This variable should be configured to reflect the configuration of your network and mail servers.

MAILPROGRAM

Tells Tripwire where to find the mail program you want it to use to send out email notifications.

SYSLOGREPORTING

Tells Tripwire whether or not it should report its findings to *syslog*. Working directly with *syslog* can help to configure this further.

Now that we've configured how Tripwire will execute and behave, let's examine the configuration file that controls how and what it analyzes.

Tripwire's Policy Configuration File

The file */etc/tripwire/twpol.txt* tells Tripwire how you want your filesystem monitored. This file can seem overwhelming at first, but don't panic! It's actually quite straightforward once you know what you're looking at. Tripwire includes a sample configuration file on which you can base your configuration. In our case some tweaking will be needed, as this template file is geared toward a default Red Hat system.

The first part of the configuration file that you should pay attention to is the section labeled @@section FS. This section provides the details that should be taken into account when checking different types of files. For instance, SIG_HI is used to monitor files that are critical aspects of a system's overall vulnerability, including binaries devoted to kernel modification, IP and routing commands, and a host of other applications. Another good one to pay attention to is SEC_LOG, which notes ownership permissions, inodes, and other attributes. Files watched by this parameter will not trip the alarm if their file sizes change, as log files often do.

The best way to learn the syntax of the Tripwire policy file is by modifying an existing config file. We won't go into much detail here—Tripwire is powerful and complex enough that a complete explanation of effective Tripwire policies deserves a book of its own—but we will go through one simple modification.

Since this file is based on a default Red Hat installation, *YaST* would not be protected if we were to install it on a SUSE box. Let's make some minor changes to the *twpol.txt* file to fix that:

```
#protect the yast binaries
(
rulename = "Watch Yast Binaries"
severity = $(SIG_CRIT)
)
{
/sbin/yast        ->  $ (SEC_CRIT) ;
/sbin/yast2       ->  $ (SEC_CRIT) ;
/sbin/zast        ->  $ (SEC_CRIT) ;
/sbin/zast2       ->  $ (SEC_CRIT) ;
}
```

This is a very simple rule that doesn't take advantage of even a quarter of Tripwire's customization features. In this case, the entries between the opening parentheses define the name of the rule and its severity. The parentheses are followed by a list of binaries to check, enclosed within curly braces.

As you can imagine, creating a perfect Tripwire policy will take some trial and error. You'll need to take into account every application that you have installed and make sure that they're being adequately monitored. Start with the sample policy, and begin adding and modifying from there. It will take a few runs, but sooner or later you'll end up with a perfect policy for your system. For more information on generating a strong policy and a full explanation of the features, consult the man page for Tripwire and the official open source Tripwire documentation at *http://sourceforge.net/project/shownotes.php?release_id=18142*.

Preparing Tripwire for Use

Once you have Tripwire configured, you need to perform a couple of steps before you can run it. To begin, cd to */etc/tripwire* and run the Tripwire installation script:

```
# ./twinstall.sh
```

Once you've done this, you'll need to accept the license agreement by typing accept at the prompt. After you've accepted the license terms, you'll then move on to generating the site and local keys. These are keys that Tripwire uses to sign your configuration files, policies, and the filesystem database. Be sure to use good, strong keys for this:

```
----------------------------------------------
Creating key files...

(When selecting a passphrase, keep in mind that good passphrases typically
have upper and lower case letters, digits and punctuation marks, and are
at least 8 characters in length.)

Enter the site keyfile passphrase:
Verify the site keyfile passphrase:
Generating key (this may take several minutes)...Key generation complete.
```

Once the key files have been generated, you'll have to enter your site and local passphrases again so that Tripwire can sign your configuration files. Using your unique passphrase to generate a key to sign the important application files ensures that no one will be able to replace your configuration files with doctored ones that might ignore suspicious activity. Signing them also keeps them from being read in plain text.

Once everything is installed, the next step is to initialize your Tripwire database. Do this by running the following command:

```
# /usr/sbin/tripwire -init
```

When you do this for the first time, you're likely to get a lot of errors. This is OK; you'll just need to note what errors come up and fix them in the policy file. It might take several minutes to fully initialize your Tripwire database, so don't worry if you think it's taking too long.

Running Your First Filesystem Integrity Check

Once the database has been initialized, you'll want to run your first integrity check:

```
# /usr/sbin/tripwire -check
```

Again, this will take a few minutes, but when it's done you can examine the report that it generates on *stdout* for changes that have occurred within your filesystem.

Once you've done that, there's not much to do but fine-tune your policy file and add Tripwire to cron to run as often as you want. To add Tripwire to root's list of nightly cron jobs, run the following command as root:

```
# crontab -e
```

This will open root's crontab file in your default text editor. Add the following line, substituting the appropriate path:

```
0 1 * * * /path/to/tripwire -check
```

This will schedule Tripwire to run every night at 1 A.M. Running Tripwire once per night is usually sufficient (especially because, depending on the complexity of your Tripwire configuration file, it can take a long time to run).

As you make changes to your *twpolicy.txt* and *twcfg.txt* files, you'll need to use the *twadmin* tool to re-encrypt them with your passphrase. To recreate your policy, use the following syntax:

```
# /usr/sbin/twadmin -create-polfile -S site.key /etc/tripwire/twpol.txt
```

TripWire Tips

You should follow a few simple policies and procedures in order to keep your Tripwire installation secure. First, don't leave the *twpol.txt* and *twcfg.txt* files that you used to generate your Tripwire database on your hard drive. Instead, store them somewhere off the server. If your system's security is compromised, as long as these files aren't available the intruder will not be able to view them to identify any unmonitored parts of your filesystem. Second, it's a good idea to change the Tripwire configuration and policy files so that your database is stored on some form of read-only media, such as a CD. This prevents anyone from being able to recreate your database with modifications, thus hiding root-kits or other malware. And finally, don't wait until your machine has been exposed to the Internet to install and configure Tripwire. It will serve you best when it's been installed on a clean machine and is able to begin keeping track of your filesystem from a fresh install. This way, you can be assured that you're not monitoring a system that has already been compromised.

While it might seem at first that Tripwire is too overwhelming to bother with, this is not actually the case. The policy file is good at scaring people off, and the default settings and initial setup can generate a lot of noise and strange error messages. However, with a little bit of work and some explora-tion of your own filesystem, you can learn quite a bit about how your sys-tem operates while you configure Tripwire. In addition, Tripwire has many uses outside the security realm. For example, you can use Tripwire to ensure that an application uninstalls all of its components or to identify all the changes made when you install an RPM. The possible uses for Tripwire are endless, and after you've mastered it, it can be an incredibly powerful tool for monitoring and maintaining your systems.

—Brian Warshawsky

HACK #67   Verify Fileystem Integrity with Afick
Monitor filesystem integrity with this easy-to-use tool.

Online security concerns grow every day as new viruses and worms are released. Because of this, it is now more important than ever to monitor your server's filesystem for signs of compromise. "Tame Tripwire" **[Hack #66]** introduced intrusion detection systems and discussed using the filesystem integrity checker Tripwire to monitor the multitude of changes that occur within your filesystem. Tripwire is an excellent tool, but to many people the steep learning curve is a big turnoff in deploying it. If for whatever reason Tripwire isn't for you, other integrity checkers are available. This is Linux, after all! *Afick* (Another File Integrity Checker) is one such tool that pro-vides numerous configuration methods, including a *perl/tk* GUI and a Web-min module. This hack will get you up and running using Afick while your other sysadmin friends are still reading the Tripwire manual.

Installing Afick

There are few dependencies involved in deploying Afick. Since Afick is written in Perl, you'll obviously need to have Perl and its libraries installed. Beyond that, simply download the source code from *http://afick.sourceforge.net*, unpack it to your favorite build location, and run the installation as follows:

```
# perl Makefile
```

If you don't want to install the *perl/tk* GUI, you can ignore any warnings you may see regarding missing *perl/tk* modules.

Once Perl has finished processing the Makefile, run the following command to actually install the software:

```
# make install
```

Now that we've built and installed Afick, let's configure it and put it through its paces.

Configuring Afick to Match Your System

The first step in configuring Afick to suit your filesystem is editing the Afick configuration file, which determines what attributes of your filesystem Afick pays attention to when scanning, and thus how it knows when to alert you to specific changes. Afick provides a default configuration file, but as every system is different, you should not depend on it to keep your server safe. Ultimately, fine-tuning Afick to match your filesystem will be a process of trial and error.

To start this process, first take a look at the Afick configuration file, which is called *linux.conf* and is located in the directory where you unpacked Afick. The configuration file contains several sections, two of which are of particular interest to us. The file is presented and laid out in a very user-friendly manner, making the sections of the file very easy to differentiate.

The first section we're interested in is the alias section. In this section, we'll set up the different combinations of file checks that Afick can perform. We will later apply the aliases defined here to specific types of files and directories. Here are some common aliases:

```
# alias :
#########
DIR = p+i+n+u+g
ETC = p+d+i+u+g+s+md5
Logs = p+n+u+g
MyRule = p+d+i+n+u+g+s+b+md5+m
```

The first part of each directive is simply the name of the alias being defined. You'll use this later to assign these aliases to specific files and directories. The second part of each alias is a list of the filesystem checks to be performed, separated by plus signs. A list of these options is presented in Table 7-1 for your reference.

Table 7-1. Afick filesystem check options

Option	Associated filesystem check
md5	Verify md5 checksum of file contents
sha1	Verify sha1 checksum of file contents
d	Verify major and minor number of device
i	Verify inode number
p	Verify file permissions
n	Verify number of links
u	Verify file ownership (user)
g	Verify file ownership (group)
s	Verify file size
b	Verify number of blocks allocated to file
m	Verify last modidication time (mtime)
c	Verify last change time (ctime)
a	Verify last access time (atime)

The second part of the configuration file we're interested in is the Files to Scan section. In this section, you can define which individual Afick checks or combinations of them that you defined as aliases will be performed against specific files and directories on your filesystem. Here are some examples for you to use to start the process of tuning your configuration:

```
/etc/adjtime ETC
/etc/aliases.db ETC -md5
/etc/mail/statistics ETC -md5
/etc/dhcpd.conf c+sha1+s+p
!/etc/cups/certs/0
```

This excerpt highlights much of the syntax of the config file. Each of the first three files uses the predefined *ETC* alias to specify what attributes should be checked. However, the second two use the -md5 directive to tell Afick to use the *ETC* alias minus the md5 checking option. This approach is useful if you'd like to specify a generic alias to work from with a little modification for different files. The fourth entry checks only the last modification time, sha1 checksum, file size, and permissions of the file */etc/dhcpd.conf*. The final entry listed above uses the ! option (or bang, for you old school *nix-ers out there), which tells Afick not to check the specified file or directory at all. This option should be used sparingly, and only where truly necessary.

Running Afick

Once you've taken a few minutes to adjust the configuration file to suit your filesystem, you're ready to run Afick for the first time. Afick operates by creating a snapshot of your filesystem in the form of a database. When you run

Afick for the first time, this database will be initialized, stored, and used as the basis for comparison in later integrity checks. To create the database, run the following command:

```
# afick -c /path_to_linux.conf/linux.conf -i
```

The -c directive tells Afick where to find the configuration file it should use, while the -i tells Afick to create an initial database. This operation may take a few minutes, but when it completes you'll find the database in the location specified in the first directive within your *linux.conf* file. Once the initial database is created, wait a few moments and rerun Afick, this time with the -k option:

```
# afick -c /path_to_linux.conf/linux.conf -k
```

The -k option tells Afick to compare the existing filesystem against the snapshot in the database and report any errors. It is at this point that you'll begin the trial-and-error phase of your Afick configuration. As errors and changes are reported, sort through them and modify your configuration file accordingly. As long as you aren't changing things, and your system is in a quiet state, what will show up are things on your system that are probably constantly changing. In some cases it will be appropriate to continue monitoring attributes such as ownership and inodes, but not mtime or atime values. Experiment and adjust your config file accordingly. Once you can run Afick without returning a flood of alerts, you're ready to add it to root's crontab to automate it to run on a schedule. To have Afick added to root's crontab, run the following command as root:

```
# crontab -e
```

This will open root's crontab in your default text editor. Add the following line, substituting the appropriate path:

```
0*/8 * * * root /path_to_afick.cron/afick.cron
```

This will schedule Afick to run every eight hours, emailing root with any changes that occur.

Securing Afick

Once you've reached this point in your configuration, you should consider moving your database to a read-only storage medium. In my experience, an old zip disk is an excellent choice (although you can also use a CD-R or DVD). To move your database to a zip disk, first mount the zip drive and then run the following command:

```
# mv /var/lib/afick/afick.pag /mnt/zip/afick.pag
```

Once you've done this, make sure you modify your configuration file to point to your newly moved database using a database := /path/to/database entry. You can then move your configuration file over to the zip disk as well, and flip the switch on the back of the zip disk to mark the disk as being read-only. By doing this, you're protecting your database and configuration file from being modified by anyone without physical access to the server.

Updating Your Database

When you make changes to your filesystem, you'll need to update your database. You can do this by issuing the following command:

```
# afick -c /path_to_linux.conf/linux.conf -u
```

Once the command finishes executing, your database is updated. You should perform an update any time you upgrade an application, apply new software or kernel patches, or perform any other activity that will alter your filesystem.

Conclusion

As you can probably tell, Afick is a less complicated version of Tripwire. The two applications share many similarities, but I find Afick to be the more useful and user-friendly of the two. In my experience with Afick, I've found a few other uses for it beyond ensuring my system isn't compromised. Among these uses are ensuring that applications properly uninstall themselves as well as tracking the exact changes made by running applications. There are many other uses to be found for this and other integrity checkers, and just a little bit of experimentation is guaranteed to reveal one or two that are relevant to you.

See Also

- "Tame Tripwire" [Hack #66]
- *http://afick.sourceforge.net*

—*Brian Warshawsky*

HACK #68 Check for Rootkits and Other Attacks

Let chkrootkit automatically check your externally facing machines for rootkits and other attacks.

A *rootkit* is a software package that enables an unauthorized user to obtain root or administrative privileges on a machine. Rootkits are usually installed by exploiting a known security problem. Once installed, they can capture passwords, monitor system status, send system authentication information to other hosts, and even execute programs at scheduled intervals.

While rootkits are conceptually quite interesting, being "rooted" (the term for being compromised such that unauthorized people have root access to your system) is not. Luckily, just as there are plenty of scripts that automate installing rootkits, there are also some great software packages that detect rootkits and identify compromised systems and applications. Some packages, such as Tripwire [Hack #66] and Afick [Hack #67], generally monitor file sizes and signatures and let you know if something has changed that shouldn't have. This hack explores *chkrootkit*, one of the most powerful and popular software packages for actually detecting rootkits themselves and discusses how to install and use it to detect and close down invasions.

Types of Rootkits

Linux rootkits work in various ways, usually as kernel modules, user-space software packages that replace system binaries, or a combination of both. Kernel rootkits insert loadable kernel modules that replace system calls with hacked versions that capture information and often hide information about specific processes from the user, whereas user-space rootkits generally replace system binaries such as *ps*, *login*, *passwd*, and so on with hacked versions that also capture information and hide information about specific processes and directories. For example, the t0rn rootkit mentioned in the "True Confessions" sidebar replaces system binaries such as *ps*, *top*, and *ls* with versions that won't list anything that is running from its */usr/src/.puta* directory. Pretty clever, actually.

chkrootkit runs on Linux systems using any 2.x kernel and has also been used and tested on FreeBSD 2.2.x, 3.x, 4.x and 5.x systems; OpenBSD 2.x and 3.x systems; NetBSD 1.6.x systems; Solaris 2.5.1, 2.6, 8.0, and 9.0 systems; and various HP-UX, Tru64, and BSDI system releases. At the time that this book was written, *chkrootkit* could detect rootkits such as 55808.A Worm, Adore LKM, Adore Worm, AjaKit, Anonoying, Aquatica, ARK, Bobkit, dsc-rootkit, duarawkz, Ducoci, ESRK, Fu, George, Gold2, Hidrootkit, Illogic, Kenga3, kenny-rk, knark LKM, Lion Worm, LOC, LPD Worm, lrk, Madalin, Maniac-RK, MithRa's Rootkit, Monkit, Omega Worm, OpenBSD rk v1, Optickit, Pizdakit, Ramen Worm, rh-shaper, RK17, Romanian, RSHA, RST.b trojan, Scalper, Sebek LKM, ShitC Worm, Shkit, Showtee, shv4, SK, Slapper A-D, SucKIT, TC2 Worm, t0rn, TRK, Volc, Wormkit Worm, x.c Worm, zaRwT, and ZK.

A basic problem in rootkit detection is that any system on which a rootkit has been installed can't be trusted to detect rootkits. This can be resolved by

True Confessions

Hi, my name is Bill, and one of my systems was rooted once. Where better to confess my sysadmin indiscretions than in a book that will hopefully be read by zillions of people?

Years ago, long before home gateways and Network Address Translation (NAT) boxes were sub-$100 consumer electronics devices, I built my own home gateway, like most Linux geeks. By putting an extra Ethernet card in an ancient Pentium box and writing a few *ipfwadm* rules (the ancestor of yesterday's *ipchains* and today's *iptables*), I could do NAT and masquerading of my internal systems through my external network interface. This worked fine 24x7 for quite a while, modulo the occasional power failure, and I used it to run my home name server and route to external DNS servers. I never updated any of the software on the box, based on the "don't fix it if it isn't broken" rule (which is a very bad rule for sysadmins to follow when it comes to security updates). One day, I logged in on the box to check something and noticed that the output from my favorite invocation of the ps command didn't display output in the same way that it usually did. So I checked */var/log/messages* and found a few messages that indicated that someone had been probing my DNS server, attempting to induce a buffer overflow. I poked around a bit and—no big surprise—found that the machine had been hacked and the t0rn rootkit (*http://www.sans.org/y2k/t0rn.htm*) was installed.

My reaction to this was different than most. Since none of my home machines themselves were hacked (I checked) and I was curious, I changed all of my passwords on systems that I might have contacted since the rootkit had been installed (from work, of course, not from home), and stopped doing anything at home that required a remote password for a few days. I then put a *README.txt* file in */usr/src/.puta*, which is where t0rn puts most of its files, saying something along the lines of "Hi there, congrats, and how'd you get in?" I got mail within a day or so from the guy who'd hacked my box, we exchanged a few mail messages through the anonymous remailer he was using, and he turned me on to some of the rootkits that he had access to. I would have been completely anal about this if this was a work machine, but as it was, he seemed like a pretty smart guy and I learned a few things. I rebuilt the machine (with updated software) within a week or two, anyway—I'm friendly, but not suicidal.

The point here is not that my system was hacked, but rather that the potential is always out there. Crackers can often exploit newly discovered or unpatched problems in system software to install rootkits on your system, some of which are both fast and clever. Adding *chkrootkit* to your system's toolbox can help you detect this sort of invasion and shut it down as quickly as possible.

doing regular system maintenance by running *chkrootkit* from a bootable CD. We'll come back to that later. For now, let's install *chkrootkit* and put it through its paces.

Obtaining, Building, and Installing chkrootkit

chkrootkit is open source and is freely available from *http://www.chkrootkit.org/ download*. The current version at the time this book was written was 0.45. Newer versions are better, since each version of *chkrootkit* adds software and support for detecting more and more rootkits. The *chkrootkit* executable is a shell script that runs the binaries and other scripts that are included as part of the *chkrootkit* package.

After downloading the source tarball, you can build *chkrootkit* as shown in the following example:

```
$ tar zxf chkrootkit.tar.gz
$ cd chkrootkit-0.45
$ make
*** stopping make sense ***
make[1]: Entering directory `/home/wvh/src/chkrootkit-0.45'
gcc -DHAVE_LASTLOG_H -o chklastlog chklastlog.c
gcc -DHAVE_LASTLOG_H -o chkwtmp chkwtmp.c
gcc -DHAVE_LASTLOG_H   -D_FILE_OFFSET_BITS=64 -o ifpromisc ifpromisc.c
gcc   -o chkproc chkproc.c
gcc   -o chkdirs chkdirs.c
gcc   -o check_wtmpx check_wtmpx.c
gcc -static  -o strings-static strings.c
gcc   -o chkutmp chkutmp.c
make[1]: Leaving directory `/home/wvh/src/chkrootkit-0.45'
```

chkrootkit's *Makefile* doesn't provide an install target, so you must either manually copy its binaries somewhere or run it from the directory in which you built it. If you do the latter, I'd suggest removing all the source code files to make it harder for anyone who has cracked your system to hack your *chkrootkit* installation—not impossible, just harder.

Running chkrootkit

Once you've built *chkrootkit*, you simply run it from wherever you've put the binaries by executing *./chkrootkit* or by invoking the full pathname to the *chkrootkit* shell script. You must execute *chkrootkit* as the root user or via sudo. The output from a run of *chkrootkit* looks like the following:

```
# ./chkrootkit
ROOTDIR is '/'
Checking 'amd'... not found
Checking 'basename'... not infected
Checking 'biff'... not found
```

```
Checking 'chfn'... not infected
Checking 'chsh'... not infected
Checking 'cron'... not infected
Checking 'date'... not infected
Checking 'du'... not infected
Checking 'dirname'... not infected
Checking 'echo'... not infected
Checking 'egrep'... not infected
Checking 'env'... not infected
Checking 'find'... not infected
Checking 'fingerd'... not found
Checking 'gpm'... not infected
Checking 'grep'... not infected
Checking 'hdparm'... not infected
Checking 'su'... not infected
Checking 'ifconfig'... not infected
Checking 'inetd'... not tested
Checking 'inetdconf'... not found
Checking 'identd'... not found
Checking 'init'... not infected
Checking 'killall'... not infected
Checking 'ldsopreload'... not infected
Checking 'login'... not infected
Checking 'ls'... not infected
Checking 'lsof'... not infected
Checking 'mail'... not infected
Checking 'mingetty'... not infected
Checking 'netstat'... not infected
Checking 'named'... not infected
Checking 'passwd'... not infected
Checking 'pidof'... not infected
Checking 'pop2'... not found
Checking 'pop3'... not found
Checking 'ps'... not infected
Checking 'pstree'... not infected
Checking 'rpcinfo'... not infected
Checking 'rlogind'... not found
Checking 'rshd'... not found
Checking 'slogin'... not infected
Checking 'sendmail'... not infected
Checking 'sshd'... not infected
Checking 'syslogd'... not infected
Checking 'tar'... not infected
Checking 'tcpd'... not infected
Checking 'tcpdump'... not infected
Checking 'top'... not infected
Checking 'telnetd'... not found
Checking 'timed'... not found
Checking 'traceroute'... not infected
Checking 'vdir'... not infected
Checking 'w'... not infected
Checking 'write'... not infected
Checking 'aliens'... no suspect files
```

```
Searching for sniffer's logs, it may take a while... nothing found
Searching for HiDrootkit's default dir... nothing found
Searching for t0rn's default files and dirs... nothing found
Searching for t0rn's v8 defaults... nothing found
Searching for Lion Worm default files and dirs... nothing found
Searching for RSHA's default files and dir... nothing found
Searching for RH-Sharpe's default files... nothing found
Searching for Ambient's rootkit (ark) default files and dirs...nothing found
Searching for suspicious files and dirs, it may take a while...
   /usr/lib/jvm/java-1.4.2-sun-1.4.2.08/jre/.systemPrefs
   /usr/lib/perl5/5.8.6/x86_64-linux-thread-multi/.packlist
Searching for LPD Worm files and dirs... nothing found
Searching for Ramen Worm files and dirs... nothing found
Searching for Maniac files and dirs... nothing found
Searching for RK17 files and dirs... nothing found
Searching for Ducoci rootkit... nothing found
Searching for Adore Worm... nothing found
Searching for ShitC Worm... nothing found
Searching for Omega Worm... nothing found
Searching for Sadmind/IIS Worm... nothing found
Searching for MonKit... nothing found
Searching for Showtee... nothing found
Searching for OpticKit... nothing found
Searching for T.R.K... nothing found
Searching for Mithra... nothing found
Searching for OBSD rk v1... nothing found
Searching for LOC rootkit... nothing found
Searching for Romanian rootkit... nothing found
Searching for Suckit rootkit... nothing found
Searching for Volc rootkit... nothing found
Searching for Gold2 rootkit... nothing found
Searching for TC2 Worm default files and dirs... nothing found
Searching for Anonoying rootkit default files and dirs... nothing found
Searching for ZK rootkit default files and dirs... nothing found
Searching for ShKit rootkit default files and dirs... nothing found
Searching for AjaKit rootkit default files and dirs... nothing found
Searching for zaRwT rootkit default files and dirs... nothing found
Searching for Madalin rootkit default files... nothing found
Searching for Fu rootkit default files... nothing found
Searching for ESRK rootkit default files... nothing found
Searching for anomalies in shell history files... nothing found
Checking 'asp'... not infected
Checking 'bindshell'... not infected
Checking 'lkm'... chkproc: nothing detected
Checking 'rexedcs'... not found
Checking 'sniffer'...
   eth0: not promisc and no PF_PACKET sockets
   vmnet8: not promisc and no PF_PACKET sockets
   vmnet1: not promisc and no PF_PACKET sockets
Checking 'w55808'... not infected
Checking 'wted'... chkwtmp: nothing deleted
Checking 'scalper'... not infected
Checking 'slapper'... not infected
```

```
Checking 'z2'... chklastlog: nothing deleted
Checking 'chkutmp'... chkutmp: nothing deleted
```

It seems like I'm clean, and that's a lot of tests! As you can see, *chkrootkit* first checks a variety of system binaries for strings that would indicate that they've been hacked, then checks for the indicators of known rootkits, checks network ports for spurious processes, and so on. I feel better already.

 If you are running additional security software such as PortSentry (*http://sourceforge.net/projects/sentrytools/*), you may get false positives (i.e., reports of problems that aren't actually problems) from the *bindshell* test, which looks for processes that are monitoring specific ports.

If you want to be even more paranoid than *chkrootkit*'s normal behavior, you can run *chkrootkit* with its -x (expert) option. This option causes *chkrootkit* to display detailed test output in order to give you the opportunity to detect potential problems that may be evidence of rootkits that the version of *chkrootkit* that you're using may not (yet) be able to identify.

Automating chkrootkit

Running *chkrootkit* "every so often" is a good idea, but running it regularly via cron is a better one. To run *chkrootkit* automatically, log in as root, su to root, or use sudo to run crontab -e and add *chkrootkit* to root's list of processes that are run automatically by cron. For example, the following entry would run *chkrootkit* every night at 1 A.M. and would mail its output to *root@hq.vonhagen.org*:

```
0 3 * * * (cd /path/to/chkrootkit; ./chkrootkit 2>&1 | mail -s "chkrootkit \
output" root@hq.vonhagen.org)
```

Summary

A basic problem in rootkit detection is that any system on which a rootkit has been installed can't be trusted to detect rootkits. Even if you follow the instructions in this hack and run *chkrootkit* via cron, you only have a small window of opportunity before the clever cracker checks root's crontab entry and either disables or hacks *chkrootkit* itself. The combination of *chkrootkit* and software such as Tripwire or Afick can help make this window as small as possible, but regular system security checks of externally facing machines from a bootable CD that includes *chkrootkit*, such as Inside Security's *Insert Security Rescue CD* (*http://sourceforge.net/projects/insert/*), is your best solution for identifying rootkits so that you can restore compromised systems.

See Also

- *http://www.chkrootkit.org*
- "Tame Tripwire" **[Hack #66]**
- "Verify Fileystem Integrity with Afick" **[Hack #67]**
- Insert Security Rescue CD: *http://www.inside-security.de/insert_en.html*
- Rootkit Hunter: *http://www.rootkit.nl*
- Windows users: *http://research.microsoft.com/rootkit/*
- Windows users: *http://www.sysinternals.com/utilities/rootkitrevealer.html*

Troubleshooting and Performance

Hacks 69–77

You'd be amazed at how often "optimizing performance" really translates into "troubleshooting." If something is misconfigured or otherwise broken, it's likely that your first inkling that something is wrong is a result of poor performance, either of the service in question or the host on which it's running.

Performance is a relative term. It's important to know what a system looks like when it's running under no load in order to be able to measure the impact of adding incrementally more users and services.

In this chapter, we'll give you the tools and techniques to troubleshoot your way to better performance, to optimize resources the system reserves for its slated tasks, and to deal with resource hogs on your systems and networks.

HACK
#69
Find Resource Hogs with Standard Commands

You don't need fancy, third-party software or log analyzers to find and deal with a crazed user on a resource binge.

There are times when users will consume more than their fair share of system resources, be it CPU, memory, disk space, file handles, or network bandwidth. In environments where users are logging in on the console (or invoking the *login* utility by some other means), you can use *pam_limits*, or the *ulimit* utility to keep them from going overboard.

In other environments, neither of these is particularly useful. On development servers, for example, you could be hosting 50 developers on a single machine where they all test their code before moving it further along toward a production rollout. Machines of this nature are generally set up to allow for things like cron jobs to run. While it's probably technically possible to limit the resources the cron utility can consume, that might be asking for trouble, especially when you consider that there are many jobs that run out of cron on behalf of the system, such as *makewhatis* and *LogWatch*.

Find Resource Hogs with Standard Commands

In general, the developers don't want to hog resources. Really, they don't. It makes their work take longer, and it causes their coworkers to unleash a ration of grief on them. On top of that, it annoys the system administrators, who they know can make their lives, well, "challenging." That said, resource hogging is generally not a daily or even weekly occurrence, and it hardly justifies the cost of third-party software, or jumping through hoops to configure for every conceivable method of resource consumption.

Usually, you find out about resource contention either through a monitoring tool's alert email or from user email complaining about slow response times or login shells hanging. The first thing you can do is log into the machine and run the top command, which will show you the number of tasks currently running, the amount of memory in use, swap space consumption, and how busy the CPUs are. It also shows a list of the top resource consumers, and all of this data updates itself every few seconds for your convenience. Here's some sample output from top:

```
top - 21:17:48 up 26 days,  6:37,  2 users,  load average: 0.18, 0.09, 0.03
Tasks:  87 total,   2 running,  83 sleeping,   2 stopped,   0 zombie
Cpu(s): 14.6% us, 20.6% sy,  0.0% ni, 64.1% id,  0.0% wa,  0.3% hi,  0.3% si
Mem:   2075860k total,  1343220k used,   732640k free,   216800k buffers
Swap:  4785868k total,        0k used,  4785868k free,   781120k cached

  PID USER      PR  NI  VIRT  RES  SHR S %CPU %MEM    TIME+  COMMAND
 3098 jonesy     25   0  4004 1240  956 S  8.7  0.1   0:11.42 hog.sh
30033 jonesy     15   0  6400 2100 1656 S  0.7  0.1   0:02.57 sshd
 8083 jonesy     16   0  2060 1064  848 R  0.3  0.1   0:00.06 top
    1 root       16   0  1500  516  456 S  0.0  0.0   0:01.91 init
```

As you can see, the top resource consumer is my *hog.sh* script. It's been running for about 11 seconds (shown in the TIME+ column), has a process ID of 3098, and uses 1240K of physical memory. A key field here is the NI field. This is referred to as the *nice value*. Users can use the *renice* utility to give their jobs lower priorities, to help ensure that they do not get in the way of other jobs scheduled to be run by the kernel scheduler. The kernel runs jobs based on their priorities, which are indicated in the PR field. As an administrator in the position of trying to fix problems without stepping on the toes of your usership, a first step in saving resources might be to renice the *hog.sh* script. You'll need to run top as root to renice a process you don't own. You can do this by hitting R on your keyboard, at which point top will ask you which process to reprioritize:

```
top - 21:19:07 up 26 days,  6:38,  2 users,  load average: 0.68, 0.26, 0.09
Tasks:  88 total,   4 running,  82 sleeping,   2 stopped,   0 zombie
Cpu(s): 19.6% us, 28.9% sy,  0.0% ni, 49.8% id,  0.0% wa,  1.0% hi,  0.7% si
Mem:   2075860k total,  1343156k used,   732704k free,   216800k buffers
Swap:  4785868k total,        0k used,  4785868k free,   781120k cached
PID to renice: 3098
```

```
  PID USER      PR  NI  VIRT  RES  SHR S %CPU %MEM   TIME+  COMMAND
 3098 jonesy    25   0  4004 1240  956 R 14.3  0.1   0:22.37 hog.sh
```

Typing in the process ID and pressing Enter will cause top to ask you what value you'd like to nice the process to. I typed in 15 here. On the next refresh, notice the change in my script's statistics:

```
top - 21:20:22 up 26 days,  6:39,  2 users,  load average: 1.03, 0.46, 0.18
Tasks:  87 total,   1 running,  84 sleeping,   2 stopped,   0 zombie
Cpu(s):  1.3% us, 22.3% sy, 13.6% ni, 61.5% id,  0.0% wa,  0.7% hi,  0.7% si
Mem:   2075860k total,  1343220k used,   732640k free,   216800k buffers
Swap:  4785868k total,        0k used,  4785868k free,   781120k cached

  PID USER      PR  NI  VIRT  RES  SHR S %CPU %MEM   TIME+  COMMAND
 3098 jonesy    39  15  4004 1240  956 S 12.0  0.1   0:31.34 hog.sh
```

Renicing a process is a safety precaution. Since you don't know what the code does, you don't know how much pain it will cause the user if you kill it outright. Renicing will help make sure the process doesn't render the system unusable while you try to dig for more information.

The next thing to check out is the good old ps command. There are actually multiple ways to find out what else a given user is running. Try this one:

```
$ ps -ef | grep jonesy
jonesy  28820     1  0 Jul31 ?        00:00:00 SCREEN
jonesy  28821 28820  0 Jul31 pts/3    00:00:00 /bin/bash
jonesy  30203 28821  0 Jul31 pts/3    00:00:00 vim XF86Config
jonesy  30803     1  0 Jul31 ?        00:00:00 SCREEN
jonesy  30804 30803  0 Jul31 pts/4    00:00:00 /bin/bash
jonesy  30818     1  0 Jul31 ?        00:00:00 SCREEN -l
jonesy  30819 30818  0 Jul31 pts/5    00:00:00 /bin/bash
```

This returns a full listing of all processes that contain the string *jonesy*. Note that I'm not selecting by user here, so if some other user is running a script called "jonesy-is-a-horrible-admin," I'll know about it. Here I can see that the user *jonesy* is also running a bunch of other programs. The PID of each process is listed in the second column, and the parent PID (PPID) of each process is listed in the third column. This is useful, because I can tell, for example, that PID 28821 was actually started by PID 28820, so I can see here that I'm running an instance of the *bash* shell inside of a *screen* session.

To get an even better picture that shows more clearly the relationship between child and parent processes, try this command:

```
$ ps -fHU jonesy
```

This will show the processes owned by user *jonesy* in hierarchical form, like this:

```
UID        PID  PPID  C STIME TTY         TIME CMD
jonesy 25760 25758  0 15:34 ?        00:00:00 sshd: jonesy@notty
```

```
jonesy 25446 25444  0 Jul29 ?       00:00:06 sshd: jonesy@notty
jonesy 20761 20758  0 16:28 ?       00:00:03 sshd: jonesy@pts/0
jonesy 20812 20761  0 16:28 pts/0   00:00:00  -tcsh
jonesy 12543 12533  0 12:11 ?       00:00:00 sshd: jonesy@notty
jonesy 12588 12543  0 12:11 ?       00:00:00   tcsh -c /usr/local/libexec/sft
jonesy 12612 12588  0 12:11 ?       00:00:00     /usr/local/libexec/sftp-serv
jonesy 12106 12104  0 10:49 ?       00:00:01 sshd: jonesy@pts/29
jonesy 12135 12106  0 10:49 pts/29  00:00:00  -tcsh
jonesy 12173 12135  0 10:49 pts/29  00:00:01    ssh livid
jonesy 10643 10641  0 Jul28 ?       00:00:07 sshd: jonesy@pts/41
jonesy 10674 10643  0 Jul28 pts/41  00:00:00  -tcsh
jonesy   845 10674  0 15:49 pts/41  00:00:06    ssh newhotness
jonesy  7011  6965  0 10:15 ?       00:01:39 sshd: jonesy@pts/21
jonesy  7033  7011  0 10:15 pts/21  00:00:00  -tcsh
jonesy 17276  7033  0 11:01 pts/21  00:00:00    -tcsh
jonesy 17279 17276  0 11:01 pts/21  00:00:00      make
jonesy 17280 17279  0 11:01 pts/21  00:00:00        /bin/sh -c bibtex paper;
jonesy 17282 17280  0 11:01 pts/21  00:00:00          latex paper
jonesy 17297  7033  0 11:01 pts/21  00:00:00    -tcsh
jonesy 17300 17297  0 11:01 pts/21  00:00:00      make
jonesy 17301 17300  0 11:01 pts/21  00:00:00        /bin/sh -c bibtex paper;
jonesy 17303 17301  0 11:01 pts/21  00:00:00          latex paper
jonesy  6820  6816  0 Jul28 ?       00:00:03 sshd: jonesy@notty
jonesy  6209  6203  0 22:15 ?       00:00:01 sshd: jonesy@pts/31
jonesy  6227  6209  0 22:15 pts/31  00:00:00  -tcsh
```

As you can see, I have a lot going on! These processes look fairly benign, but this may not always be the case. In the event that a user is really spawning lots of resource-intensive processes, one thing you can do is renice every process owned by that user in one fell swoop. For example, to change the priority of everything owned by user *jonesy* to run only when nothing else is running, I'd run the following command:

```
$ renice 20 -u jonesy
1001: old priority 0, new priority 19
```

Doing this to a user who has caused the system load to jump to 50 or so can usually get you back down to a level that makes the system usable again.

What About Disk Hogs?

The previous commands will not help you with users hogging disk space. If your user home directories are all on the same partition and you're not enforcing quotas, anything from a runaway program to a penchant for music downloads can quickly fill up the entire partition. This will cause common applications such as email to stop working altogether. If your mail server is set up to mount the user home directories and deliver mail to folders in the home directories, it won't be amused!

When a user calls to say email is not working, the first command you'll want to run is this one:

```
$ df -h
Filesystem              Size  Used Avail Use% Mounted on
fileserver:/export/homes
                        323G  323G    0G 100% /.autofs/u
```

Well, that's a full filesystem if I ever saw one! The df command shows disk usage/free disk statistics for all mounted filesystems by default, or for whatever filesystems it receives as arguments. Now, to find out the identity of our disk hog, become root, and we'll turn to the du command:

```
# du -s -B 1024K /home/* | sort -n
```

The du command above produces a summary (-s) for each directory under *home*, presenting the disk usage of each directory in 1024K (1 MB) blocks. We then pipe the output of the command to the sort command, which we've told to sort it numerically instead of alphabetically by feeding it the -n flag. With this output, you can see right away where the most disk space is being used, and you can then take action in some appropriate fashion (either by contacting the owner of a huge file or directory, or by deleting or truncating an out-of-control log file [Hack #51].

Bandwidth Hogging

Users who are hogging network bandwidth are rarely difficult to spot using the tools we've already discussed. However, if the culprit isn't obvious for some reason, you can lean on a core fundamental truth about Unix-like systems that goes back decades: everything is a file.

You can probe anything that can be represented as a file with the lsof command. To get a list of all network files (sockets, open connections, open ports), sorted by username, try this command:

```
$ lsof -i -P| sort -k3
```

The -i flag to lsof says to select only network-related files. The -P flag says to show the port numbers instead of trying to map them to service names. We then pipe the output to our old friend sort, which we've told this time to sort based on the third field or "key," which is the username. Here's some output:

```
sshd      1859   root   3u  IPv6   5428     TCP *:22 (LISTEN)
httpd     1914   root   3u  IPv6   5597     TCP *:80 (LISTEN)
sendmail  16643  root   4u  IPv4   404617   TCP localhost.localdomain:
25 (LISTEN)
httpd     1914   root   4u  IPv6   5598     TCP *:443 (LISTEN)
dhcpd     5417   root   6u  IPv4   97449    UDP *:67
```

```
sshd      24916   root    8u  IPv4 4660907       TCP localhost.localdomain:
6010 (LISTEN)
nmbd       7812   root    9u  IPv4  161622       UDP *:137
snmpd     25213   root    9u  IPv4 4454614       TCP *:199 (LISTEN)
sshd      24916   root    9u  IPv6 4660908       TCP localhost:6010 (LISTEN)
COMMAND    PID   USER    FD   TYPE  DEVICE SIZE NODE NAME
```

These are all common services, of course, but in the event that you catch a port or service here that you don't recognize, you can move on to using tools such as an MRTG graph **[Hack #79]**, *ngrep*, *tcpdump*, or *snmpget/snmpwalk* **[Hack #81]** to try to figure out what the program is doing, where its traffic is headed, how long it has been running, and so on. Also, since lsof shows you which processes are holding open which ports, problems that need immediate attention can be dealt with using standard commands to renice or kill the offending process.

HACK #70   Reduce Restart Times with Journaling Filesystems

Large disks and filesystem problems can drag down the boot process unless you're using a journaling filesystem. Linux gives you plenty to choose from.

Computer systems can only successfully mount and use filesystems if they can be sure that all of the data structures in each filesystem are consistent. In Linux and Unix terms, consistency means that all of the disk blocks that are actually used in some file or directory are marked as being in use, all deleted blocks aren't linked to anything other than the list of free blocks, all directories in the filesystem actually have parent directories, and so on. This check is done by filesystem consistency check applications, the best known of which is the standard Linux/Unix *fsck* application. Each filesystem has its own version of *fsck* (with names like *fsck.ext3*, *fsck.jfs*, *fsck.reiserfs*, and so on) that understands and "does the right thing" for that particular filesystem.

When filesystems are mounted as part of the boot process, they are marked as being in use ("dirty"). When a system is shut down normally, all its on-disk filesystems are marked as being consistent ("clean") when they are unmounted. When the system reboots, filesystems that are marked as being clean do not have to be checked before they are mounted, which saves lots of time in the boot process. However, if they are not marked as clean, the laborious filesystem consistency check process begins. Because today's filesystems are often quite large and therefore contain huge chains of files, directories, and subdirectories, each using blocks in the filesystem, verifying the consistency of each filesystem before mounting it is usually the slowest part of a computer's boot process. Avoiding filesystem consistency checks is therefore the dream of every sysadmin and a goal of every system or filesystem designer. This hack explores the basic concepts of how a special type of filesystem, known as a *journaling filesystem*, expedites system restart times by largely eliminating the need to check filesystem consistency when a system reboots.

Journaling Filesystems 101

Some of the more inspired among us may keep a journal to record what's happening in our lives. These come in handy if we want to look back and see what was happening to us at a specific point in time. Journaling filesystems operate in a similar manner, writing planned changes to a filesystem in a special part of the disk, called a *journal* or *log*, before actually applying them to the filesystem. (This is hard to do in a personal journal unless you're psychic.) There are multiple reasons journaling filesystems record changes in a log before applying them, but the primary reason for this is to guarantee filesystem consistency.

Using a log enforces consistency, because sets of planned changes are grouped together in the log and are replayed transactionally against the filesystem. When they are successfully applied to the filesystem, the filesystem is consistent, and all of the changes in the set are removed from the log. If the system crashes while transactionally applying a set of changes to the filesystem, the entries remain present in the log and are applied to the filesystem as part of mounting that filesystem when the system comes back up. Therefore, the filesystem is always in a consistent state or can almost always quickly be made consistent by replaying any pending transactions.

 I say "almost always" because a journaling filesystem can't protect you from bad blocks appearing on your disks or from general hardware failures, which can cause filesystem corruption or loss. See "Recover Lost Partitions" **[Hack #93]**, "Recover Data from Crashed Disks" **[Hack #94]**, and "Repair and Recover ReiserFS Filesystems" **[Hack #95]** for some suggestions if *fsck* doesn't work for you.

Journaling Filesystems Under Linux

Linux offers a variety of journaling filesystems, preintegrated into the primary kernel code. Depending on the Linux distribution that you are using, these may or may not be compiled into your kernel or available as loadable kernel modules. Filesystems are activated in the Linux kernel on the File Systems pane of your favorite kernel configuration mechanism, accessed via make xconfig or (for luddites) make menuconfig. The options for the XFS journaling filesystem are grouped together on a separate pane, XFS Support.

The journaling filesystems that are integrated into the Linux kernel at the time this book was written are the following:

ext3
> *ext3* adds high-performance journaling capabilities to the standard Linux *ext2* filesystem on which it's based. Existing *ext2* filesystems can easily be converted to *ext3*, as explained later in this hack.

JFS

> The Journaled File System (JFS) was originally developed by International Business Machines (IBM) for use on their OS/2 and AIX systems. JFS is a high-performance journaling filesystem that allocates disk space as needed from pools of available storage in the filesystem (known as *allocation groups*) and therefore creates inodes as needed, rather than preallocating everything as traditional Unix/Linux filesystems do. This provides fast storage allocation and also removes most limitations on the number of inodes (and therefore files and directories) that can be created in a JFS filesystem.

ReiserFS

> Written by Hans Reiser and others with the financial support of companies such as SUSE, Linspire, mp3.com, and many others, ReiserFS is a high-performance, space-efficient journaling filesystem that is especially well suited to filesystems that contain large numbers of files. ReiserFS was the first journaling filesystem to be integrated into the Linux kernel code and has therefore been popular and stable for quite a while. It is the default filesystem type on Linux distributions such as SUSE Linux.

Reiser4

> Written by Hans Reiser and others with the financial support of the Defense Advanced Research Projects Agency (DARPA), Reiser4 is the newest of the journaling filesystems discussed in this hack. Reiser4 is a very high-performance, transactional filesystem that further increases the extremely efficient space allocation provided by ReiserFS. It is also designed to be extended through plug-ins that can add new features without changing the core code.

XFS

> Contributed to Linux by Silicon Graphics, Inc. (SGI), XFS (which doesn't really stand for anything) is a very high-performance journaling filesystem that dynamically allocates space and creates inodes as needed (like JFS), and supports a special (optional) real-time section for files that require high-performance, real-time I/O. The combination of these features provides a fast filesystem without significant limitations on the number of inodes (and therefore files and directories) that can be created in an XFS filesystem.

Each of these filesystem has its own consistency checker, filesystem creation tool, and related administrative tools. Even if your kernel supports the new type of filesystem that you've selected, make sure that your filesystems also include its administrative utilities, installed separately through your distribution's package manager, or you're in for a bad time the next time you reboot and a filesystem check is required.

The purpose of this hack is to explain why journaling filesystems are a good idea for most of the local storage that is attached to the systems you're responsible for, and to provide some tips about integrating journaling filesystems into existing systems. I can't really say more about these here without turning this hack into a tome on Linux filesystems—which I already wrote a few years ago (*Linux Filesystems*, SAMS Publishing), though it's now somewhat dated. All of these journaling filesystems are well established and have been used on Linux systems for a few years. Reiser4 is the newest of these and is therefore the least time-tested, but Hans assures us all that no one does software engineering like the Namesys team.

Converting Existing Filesystems to Journaling Filesystems

Traditional Linux systems use the *ext2* filesystem for local filesystems. Because the journaling filesystems available for Linux all use their own allocation and inode/storage management mechanisms, the only journaling Linux filesystem that you can begin using with little effort is the *ext3* filesystem, which was designed to be compatible with *ext2*.

To convert an existing *ext2* filesystem to an *ext3* filesystem, all you have to do is add a journal and tell your system that it is now an *ext3* filesystem so that it will start using the journal. The command to create a journal on an existing *ext2* filesystem (you must be root or use sudo) is the following:

```
# tune2fs -j /dev/filesystem
```

> If you create a journal on a mounted *ext2* filesystem, it will initially be created as the file *.journal* in the root of the filesystem and will automatically be hidden when you reboot or remount the filesystem as an *ext3* filesystem.

You will need to update */etc/fstab* to tell the mount command to mount your converted filesystem as an *ext3* filesystem and reboot to verify that all is well.

In general, if you want to begin using any of the non-*ext3* journaling filesystems discussed in this chapter with any existing system, you'll need to do the following:

- Build support for that journaling filesystem into your Linux kernel, make it available as a loadable kernel module, or verify that it's already supported in your existing kernel.

- Make sure you update the contents of any initial RAM disk you used during the boot process to include any loadable kernel modules for the new filesystem(s) that you are using.

- Install the administrative tools associated with the new filesystem type, if they aren't already available on your system. These include a minimum of new *mkfs.filesystem-type* and *fsck.filesystem-type* utilities, and may also include new administrative and filesystem repair utilities.

- Manually convert your existing filesystems to the new journaling filesystem format by creating new partitions or logical volumes that are at least as large as your existing filesystems, formatting them using the new filesystem format, and recursively copying the contents of your existing filesystems into the new ones.

- Go to single-user mode, unmount your existing filesystems, and update the entries in */etc/fstab* to reflect the new filesystem types (and the new disks/volumes where they are located unless you're simply replacing an existing disk with one or more new ones).

When migrating the contents of existing partitions and volumes to new partitions and volumes in different filesystem formats, *always* back up everything first and test each of the new partitions before wiping out its predecessor. Forgetting any of the steps in the previous list can turn your well-intentioned system improvement experience into a restart nightmare if your system won't boot correctly using its sexy new filesystems.

Summary

Journaling filesystems can significantly improve system restart times, provide more efficient use of the disk space available on your partitions or volumes, and often even increase general system performance. I personally tend to use *ext3* for system filesystems such as / and */boot*, since this enables me to use all of the standard *ext2* filesystem repair utilities if these filesystems become corrupted. For local storage on SUSE systems, I generally use ReiserFS, because that's the default there and it's great for system partitions (such as your mail and print queues) because of its super-efficient allocation.

I tend to use XFS for physical partitions on Linux distributions other than SUSE Linux, because I've used it for years on Linux and SGI boxes, it has always been stable in my experience, and the real-time section of XFS filesystems is way cool. I generally use *ext3* on logical volumes because the dynamic allocation mechanisms used by JFS and XFS and ReiserFS's tree-balancing algorithms place extra overhead on the logical volume subsystem. They all still work fine on logical volumes, of course.

See Also

- "Recover Lost Partitions" [Hack #93]
- "Recover Data from Crashed Disks" [Hack #94]
- "Repair and Recover ReiserFS Filesystems" [Hack #95]
- man tune2fs
- *ext3* home page: *http://e2fsprogs.sourceforge.net/ext2.html*
- JFS home page: *http://jfs.sourceforge.net*
- ReiserFS/Reiser4 home page: *http://www.namesys.com*
- XFS home page: *http://oss.sgi.com/projects/xfs/*

Grok and Optimize Your System with sysctl

#71

Instead of interacting directly with /proc files, you can get and set kernel options in a flash with the sysctl command.

In days of old, *sysctl* referred to a header file or system call that C programmers could use to change kernel settings from a program. The files under */proc/sys/* are often collectively referred to as the *sysctl* interface, because they can be written to, and changes made to the files will be picked up by the running kernel without rebooting. This feature was implemented in the kernel as early as Version 2.0 (but don't quote me).

These days, *sysctl* is a kernel call, an interface, and a command that allows administrators to easily interact with the kernel. It also allows for a proper startup configuration file, so you don't have to rebuild kernels everywhere to disable IP forwarding, for example. Enabling and disabling IP forwarding was one of the first things I ever used the *sysctl* interface for. Enabling IP forwarding for your Linux router used to be done with a command like this:

```
# echo 1 > /proc/sys/net/ipv4/ip_forward
```

The content of the file was "0" by default, indicating that forwarding was not turned on. Echoing a "1" into the file turned it on.

Enter the sysctl command. Now we can all easily see every single setting available to us through the interface with a simple command:

```
# sysctl -a
net.ipv4.tcp_keepalive_time = 7200
net.ipv4.ipfrag_time = 30
net.ipv4.ip_dynaddr = 1
net.ipv4.ipfrag_low_thresh = 196608
net.ipv4.ipfrag_high_thresh = 262144
net.ipv4.tcp_max_tw_buckets = 180000
net.ipv4.tcp_max_orphans = 16384
net.ipv4.tcp_synack_retries = 5
```

```
net.ipv4.tcp_syn_retries = 5
net.ipv4.ip_nonlocal_bind = 0
net.ipv4.ip_no_pmtu_disc = 0
net.ipv4.ip_autoconfig = 0
net.ipv4.ip_default_ttl = 64
net.ipv4.ip_forward = 0
...
```

On my desktop Debian system, this returned over 400 "key=value"-formatted records. The keys on the left are dotted representations of file paths under */proc/sys*. For example, the setting for *net.ipv4.ip_forward* can be found in */proc/sys/net/ipv4/ip_forward*. If you know what you're looking for, though, you can specify what you want as an argument to sysctl:

```
# /sbin/sysctl net.ipv4.ip_forward
net.ipv4.ip_forward = 0
```

So if you always wanted to know more about your kernel, consider it done. How about customizing the kernel settings? You have choices. You can make temporary changes to the kernel using the -w flag to "write" a new setting:

```
# sysctl -w net.ipv4.ip_forward=1
```

On the other hand, if you want to make a more permanent change, you can put your custom settings into the */etc/sysctl.conf* file, which will ensure that your settings are applied automatically when the kernel boots. (Actually, it's not read right when the kernel is launched, per se, but at some point before a login prompt is displayed to the console. Exactly when the variables are set varies from distribution to distribution, but if you grep for sysctl under */etc/ init.d*, you're sure to find it in a hurry!)

The configuration file consists of records that look identical to the output of sysctl -a. Here's an example configuration file:

```
# Controls IP packet forwarding
net.ipv4.ip_forward = 0

# Controls source route verification
net.ipv4.conf.default.rp_filter = 1

# Controls the System Request debugging functionality of the kernel
kernel.sysrq = 0

# Controls whether core dumps will append the PID to the core filename.
# Useful for debugging multi-threaded applications.
kernel.core_uses_pid = 1

# Decrease the time default value for tcp_fin_timeout connection.
net.ipv4.tcp_fin_timeout = 30
```

```
# Decrease the time default value for tcp_keepalive_time connection
net.ipv4.tcp_keepalive_time = 1800

# Turn off tcp_window_scaling
net.ipv4.tcp_window_scaling = 0

# Turn off the tcp_sack
net.ipv4.tcp_sack = 0

# Turn off tcp_timestamps
net.ipv4.tcp_timestamps = 0

# Increase transport socket buffers to improve performance of nfs (and
networking
# in general)
# 'rmem' is 'read memory', 'wmem' is 'write memory'.
net.core.rmem_max = 262143
net.core.rmem_default = 262143
net.core.wmem_max = 262143
net.core.wmem_default = 262143

net.ipv4.tcp_rmem = 4096         87380    8388608
net.ipv4.tcp_wmem = 4096      87380    8388608

# These are for both security and performance

net.ipv4.icmp_echo_ignore_broadcasts = 1
net.ipv4.icmp_ignore_bogus_error_responses = 1
```

When all is said and done, the hardest part of using the *sysctl* interface is learning what all the variables actually mean and how they apply to your particular situation. I hope the comments in my sample file can help out a bit. Also check out the documentation of the */proc* files that comes with the kernel source distribution to get started.

Get the Big Picture with Multiple Displays

Using two monitors with a single system gives you more room to work. The latest versions of the X Window System make this easier than ever before.

Many of the hacks in this book discuss how to better monitor system and process status, how to use the Web for basic computing infrastructure functions, and so on. This hack explains how to get enough display space so that you can actually see all of that information by attaching two video cards and two monitors to any Linux system and configuring the XFree86 or X.org X Window System for what is known as *multi-head* display.

Whenever possible, add a second graphics card of the same type as the one that is already in your system, or replace your existing graphics card with one that supports two monitors. This will enable you to use the same X server to control both graphics cards and their associated displays. Similarly, it's a good idea to add a second monitor of exactly the same size and with exactly the same maximum display resolution as your existing monitor. This will simplify synchronizing graphics modes across the two monitors (and in the X Window System configuration sections for each display).

This hack creates two separate displays, one on each of your monitors. An alternate approach would be to use the X Window System's Xinerama extension to create one single display that spans two monitors. (See *http://www.tldp.org/HOWTO/Xinerama-HOWTO/* for more information about Xinerama.) With two separate displays you cannot move windows from one to the other, though you can create windows on a specific display by specifying the display that you want to use on an X application's command line. I find Xinerama disconcerting because windows can be split across the two displays, which makes them a tad hard to read because of the casing on my monitors. I find separate displays easier to use and cleaner looking. Your mileage may vary.

X Window System configuration information is stored in the file */etc/X11/xorg.conf* if you are using the X11 server from X.org, or in */etc/X11/XF86Config* if you are using an XFree86-based X11 server. After adding the hardware to your system and booting in a nongraphical, multi-user mode such as runlevel 3, the procedure for modifying this file to use a multi-head display is as simple as the following few steps.

First, you need to create two Monitor sections in your X server's configuration file. Make sure you use a unique Identifier name for each monitor:

```
Section "Monitor"
        Identifier   "Monitor 0"
        VendorName   "Monitor Vendor"
        ModelName    "Model X"
        HorizSync    30.0 - 50.0
        VertRefresh  60.0 - 60.0
EndSection

Section "Monitor"
        Identifier   "Monitor 1"
        VendorName   "Monitor Vendor"
        ModelName    "Model Y"
        HorizSync    30.0 - 50.0
        VertRefresh  60.0 - 60.0
EndSection
```

Next, create a Device section for each graphics card in your system. As with the monitors, be sure to use a unique Identifier for each graphics card:

```
Section "Device"
        Identifier  "VideoCard 0"
        Driver      "drivername"
        VendorName  "Vendor"
        BusID       "PCI:00:15:0"
EndSection

Section "Device"
        Identifier  "VideoCard 1"
        Driver      "drivername"
        VendorName  "Vendor"
        BusID       "PCI:1:0:0"
EndSection
```

The BusID enables the X server to correctly and uniquely define each display in your configuration file, and its value can be found from the output of the *lspci* command. The BusID can be found at the beginning of the first line of *lspci* output that identifies the graphics card. The format is slightly different than what you will need to put in your configuration file: *lspci* reports in hexadecimal, while you must use decimal notation in your configuration file. The output of the *lspci* command is also *xx:yy.z*, which you must express as *xx:yy:z* in your configuration file—note that the period in the *lspci* output must be replaced with a colon in your configuration file.

```
# lspci | grep VGA
00:0f.0 VGA compatible controller: nVidia Corporation NV11 [GeForce2 MX/MX
400] (rev b2)
01:00.0 VGA compatible controller: nVidia Corporation NV15 [GeForce2 GTS/
Pro] (rev a4)
```

My favorite tool for converting hex to decimal is the standard Linux *bc* utility. You can specify *bc*'s input base using the ibase=*base* command and leave its output set to decimal (the default). For example, the following shows how to convert 10 hex to decimal (OK, that's not very hard, but this is an example, and a simple example does make things clear):

```
$ bc -q
ibase=16
10
16
```

After specifying the input base, you simply enter a hex value and press Return, and *bc* displays the decimal equivalent. Type Ctrl-D to exit *bc*.

The next thing to add to your X server's configuration file is two Screen sections. Each section will use one of the Monitor and Device stanzas that you defined previously. The resolution and color depth of the two can be different if you so desire but are usually the same:

```
Section "Screen"
        Identifier "Screen 0"
        Device     "VideoCard 0"
        Monitor    "Monitor 0"
        DefaultDepth    24
        SubSection "Display"
                Depth    24
                Modes    "800x600" "640x480"
        EndSubSection
EndSection

Section "Screen"
        Identifier "Screen 1"
        Device     "VideoCard 1"
        Monitor    "Monitor 1"
        DefaultDepth    24
        SubSection "Display"
                Depth    24
                Modes    "1024x768" "800x600" "640x480"
        EndSubSection
EndSection
```

Now, you must tie all of these pieces together in the ServerLayout section (normally at the top of your configuration file):

```
Section "ServerLayout"
        Identifier    "Multihead layout"
        Screen      0 "Screen 0" 0 0
        Screen      1 "Screen 1" RightOf "screen 0"
        InputDevice   "Mouse0" "CorePointer"
        InputDevice   "Keyboard0" "CoreKeyboard"
        InputDevice   "DevInputMice" "AlwaysCore"
EndSection
```

The 0 0 next to Screen 0 means that this screen will start at position 0,0. Screen 1 will be located to the right of Screen 0.

Now that that's done, start the X Window System using your favorite startx or xinit command. If X does not start correctly, double-check the entries that you added to your configuration file for syntax errors, paying particular attention to the BusID values in the Device stanzas.

> Redirecting the output of the startx or xinit command to a file can help capture error messages that you can use to debug your configuration files. Executing xinit >& x_startup.txt can be extremely useful, unless you can read much faster than I can.

Once X is working correctly, you can start a graphical application so that it starts on the screen of your choice by using the -display option that is accepted by almost every X Window System command. For example, to start an *xterm* on Screen 1, you would execute the command xterm -display :0.1. This display value specifies that the application use Screen 1 of the current display (display 0) on the current host. The general form of a display value is the following:

```
hostname:displaynumber.screennumber
```

Using a multi-head display may be a bit disconcerting at first, especially when your mouse pointer crosses from one monitor to the other, but you'll quickly find that the additional display real estate is well worth any amount of acclimation.

See Also

- "Monitor Network Traffic with MRTG" [Hack #79]

—Lance Tost

Maximize Resources with a Minimalist Window Manager

Using window managers rather than desktop environments can improve the performance of slower systems or simply leave more system resources available for actual computing.

Graphical user interfaces such as KDE and GNOME are slick and easy to use, but all that eye candy has a price—executing and managing all of those graphical bells and whistles requires a certain percentage of system resources. A typical idle KDE desktop on SUSE 9 Enterprise occupies around 370 MB of RAM. For today's servers with multiple gigabytes of RAM, this may not be an issue. However, if you're running a legacy server that contains less than a gig of RAM, you could certainly benefit from the use of a more modest graphics system, known as a *window manager*. Window managers focus on displaying and managing windows, not drag and drop and other luxuries. One of the best lightweight window managers is *Fluxbox*, an open source software package available online and derived from the *Blackbox* window manager, which is itself an open source clone of the window manager used on old workstations from NeXT. Using Fluxbox can decrease the amount of RAM required by your GUI by over 100 MB, and also eliminates the ten zillion background processes that desktop environments such as KDE start to support things like drag and drop, automatic file associations, and so on. This hack explains how to build and install Fluxbox so that you can devote more of your system's memory to the applications that you actually want to run.

Getting and Installing Fluxbox

As usual, the easiest method of installing Fluxbox is via an RPM packaged for your distribution. These can be found on the Fluxbox home page, *http://Fluxbox.sourceforge.net*. In this example, we'll compile from source so that we can pass a few options to make Fluxbox a little more familiar. Grab the tarball from the home page, and extract it to a working directory. Navigate into the newly created directory, and run *configure* as follows:

```
$ ./configure -with kde -with-gnome
```

This will allow Fluxbox to use the KDE and GNOME panel icons. Once the *configure* script has finished, run the following command as root to build Fluxbox:

```
# make && make install
```

This will compile Fluxbox (which doesn't require root privileges) and install it for you (which requires root privileges, since you have to be able to write to subdirectories of */usr/local*). The name of the actual executable for Fluxbox is *fluxbox* (no initial cap). Now we just need to configure X to start Fluxbox as your window manager.

Start Me Up, Scotty!

If you installed on a SUSE or Red Hat system using an RPM, you can simply select Fluxbox as your session type from the login screen. Otherwise, navigate to your home directory and find a file called either *.xsession* or *.xinitrc*. If a file matching one of those names doesn't exist, you'll need to create one. Which one you create depends largely on how your system starts X—see the Fluxbox documentation for more information.

In this case, we'll edit *.xinitrc*. Open it with your favorite text editor and enter the following line:

```
exec /usr/local/bin/fluxbox
```

where */usr/local/bin* is the directory in which you installed your *fluxbox* executable (*/usr/local/bin* is usually the default installation location). You'll then need to change the file ownership properties via chmod:

```
$ chmod 700 .xinitrc
```

You can now log out and right back in. Depending on your distribution, either *fluxbox* will start automatically, or you'll be able to select it as your session type from the login manager. Either way, upon logging in you'll be greeted (very quickly!) by a plain-looking screen. Right-clicking on the desktop brings up a menu with various options on it. If you configured it with the KDE and GNOME options as I suggested, some of the tools from those environments might be available to you right away. Figure 8-1 shows a sample Fluxbox screen running a single *xterm* with the Firefox web browser open, and displaying my default Fluxbox menu as the result of a right-click on the background.

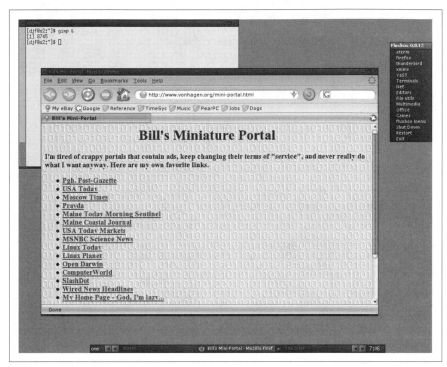

Figure 8-1. Fluxbox in all its minimal glory

Configure Fluxbox

The next step is to begin customizing Fluxbox to your liking. As you can see from Figure 8-1, Fluxbox is highly configurable. The biggest piece of Fluxbox configuration is customizing its main menu. This is the menu that is displayed whenever you click on the desktop, and it is completely configurable. The menu is controlled via a text file called *menu*. This file is located in your *.fluxbox* directory, which is automatically created in your home directory the first time you run Fluxbox. The layout of the file is very simple:

```
[begin] (Fluxbox)
    [exec] (xterm) {xterm}
    [exec] (mozilla) {mozilla}
    [exec] (Run) {fbrun}
[submenu] (Terminals)
    [exec] (xterm) {xterm}
```

```
        [exec] (gnome-terminal) {gnome-terminal}
        [exec] (console) {console}
    [end]
    [submenu] (Net)
    [submenu] (Utilities)
        [exec]  (Ethereal) {ethereal}
    [submenu] (Browsers)
        [exec] (mozilla) {mozilla}
        [exec] (conqueror) {kfmclient openProfile webbrowsing}
    [end]
    [end]
```

This example is a sample section from my Fluxbox *menu* file. As you can see, this is a fairly simple configuration file. The top line is the title of my menu. In this example, each menu item is preceded by the [exec] command, which tells Fluxbox that this is a system command that it should actually execute. The first argument in the regular parentheses is the name you want displayed for the application, while the text within the curly braces specifies the command you would run from the command line to execute the program. Note that if the application you're trying to add to your menu isn't located within your default path, you'll need to specify the full path to the executable. Each sequentially lower portion of your menu is marked by the [submenu] command. Specify the end of a menu with the [end] command. Items that you want directly available can be placed at the top, under the title.

Fluxbox startup files can also invoke internal Fluxbox commands, which are identified within square brackets just like the [exec] instruction, as in the following example:

```
    [exit] (Exit)
```

This creates an Exit menu item that executes the internal Fluxbox exit command. When deploying systems that run Fluxbox for users and start in graphical runlevels, you may find Fluxbox menu commands like the following to be quite handy:

```
    [exec] (Shut Down System) {sudo shutdown -h now}
    [exec] (Reboot System) {sudo shutdown -r now}
    [exit] (Log Out)
```

These assume that the user has been granted certain privileges in the *sudo* application, and create the standard sorts of menu items that users who may be unfamiliar with Linux typically expect to see in their graphical user interface.

> The options discussed in this section are only the tip of the Fluxbox configuration iceberg. See the Fluxbox man page for a complete list of available Fluxbox configuration commands and options.

The Slit

The Slit is one of the coolest features of Fluxbox. You can think of the Slit as a version of the OS X Dashboard that's always available. It contains small dockable applications (commonly known as *dock apps*) that are able to run in withdrawn mode, which simply means that they run independently in the background. This is typically designated by a -w flag when running the application from the command line. Note that not all applications can run in this manner, but many are specifically designed to run this way. I typically start any dock apps that I want to run by putting them in my *.xinitrc* file, starting them in the background before actually starting the Fluxbox window manager. The order in which applications appear in the Slit is defined by putting their names in the desired order in the *slitlist* file in your *.fluxbox* directory.

The Slit is an exceptional way to display statistics such as memory and processor utilization using the proper dock apps. You can find dock apps at *http://freshmeat.net* and *http://www.dockapps.org*.

Make It Pretty!

There is a large community of people on the Internet who devote a lot of time to creating custom Fluxbox themes. These themes can be found at the Fluxbox home page, as well as around the Net. Installing a theme is as simple as downloading it and adding it to the *~/.fluxbox/styles* directory. These styles will then be selectable from the Fluxbox → Menu submenu. If such a directory doesn't exist, search for your global Fluxbox share directory (usually */usr/local/share/*Fluxbox). The location of this directory will vary depending on your method of installation.

Minimal Hassle

After a little bit of configuration, you might find that you prefer the simple layout of Fluxbox to heavier window managers such as GNOME and KDE. In addition to preserving server resources, Fluxbox is a great application to use to extend the life of an old laptop or desktop that just can't hack the high demands of a heavier desktop solution.

Another memory-saving tip related to GUIs is to start your system in a nongraphical runlevel (typically, runlevel 3) and then manually start your window manager by using the xinit or startx commands after you've logged in. This eliminates the memory overhead of the *xwm*, *kdm*, or *gdm* display managers, which are the processes that provide support for graphical logins, and can save you another 80 MB or so of memory. See the man page for xinit for more information.

See Also

- *http://fluxbox.sourceforge.net*
- *http://www.dockapps.org*
- man fluxbox
- man xinit
- man sudo

—Brian Warshawsky

Profile Your Systems Using /proc

The /proc filesystem holds a wealth of information—and with a little bit of scripting you can use it to create profiles of your servers.

The key to recognizing anomalies on your server is to have a good understanding and knowledge of what things look like when it's healthy. A great place to start hunting for information is the */proc* filesystem. This filesystem is a portal into the depths of what the running kernel and the system load look like, and it provides a full profile of the hardware in use on the local system.

When I install a new server, one of the first things I do is take a sort of profile "snapshot," so that I can get a good picture of what the system resources look like on an idle system. I also do this just before and after I install or fire up new software or system services, so I can get a measure of an application's impact on the availability of system resources and so that I have a "cheat sheet" for looking up the system's installed hardware.

The script I use is very rough around the edges and wasn't written for the purpose of working on any machine you might ever run across, but it does work on a good number of Linux servers I've encountered. Let's have a look at each part of the script, along with the output it produces.

The first thing the script does is record the hostname and kernel version information, along with the first several lines of output from the top command, so I can see the load, number of users/processes, and so on:

```
#!/bin/bash
echo ""
echo "#########BASIC SYSTEM INFORMATION########"
echo HOSTNAME: `cat /proc/sys/kernel/hostname`
echo DOMAIN: `cat /proc/sys/kernel/domainname`
echo KERNEL: `uname -r`
top -b | head -8
```

Here's the output for this part of the script:

```
##########BASIC SYSTEM INFORMATION########
HOSTNAME: willy
DOMAIN: pvt
KERNEL: 2.4.21-32.0.1.ELsmp


 22:53:14  up 7 days, 15:36, 12 users,  load average: 0.00, 0.02, 0.00
114 processes: 113 sleeping, 1 running, 0 zombie, 0 stopped
CPU states:  cpu    user   nice  system    irq  softirq  iowait    idle
           total   0.0%   0.0%    0.4%   0.0%    0.0%    6.8%    92.6%
           cpu00   0.0%   0.0%    0.9%   0.0%    0.0%    7.8%    91.1%
           cpu01   0.0%   0.0%    0.0%   0.0%    0.0%    7.8%    92.1%
```

The hostname information is there so I'll know what I'm looking at when I
refer back to the output again in the future. The domain listed here is actually the NIS domain to which the box is bound. Depending on the environment, this can be an important bit of troubleshooting information—but if
you're in an NIS environment, you already knew that. What you're probably wondering is why I bothered to use /proc for this instead of system commands to get the hostname and domain name information. The answer is
because I've found that using files under /proc is more reliable than assuming that system commands are in your default path. For things like hostname,
chances are it's there, but three different tools can be installed for domain
name information. A typical Red Hat host has domainname, ypdomainname,
and dnsdomainname. On Red Hat systems, these are all symlinks to the
hostname command. On my Debian stable box, there is no domainname command at all. However, the /proc/sys/kernel/domainname file is on most
machines I come across, so using it makes the script more flexible.

Next up, let's have a look at the part of the script that gathers filesystem
information:

```
echo "######## FILESYSTEM INFORMATION #########"
echo ""
echo "SUPPORTED FILESYSTEM TYPES:"
echo ---------------------
echo `cat /proc/filesystems | awk -F'\t' '{print $2}'`
echo ""
echo "MOUNTED FILESYSTEMS:"
echo ---------------------
cat /proc/mounts
```

Again, here's the output:

```
SUPPORTED FILESYSTEM TYPES:
---------------------
sysfs rootfs bdev proc sockfs pipefs futexfs tmpfs eventpollfs devpts ext2
ramfs iso9660 devfs mqueue usbfs ext3 reiserfs supermount vfat
```

```
MOUNTED FILESYSTEMS:
----------------------
/dev/root / reiserfs rw 0 0
none /dev devfs rw 0 0
none /proc proc rw,nodiratime 0 0
sysfs /sys sysfs rw 0 0
devpts /dev/pts devpts rw 0 0
tmpfs /dev/shm tmpfs rw 0 0
usbfs /proc/bus/usb usbfs rw 0 0
none /dev/shm tmpfs rw 0 0
/dev/hdb1 /mnt/hdb1 ext3 rw,noatime 0 0
/dev/hdb2 /mnt/hdb2 reiserfs rw,noatime 0 0
```

This is not information that's likely to change on a standalone server, but in a large environment with many NFS mounts and running automounters, it can be useful information to have. The supported filesystem information is also handy if you're in a shop that builds its own kernels, because it'll let you know if your new junior admin made the novice mistake of forgetting to add *ext3* or *vfat* support to the kernel.

This next bit is only slightly more complex. It summarizes information about IDE devices, their model numbers, the devices they're assigned to on the system (*hda*, *hdb*, etc.), and, in case you don't recognize the models, exactly what kinds of devices they are. Here's the IDE device portion of the script:

```
echo "IDE DEVICES BY CONTROLLER"
echo ------------------------
for i in `ls /proc/ide | grep ide`
do
        echo $i:
        for j in `ls /proc/ide/$i | grep hd`
        do
                echo ""
                echo "    $j"
                echo "    --------"
                echo "    model: `cat /proc/ide/$i/$j/model`"
                echo "    driver: `cat /proc/ide/$i/$j/driver`"
                echo "    device type: `cat /proc/ide/$i/$j/media`"
                if [ -e /proc/ide/$i/$j/geometry ]; then
                        echo "    geometry:" `cat /proc/ide/$i/$j/geometry`
                fi
                echo ""
        done
done
```

And here's the output:

```
###### IDE SUBSYSTEM INFORMATION ########


IDE DEVICES BY CONTROLLER
-------------------------
ide0:
```

```
    hdb
    --------
    model: ST3200822A
    driver: ide-disk version 1.18
    device type: disk

ide1:

    hdd
    --------
    model: FX4830T
    driver: ide-cdrom version 4.61
    device type: cdrom
```

This tells me that there are two IDE controllers, a CD-ROM drive, and one IDE hard drive on the machine. I also know that the CD drive is going to be mountable as */dev/hdd* (something that might be less obvious on a machine with lots of IDE devices). Keep in mind that I could've gotten even more information if I wanted to require root privileges to run this script! For example, to see the settings for */dev/hdb*, I need to be root. I can then run this command:

```
# cat /proc/ide/hdb/settings
```

This will give me more information than I could ever want to know about my hard drive. Here's a sampling:

name	value	min	max	mode
acoustic	0	0	254	rw
address	1	0	2	rw
bios_cyl	24321	0	65535	rw
bios_head	255	0	255	rw
bios_sect	63	0	63	rw
bswap	0	0	1	r
current_speed	66	0	70	rw
failures	0	0	65535	rw
init_speed	66	0	70	rw
io_32bit	1	0	3	rw
keepsettings	0	0	1	rw
lun	0	0	7	rw
max_failures	1	0	65535	rw
multcount	16	0	16	rw
nice1	1	0	1	rw
nowerr	0	0	1	rw
number	1	0	3	rw
pio_mode	write-only	0	255	w
unmaskirq	1	0	1	rw
using_dma	1	0	1	rw
wcache	1	0	1	rw

Profile Your Systems Using /proc

There's a ton of information in the files under */proc*. Scripts like this one can be greatly expanded upon and make a wonderful tool for consulting administrators. Send it to a client and have him send you the output via email, or use it to take a snapshot of a machine when you set it up so that when a client calls up you're ready with the information about the host in question.

The Code

Here's a copy of the entire script in one place, for easy review:

```
#!/bin/bash
echo ""
echo "#########BASIC SYSTEM INFORMATION########"
echo HOSTNAME: `cat /proc/sys/kernel/hostname`
echo DOMAIN: `cat /proc/sys/kernel/domainname`
echo KERNEL: `uname -r`
top -b | head -8
echo "######## FILESYSTEM INFORMATION #########"
echo ""
echo "SUPPORTED FILESYSTEM TYPES:"
echo ---------------------
echo `cat /proc/filesystems | awk -F'\t' '{print $2}'`
echo ""
echo "MOUNTED FILESYSTEMS:"
echo ---------------------
cat /proc/mounts
echo "IDE DEVICES BY CONTROLLER"
echo ------------------------
for i in `ls /proc/ide | grep ide`
do
        echo $i:
        for j in `ls /proc/ide/$i | grep hd`
        do
                echo ""
                echo "    $j"
                echo "    --------"
                echo "    model: `cat /proc/ide/$i/$j/model`"
                echo "    driver: `cat /proc/ide/$i/$j/driver`"
                echo "    device type: `cat /proc/ide/$i/$j/media`"
                if [ -e /proc/ide/$i/$j/geometry ]; then
                        echo "    geometry:" `cat /proc/ide/$i/$j/geometry`
                fi
                echo ""
        done
done
```

HACK #75 Kill Processes the Right Way

The Linux kill command enables you to terminate processes normally or by using a sledgehammer.

If you spend much time as a Linux user or administrator, sooner or later you're going to have to end a process (often simply a program that no longer responds to user input or that just won't seem to go away). The safest way to kill a process is to simply use the kill command, with no modifiers or flags. First use the ps –ef command to determine the process ID (PID) of the process you want to kill, and then simply type this command:

```
# kill -pid
```

The standard kill command usually works just fine, terminating the offending process and returning its resources to the system. However, if your process has started child processes, simply killing the parent can potentially leave the child processes running, and therefore still consuming system resources. In order to prevent such so-called "zombie processes," you should make sure that you kill any and all child processes before you kill their respective parent processes.

Killing Processes in the Right Order

You can identify child process and their parents by using the Linux ps -ef command and examining each entry, looking at the column labeled PPID (parent process ID). However, if you're only interested in a specific family of processes, using the grep command makes life easier.

Let's look at an example. If we're trying to kill the *httpd* process, we'll need to kill its child processes before we can kill the parent. As a shortcut, use the following command to determine the PIDs that we'll need to terminate:

```
# ps –ef | grep httpd
[root@aardvark kida]# ps -ef | grep httpd
root      23739     1  0 Jun06 ?        00:00:07 /usr/sbin/httpd
apache    24375 23739  0 Jul17 ?        00:00:01 /usr/sbin/httpd
apache    24376 23739  0 Jul17 ?        00:00:00 /usr/sbin/httpd
apache    24377 23739  0 Jul17 ?        00:00:01 /usr/sbin/httpd
apache    24378 23739  0 Jul17 ?        00:00:00 /usr/sbin/httpd
apache    24379 23739  0 Jul17 ?        00:00:00 /usr/sbin/httpd
apache    24380 23739  0 Jul17 ?        00:00:01 /usr/sbin/httpd
apache    24383 23739  0 Jul17 ?        00:00:00 /usr/sbin/httpd
apache    24384 23739  0 Jul17 ?        00:00:01 /usr/sbin/httpd
```

The first column tells us the user that owns each process, and the second and third columns tell us their PIDs and PPIDs, respectively. The first process listed, with the PPID of 1, is the parent process. When a process has a PPID of 1, that means it was started by *init* at boot time.

The first thing to try now that we have the parent process ID is to try to gracefully take it down by using the following command:

```
# kill -1 23739
```

The -1 option tells the kill command to attempt to end the process as if the user who started it has logged out. When you use this option, the kill command also attempts to go through and kill child processes left behind. This won't always work, though—you may still need to go through and kill child processes manually first, before killing the parent process. To kill more than one process at a time, simply separate the PIDs with spaces on the kill command line:

```
# kill 24384 24383 24380
```

A second option is to send a TERM signal to the parent process in an attempt to kill it and its child processes. This can be done using the following command:

```
# kill -TERM 23739
```

Alternatively, you can attempt to kill all the processes within the same process group using killall. The killall command enables you to specify the names of the processes you want to terminate, rather than their PIDs, which can save you a lot of ps commands and eyestrain:

```
# killall httpd
```

Stopping and Restarting a Process

At some point, you might find yourself wanting to simply stop and restart a process. Instead of issuing the sequence of commands to manually kill and then restart your process, try using the following command:

```
# kill -HUP 23739
```

This will have Linux perform the process shutdown gently, and then restart it immediately. This is especially handy when you're working on configuring an application that needs its process restarted after changes to its configuration files.

The Last Resort

If the regular kill or kill -1 commands don't work, you can always bring out the all-powerful kill -9 command:

```
# kill -9 23739
```

This extremely powerful and dangerous command forces a process to stop in its tracks, without allowing it to clean up after itself. This can lead to unutilized system resources and is generally not recommended unless all other options have failed.

After using the `kill -9` (or the synonymous `kill -s SIGKILL`) command, be sure to use `ps -ef` again to make sure you don't have any zombie processes left. You can only eliminate a zombie process by terminating its parent process, which is fine if the parent process can safely be terminated or restarted but problematic if the zombie process has ended up being owned by the *init* process (PID 1). You do *not* want to kill the *init* process unless you know its implications and really mean to do that, because killing *init* will shut down your system. If you have zombie processes whose parent is *init*, and they are consuming significant amounts of system resources, you will need to reboot the machine at some point in order to clean up the process table.

See Also

- `man kill`
- `man ps`

—Brian Warshawsky

HACK #76 Use a Serial Console for Centralized Access to Your Systems

Keep a secret backdoor handy for midnight emergencies.

Imagine the following scenario. It's 3 A.M., and you're the administrator on call. All of a sudden, you're jolted awake by the pager rattling itself off the side of your nightstand. A critical server isn't responding to network polls, and you're unable to SSH into it to determine what the problem is. You are now faced with a tough decision—no one wants to get dressed and head into the office at 3 A.M., but this server is essential to your company's online presence. What do you do? The good news is that with proper fore-sight and planning, you can avoid this kind of decision altogether with a console server.

A *console server* is a device to which you can connect the consoles of multiple systems. You can then connect to the console server to get easy access to any of those systems. Devices that enable you to connect multiple serial ports and quickly switch between them are readily available from many different vendors. A quick Google search for "serial console server" will list more potential vendors than you probably want to know about.

This hack explains how to configure your Linux systems so that they can use serial ports for console output rather than the traditional graphical displays that we're used to on Linux systems. Not only are serial consoles inexpensive compared to multiple graphical displays, but they are easy to access remotely and fast because there is no graphical overhead.

The Options

Before you rush off to implement a console server, you need to consider several options. Various commercial options are available that provide many different flavors of console server. However, the method we're going to discuss here is a bit more do-it-yourself, and can ultimately be much cheaper to implement than a commercial option.

Another option to explore is whether or not your hardware already supports serial port console access via the BIOS. If it does, this might all be a moot point for you. However, this kind of hardware support is fairly rare, so odds are you're going to have to decide between an expensive proprietary method, or an easy-to-implement open source method.

If you're still reading, it would appear that you've decided to go the easy open source route. Good for you! The first thing to keep in mind when designing your console server is its physical deployment. The server will need to be kept fairly close to your critical servers. It will also need to have one or more serial ports available. A variety of vendors provide multi-serial-port PCI cards, so find the one that seems to best suit your situation and stay with it. If you only need to connect to one or two devices, consider sticking with the onboard serial ports typically found on most servers.

Start at the Beginning: The Bootloader

We'll now begin the process of configuring the console client, which, confusingly enough, is your production server. We need to configure the bootloader to both send output and receive input via the serial port. This isn't as difficult as it might sound, so have no fear. Several bootloaders are available for Linux, but by far the most prevalent are GRUB and LILO. In this hack we'll cover setting up console access through GRUB. Though LILO is certainly an effective bootloader and is capable of performing the same functions as GRUB, it doesn't contain as many of the features that make GRUB an attractive choice for this application.

When we configure the bootloader to redirect system input and output, we're actually indirectly configuring the Linux kernel to redirect the system's I/O. These configurations are made by modifying the configuration files for GRUB, thereby changing the way that GRUB boots the Linux kernel. GRUB's configuration file can be found under the *etc* (or sometimes *boot/grub*) directory, and is aptly named *grub.conf* (on some distributions this file may be named *menu.lst*).

Before we dive into configuring the bootloader, let's take a moment to examine a typical *grub.conf* file:

```
# grub.conf generated by anaconda
#
# Note that you do not have to rerun grub after making changes to this file
# NOTICE:  You have a /boot partition. This means that
#          all kernel and initrd paths are relative to /boot/, eg.
#          root (hd0,0)
#          kernel /vmlinuz-version ro root=/dev/hda3
#          initrd /initrd-version.img
#boot=/dev/hda
default=0
timeout=5
splashimage=(hd0,0)/grub/splash.xpm.gz
hiddenmenu
title Fedora Core (2.6.11-1.27_FC3)
        root (hd0,0)
        kernel /vmlinuz-2.6.11-1.27_FC3 ro root=LABEL=/
        initrd /initrd-2.6.11-1.27_FC3.img
```

Some people recommend removing the splashimage directives, because graphical images are not appropriate for serial consoles. However, I've never had an issue with this. Whether or not you'll need to remove these directives will largely depend on the version of GRUB you're using. If it's fairly recent, it should be able to ignore these lines without an issue. Otherwise, simply comment out or remove the splashimage reference.

Now that you have that worked out, let's modify the configuration file to redirect all input and output to the serial port. The standard settings for serial port communications are 9,600 baud, no parity, and 8 bits. It's important to remember these settings, as they will become necessary later when you need to configure the console server to communicate with the client. To pass these settings on to the kernel, add the following lines to the top of your *grub.conf* file.

```
serial --unit=0 --speed=9600 --word=8 --parity=no --stop=1
terminal --timeout=30 serial console
```

These lines should appear directly above your default directive. Most of the flags passed are self-explanatory, but let's look at the ones that may not be so clear. The --unit flag tells the kernel to redirect everything to the first serial port the kernel can identify. This will remain the same boot after boot, so you don't need to worry about it changing. The --word directive is used to set the number of bits that are to be used in communications with the console server. This can be set to 5, 6, 7, or 8. Take note that almost everything communicates using either 7 or 8 bits, and 8 bit is a nearly industry-wide standard. Using a lower number for this option can end up coming back to bite you should ASCII values greater than 127 be displayed. The --parity flag is used in this case to disable the use of parity error checking of the data transmitted from one end of the null modem connection to the other. The --stop directive is used to set the method by which a null modem data transmission is terminated.

The second line we added instructs the kernel to use both the serial port and the console to display output. Whichever one receives input first becomes the default console. Herein lies one of the above-mentioned features that makes GRUB an excellent choice for this project. By specifying both the serial and console options, we are able to effectively utilize two different devices as the console.

Once you've made the changes, reboot the server so the new GRUB directives can take effect. We'll now move on to configuring your console server to communicate with the client.

Putting It All Together

First, you need to make sure you have a serial cable connecting your console server to the client. (Be sure to connect the serial cable to the same port you configured the kernel to redirect I/O to, or you'll end up staring at a whole lot of nothing!) Then you'll need a program to communicate via the null modem. There are several available, but for overall ease of use and maximum features, I recommend *minicom*. To start *minicom*, run the following command as root:

```
# minicom -s
```

This will bring you directly into the *minicom* configuration screen. Select "Serial Port Setup" and change the configuration to match what you set up earlier in GRUB. Once that's done, save your changes and exit. You should be taken to the main *minicom* screen. If you don't see anything, hit Return once, and you should be greeted with the login prompt for your server. Congratulations—as long as your network remains alive, you now have remote console access to your server!

> For more information about installing and configuring *minicom*, see "Turn Your Laptop into a Makeshift Console" [Hack #37].

Once everything is assembled and *minicom* is installed, all you have to do it to SSH to your console server, start *minicom* with the correct serial device, and access the console of your troubled system. Voilà! What could be easier?

Where to Go from Here

What we've created here is the most basic application of a console server. As I mentioned earlier, this can be expanded with the addition of a multi-port serial card. With a little extra time spent cabling and configuring your bootloaders, you can effectively deploy console servers across your entire network. Another trick to keep in mind is the deceptively simple RJ45 to DB9 serial adaptor. These little guys allow you to use a strand of cat5 network cable to connect to a serial port. I have actually used them in conjunction with patch panels to provide myself console access to network equipment from my desk. You can pick up one of these lifesaving gadgets from any networking supply company for under a few dollars.

Another way to increase the usefulness of your console server is to include a modem attached to the console server in your setup. This can be configured to accept incoming calls, thereby allowing you to connect to your console server over the phone line in the event of a network outage. I would highly recommend this, as the remote console server does you no good if your problem lies somewhere else on the network.

You'll only need to use a serial console server once to prove to yourself that it's well worth the half-hour or so it might take you to get it configured. At 3 A.M., when you're able to reboot a server remotely and bring it back online without so much as putting on a pair of pants, you'll agree that the foresight for such an occasion is priceless.

See Also

- *http://www.linuxjournal.com/article/7206*

—Brian Warshawsky

HACK #77 Clean Up NIS After Users Depart

Don't let your NIS maps go stale! The NIS password map obviously needs maintenance, but don't forget to remove departed users from the groups they belonged to as well.

Many sites use NIS, in part because it's been there for many years and is an extremely reliable, acceptably fast, and relatively low-overhead way to run a centralized authentication directory. Over the years, tons of systems software has been written to take advantage of information supplied by NIS servers for the purposes of providing information or security to the client systems.

Though there are tools available to take care of most user-management tasks when the users reside on the local system, many of these tools don't have full support for NIS, and NIS-specific versions of these tools have yet to appear. As a result, certain portions of your NIS directory can become stale.

The NIS group map is a perfect example of this occurrence. The standard userdel command doesn't support NIS, and the groupmod command doesn't support removing a user from a group, let alone an NIS group. Most of the NIS-specific commands are either for searching the maps (e.g., ypmatch and ypcat), getting information about your client system (e.g., ypwhich and ypdomainname), or getting information about the NIS server (e.g., yppoll). No tools are available for grooming the NIS maps without opening an editor and removing entries by hand.

Therefore, if you haven't been vigilant about maintaining the maps to ensure that they're always consistent with reality, you can build up lots of stale accounts. Many sites are very vigilant about removing users from the password map, but even that is often a manual process involving opening the map in an editor and deleting the line corresponding to the departed user. What I've found, though, is that the group map is often forgotten, so you may wind up with 40 or 50 users who are assigned to groups, but whose accounts no longer exist. This makes the data in that map less usable, and depending on how the data is used, it could cause problems over time.

Take, for example, a mail server that uses the group map to create mail aliases corresponding to group names. A stale group map will place a bunch of nonexistent users in your mail aliases, which will cause your mail logs to grow out of control logging errors about nonexistent users—not to mention that mail to a "stale" alias will cause end users to receive bounce errors from the mail server.

I've written a Perl script to take care of cleaning up after user accounts that no longer exist. It sifts through the group map, and for each user, it checks for the existence of that user's account in the password map. Any users that aren't listed in the password map are neatly removed from the group map. I call the script *cleangroup*.

The Code

```
#!/usr/bin/perl

## looks up all members of each group via 'ypmatch $user passwd' and
## deletes any users from a given group file which aren't found.
## Output goes to STDOUT!

if($#ARGV < 0) {
 die "Must specify group file.\n" ;
}
$grpfile = $ARGV[0] ;
open(GRPFILE, "<$grpfile") || die "can't read $grpfile: $!\n" ;

while(<GRPFILE>) {
        chomp ;
        ($group,$pwd,$id,$members) = split(/:/) ;
        @unames = split(/,/, $members);
        foreach $i (@unames){
                if($i ne "root"){
```

```
                        if(! `ypmatch $i passwd 2>/dev/null`){
                                $members =~ s/\b$i\b//g ;
                        }
                }
        }
$members =~ s/,,/,/ ;
$members =~ s/,$// ;
$members =~ s/^,// ;
print "$group:$pwd:$id:$members\n" ;
}
close(GRPFILE) ;
```

Running the Code

I run *cleangroup* in the directory containing the NIS maps. For safety's sake, I have the script output to *stdout* instead of changing the map in-place. I redirect the output to a file, run a quick diff to see what was changed, and then copy the new map over the old one. Here are the commands I use:

```
# ./cleangroup groupmap > newgroupmap
# diff groupmap newgroupmap
```

This should output lines similar to the following:

```
  104c104
< stuff:*:20205:ken,maria,mike,tier,matt,jonesy,russ,allen
---
> stuff:*:20205:ken,maria,mike,tier,matt,russ,allen
252c252
< things:*:140:dan,chase,chandler,christian,chance,steph,jonesy
---
> things:*:140: dan,chase,chandler,christian,chance,steph
```

You'll notice that in each case the account *jonesy* was removed, once from the middle of the list and once from the end. I've yet to have any problems with this script, so I hope you find it as useful as I have!

Logfiles and Monitoring
Hacks 78–88

The only thing worse than disastrous disk failures, runaway remote hosts, and insidious security incidents is the gut-wrenching feeling that comes with the realization that they probably could've been avoided.

To avert catastrophe, often the best tool you can have is access to data that enables you to take proactive steps. Whether it's having a disk tell you when it's about to expire or being informed of network or service outages, tools that aggregate data and alert you to anomalies are invaluable to system and network administrators. The goal of this chapter is to show you how to get data you don't currently have, and how to use data you do have in more useful ways.

HACK #78 Avoid Catastrophic Disk Failure

Access your hard drive's built-in diagnostics using Linux utilities to predict and prevent disaster.

Nobody wants to walk in after a power failure only to realize that, in addition to everything else, because of a dead hard drive they now have to rebuild entire servers and grab backed-up data from tape. Of course, the best way to avoid this situation is to be alerted when something is amiss with your SCSI or ATA hard drive, before it finally fails. Ideally the alert would come straight from the hard drive itself, but until we're able to plug an RJ-45 directly into a hard drive we'll have to settle for the next best thing, which is the drive's built-in diagnostics. For several years now, ATA and SCSI drives have supported a standard mechanism for disk diagnostics called "Self Monitoring, Analysis, and Reporting Technology" (SMART), aimed at predicting hard drive failures. It wasn't long before Linux had utilities to poll hard drives for this vital information.

The *smartmontools* project (*http://smartmontools.sourceforge.net*) produces a SMART monitoring daemon called *smartd* and a command-line utility called *smartctl*, which can do most things on demand that the daemon does in the background periodically. With these tools, along with standard Linux file-system utilities such as *debugfs* and *tune2fs*, there aren't many hard drive issues you can't fix.

But before you can repair anything or transform yourself into a seemingly superpowered hard-drive hero with powers on loan from the realm of the supernatural, you have to know what's going on with your drives, and you need to be alerted to changes in the status of the health of your drives.

First, you should probably get to know your drives a bit, which *smartctl* can help out with. If you know that there are three drives in use on the system, but you're not sure which one the system is labeling */dev/hda*, run the following command:

```
# smartctl -i /dev/hda
```

This will tell you the model and capacity information for that drive. This is also very helpful in figuring out which vendor you'll need to call for a replacement drive if you bought the drive yourself. Once you know what's what, you can move on to bigger tasks.

Typically, before I even set up the *smartd* daemon to do long-term, continuous monitoring of a drive, I first run a check from the command line (using the *smartctl* command) to make sure I'm not wasting time setting up monitoring on a disk that already has issues. Try running a command like the following to ask the drive about its overall health:

```
# smartctl -H /dev/hda
smartctl version 5.33 [i386-redhat-linux-gnu] Copyright (C) 2002-4 Bruce
Allen
Home page is http://smartmontools.sourceforge.net/

=== START OF READ SMART DATA SECTION ===
SMART overall-health self-assessment test result: PASSED
```

Well, this is good news—the drive says it's in good shape. However, there really wasn't much to look at there. Let's get a more detailed view of things using the -a, or "all," flag. This gives us lots of output, so let's go over it in pieces. Here's the first bit:

```
# smartctl -a /dev/hda
smartctl version 5.33 [i386-redhat-linux-gnu] Copyright (C) 2002-4 Bruce
Allen
Home page is http://smartmontools.sourceforge.net/

=== START OF INFORMATION SECTION ===
Device Model:     WDC WD307AA
Serial Number:    WD-WMA111283666
Firmware Version: 05.05B05
```

```
User Capacity:     30,758,289,408 bytes
Device is:         In smartctl database [for details use: -P show]
ATA Version is:    4
ATA Standard is:   Exact ATA specification draft version not indicated
Local Time is:     Mon Sep  5 17:48:09 2005 EDT
SMART support is: Available - device has SMART capability.
SMART support is: Enabled
```

This is the exact same output that smartctl -i would've shown you earlier. It tells you the model, the firmware version, the capacity, and which version of the ATA standard is implemented with this drive. Useful, but not really a measure of health per se. Let's keep looking:

```
=== START OF READ SMART DATA SECTION ===
SMART overall-health self-assessment test result: PASSED
```

This is the same output that smartctl -H showed earlier. Glad we passed, but if we just barely made it, that's not passing to a discriminating administrator. More!

```
General SMART Values:
Offline data collection status:   (0x05) Offline data collection activity
                                         was aborted by an interrupting
command
                                         from host.
                                         Auto Offline Data Collection:
Disabled.
Self-test execution status:       ( 113) The previous self-test completed
having
                                         the read element of the test failed.
```

These are the values of the SMART attributes the device supports. We can see here that offline data collection is disabled, which means we can't run "offline" tests (which run automatically when the disk would otherwise be idle). We can enable it using the command smartctl -o on, but this may not be what you want, so let's hold off on that for now. The self-test execution status shows that a read operation failed during the last self-test, so we'll keep that in mind as we continue looking at the data:

```
Total time to complete Offline
data collection:                  (2352) seconds.
Offline data collection
capabilities:                     (0x1b) SMART execute Offline immediate.
                                         Auto Offline data collection on/off
                                         support.
                                         Suspend Offline collection upon new
                                         command.
                                         Offline surface scan supported.
                                         Self-test supported.
                                         No Conveyance Self-test supported.
                                         No Selective Self-test supported.
```

```
SMART capabilities:            (0x0003) Saves SMART data before entering
                                        power-saving mode.
                                        Supports SMART auto save timer.
Error logging capability:      (0x01) Error logging supported.
                                        No General Purpose Logging support.
```

This output is just a list of the general SMART-related capabilities of the
drive, which is good to know, especially for older drives that might not have
all of the features you would otherwise assume to be present. Capabilities
and feature support in the drives loosely follow the version of the ATA standard in place when the drive was made, so it's not safe to assume that an
ATA-4 drive will support the same feature set as an ATA-5 or later drive.

Let's continue on our tour of the output:

```
Short self-test routine
recommended polling time:      (   2) minutes.
Extended self-test routine
recommended polling time:      ( 42) minutes.
```

When you tell this drive to do a short self-test, it'll tell you to wait two minutes for the results. A long test will take 42 minutes. If this drive were new
enough to support other self-test types (besides just "short" and
"extended"), there would be lines for those as well. Here's the next section
of output:

```
SMART Attributes Data Structure revision number: 16
Vendor Specific SMART Attributes with Thresholds:
ID# ATTRIBUTE_NAME          FLAG    VALUE WORST THRESH TYPE      UPDATED
WHEN_FAILED RAW_VALUE
  1 Raw_Read_Error_Rate     0x000b  200   200   051    Pre-fail  Always
-       0
  3 Spin_Up_Time            0x0006  101   091   000    Old_age   Always
-       2550
  4 Start_Stop_Count        0x0012  100   100   040    Old_age   Always
-       793
  5 Reallocated_Sector_Ct   0x0012  198   198   112    Old_age   Always
-       8
  9 Power_On_Hours          0x0012  082   082   000    Old_age   Always
-       13209
 10 Spin_Retry_Count        0x0013  100   100   051    Pre-fail  Always
-       0
 11 Calibration_Retry_Count 0x0013  100   100   051    Pre-fail  Always
-       0
 12 Power_Cycle_Count       0x0012  100   100   000    Old_age   Always
-       578
196 Reallocated_Event_Count 0x0012  196   196   000    Old_age   Always
-       4
197 Current_Pending_Sector  0x0012  199   199   000    Old_age   Always
-       10
198 Offline_Uncorrectable   0x0012  199   198   000    Old_age   Always
-       10
```

```
199 UDMA_CRC_Error_Count    0x000a   200   253   000   Old_age   Always
-       0
200 Multi_Zone_Error_Rate   0x0009   200   198   051   Pre-fail  Offline
-       0
```

Details on how to read this chart, in gory-enough detail, are in the *sysctl* manpage. The most immediate values to concern yourself with are the ones labeled Pre-fail. On those lines, an indicator of the need for immediate action is if the VALUE column output descends to or below the value in the THRESH column. Continuing on:

```
SMART Error Log Version: 1
No Errors Logged

SMART Self-test log structure revision number 1
Num  Test_Description   Status                    Remaining  LifeTime(hours)
LBA_of_first_error
# 1  Extended offline   Completed: read failure      10%         97
57559262
# 2  Extended offline   Aborted by host              50%         97        -
# 3  Short offline      Completed without error      00%         97        -

Device does not support Selective Self Tests/Logging
```

This output is the log output from the last three tests. The numbering of the tests is actually the reverse of what you might think: the one at the top of the list, labeled as # 1, is actually the most recent test. In that test we can see that there was a read error, and the LBA address of the first failure is posted (57559262). If you want to see how you can associate that test with an actual file, Bruce Allen has posted a wonderful HOWTO for this at *http:// smartmontools.sourceforge.net/BadBlockHowTo.txt*.

Now that you've seen what *smartctl* can find out for us, let's figure out how to get *smartd* configured to automate the monitoring process and let us know if danger is imminent.

Fortunately, putting together a basic configuration takes mere seconds, and more complex configurations don't take a great deal of time to put together, either. The *smartd* process gets its configuration from */etc/smartd.conf* on most systems, and for a small system (or a ton of small systems that you don't want to generate copious amounts of mail), a line similar to the following will get you the bare essentials:

```
/dev/hda -H -m jonesy@linuxlaboratory.org
```

This will do a (very) simple health status check on the drive, and email me only if it fails. If a health status check fails, it means the drive could very well fail in the next 24 hours, so have an extra drive handy!

There are more sophisticated setups as well that can alert you to changes in the status that don't necessarily mean certain death. Let's look at a more complex configuration line:

```
/dev/hda -l selftest -l error -I 9 -m jonesy@linuxlaboratory.org -s L/../../
7/02
```

This one will look for changes in the self-test and error logs for the device, run a long self-test every Sunday between 2 and 3 A.M. and send me messages about any attribute except for ID 9, the Power_On_Hours attribute, which I don't care about for the purposes of determining whether a disk is bad (you can check the sysctl -a output to determine an attribute's ID). The -I attribute is often used with attribute numbers 194 or 231, which usually is the temperature. It would be bad to get messages about the constantly changing temperature of the drive!

Once you have your configuration file in order, the only thing left to do is start the service. Inevitably, you'll get more mail than you'd like in the first initial runs, but as time goes on (and you read more of the huge manpage) you'll learn to get what you want from *smartd*. For me, just the peace of mind is worth the hours I've spent getting a working configuration. When you're able to avert certain catastrophe for a client or yourself, I'm sure you'll say the same.

HACK #79 Monitor Network Traffic with MRTG

The Multi-Router Traffic Grapher provides a quick visual snapshot of network traffic, making it easy to find and resolve congestion.

There are many reasons it's a good idea to capture data pertaining to your network and bandwidth usage. Detailed visual representations of such data can be incredibly useful in determining the causes of network outages, bottlenecks, and other issues. Collecting such detailed data used to require sophisticated and expensive equipment, but with the advent of Linux and the widespread use of SNMP, we now have a new tool to simplify and expand the possibilities of bandwidth monitoring. This tool is called the *Multi-Router Traffic Grapher* (MRTG), and this hack shows you how to set it up and use it.

Requirements

MRTG has a few simple dependencies that you may need to fulfill before you dive right into the installation. For starters, you need to have a web server up and running. Apache is typically recommended, but you may be able to get it to work with other web servers. You'll also need Perl installed and working on your system, and MRTG will require three libraries to build its graphs. The first, *gd*, is used to generate the graphs that make MRTG what it is. The second is *libpng*, which is used to generate the images of the graphs. Finally, to compress these images, you'll need the *zlib* library. Download locations for all three of these libraries can be found at the MRTG home page (*http://people.ee.ethz.ch/~oetiker/webtools/mrtg/*).

Installation

Once you have the dependencies installed, you can begin the MRTG installation. First, download and untar the source to your build location. Start the MRTG installation with the following command:

```
$ ./configure -prefix=/usr/local/mrtg-2
```

If this produces an error message, you may have to specify where you installed the previously mentioned libraries:

```
# ./configure -prefix=/usr/local/mrtg-2 --with-gf=/path/to/gd \
--with-z=/path/to/z --with-png=/path/to/png
```

If you need help determining where those libraries were installed, run the following command for each library to find its location:

```
# find / -type f -name libpng
```

Once configuration is complete, follow it up with a typical make install:

```
# make && make install
```

The next step is to create the *mrtg.cfg* file that MRTG will use to determine which devices on your network to query. If you had to create this by hand, things could get a little hairy. Fortunately for us, however, MRTG comes with a command-line configuration tool called *cfgmaker* that greatly simplifies the creation of the *.cfg*. Detailed documentation on *cfgmaker* is available at the MRTG home page, but the following example should be enough to get you started:

```
# cfgmaker -global 'WorkDir: /path/to/web/root/mrtg' \
    --output=/etc/mrtg.cfg \
    --global'Options[_]: bits, growright' --output=/etc/mrtg.cfg \
    SNMP-community-name@address.router1 \
    SNMP-community-name@address.router2 \
    Global 'Options[_]: bits, growright' --ifref=descry \
    --ifdescr=alias SNMP-community-name@address.switch.1
```

This will create the configuration file */etc/mrtg.cfg*, which will tell MRTG to create bandwidth graphs for *router1*, *router2*, and *switch1*. The graphs will use bits as the primary measurement on the y-axis and will grow toward the righthand side. The -global options add entries that apply to this configuration as a whole, while those that are not specified as global apply only to the devices in which we specify them. The location of the configuration file to create is specified by the -output option.

With a valid config file in hand, we can now run MRTG for the first time. Each time you run MRTG, you'll need to specify the location from which you want it to read the config file. Also, unless you've added it to your path, you'll need to type out the full path to the executable.

```
# /usr/local/bin/mrtg-2/bin/mrtg /etc/mrtg.cfg
```

You will see some errors the first two times you run MRTG, but pay them no mind—it's simply complaining because it can't find any previous MRTG data. After running the command, your MRTG web root should be filled with PNG files. This is great, except it's a pain to look at them like this, and they're not exactly labeled in a human friendly format. The solution to this problem can be found in the *indexmaker* tool. *indexmaker* works just like the *cfgmaker* tool, only instead of generating config files, it generates an HTML template with which we can display our MRTG graphs:

```
# indexmaker -output=/path/to/web/root/index.html \
    -title="My Network MRTG" -sort=title
```

This will create an *index.html* file that sorts and displays our data in a much more user-friendly format, as shown in Figure 9-1. You can then modify the index file just as you would any HTML file to make it display any other information you wish.

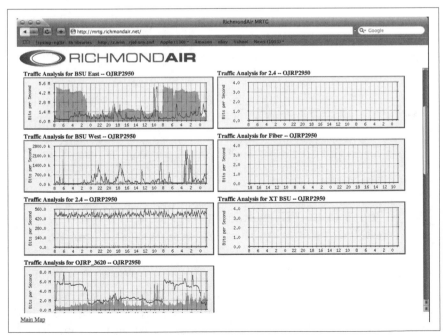

Figure 9-1. Network traffic graphs created from MRTG data

Automating MRTG

The only thing left to do is to automate the process. MRTG wouldn't be very useful if you had to start it manually every time, so we'll have to automate it by adding it to cron. Add the following entry to root's crontab to run MRTG every five minutes:

```
*/5 * * * * /usr/local/mrtg-2/bin/mrtg /etc/mrtg.cfg \
    --logging /var/log/mrtg.log
```

Don't get impatient waiting to see your pretty new graphs. It will take a day or so for them to begin displaying truly useful data. Once you've had them running for a while, though, you'll be able to pick out all kinds of useful trends in your bandwidth utilization. For instance, you might notice that your bandwidth tends to spike between 8:30 and 9:00 A.M., and then again after lunch. This will help you better understand the utilization of your network, and in turn better serve it. It can be fascinating to simply watch your bandwidth utilization materialize, and then use the information to track and follow trends in network activity. MRTG will create yearly graphs as well as hourly, monthly, and daily graphs. Having such detailed information at your fingertips can help you understand just how much traffic you gained after your web site was Slashdotted, and how your popularity increased even after the story ran.

MRTG has a million uses, and they're not just limited to tracking bandwidth utilization. With a little modification, you can use it to measure almost anything you want. For more information on modifying MRTG to display other statistics, see the MRTG home page.

See Also

- *http://people.ee.ethz.ch/~oetiker/webtools/mrtg/*
- "Monitor Service Availability with Zabbix" [Hack #85]

—Brian Warshawsky

H A C K   Keep a Constant Watch on Hosts
#80
Monitor load or other statistics for multiple hosts on your desktop or on the command line.

rstatd is an RPC-based kernel statistics server that is either included with or available for every form of Unix I've ever used. It isn't something new. In fact, I suspect that its age might cause it to slip under the radar of younger admins, who might not know it if it hasn't appeared on the front page of Freshmeat recently. Hopefully, the information here will pique your interest in this very useful tool.

When I say that *rstatd* provides "kernel statistics," I'm referring to things such as CPU load, page swapping statistics, network IO statistics, and the like. Of course, providing this information to administrators in a way that is useful can sometimes be challenging, but there are a few tools available to help.

To make these tools useful, you must have a running *rstatd* daemon. Note that *rstatd* is dependent on the *portmap* daemon, which should already be running if you're using other RPC-based services such as NIS or NFS. To do a quick check to make sure these are running, you can run the following command:

```
$ rpcinfo -p
   program vers proto    port
   100000   2   tcp      111   portmapper
   100000   2   udp      111   portmapper
   100001   3   udp      646   rstatd
   100001   2   udp      646   rstatd
   100001   1   udp      646   rstatd
```

Without any other arguments, this will show you the status of the local host. If you put a hostname on the end of the above command, it will show you the status of a remote host. Now we're ready to point some tools at this host!

First and foremost among these tools is the standard rup command, which is available on Linux and other Unix platforms. It's a simple *rstatd* client utility, but with the right tools you can use it to produce output similar to that produced by the top command—only instead of monitoring processes on the local host, you can monitor the load on multiple machines. Here's a command you can run to have a list of hosts, sorted by load average, updated every five seconds:

```
$ watch -n 5 rup -l host1 host2 host3 host4 host5
     host3   up 12 days,  7:33,   load average: 0.00, 0.00, 0.00
     host4   up 12 days,  7:28,   load average: 0.00, 0.00, 0.00
     host1   up 12 days,  6:11,   load average: 0.05, 0.04, 0.05
     host2   up 12 days,  6:11,   load average: 0.05, 0.04, 0.05
     host5   up 12 days,  7:29,   load average: 0.09, 0.06, 0.01
```

This is okay if you have no access to any kind of graphical environment. Of course, it takes over your terminal, so you'll at least need to run it inside a *screen* session **[Hack #34]** or in a separate virtual terminal. Another problem here is that it's just simple raw data output; it doesn't alert you to any events, like *host4*'s load going through the stratosphere.

For that, we can move into graphical clients. An old favorite of mine is *xmeter*, which was developed long ago and has since seemingly been forgotten and abandoned. Its configuration takes a little time to sift through (it's not graphical), but it does come with a manpage to help out, and once it's configured the only thing you'll ever have to change is the list of hosts to monitor. It provides configuration options to change the color of the output based on thresholds, so if the load of a machine gets to be a bit out of control, the color change is likely to catch your eye. Figure 9-2 shows a shot of *xmeter* monitoring the load on multiple hosts.

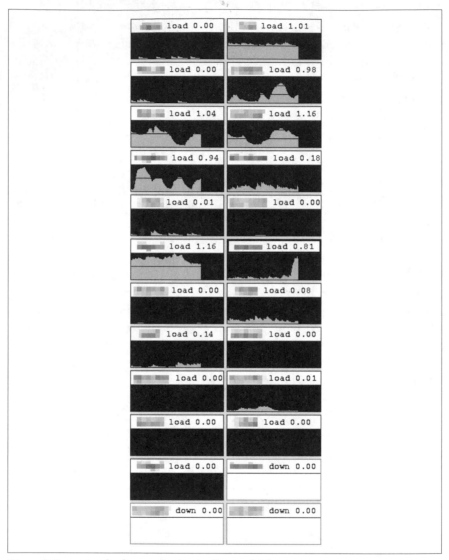

Figure 9-2. xmeter display monitoring load on multiple servers

A more recent development in the world of *rstatd* data-collection tools is *jperfmeter*, which is a Java-based, cross-platform monitor with a more polished interface and a graphical configuration tool. It does not yet (at the time of writing) support thresholds, and it's missing a few other finer details, but it's a brand new tool, so I'm sure it will get there at some point.

There are other tools available for remote server statistics monitoring, but you may also want to look into building your own, using either the Rstat::Client Perl module or the RPC or *rstat* interfaces for other languages, such as Python, Java, or C/C++.

Remotely Monitor and Configure a Variety of Networked Equipment

Using SNMP, you can collect information about almost any device attached to your network.

For everything that has a network interface, chances are there's some form of Simple Network Management Protocol (SNMP) daemon that can run on it. Over the years, SNMP daemons have been added to everything from environmental sensors to UPSs to soda vending machines. The point of all of this is to be able to remotely access as much information about the host as humanly possible. As an added bonus, proper configuration can allow administrators to change values on the host remotely as well.

SNMP daemon packages are available for all of the widely used distributions, along with possibly separate packages containing a suite of SNMP command-line tools. You might have come across the snmpwalk or snmpget commands before in your travels, or you might've seen similarly named functions in scripting languages such as Perl and PHP.

Let's have a look at a small bit of a "walk" on an SNMP-enabled Linux host and use it to explain how this works:

```
$ snmpwalk -v2c -c public livid interfaces
IF-MIB::ifNumber.0 = INTEGER: 4
IF-MIB::ifIndex.1 = INTEGER: 1
IF-MIB::ifIndex.2 = INTEGER: 2
IF-MIB::ifIndex.3 = INTEGER: 3
IF-MIB::ifIndex.4 = INTEGER: 4
IF-MIB::ifDescr.1 = STRING: lo
IF-MIB::ifDescr.2 = STRING: eth0
IF-MIB::ifDescr.3 = STRING: eth1
IF-MIB::ifDescr.4 = STRING: sit0
IF-MIB::ifType.1 = INTEGER: softwareLoopback(24)
IF-MIB::ifType.2 = INTEGER: ethernetCsmacd(6)
IF-MIB::ifType.3 = INTEGER: ethernetCsmacd(6)
IF-MIB::ifType.4 = INTEGER: tunnel(131)
IF-MIB::ifPhysAddress.1 = STRING:
IF-MIB::ifPhysAddress.2 = STRING: 0:a0:cc:e7:24:a0
IF-MIB::ifPhysAddress.3 = STRING: 0:c:f1:d6:3f:32
IF-MIB::ifPhysAddress.4 = STRING: 0:0:0:0:3f:32
IF-MIB::ifAdminStatus.1 = INTEGER: up(1)
IF-MIB::ifAdminStatus.2 = INTEGER: up(1)
IF-MIB::ifAdminStatus.3 = INTEGER: down(2)
```

```
IF-MIB::ifAdminStatus.4 = INTEGER: down(2)
IF-MIB::ifOperStatus.1 = INTEGER: up(1)
IF-MIB::ifOperStatus.2 = INTEGER: up(1)
IF-MIB::ifOperStatus.3 = INTEGER: down(2)
IF-MIB::ifOperStatus.4 = INTEGER: down(2)
```

As you can see, there's a good bit of information here, and I've cut out the bits that aren't important right now. Furthermore, this is only one part of one SNMP "tree" (the "interfaces" tree). Under that tree lie settings and status information for each interface on the system. If you peruse the list, you'll see separate values for each interface corresponding to things like the interface description (the name the host calls the interface), the physical address, and the interface type.

But what is this "tree" I'm speaking of? SNMP data is actually organized much like LDAP data, or DNS data, or even your Linux system's file hierarchy—they're all trees! Our output above has hidden some of the detail from us, however. To see the actual path in the tree for each value returned, we'll add an option to our earlier command:

```
$ snmpwalk -Of -v2c -c public livid interfaces
.iso.org.dod.internet.mgmt.mib-2.interfaces.ifNumber.0 = INTEGER: 4
.iso.org.dod.internet.mgmt.mib-2.interfaces.ifTable.ifEntry.ifIndex.1 =
INTEGER: 1
.iso.org.dod.internet.mgmt.mib-2.interfaces.ifTable.ifEntry.ifIndex.2 =
INTEGER: 2
.iso.org.dod.internet.mgmt.mib-2.interfaces.ifTable.ifEntry.ifIndex.3 =
INTEGER: 3
.iso.org.dod.internet.mgmt.mib-2.interfaces.ifTable.ifEntry.ifIndex.4 =
INTEGER: 4
.iso.org.dod.internet.mgmt.mib-2.interfaces.ifTable.ifEntry.ifDescr.1 =
STRING: lo
.iso.org.dod.internet.mgmt.mib-2.interfaces.ifTable.ifEntry.ifDescr.2 =
STRING: eth0
.iso.org.dod.internet.mgmt.mib-2.interfaces.ifTable.ifEntry.ifDescr.3 =
STRING: eth1
.iso.org.dod.internet.mgmt.mib-2.interfaces.ifTable.ifEntry.ifDescr.4 =
STRING: sit0
.iso.org.dod.internet.mgmt.mib-2.interfaces.ifTable.ifEntry.ifType.1 =
INTEGER: softwareLoopback(24)
.iso.org.dod.internet.mgmt.mib-2.interfaces.ifTable.ifEntry.ifType.2 =
INTEGER: ethernetCsmacd(6)
.iso.org.dod.internet.mgmt.mib-2.interfaces.ifTable.ifEntry.ifType.3 =
INTEGER: ethernetCsmacd(6)
.iso.org.dod.internet.mgmt.mib-2.interfaces.ifTable.ifEntry.ifType.4 =
INTEGER: tunnel(131)
.iso.org.dod.internet.mgmt.mib-2.interfaces.ifTable.ifEntry.ifPhysAddress.1 =
STRING:
.iso.org.dod.internet.mgmt.mib-2.interfaces.ifTable.ifEntry.ifPhysAddress.2 =
STRING: 0:a0:cc:e7:24:a0
```

```
.iso.org.dod.internet.mgmt.mib-2.interfaces.ifTable.ifEntry.ifPhysAddress.3 =
STRING: 0:c:f1:d6:3f:32
.iso.org.dod.internet.mgmt.mib-2.interfaces.ifTable.ifEntry.ifPhysAddress.4 =
STRING: 0:0:0:0:3f:32
.iso.org.dod.internet.mgmt.mib-2.interfaces.ifTable.ifEntry.ifAdminStatus.1 =
INTEGER: up(1)
.iso.org.dod.internet.mgmt.mib-2.interfaces.ifTable.ifEntry.ifAdminStatus.2 =
INTEGER: up(1)
.iso.org.dod.internet.mgmt.mib-2.interfaces.ifTable.ifEntry.ifAdminStatus.3 =
INTEGER: down(2)
.iso.org.dod.internet.mgmt.mib-2.interfaces.ifTable.ifEntry.ifAdminStatus.4 =
INTEGER: down(2)
.iso.org.dod.internet.mgmt.mib-2.interfaces.ifTable.ifEntry.ifOperStatus.1 =
INTEGER: up(1)
.iso.org.dod.internet.mgmt.mib-2.interfaces.ifTable.ifEntry.ifOperStatus.2 =
INTEGER: up(1)
.iso.org.dod.internet.mgmt.mib-2.interfaces.ifTable.ifEntry.ifOperStatus.3 =
INTEGER: down(2)
.iso.org.dod.internet.mgmt.mib-2.interfaces.ifTable.ifEntry.ifOperStatus.4 =
INTEGER: down(2)
```

Now we can clearly see that the "interfaces" tree sits underneath all of those other trees. If you replaced the dot separators with a forward slashes, it would look very much like a directory hierarchy, with the value after the last dot being the filename and everything after the equals sign being the content of the file. Now this should start to look a little more familiar—more like the output of a find command than something completely foreign (I hope).

A great way to get acquainted with an SNMP-enabled (or "managed") device is to simply walk the entire tree for that device. You can do this by pointing the snmpwalk command at the device without specifying a tree, as we've done so far. Be sure to redirect the output to a file, though, because there's far too much data to digest in one sitting! To do this, use a command like the following:

```
$ snmpwalk -Ov -v2c -c public livid > livid.walk
```

You can run the same command against switches, routers, firewalls, and even some specialized devices such as door and window contact sensors and environmental sensors that measure the heat and humidity in your machine room.

The Code

Even just sticking to Linux boxes offers a wealth of information. I've written a script in PHP, runnable from a command line, that gathers basic information and reports on listening TCP ports, using only SNMP. Here's the script:

```php
#!/usr/bin/php

<?php
snmp_set_quick_print(1);
$string = "public";
$host = "livid";
```

```
check_snmp($host);
spitinfo($host);

function check_snmp($box)//see if this box is running snmp before we throw
                        //requests at it.
{
    $string="public";
    $infocheck = @snmpget("$box", "$string", "system.sysDescr.0");
    if(! $infocheck)
    {
        die("SNMP doesn't appear to be running on $box");
    }
    else
    {
    return $infocheck;
    }
}
function spitinfo($host)//retrieves and displays snmp data.
{
        $string = "public";
        $hostinfo = @snmpget("$host","$string","system.sysDescr.0");
        list ($k)=array(split(" ", $hostinfo));
        $os = $k[0];
        $hostname = @snmpget("$host","$string","system.sysName.0");
        $user = @snmpget("$host","$string","system.sysContact.0");
        $location = @snmpget("$host","$string","system.sysLocation.0");
        $macaddr = @snmpget
                    ("$host","$string","interfaces.ifTable.ifEntry.
                      ifPhysAddress.2");
        $ethstatus =
                    @snmpget("$host","$string","interfaces.ifTable.ifEntry.
                             ifOperStatus.2");
        $ipfwd = @snmpget("$host","$string","ip.ipForwarding.0");
        $ipaddr = @gethostbyname("$host");
        $info=array("Hostname:"=>"$hostname","Contact:"=>"$user",
                "Location:"=>"$location","OS:"=>"$os","MAC Address:"=>
                "$macaddr","IP Address:"=>"$ipaddr","Network Status"=>
                "$ethstatus",
                 "Forwarding:"=>"$ipfwd");
        print "$host\n";
        tabdata($info);
        print "\nTCP Port Summary\n";
        snmp_portscan($hostname);
}
function tabdata($data)
{
    foreach($data as $label=>$value)
        {
            if($label){
                print  "$label\t";
            }else{
                    print "Not Available";
            }
```

```
            if($value){
                print   "$value\n";
            }else{
                    print "Not Available";
            }
        }
    }

    function snmp_portscan($target)
    {
            $listen_ports = snmpwalk("$target", "public", ".1.3.6.1.2.1.6.13.1.3.
    0.0.0.0");
            foreach($listen_ports as $key=>$value)
            {
                    print "TCP Port $value (" . getservbyport($value, 'tcp') . ")
    listening \n";
            }
    }

    ?>
```

Running the Code

Save this script to a file named *report.php*, and make it executable (chmod 775
report.php). Once that's done, run it by issuing the command ./report.php.

I've hard-coded a value for the target host in this script to shorten things up
a bit, but you'd more likely want to feed a host to the script as a command-
line argument, or have it read a file containing a list of hosts to prod for
data. You'll also probably want to scan for the number of interfaces, and do
other cool stuff that I've left out here to save space. Here's the output when
run against my Debian test system:

```
Hostname:       livid
Contact:        jonesy(jonesy@linuxlaboratory.org
Location:       Upstairs office
OS:     Linux
MAC Address:    0:a0:cc:e7:24:a0
IP Address:     192.168.42.44
Network Status  up
Forwarding:     notForwarding

TCP Port Summary
TCP Port 80 (http) listening
TCP Port 111 (sunrpc) listening
TCP Port 199 (smux) listening
TCP Port 631 (ipp) listening
TCP Port 649 () listening
TCP Port 2049 (nfs) listening
TCP Port 8000 () listening
TCP Port 32768 () listening
```

You'll notice in the script that I've used numeric values to search for in SNMP. This is because, as in many other technologies, the human-readable text is actually mapped from numbers, which are what the machines use under the covers. Each record returned in an snmpwalk has a numeric object identifier, or OID. The client uses the Management Information Base (MIB) files that come with the Net-SNMP distribution to map the numeric OIDs to names. In a script, however, speed will be of the essence, so you'll want to skip that mapping operation and just get at the data.

You'll also notice that I've used SNMP to do what is normally done with a port scanner, or with a bunch of calls to some function like (in PHP) fsockopen. I could've used function calls here, but it would have been quite slow because we'd be knocking on every port in a range and awaiting a response to see which ones are open. Using SNMP, we're just requesting the host's list of which ports are open. No guessing, no knocking, and much, much faster.

HACK #82 Force Standalone Apps to Use syslog

Some applications insist on maintaining their own set of logs. Here's a way to shuffle those entries over to the standard syslog facility.

The dream is this: working in an environment where all infrastructure services are running on Linux machines [Hack #44] using easy-to-find open source software such as BIND, Apache, Sendmail, and the like. There are lots of nice things about all these packages, not the least of which is that they all know about and embrace the standard Linux/Unix *syslog* facilities. What this means is that you can tell the applications to log using *syslog*, and then configure which log entries go where in one file (*syslog.conf*), instead of editing application-specific configuration files.

For example, if I want Apache to log to *syslog*, I can put a line like this one in my *httpd.conf* file:

```
ErrorLog    syslog
```

This will, by default, log to the *local7 syslog* facility. You can think of a *syslog* facility as a channel into *syslog*. You configure *syslog* to tell it where entries coming in on a given channel should be written. So, if I want all messages from Apache coming in on the *local7* channel to be written to */var/log/httpd*, I can put the following line in */etc/syslog.conf*:

```
local7.*            /var/log/httpd
```

You can do this for the vast majority of service applications that run under Linux. The big win is that if an application misbehaves, you don't have to track down its logfiles—you can always consult *syslog.conf* to figure out where your applications are logging to.

In reality, though, most environments are not 100% Linux. Furthermore, not all software is as *syslog*-friendly as we'd like. In fact, some software has no clue what *syslog* is, and these applications maintain their own logfiles, in their own logging directory, without an option to change that in any way. Some of these applications are otherwise wonderful services, but systems people are notoriously unrelenting in their demand for consistency in things like logging. So here's the meat of this hack: an example of a service that displays selfish logging behavior, and one way to go about dealing with it.

Fedora Directory Server (FDS) can be installed from binary packages on Red Hat–based distributions, as well as on Solaris and HP-UX. On other Linux distributions, it can be built from source. However, on no platform does FDS know anything about the local *syslog* facility. Enter a little-known command called logger.

The logger command provides a generic shell interface to the *syslog* facility on your local machine. What this means is that if you want to write a shell or Perl script that logs to *syslog* without writing *syslog*-specific functions, you can just call *logger* from within the script, tell it what to write and which *syslog* facility to write it to, and you're done!

Beyond that, *logger* can also take its input from *stdin*, which means that you can pipe information from another application to *logger*, and it will log whatever it receives as input from the application. This is truly beautiful, because now I can track down the FDS logs I'm interested in and send them to *syslog* with a command like this:

```
# exec tail -f /opt/fedora-ds/slapd-ldap/logs/access.log | logger -p local0.
debug &
```

I can then tell my *syslog* daemon to watch for all of the messages that have been piped to *logger* and sent to *syslog* on *local0* and to put them in, say, */var/log/ldap/access.log*.

The debug on the end of the facility name is referred to in *syslog* parlance as a *priority*. There are various priority levels available for use by each *syslog* facility, so a given application can log messages of varying severity as being of different priorities [Hack #86]. FDS is a good example of an application where you'd want to utilize priorities—the access log for FDS can be extremely verbose, so you're likely to want to separate those messages into their own logfile. Its error log is rarely written to at all, but the messages there can pertain to the availability of the service, so you might want those messages to go to */var/log/messages*. Rather than using up another whole *syslog* facility to get those messages to another file, just run a command like this one:

```
# tail -f /opt/fedora-ds/slapd-ldap/logs/error.log | logger -p local0.notice
```

Now let's tell *syslog* to log the messages to the proper files. Here are the configuration lines for the access and error logs:

```
local0.debug      /var/log/ldap/access.log
local0.notice     /var/log/messages
```

There is one final enhancement you'll probably want to make, and it has to do with `logger`'s output. Here's a line that made it to a logfile from `logger` as we ran it above, with just a -p flag to indicate the facility to use:

```
Aug 26 13:30:12 apollo logger: connection refused from 192.168.198.50
```

Well, this isn't very useful, because it lists `logger` as the application reporting the log entry! You can tell `logger` to masquerade as another application of your choosing using the -t flag, like this:

```
# tail -f access.log | logger -p local0.debug -t FDS
```

Now, instead of the reporting application showing up as `logger:`, it will show up as `FDS:`.

Of course, there are probably alternatives to using *logger*, but they sometimes involve writing Perl or PHP daemons that perform basically the same function as our *logger* solution. In the long run, you may be able to come up with a better solution for your site, but for the "here and now" fix, *logger* is a good tool to have on your toolbelt.

HACK #83 Monitor Your Logfiles

Use existing tools or simple homemade scripts to help filter noise out of your logfiles.

If you support a lot of services, a lot of hosts, or both, you're no doubt familiar with the problem of making efficient use of logfiles. Sure, you can have a log reporting tool send you log output hourly, but this information often goes to waste because of the extremely high noise-to-signal ratio. You can also try filtering down the information and using a tool such as *logwatch* to report on just those things most important to you on a daily basis. However, these reports won't help alert you to immediate, impending danger. For that, you need more than a reporting tool. What you really need is a log monitor; something to watch the logs continually and let you know about anything odd.

Log monitors in many environments come in human form: administrators often keep several terminal windows open with various logs being tailed into them, or they use something like root-tail to get those logs out of windows and right into their desktop backgrounds. You can even send your output to a Jabber client [Hack #84]. This is wonderful stuff, but again, it doesn't help filter out any of the unwanted noise in logfiles, and it's not very effective if all the humans are out to lunch (so to speak).

There are a number of solutions to this problem. One is simply to make sure that your services are logging at the right levels and to the right *syslog* facilities, and then make sure your *syslog* daemon is configured to break things up and log things to the right files. This can help to some degree, but what we want is to essentially have a real-time, always-running "grep" of our logs that will alert us to any matches that are found by sending us email, updating a web page, or sending a page.

Using log-guardian

There are a couple of tools out there that you can use for log monitoring. One is *log-guardian*, which is a Perl script that allows you to monitor multiple logfiles for various user-supplied patterns. You can also configure the action that *log-guardian* takes when a match is found. The downside to using *log-guardian* is that you must have some Perl knowledge to configure it, since actions supplied by the user are in the form of Perl subroutines, and other configuration parameters are supplied in the form of Perl hashes. All of these are put directly into the script itself or into a separate configuration file. You can grab *log-guardian* from its web site: *http://www.tifaware.com/ perl/log-guardian/*. Once downloaded, you can put the *log-guardian.pl* script wherever you store local system tools, such as under */opt* or in */var/local*. Since it doesn't come with an *init* script, you'll need to add a line similar to this one to your system's *rc.local* file:

```
/var/local/bin/log-guardian &
```

The real power of *log-guardian* comes from Perl's File::Tail module, which is a fairly robust bit of code that acts just like tail -f. This module is required for *log-guardian*. To determine whether you have it installed, you can run something like locate perl | grep Tail, or run a quick Perl one-liner like this at the command line:

```
$ perl -e "use File::Tail;"
```

If that returns a big long error beginning with "Can't find Tail/File.pm" or something similar, you'll need to install it using CPAN, which should be dead simple using the following command:

```
# perl -MCPAN -e shell
```

This will give you a CPAN shell prompt, where you can run the following command to get the module installed:

```
> install File::Tail
```

The File::Tail module is safe for use on logfiles that get moved, rolled, or replaced on a regular basis, and it doesn't require you to restart or even think about your script when this happens. It's dead-easy to use, and its more advanced features will allow you to monitor multiple logfiles simultaneously.

Here's a simple filter I've added to the *log-guardian* script itself to match on *sshd* connections coming into the server:

```
'/var/log/messages' => [
    {
        label   => 'SSH Connections',
        pattern => "sshd",
      action => sub {
                    my $line = $_[1];
                    print $line;
        }
    },
],
```

That's about as simple a filter you can write for *log-guardian*. It matches anything that gets written to */var/log/messages* that has the string sshd in it and prints any lines it finds to *stdout*. From there, you can send it to another tool for further processing or pipe it to the mail command, in which case you could run *log-guardian* like this:

```
# /var/local/bin/log-guardian | mail jonesy@linuxlaboratory.org
```

Of course, doing this will send every line in a separate email, so you might prefer to simply let it run in a terminal. You'll be able to monitor this output a little more easily than the logfiles themselves, since much of the noise has been filtered out for you.

This *sshd* filter is just one example—the "pattern" can consist of any Perl code that returns some string that the program can use to match against incoming log entries, and the "action" performed in response to that match can be literally anything you're capable of inventing using Perl. That makes the possibilities just about endless!

Using logcheck

The *logcheck* utility is not a real-time monitor that will alert you at the first sign of danger. However, it is a really simple way to help weed out the noise in your logs. You can download *logcheck* from *http://sourceforge.net/projects/sentrytools/*.

Once downloaded, untar the distribution, cd to the resulting directory, and as root, run make linux. This will install the *logcheck* files under */usr/local*. There are a few files to edit, but the things that need editing are simple one-liners; the configuration is very intuitive, and the files are very well commented.

The main file that absolutely must be checked to ensure proper configuration is */usr/local/etc/logcheck.sh*. This file contains sections that are marked with tags such as CONFIGURATION and LOGFILE CONFIGURATION, so you can easily find those variables in the file that might need changing. Probably the most obvious thing to change is the SYSADMIN variable, which tells *logcheck* where to send output.

```
SYSADMIN=user@mydomain.com
```

You should go over the other variables as well, because path variables and paths to binaries are also set in this file.

Once this is ready to go, the next thing you'll want to do is edit root's crontab file, which you can do by becoming root and running the following command:

```
# crontab -e
```

You can schedule *logcheck* to run as often as you want. The following line will schedule *logcheck* to run once an hour, every day, at 50 minutes after the hour:

```
50 * * * * /bin/sh /usr/local/etc/logcheck.sh
```

You can pick any time period you want, but once per hour (or less in smaller sites or home networks) should suffice.

Once you've saved the crontab entry, you'll start getting email with reports from *logcheck* about what it's found in your logs that you might want to know about. It figures out which log entries go into the reports by using the following methodology:

- It matches a string you've noted as significant by putting it in */usr/local/ etc/logcheck.hacking*.

- It does *not* match a string you've noted as being noise by putting it in */usr/ local/etc/logcheck.ignore*.

These two files are simply lists of strings that *logcheck* will try to match up against entries in the logs it goes through to create the reports. There is actually a third file as well, */usr/local/etc/logcheck.violations.ignore*, which contains strings that are matched only against entries that are already flagged as violations. There's an example of this in the *INSTALL* file that comes with the distribution that is more perfect than anything I can think of, so I'll reiterate it here:

```
Feb 28 21:00:08 nemesis sendmail[5475]: VAA05473: to=crowland, ctladdr=root
(0/0), delay=00:00:02, xdelay=00:00:01, mailer=local, stat=refused

Feb 28 22:13:53 nemesis rshd: refused connect from hacker@evil.com:1490

The top entry is from sendmail and is a fairly common error. The stat line
indicates that the remote host refused connections (stat=refused). This can
happen for a variety of reasons and generally is not a problem.

The bottom line however indicates that a person (hacker@evil.com) has tried
unsuccessfully to start an rsh session on my machine. This is bad (of
course you shouldn't be running rshd to begin with).
```

> The logcheck.violations file will find the word 'refused' and will flag it
> to be logged; however, this will report both instances as being bad and you
> will get false alarms from sendmail (both had the word 'refused').

To get around these false positive without also throwing out things you want to know about, you put a line like this in */usr/local/etc/logcheck. violations.ignore*:

```
mailer=local, stat=refused
```

This will match only the Sendmail log entry and will be ignored. Any other entries will be caught if they contain the string "refused".

Of course, it will likely take you some time to fine-tune the reports *logcheck* sends, but the model of forcing you to tell the tool to explicitly ignore things ensures that it ignores only what you tell it to, instead of making assumptions about your environment.

HACK #84 Send Log Messages to Your Jabber Client

Use hidden features of syslog and a quick script to send syslog messages straight to your desktop.

So you've finally gotten your machine room set up with centralized logging. Now you no longer need to open 50 different terminal windows to tail logs on all of your web servers. Instead, you just open one session to the central log host, tail the log, and go about your business.

But what if you could have the really important log messages, maybe only those going to the auth.warning facility, sent directly to your desktop in a way that will catch your attention even if you leave and come back only after the message has already scrolled by in your tail session?

You can actually accomplish this in a number of ways, but my favorite is by sending anything that comes through my *syslog* filter to my Jabber client. As most of you probably know, Jabber is an open source instant messaging protocol supported by Linux clients such as GAIM and Kopete.

This hack works because it turns out that *syslog* has the ability to send or copy messages to a named pipe (or FIFO). A pipe in the Linux world is a lot like a pipe in a plumber's world: you send something in one end, and it comes out (or is accessible through) the other end. By this logic, you can see that if I can have warnings sent to a pipe, I should be able to attach to that pipe some form of faucet from which I can access those messages. This is exactly what we'll do. For example, to send only those messages that pertain to failed login attempts (auth.warning) to a named pipe, you'd put the following line in */etc/syslog.conf*:

```
auth.warning            |/var/log/log-fifo
```

With that in place, you next need to create the *log-fifo* named pipe, which you can do with the following command:

```
# mkfifo /var/log/log-fifo
```

The next time you restart your *syslog* daemon, messages will be sent to *log-fifo*. You can quickly test that it's working by running the following command and watching the output:

```
# less -f /var/log/log-fifo
```

To get these messages to an open Jabber client, you can have a script read from *log-fifo*, wrap it in the appropriate XML, and send it off for routing to your target Jabber account. The script I use is a hacked up version of DJ Adams's original *jann* Perl script and requires the Net::Jabber module, which is readily available for (if not already installed on) most distributions. I call it *jann-log*.

The Code

This script reads *syslog* output from a FIFO and forwards it as a Jabber message:

```perl
#!/usr/bin/perl
use Net::Jabber qw(Client);
use strict;
# Announce resources
my %resource = (
  online => "/announce/online",
);
# default options
my %option = (
  server => "moocow:5222",
  user   => "admin",
  type   => "online",
);
# Default port if none specified
$option{server} = "moocow:5222";
# Ask for password if none given
unless ($option{pass}) {
  print "Password: ";
  system "stty -echo";
  $option{pass} = <STDIN>;
  system "stty echo";
  chomp $option{pass};
  print "\n";
}
# Connect to Jabber server
my ($host, $port) = split(":", $option{server}, 2);
print "Connecting to $host:$port as $option{user}\n";
my $c = new Net::Jabber::Client;
$c->Connect(
  hostname => $host,
  port     => $port,
```

```
) or die "Cannot connect to Jabber server at $option{server}\n";
my @result;
eval {
  @result = $c->AuthSend(
    username => $option{user},
    password => $option{pass},
    resource => "GAIM",
  );
};
die "Cannot connect to Jabber server at $option{server}\n" if $@;
if ($result[0] ne "ok") {
  die "Authorisation failed ($result[1]) for user $option{user} on
$option{server}\n";
}
print "Sending $option{type} messages\n";
# The message.  Change the file name in this 'open' line to
# the name of your fifo.
open(STATUS, "cat /var/log/log-fifo 2>&1 |")
     || die "UGH: there's issues:  $!";
while (<STATUS>) {
        my $xml .= qq[<subject>] .
    ($option{type} eq "online" ? "Admin Message" : "MOTD") .
    qq[</subject>];
        my $to = $host . $resource{$option{type}};
        $xml .= qq[<message to="$to">];
        $xml .= qq[<body>];
        my $message = $_;
    $xml .= XML::Stream::EscapeXML($message);
    $xml .= qq[</body>];
        $xml .= qq[</message>] ;
        $c->SendXML($xml);
        print $xml;
}
```

Running the Code

Place this script in a place accessible only by you and/or your admin team (for example, */var/local/adm/bin/jann-log*) and change the permissions so that the script is writable and executable only by your admin group. Then open up a Jabber client on your desktop and connect to your Jabber server. Once that's done, run the script. It should confirm that it has connected to the Jabber server and is awaiting messages from the FIFO.

A simple way to test your auth.warning facility on the server where *jann-log* is listening for messages is to SSH to the host and purposely use the wrong password to try to log in.

Monitor Service Availability with Zabbix

It's nice to have some warning before those help calls come flooding in. Be the first to know what's happening with critical servers on your network!

It will happen to everyone sooner or later: you'll be minding your own business, blissfully unaware that the network is crashing to its knees until a secretary claims that the Internet is down. By that time, the bosses have all noticed, and everyone wants answers. Full-blown panic kicks in, and you race around the office, pinging things at random to try to figure out what's happening. Wouldn't it be nice if you had some sort of detailed real-time network map that could monitor services and tell you what was going on? Zabbix to the rescue! Zabbix is a host monitoring tool that can do amazing things. Read on to see how you can apply it in your own network.

Dependencies

Zabbix is a complicated beast, so there are naturally a few dependencies to note before you rush headlong into the installation. Zabbix is written in PHP, so make sure you have a relatively recent version installed. If you haven't upgraded in a while, this might be the time to do so. Since Zabbix is completely web-based, you'll obviously need a web server as well. Par for the course, Apache or Apache2 is the recommended server of choice. Make sure when you install Apache that you configure it with *mod-php* enabled as well. This ensures that Apache can understand the embedded PHP that makes Zabbix what it is. Then, make sure you have the *PHP GD* library installed (available from *http://www.boutell.com/gd/*). While Zabbix will technically run without this, it's not recommended, as this is the library that generates the network maps and graphs that make Zabbix so useful. Finally, you'll need a SQL database. While Zabbix supports both PostgreSQL and MySQL, in this example we'll be using MySQL.

Installing Zabbix

Unfortunately, installing Zabbix isn't as straightforward as many applications we've discussed so far. Some parts of its installation, which I'll highlight as we go along, are optional.

The first step in getting Zabbix up and running is to download and untar the source code. You can find this at the home page (*http://www.zabbix.com*). At the time this book was written, the latest version was 1.0. Download the archive file of the latest version, untar it in your normal build location, and navigate to the new directory. First, we'll need to configure Zabbix to make use of the database choice we've selected (MySQL) and to use SNMP. Run the following command to prepare the installation:

```
$ ./configure –with-mysql –with net-snmp
```

This shouldn't take too long, so don't grab a beer just yet! Before you move on to the make, you'll need to take a second to prepare the MySQL database for Zabbix. Navigate to the *create/* directory and then start MySQL, create the Zabbix database, and concatenate the *.sql* scripts to populate the tables:

```
# mysql -u<username> -p<password>
Mysql> create database Zabbix;
Mysql> quit;
# cd create/mysql
# cat schema.sql |mysql -u<username> -p<password> Zabbix
# cd ../data
# cat data.sql |mysql -u<username> -p<password> Zabbix
```

You can now jump back to the root of the Zabbix directory and issue the make command.

Once the make completes, take a moment to copy the contents of the *bin/* directory to somewhere in your path. I tend to use */usr/local/bin*.

```
# cp bin/* /usr/local/bin
```

This is a fairly unsophisticated installation mechanism, but you're almost done. Now we have to set a few variables so that PHP knows how to properly access your database. Navigate to *frontend/php/include* in your Zabbix source directory and open the file *db.inc.php* in your favorite text editor. Make the following changes:

```
$DB_TYPE ="MySQL";
$DB_SERVER ="localhost";
$DB_DATABASE ="Zabbix";
$DB_USER ="<MySQL username here>"
$DB_PWD ="<MySQL password here>"
```

The $DB_DATABASE variable is the name of the database you created in MySQL for Zabbix earlier. Once these changes have been made, copy the PHP files to your web root:

```
# cp –R frontends/php/* /srv/www/htdocs/
```

Now make the directory */etc/zabbix* and copy the sample configuration files to it:

```
# mkdir /etc/zabbix
# cp misc/conf/zabbix_suckerd.conf /etc/zabbix/zabbix_suckerd.conf
# cp misc/conf/zabbix_trapperd.conf /etc/zabbix/zabbix_trapperd.conf
```

These sample configuration files are fine for small-time applications, but if you're planning on deploying Zabbix on a large-scale or enterprise rollout you should read the configuration files section of the online Zabbix manual, available at *http://www.zabbix.com/manual/v1.1/config_files.php*. Doing so will save you many headaches in the future. Once these files are moved, you're done with the installation! All that's left is to fire up the Zabbix daemons and ensure that they work:

```
# zabbix_suckerd
# zabbix_trapperd
```

Assuming everything went as planned, you can now point your web browser to *http://127.0.0.1* and see your new Zabbix installation. When you get to the login screen, enter Admin for your username and leave the password field blank. Once logged in, take a moment to change the default password.

Monitoring Hosts

After that installation, you certainly deserve to do something easy now! Fortunately, Zabbix seems to be designed with ease in mind. Let's start adding some hosts to monitor. The upper section of the screen has the navigation bars that you'll use to navigate around Zabbix. Click Hosts to add a new host to your monitoring. Figure 9-3 shows the fields available when adding a new host on the Hosts tab in Zabbix.

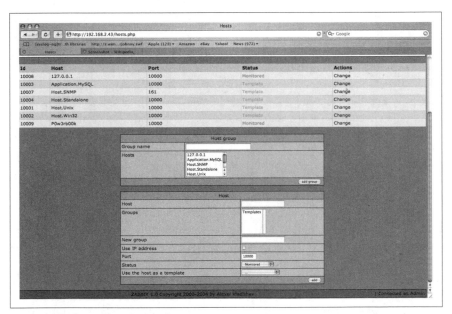

Figure 9-3. The Zabbix Hosts tab

You'll see here that you have several options when adding your new hosts. Fill in the options to suit your needs and click Add. Note that if you'd rather monitor by hostname than by DNS (which is often an excellent idea), checking the

Use IP Address box will give you an additional box to provide the IP address to monitor. For example, let's assume we want to configure Zabbix to notify us if 192.168.2.118 ever stops serving FTP traffic. To do so, on the Hosts tab, we would enter 192.168.2.118 in the Host field. We'd then change the port to 22 since we're interested in FTP traffic. Next, move over to the Items tab. We'll need to type in a description for this item, so we'll call it Home-FTP. Under Type, select "Simple check." In the Key field, enter "ftp." The rest we can leave as it is. Now wait a few minutes, and check the Latest Values tab. You should see an option there for 192.168.2.118 (or the hostname if you gave it one). Since the FTP server is running, we get a return value of 1. Had the server not been running, we would see 0 in that field. Notice that to the right you have the option to graph, trend, and compare data collected over time. This allows for detailed data analysis on the uptime and availability of your servers. It is also an excellent demonstration of the graphical qualities of Zabbix.

Mapping the Network

The last aspect of Zabbix that we'll look at is the mapping feature (shown in Figure 9-4). This is an excellent tool for providing a quick reference map of the network showing detailed status. To begin, click on the lower Network Maps button. Create a new network map by filling in the name you wish to call your new map. If you'll have a lot of hosts to monitor, change the size of the map to make it bigger. Click Add to continue. Once you've created your map, it's time to add some hosts to it. Select the host we created in the previous example, *Home-FTP*. You can then select the coordinates you wish for the icon representing *Home-FTP* to be displayed on. Select the Server icon and click Add. The page will refresh, and when it finishes loading, you'll see your icon representing *Home-FTP* on the map. You can continue adding hosts and placing them on the map until you have a full representation of your network.

The Details

What we've covered here is a fraction of the capabilities of Zabbix. If you'd like to get more in depth with it, you can install the Zabbix agents on the machines you wish to monitor. Once you've done that, you can monitor statistics such as CPU utilization, drive space, and anything else that can be monitored via SNMP. You can also define custom triggers to alert you right away to emergency situations. Trigger definition is highly detailed and can get quite elaborate and complex. If you'd like to learn more about this incredibly flexible network monitoring tool, check out the Zabbix web page at *http://www.zabbix.com* for more information. There is a fairly active forum there dedicated to helping users in need and sharing configuration tips and tricks.

—*Brian Warshawsky*

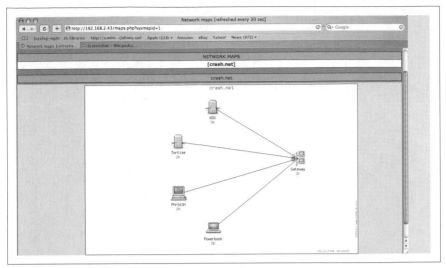

Figure 9-4. The mapping features of Zabbix

Fine-Tune the syslog Daemon

HACK #86

You can't see problems that aren't being reported. Correctly setting up the system log daemon and logging levels ensures that you always know what's going on.

Linux systems log boot information, process status information, and a significant amount of access and error information in the system logfile, */var/log/messages*, using a system daemon known as *syslog*. But when was the last time you looked at this file? If you've never spent any time fine-tuning the *syslog* daemon, your system logfile probably contains a tragically jumbled mess of cron completion notices, boot notices, MARK entries, and any number of other service or daemon log messages. Imagine if you could configure *syslog* to dump all that information where *you* wanted it, and sort it all too....Well, this *is* Linux we're talking about here, so of course you can configure *syslog* any way you want!

Making Sense of syslog.conf

A configuration file called */etc/syslog.conf* controls the *syslog* daemon. As unimaginative as the config file's name might be, learn it well because this is a file you'll need to become very familiar with if you want to master the intricacies of Linux system logging. The file may not make a whole lot of sense upon first glance, but here's a simple *syslog.conf* file that I'll use to explain the syntax further:

```
# Log all kernel messages to the console.
# Logging much else clutters up the screen.
```

```
# kern.*                               /dev/console
# Log anything (except mail) of level info or higher.
# Don't log private authentication messages!
*.info;mail.none;authpriv.none;cron.none        /var/log/messages
# The authpriv file has restricted access.
authpriv.*                             /var/log/secure
# Log all the mail messages in one place.
mail.*                                 -/var/log/maillog
# Log cron stuff
cron.*                                 /var/log/cron
# Everybody gets emergency messages
*.emerg                                *
# Save news errors of level crit and higher in a special file.
uucp,news.crit                         /var/log/spooler
# Save boot messages also to boot.log
local7.*                               /var/log/boot.log
```

As you can see in the noncommented lines in this example, there are three main parts to each active line of the configuration file. The first entry on a line is called the *facility*, which is the underlying subsystem that creates the log messages for the logfiles. There are 13 predefined system facility values: *auth*, *authpriv*, *cron*, *daemon*, *ftp*, *kern*, *lpr*, *mail*, *mark*, *news*, *syslog*, *user*, and *uucp*. In addition to these, there are also eight others, named *local0* through *local7*, which are for programs to use when implementing their own *syslog* messages. Each of the predefined facilities refers to a specific aspect of the system. For instance, *auth* refers to the Linux authorization system, including programs such as *login* and *su*. The *mark* facility is used internally for *syslog*, and should be left alone for the time being. The *daemon* facility is for other system daemons that are not listed specifically. You can represent all available facilities by using the asterisk (*) symbol.

The second part to a configuration line is the *priority*, which is separated from its associated facility by a period. Every time a part of the system sends a message to *syslog*, that message is coded with a priority. Basically, the program is letting *syslog* know how important this message is. From lowest to highest, the priority levels are *debug*, *info*, *notice*, *warning*, *err*, *crit*, *alert*, and *emerg*. The higher the priority, the more important the message is. Once you hit the *emerg* priority, the system is rapidly approaching a kernel panic and is probably unusable. You can represent messages of any priority by using the asterisk symbol. For example, *local7.** means "messages of any priority from the *local7* facility."

The third and final aspect of the configuration line is the *action*. This is basically just a short section that tells *syslog* what to do with the information it has received. To better explain this, let's look at an example line from the sample configuration file provided above:

```
# Log cron stuff
cron.*                                 /var/log/cron
```

Few things are more annoying than scrolling through */var/log/messages* and having to wade through all the cron messages, so this kind of configuration option comes in handy. This example means that messages of all priorities issued by the cron facility should be sent to the */var/log/cron* logfile. As mentioned previously, the asterisk is a wildcard feature that tells *syslog* to apply the same rule to every message from cron, regardless of its priority. You can do similar things with the asterisk wildcard for the facility, such as instructing *syslog* to send every message of priority warning or higher to a specific logfile:

```
*.warning                      /var/log/problems
```

Real-Time Alerts from the System Log

Other wildcard features that can be used include the at sign (@), for sending messages to remote *syslog* hosts; a dash (-), for telling *syslog* not to sync the disks after every message; and an asterisk in the actions section of the configuration to alert everyone on the system to an issue. For instance, look at the following example from the sample configuration file:

```
# Everybody gets emergency messages
*.emerg                                       *
```

The final asterisk on this line tells *syslog* to send a message out to every user online via the wall (Write to ALL users) command to let them know of any emergency conditions. These messages will appear in every active terminal window on the system. You can think of configurations like this as Linux's emergency broadcast system.

Another interesting line in the example *syslog.conf* file shown earlier in this hack is the line that addresses kernel *syslog* messages. Rather than being sent to a logfile, all these messages are sent to the console instead. One popular trick using this feature is to direct many of the *syslog* messages to a virtual console instead of the main console. I often do this on machines that aren't used much for local work but still have monitors. For example, specifying this line:

```
auth,kern.*                    /dev/tty5
```

allows me to see the *syslog* messages of everyone who logs on—and any issues with the kernel—simply by switching the machine to virtual console 5 (Alt-F5) and leaving it there with the monitor on. Now, whenever I walk by that machine, I can keep track of users logging on and off, or anything else I've set it up to do. When I need to work on the server and that would be in the way, I just switch back to my primary console (Alt-F1), and the messages continue to be sent to console 5.

Centralizing Logs for Convenient Access

Another interesting *syslog* option is remote logging. While *syslog* itself allows for remote logging, there is a more robust solution to be found in *syslog-ng* **[Hack #87]**, a new version of *syslog*. *syslog* allows you to send messages to remote hosts, but it does so in plain text across the network, so you should use this feature with caution. Here's how it works: by adding an at sign and a hostname or IP address in the action section of the configuration file, you can specify that *syslog* send its messages to another waiting remote *syslog* server. The remote *syslog* server will need to have the *syslog* daemon started with the -r option to allow it to listen on port 514 for incoming *syslog* messages. The following line shows an example of sending all critical kernel messages to the remote machine *aardvark* for safekeeping.

```
kern.crit                       @aardvark
```

Remote logging can be extremely helpful in the event of a system crash, as it allows you to see log messages that you might otherwise be unable to access (since the system that issued them is down). As previously mentioned, these messages are sent in plain text across the network, so be sure to use *syslog*'s remote logging with caution—and never do it across the Internet. Also, note that if you send certain types of messages to a remote log server, they are not recorded locally unless you create another entry that also sends those same messages to the local log, as in the following example:

```
kern.crit                       @aardvark
kern.crit                       /var/log/messages
```

 Another interesting potential security issue with *syslog*'s remote logging is that starting the *syslog* daemon with the -r option to receive remote log entries means that any host can send a log message to that host. The *syslog* facility doesn't have a way of identifying specific hosts that it should receive messages from, so it just holds up a big electronic catcher's mitt and accepts anything that comes its way.

The *syslog* daemon can be customized in many different ways, but it's somewhat dated in terms of both capabilities and security. "Centralize System Logs Securely" **[Hack #87]** provides newer and even more configurable approach to system logging.

See Also

- man syslog
- "Centralize System Logs Securely" **[Hack #87]**

—*Brian Warshawsky*

Centralize System Logs Securely

Protect your valuable logfiles from prying eyes

In "Fine-Tune the syslog Daemon" [Hack #86], we discussed configuration of the *syslog* daemon. As useful and even necessary as this logging service is, though, it's beginning to show its age. In response to that, a company name BalaBit has devoted both time and resources to bringing us the next generation of *syslog*, *syslog-ng*, which addresses many of the problems that plague the original. Improvements include using TCP instead of UDP to communicate with remote log hosts and a much more configurable interface to your system's logging capabilities. From a security standpoint, the implementation of TCP is a great advancement—that allows us to use additional applications such as *stunnel* to create encrypted tunnels to protect the contents of logfiles as they are sent to the central log host. In this hack, we examine such a deployment.

Getting Started

To implement encrypted remote logging, you'll need to download and compile three programs. Let's start with *stunnel*. Grab the latest instance of the source code from *http://www.stunnel.org/download/source*. Once you've got the tarball, unpack it and navigate to your newly created directory. You can now follow the typical installation procedure:

```
$ ./configure
$ make
# make install
```

You'll now need to grab the source for *syslog-ng* and *libol*, a library required by *syslog-ng*. You can download each of these from *http://www.balabit.com/downloads/syslog-ng/*. Untar and install *libol* first, then *syslog-ng*. Installation of these two applications uses the previous typical source install three-step.

Once you've successfully installed *stunnel*, *syslog-ng*, and *libol*, you'll need to create encryption certificates for all the machines between which you want to transfer secure log information.

Creating Your Encryption Certificates

To transfer log data securely between a remote host and a central log host, communication between the two must be encrypted. In order to successfully use encryption, both hosts must be able to verify their identities and share the encryption keys used for reading and writing the encrypted data. This information is provided by SSL certificates, which can either be granted by a third party or created yourself for use within your organization. (For more than you probably want to know about SSL and certificates, see the SSL HOWTO at *http://www.tldp.org/HOWTO/SSL-Certificates-HOWTO/*.)

At this point, you must create multiple certificates: one for use by the central log server, and one for each client that sends log information to the server. Later in this section, you'll install the server certificate on your server and distribute the client certificates to the hosts for which they were created.

The process for creating certificates varies slightly based on the Linux distribution you're using. For a Red Hat system, it is as follows:

```
# cd /usr/share/ssl/certs
# make syslog-ng-server.pem
# make syslog-ng-client.pem
```

As each certificate is generated, the script will ask you several questions regarding your location, hostname, organization, and email address. Once all the questions have been answered, your certificates are generated. Your next step is to verify that only root has access to them:

```
[root@aardvark certs]# ls -l *.pem
-rw-------  1 root root 2149 Aug 14 12:12 syslog-ng-client.pem
-rw-------  1 root root 2165 Aug 14 12:12 syslog-ng-server.pem
[root@aardvark certs]#
```

There is one last thing you'll need to do before you start distributing your certificates: extract the CERTIFICATE section from each certificate that is going to a client machine and concatenate the extracted sections into a single file named *syslog-ng-client.pem*, which you will put on your server along with the server key. The CERTIFICATE key data in a certificate file is the information between the following two lines:

```
-----BEGIN CERTIFICATE-----
-----END CERTIFICATE-----
```

Copy the *syslog-ng-client.pem* file over to the */etc/stunnel* directory on the server and place a copy of each client's own certificate in that client's */etc/stunnel* directory. This may sound somewhat complicated, so let's summarize: all you're doing here is extracting the CERTIFICATE from each client's certificate file, concatenating that information into one large client certificate that will reside on your server (along with the server's certificate), and then copying the individual client certificates to the hosts for which they were intended.

Configuring stunnel

Now, on the server side, edit your *stunnel.conf* file to read as follows:

```
cert = /etc/stunnel/syslog-ng-server.pem
CAfile = /etc/stunnel/syslog-ng-client.pem
verify = 3
[5140]
        accept = your.server.ip:5140
        connect = 127.0.0.1:514
```

Then make similar changes to *stunnel.conf* on the client side:

```
client = yes
cert = /etc/stunnel/syslog-ng-client.pem
CAfile = /etc/stunnel/syslog-ng-server.pem
verify = 3
[5140]
        accept = 127.0.0.1:514
        connect = your.server.ip:5140
```

Configuring syslog-ng

Once those changes have been made, it's time to start working on creating your *syslog-ng.conf* file. The syntax of this file has a steep learning curve and is well beyond the scope of this hack, so use what I'm about to show you as a starting point, and work from there. Far more detail can be found online and in the manpages. On your central log server, add the following to */etc/syslog-ng/syslog-ng.conf*:

```
options {   long_hostnames(off);
            sync(0);
            keep_hostname(yes);
            chain_hostnames(no);   };
    source src {unix-stream("/dev/log");
             pipe("/proc/kmsg");
             internal();};
    source stunnel {tcp(ip("127.0.0.1")
             port(514)
             max-connections(1));};
    destination remoteclient {file("/var/log/remoteclient");};
    destination dest {file("/var/log/messages");};
    log {source(src); destination(dest);};
    log {source(stunnel); destination(remoteclient);};
```

Then, add the following to your *syslog-ng.conf* file on each client:

```
options {long_hostnames(off);
            sync(0);};
    source src {unix-stream("/dev/log"); pipe("/proc/kmsg");
            internal();};
    destination dest {file("/var/log/messages");};
    destination stunnel {tcp("127.0.0.1" port(514));};
    log {source(src);destination(dest);};
    log {source(src);destination(stunnel);};
```

Testing

Once you've done all this, you can start *stunnel* and *syslog-ng* to see if everything is working. Before you do so, though, make sure you stop the *syslogd* service. You don't want the two of them stepping on each other. To test whether your remote logging is working, use the logger command:

```
# logger This is a Test
```

Then, on your log server, search (or grep) */var/log/messages* (or wherever you have remote logs) for "This is a Test". If you get a response, congratulations—everything is working fine, and you now have encrypted remote logging!

Where Next?

While remote logging has always been a useful and even necessary process, sending valuable system information unencrypted across the void has long been a security risk. Thanks to *syslog-ng* and *stunnel*, we no longer have to worry about that. In addition, the flexibility of *syslog-ng* has moved leaps and bounds beyond what *syslogd* was ever capable of. It truly is the Next Generation of system logging daemons.

That flexibility comes with a price, though—the *syslog-ng* configuration file is a complex beast. If you spend a little time getting to know it, however, you'll find that it's not quite as hard as it looks. I can assure you that the complexity of the syntax is proportional to its adaptability once you understand it. Listed below are some resources you can consult online for help in configuring your *syslog-ng* instance to meet your needs.

See Also

- *http://www.balabit.hu/static/syslog-ng/reference/book1.html*
- *http://www.stunnel.org/examples/syslog-ng.html*
- "Fine-Tune the syslog Daemon" [Hack #86]

—*Brian Warshawsky*

H A C K   Keep Tabs on Systems and Services
#88   Consolidate home-grown monitoring scripts and mechanisms using Nagios.

Monitoring is a key task for administrators, whether you're in a small environment of 50–100 servers or are managing many sites globally with 5,000 servers each. At some point, trying to keep up with the growth in the number of new services and servers deployed, and reflecting changes across many disparate monitoring solutions, becomes a full-time job!

Admins often monitor not only the availability of a system (using simple tools such as *ping*), but also the health of the services running on the system—the network devices that connect the systems to each other; peripheral devices such as printers, copiers, uninterruptible power supplies (UPSs); and even air conditioners and other equipment. Often, these tools perform simple connections to services and use SNMP and *rstatd* data collection and specialized environmental monitoring devices to gain a complete view of the data centers.

While there are plenty of solutions out there for collecting and aggregating this data in some sane way, I've found Nagios to provide the perfect balance between simplicity and power. Nagios is a solution that meets the requirements of our mid-sized organization's computing environment quite well, for reasons such as these:

Dependency checking

> If all your printers are on a single switch, and that switch goes down, would you rather get a page about each of 50 unavailable printers or a single page saying "the printer switch is down"? Nagios can be configured (or not) to follow a logical path, so that one unreachable device triggers the checking of other devices upon which the first failure is dependent. If a printer is down, Nagios first checks to make sure the printer switch is up before notifying anyone. If that printer switch is up and someone is running around unplugging printers, you'll get a lot of pages, but if the switch is down you'll be notified of the larger problem, not its consequences. Further, if that printer switch is unreachable because a router between Nagios and the printer switch is down or unavailable, you'll get that message instead, which can save you some troubleshooting time and makes the pages far more interesting and useful.

Downtime scheduling

> When you have a host of different tools monitoring your environment, or a single tool that doesn't allow for downtime scheduling, your pager will go nuts as you bring down your environment and possibly again on the way back up. Mix this with a situation in which there is no dependency checking and you'll soon find a group of administrators walking around while their pagers lie vibrating in their desk drawers. With Nagios, you can schedule downtimes and avoid the hassle.

Recovery notification

> Many people use monitoring solutions that do simple "ping" monitoring, which tells you if a machine is unreachable. However, if it was unreachable because of a temporary power glitch that caused a switch to momentarily freak out, and the agent never lets you know that the machine became available again one minute later, you could be wasting gobs of time driving over to the site for a problem that has already corrected itself. Nagios will notify you of recoveries.

A lot of solutions don't provide these benefits. Throw in solutions that are tough to customize, don't provide service checks for specialized appliances or services, and are tough to integrate with the few tools you might have that *do* work well, and you have big headaches and a downhill trend in the morale of your administrators.

Enter Nagios

I've found that Nagios provides an extremely simple way of taking many of our disparate scripts, notification modules, ping checkers, and other tools, and putting them all under the Nagios umbrella as "plug-ins" without my having to change much of anything. In fact, the monitoring functionality that comes preconfigured with Nagios is all handled through shell, Perl, or C programs that Nagios calls in the background.

The barrier to entry was actually so low that within a day I had a very basic Nagios configuration up and running, with a web interface, email notifications, and basic service and host checks working. By the end of the week, I had configured Nagios to be more discriminating in its notifications (e.g., notify only the DBA if the database *service* became unavailable, but only the Sun admins if the database *server* went down). I had also configured host and service dependencies, and told it about our next two scheduled downtimes. I had even found existing plug-ins for Nagios that allowed for the retirement of a couple of our home-grown scripts for monitoring things like a NetApp filer and a MySQL database. Things were looking up!

What's more is that the Nagios web interface, while it keeps useful enough statistics to help pinpoint when a problem started or predict your disk needs on a file server over the next year, can also easily be integrated with standard tools such as MRTG [Hack #79] or Cacti.

If you want to get really hardcore, you can also use Nagios to collect SNMP traps, or go fully distributed by using Nagios agents, rather than a central polling mechanism, across your machine room.

The only downside to Nagios that I've found so far is that, while configuration is pretty brainless, there is no configuration GUI or automation, so it all has to be done by hand (which can be somewhat cumbersome and very time-consuming). The payoff is there, though, so let's check out some configuration details. I'll cover only the most basic configuration, because documenting a full-blown Nagios deployment could be another book unto itself!

First you'll need to install Nagios, either using your distribution's package management system (for a binary install) or by going to *http://www.nagios.org* to grab the source and installing according to the plentiful documentation.

Hosts, Services, and Contacts, Oh My!

We'll start simple. Your machine room consists of hosts. These hosts run services. If either a host or a service that it runs becomes unavailable, you'll want Nagios to notify a contact. Thus, the first thing to do is tell Nagios about these entities. To do this, we add entries in the *hosts.cfg*, *services.cfg*, and *contacts.cfg* files. These files may be located under */etc/nagios* if your installation was preconfigured (as on a SUSE system or a Red Hat RPM install), or wherever you told it to put configuration files during a source install (*/usr/local/etc/nagios*, by default).

Here's a simple *hosts.cfg* entry that tells Nagios some basic information about a host:

```
define host{
        use             generic-host
        host_name       newhotness
        alias           Jonesy's Desktop
        address         128.112.9.52
        parents         myswitch
        }
```

You'll notice that all this information is specific to my desktop machine. There's nothing here about how to check the availability of the host, when to check it, or anything else. This is because Nagios allows you to configure a template host entry to hold all of that information (since it's likely to be identical for large numbers of hosts). The template used in the above entry is called *generic-host*, and can be found near the top of the *hosts.cfg* file. The *generic-host* template entry looks like this:

```
define host{
        name                         generic-host
        notifications_enabled        1
        event_handler_enabled        1
        flap_detection_enabled       1
        process_perf_data            1
        notification_interval        360
        notification_period          24x7
        notification_options         d,u,r
        contact_groups               sysstaff
        check_command                check-host-alive
        max_check_attempts           10
        retain_status_information    1
        retain_nonstatus_information 1
        register                     0
        }
```

This one entry does all the heavy lifting for the rest of the devices that reference this template. They will all be checked using the check-host-alive check command, which is a scripted ping command. Per the notification_ period key's value, they'll be monitored 24 hours a day, 7 days a week. The notification_options line says to send notifications if the status of the machine is either down (d), unreachable (u), or recovered (r). The flap_ detection_enabled option is turned on here, as well. This is a feature of Nagios that seeks to save you from getting pages from services or hosts that change state frequently due to temporary aberrations in network connectivity, host response times, or services that are purposely restarted to pick up automated updates. You have to admit, putting all this detail into one entry is better than putting it into every host entry!

Let's move on to services. A typical *services.cfg* entry looks like this:

```
define service{
        use                             generic-service
        host_name                       ftpserver
        service_description             FTP
        is_volatile                     0
        check_period                    24x7
        max_check_attempts              3
        normal_check_interval           5
        retry_check_interval            1
        contact_groups                  sysstaff
        notification_interval           120
        notification_period             24x7
        notification_options            w,u,c,r
        check_command                   check_ftp
        }
```

This is the entry for my FTP server. Again, it includes only the information specific to the FTP server; all the rest of the information comes from the template named *generic-service*, whose settings are applied to all of the services whose entries refer to it using the use generic-service directive. Notice that I use a service-specific check command called check_ftp. The check_ftp command is just a shell script that attempts to make a connection to the FTP service on *ftpserver*.

You've no doubt noticed that both the host and service checks send mail to *sysstaff* if there's a problem. But what is *sysstaff*? It's actually not an email alias (although you can use one if you like). Instead, it's configured within Nagios itself, in the *contacts.cfg* and *contactgroups.cfg* files. Let's have a look! Here's an entry for a contact from the *contacts.cfg* file:

```
define contact{
        contact_name                    jonesy
        alias                           Jonesy
        service_notification_period     24x7
        host_notification_period        24x7
        service_notification_options    c,r
        host_notification_options       d,r
        service_notification_commands   notify-by-email
        host_notification_commands      host-notify-by-email
        email                           jonesy@linuxlaboratory.org
        }
```

This is my contact entry. It says that I'm to be notified of any host or service failures 24 hours a day, 7 days a week. However, I've hacked my entry so that instead of being notified of every change in state, I'm only notified when services (service_notification_options) are critical (c) and when they recover (r), and when hosts (host_notification_options) are down (d) and when they recover (r). There's an entry like this for everyone who will receive notifications about service or host status from Nagios.

Once all of the contacts are defined, you can group them together to form Nagios-specific groups in *contactgroups.cfg*. Here's an example:

```
define contactgroup{
        contactgroup_name       sysstaff
        alias                   The Systems Guys
        members                 jonesy,bill,joe
        }
```

That wasn't so hard, was it? Just remember that anyone in a contact group must first be defined as a contact in *contacts.cfg*.

At this point you have only a very simple configuration, but it's enough to fire up Nagios and have it monitor the hosts and services you defined and notify those who are defined as contacts. Before you do that, though, you should run the following command to do a syntax check:

```
$ nagios -v /etc/nagios/nagios.cfg
```

This runs Nagios in "verify" mode, and we've fed it the main Nagios configuration file, which contains a line for every other configuration file in use. If there's a problem, Nagios will spit out plenty of information for you to find, check out, and fix the problem. In these early stages, the most common issues will probably be related to configuration files defined in *nagios.cfg* that are not yet being used. For example, since we haven't used the dependency configuration file, you'll want to comment out any references to it in *nagios.cfg*.

If you received no errors, you're in good shape. You might see "warnings" that point out possible problems to you during config verification, but in many cases these warnings are for things that are intentional, such as contacts that are not assigned to a contact group (which is not required and not always desirable). Once you've verified that the warnings are harmless, or fixed whatever issues existed and reverified things, you can fire up Nagios and begin receiving notifications via email about the hosts and services you've configured.

See Also

- *http://www.nagios.org*

## CHAPTER TEN

System Rescue, Recovery, and Repair
Hacks 89–100

No computing system survives contact with the environment. The excellence of your sysadmin skills can't stop hardware from failing—it can only help you best recover from failed disk drives, controllers, and other calamities that drown your inbox with support requests (if anyone can send mail at all) and result in long lines of cranky users standing outside your office like shoppers trying to return broken gifts after the holiday season. "You do have backups from 10 minutes ago, don't you?" you hear them cry.

Data recovery is more critical today than ever, since the loss of a single disk or filesystem can mean hundreds of gigabytes of lost data. But don't worry—all is not necessarily lost. You can come out of many systems failures with your wizard hat fully intact, and perhaps even sporting a few new stars.

The hacks in this chapter provide a variety of hard-won tips on how to deal with systems that suddenly won't boot on their own, how to bring into line balky filesystems that you can't access or unmount, and even how to recover deleted files or data from failed hard drives. Some of the techniques in this chapter have retrieved data from Linux systems whose disks more closely resembled blocks of wood than advanced storage devices.

As an interesting spin on recovery and restoration, this chapter also includes hacks on how to permanently delete files and wipe hard disks so that they can safely be disposed of without donating your corporate secrets to the competition or your music collection to the RIAA. We stop short of describing how to *physically* wipe hard disks, though (i.e., using a hammer)—most people can work that one out (and we looked a tad too gleeful in the figures we submitted).

Resolve Common Boot and Startup Problems

Malicious crackers, overenthusiastic software updates, or simple hardware failures can prevent you from rebooting or accessing a system. The first thing to do is to relax and try a few standard tips and tricks to get your ailing system back on its feet.

Sooner or later—usually just before one of your users is about to submit her thesis or you have a meeting to present the IT strategy document you've been working on for weeks—you'll find that attempting to boot one of your systems results in a variety of cryptic error messages, a blinking cursor, or a graphical user interface that won't accept any keyboard or mouse input. In other words, not the standard Linux login you're used to at all. Of course, you have backups of your critical files elsewhere, but if your system isn't running for one reason or another, backups are just a distant security blanket. In all likelihood, your data is probably still present on the host formerly known as "your desktop machine," but you just can't boot the box to get to it. What's a girl to do?

Depending on the types of errors you're seeing, you may need anything from a crash course in BIOS settings, a PhD in the use of *fsck* and its friends, or some way of booting your system and accessing your data quickly. This hack discusses some of the standard tips and tricks for trying to get your box running on its own. If the tips in this hack aren't sufficient, see "Rescue Me!" [Hack #90] for the big hammer, which is creating a bootable CD containing a Linux distribution that provides the tools you need to repair an ailing Linux box. You can then apply the tools provided on that CD to repair your filesystems, recover partitions, and perform the other hacks listed at the end of this one that will enable you to get your system back and booting on its own.

Check BIOS Settings

If your system doesn't boot at all, the first thing to check is whether it's actually finding the device from which you expect it to boot. If you've recently added a disk to your system or changed its hardware configuration in any way, chances are that your BIOS settings are simply wrong. For example, I have a 64-bit server with a variety of removable drives that boots off an internal disk. For some reason, each time I add, remove, or change one of the removable drives, the BIOS forgets that it's supposed to boot off an internal SATA drive and insists on trying to boot from one of my music archives or one of the disks containing user home directories. Crap.

The standard symptoms of a system that has become confused about its boot settings are a blinking cursor after the system has tried to initiate the boot process, or a message saying something like "No bootable devices found." To make sure that your system is actually attempting to boot from the right device, you'll have to investigate its Basic Input/Output System (BIOS) settings.

On many systems, either there's a boot splash screen that hides the command needed to enter the BIOS, or the display comes up after this information has already been displayed. Most modern systems enable you to access their BIOS settings by pressing the Delete key (the one in the cluster of keys with Home, End, Page Up, and Page Down) as soon as the system powers up. The system will still perform some initial checks, but it will then display a BIOS settings screen. If pressing Delete does not provide access to your system's BIOS, other popular keys/key combinations to try (in order) are F2, F1, F3, F10, Esc, Ctrl-Alt-Esc, Ctrl-Alt-Insert, and Control-Alt-S. One of these should give you access to your system's BIOS, though trying them all can be somewhat tedious and time-consuming.

Most modern x86 boxes feature one of a small number of different BIOS types. Two of the more popular BIOS types are the different Award BIOS screens shown in Figures 10-1 and 10-2.

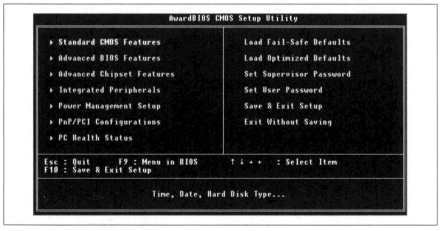

Figure 10-1. An Award BIOS with vertical menus

In the BIOS shown in Figure 10-1, the boot settings are stored in the Advanced Settings screen, which you can navigate to using the down arrow key. Press Return to display this screen once its name is highlighted. On the Advanced Settings screen, use the down arrow key to navigate to the First Boot Device entry, and press Return to display your choices. Use the arrow keys to select the entry corresponding to your actual boot drive, and press Return. You can then press the Escape key to exit this screen, and press F10 to save the new settings, exit the BIOS settings screen, and reboot.

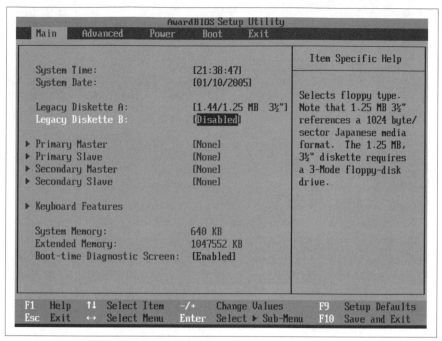

Figure 10-2. An Award BIOS with horizontal menus

In the BIOS shown in Figure 10-2, the boot settings are stored in the Boot screen, which you can navigate to using the right arrow key. Press Return to display this screen once its name is highlighted. On the Boot screen, use the down arrow key to navigate to the Hard Drive entry, and press Return to display a list of available drives. You can then highlight the correct drive using the arrow keys and press Return to select it. Once the correct hard drive is selected, you can use the plus symbol to move that entry to be the first bootable device, and then press F10 to save the new settings, exit the BIOS settings screen, and reboot.

> If the BIOS boot settings for the system on which you're having problems appear to be correct, this is probably not the root of your problem, and you should change these settings only as a last resort. Changing too many variables at one time is a normal reaction to an unbootable system, but it's rarely the right one.

Depending on the types and configuration of the drives in your system, you may have to experiment a bit with BIOS boot device settings before your system will boot correctly. If the BIOS doesn't find a drive that you know to be physically present, the drive may have failed, in which case there isn't all that much you can do without drive-specific hardware recovery techniques that are outside the scope of this book. If the BIOS finds the drive but you can't read the disk's partition table using the rescue CD, see "Recover Lost Partitions" [Hack #93] for suggestions about recreating the partition table. If the partition table is fine but you can't mount or repair one or more partitions, see "Recover Data from Crashed Disks" [Hack #94] for suggestions about recovering data from the disk.

Fixing Runlevel or X Window System Problems

Most Linux distributions nowadays provide some sort of free online update service. These are great for keeping your system up to date with the newest, brightest, shiniest software available for your distribution. If you get a bogus update, however, they can also incapacitate your system—and some of the more common bogus updates that I've seen are updates to the X Window System (for X.org or, in the past, XFree86). Unfortunately, the fix that corrects someone else's problem may take your GUI to its knees, where it doesn't accept keyboard or mouse input. If you can't get your X Window System display to respond to keyboard or mouse input, try the following:

- Switch to another virtual console by pressing Ctrl-Alt-F1 or Ctrl-Alt-F2, log in there, and edit */etc/inittab* to start at another runlevel until you can correct the problem. The specific *inittab* line you are looking for is:

      id:5:initdefault:

  You need to change the 5 to another runlevel (usually 3). Some distributions, such as Ubuntu and Gentoo, merely require you to stop the display manager from running, which usually means removing the *xdm*, *gdm*, or *kdm* service from the boot process. Once you've done this, reboot.

- Go to another machine and SSH or telnet into the system where you're having problems. Once logged in, su and edit */etc/inittab* to start at another runlevel (usually 3) until you can correct the problem. Reboot.

- If you can't do either of the previous suggestions (for example, if no other machine is handy or you've disabled virtual consoles and gettys to optimize performance), use the information provided later in this hack to reboot in single-user mode. You can then edit */etc/inittab* to start at another runlevel until you can correct the problem. Reboot.

Once you're in a nongraphical runlevel, you can perform repair tasks such as running filesystem repair utilities, repairing your X Window System configuration, and so on.

Regenerating a Default X Window System Configuration File

If you can boot your system successfully in a nongraphical runlevel but cannot start the X Window System automatically or manually, your configuration file may simply be hosed (in technical terms). Whether this happened because you've installed an updated version of the X Window System, your root filesystem took a hit and the file was deleted, or you've "fine-tuned" your configuration files to the point where X won't start any more, you can start from scratch by generating a default X Window System configuration file that you can then use as a starting point to correct the problems you're seeing. Both the X.org and XFree86 implementations of the X Window System provide a -configure option that enables you to generate a default configuration file. Depending on which X Window System server you have on your Linux system, log in as root and execute one of the following two commands to generate a default configuration file:

```
# Xorg -configure
# XFree86 -configure
```

These commands cause the X server to probe your graphics hardware and generate a default X Window System configuration file in the */root* directory called *xorg.conf.new* or *XF86Config.new*. You can then test this generic configuration file by starting your X server with the following command:

```
# X -config /root/filename
```

If the X server starts correctly, replace your default X configuration file with the new one and (after creating a backup copy) resume normal use or fine-tuning. One common failing is that X won't start because it can't detect your mouse. If this happens, check the InputDevice section of the configuration file you created for the value of the Device option. If this is simply /dev/mouse, try changing it to /dev/input/mice and restarting X using the updated configuration file.

If you're having problems starting or configuring X in general, your video card may use a chipset that is not yet supported by the version of the X Window System that you're using. If this happens, you can try using a lowest common denominator as a fallback. Video Electronic Standards Association (VESA) is supported by most cards and should enable X to work at lower resolutions on almost any system with graphical capabilities. To use VESA, simply set the Driver line in your Device section to be vesa.

Booting to Single-User Mode

If you're having problems booting to a specified runlevel, you may need to boot to single-user mode in order to repair your system. This can happen for a number of reasons, most commonly because of filesystem consistency problems, but also because of things such as the failure of any of the low-level system initialization scripts.

If you're using the GRUB bootloader, press any key to interrupt the standard GRUB boot process, use the arrow keys to select the kernel you want to boot, and press the e key to edit the boot options for that kernel. Select the line containing the actual boot options (usually the first line), press e again to edit that command line, and append the command single to the end of the command line. You can then press b to boot with those boot options, and your system will go through the standard boot process but terminate either at a root shell prompt or by prompting you for your root password before starting that shell.

If you're still using the LILO bootloader, you can do the same thing by entering the name of the boot stanza that you want to boot (usually linux), followed by a space and the -s directive. Again, you should get a root shell prompt or a request for the root password in a few seconds.

If you're having problems starting a single-user shell, there may still be a problem in some low-level aspect of your boot process, or (gasp) you may have forgotten or be unable to supply the root password. In this case, see "Bypass the Standard Init Sequence for Quick Repairs" **[Hack #91]** for a quick way of bypassing the */sbin/init* process and starting a shell directly.

Resolving Filesystem Consistency Problems

When a system doesn't boot because it claims that one or more of your partitions is inconsistent and therefore needs to be repaired, you're in luck—it's hard to see disk corruption as a good thing, but it beats some of the alternatives. At least your system found the boot sector, booted off the right drive, and got to the point where it found enough applications to try to check your filesystems.

One of the most common problems when booting a system is resolving filesystem consistency problems encountered during boot time. When you shut down a system normally, the system automatically unmounts all of its filesystems, marking them as "clean" so that it can recognize that they are in a consistent state when you next boot the system. If a system crashes for some reason, the filesystems are not marked as clean and must therefore be checked for consistency and correctness the next time you boot the system. Different types of filesystems each have their own filesystem consistency verification and repair utilities. In most cases, your system will automatically run these for you as part of the boot process and will correct any filesystem consistency problems that these utilities detect. Sometimes, however, you're not so lucky, and you'll have to run these utilities manually to correct serious filesystem problems.

Similarly, if you're using the XFS filesystem, all the vanilla repair utility does is return TRUE, since it expects that the XFS filesystem can correctly replay the journal and fix any problems as part of its mount process. If that's not the case, you can find yourself in single-user mode if the boot and root partitions are OK. If not, see "Rescue Me!" [Hack #90] for information about getting a rescue CD, because you're going to need it.

The details of manually running each filesystem's consistency-checking utility are outside the scope of this hack, but it's at least useful to know which utility to use if you have to manually repair a filesystem. Table 10-1 shows the filesystem consistency utilities that you use to manually repair various types of Linux filesystems.

Table 10-1. Repair utilities for different Linux filesystems

Filesystem	Utility
ext2, ext3	e2fsck
JFS	jfs_fsck
reiserfs	reiserfsck
XFS	xfs_check, xfs_repair

In the case of the XFS filesystem, *xfs_check* is a shell script that simply identifies problems in a specified filesystem, which you must then use the *xfs_repair* utility to correct.

See Also

- RIP home page: *http://www.tux.org/pub/people/kent-robotti/looplinux/rip/*
- "Rescue Me!" [Hack #90]
- "Bypass the Standard Init Sequence for Quick Repairs" [Hack #91]

HACK #90   Rescue Me!

So you've tried all the standard tips and tricks to get your system to boot on its own, and nothing has worked. In that case, a bootable Linux system on a CD may be your new best friend.

Hardware failure, filesystem corruption, overzealous upgrades, and significant tweaking of your system's startup process are among the things that can cause your system to fail to boot successfully. Assuming you've gotten to this point and the suggestions in "Resolve Common Boot and Startup Problems" [Hack #89] didn't work out, your next good alternative is to download, burn, and boot from what is known as a "rescue disk."

It's always a good idea to keep a bootable rescue disk handy. Download and burn one before you have problems, so that you'll have one to use should you ever need it.

A rescue disk is a small Linux distribution that boots and runs from a CD and provides the kernel and operating system capabilities that you need to access your hardware, as well as the tools you need to resolve problems with the interaction between that hardware and the desktop or server system you're trying to boot. The things that a rescue disk must provide fall into four general categories:

- A kernel and drivers for the storage devices attached to your system and, preferably, at least one of the network interface(s) available on that system.

- Disk repair utilities for various types of filesystems, including logical volume management (LVM) utilities.

- System utilities such as *mount* that enable you to access data from the filesystems on the ailing machine, boot tools such as GRUB that enable you to verify (and optionally update) the system's boot process, and so on. These often include the tools used to recover from systems problems, as discussed in "Recover Lost Partitions" [Hack #93] (*gpart*) and "Recover Data from Crashed Disks" [Hack #94] (*ddrescue*).

- Standard utilities, such as a text editor to correct and update text files used by the system during the boot process (such as */etc/inittab*), the configuration files used by various services, and the system startup scripts in the */etc/rc.d* or */etc/init.d* directory (depending on your distribution)

Though there are plenty of rescue disks around, including many graphical Live-CD Linux distributions, my personal favorite for years has been Kent Robotti's RIP (Recovery Is Possible!) disk, available from *http://www.tux.org/pub/people/kent-robotti/looplinux/rip/*. This is a relatively small (25 MB) rescue disk that does not offer any graphical user interface but does provide a complete set of up-to-date filesystem repair utilities for *ext2*, *ext3*, JFS, *reiserfs*, *reiser4*, and XFS filesystems, as well as the LVM2 utilities for mounting and managing logical volumes. As a nongraphical rescue disk, it targets experienced sysadmins who are comfortable at the command line, which you should be when trying to rescue or recover data from an ailing system.

Downloading and Burning the Rescue Disk

The two ISO images on the RIP page differ in terms of the bootloaders they use—one uses GRUB, and the other uses the standard ISOLINUX bootloader. I prefer to use the latter because it is simpler, so I always retrieve the file *RIP-13.4.iso.bin*, which is a binary CD image that you can burn directly to CD and then use to boot your system.

The standard Linux command-line CD-burning utility is called *cdrecord*. Prior to the 2.6 Linux kernel, using an IDE CD writer with *cdrecord* required the use of a loadable kernel module that provided SCSI emulation for IDE, because *cdrecord* expected SCSI identifiers when specifying the target output device. With the 2.6 kernel, CD-burning utilities can use ATA CD drives directly, without any special modules.

Once you've retrieved the file, you'll need to identify your system's CD burner(s). To do this, su to root and then execute the cdrecord -scanbus command. This causes *cdrecord* to probe the system for suitable devices and display the information that you'll need to supply in order to write to them. Here's an example:

```
# cdrecord -scanbus
Cdrecord 2.0 (i686-pc-linux-gnu) Copyright (C) 1995-2002 J#rg Schilling
Linux sg driver version: 3.1.24
Using libscg version 'schily-0.7'
scsibus0:
        0,0,0     0) 'TOSHIBA ' 'DVD-ROM SD-R1202' '1026' Removable CD-ROM
        0,1,0     1) *
        0,2,0     2) *
        0,3,0     3) *
        0,4,0     4) *
        0,5,0     5) *
        0,6,0     6) *
        0,7,0     7) *
```

Once you've identified the device associated with your CD burner, burn the CD image to a writable CD-ROM using a command such as the following:

```
# cdrecord -v dev=0,0,0 speed=4 RIP-13.4.iso.bin
```

This command will produce very verbose output (due to the use of the -v option) and will wait nine seconds before actually starting to write to the disc, just in case you change your mind. Once writing begins, the *cdrecord* command displays a status line that it continues to update until the entire file is written to the CD.

Using the Rescue CD

Once you've created the rescue CD, you need only put it in the ailing system and reboot. If your system is not configured to boot from the CD drive before booting from a hard disk partition, you may need to change your system's boot sequence in the BIOS settings in order to get the system to boot from the CD.

Once you've booted from the rescue CD, you can quickly and easily perform tasks such as the following:

- Run standard system repair commands to repair filesystem consistency [Hacks #89 and #95].

- Configure your system's network interface so that you can bring the system up on your network.

- Create archive files of critical files and directories and transfer those files to other systems using the *ncftp* utility supplied on the rescue disk.

- Correct other boot problems [Hack #89].

See Also

- RIP home page: *http://www.tux.org/pub/people/kent-robotti/looplinux/rip/*

HACK #91 Bypass the Standard Init Sequence for Quick Repairs

Get as close to the metal as you can when resolving startup problems.

If you're having problems booting a system to single-user mode, both the LILO and GRUB Linux bootloaders provide a great shortcut to help you get a shell prompt on an ailing system. This hack is especially useful if your password or shadow file has been damaged, a critical system binary is damaged or missing, or—heaven forbid—you've actually forgotten the root password on one of your systems.

By default, Linux systems use the */sbin/init* process to start all other processes, including the root shell that you get when you boot a system in single-user mode. Both LILO and GRUB enable you to specify an alternate binary to run instead of the init process, though, using the init=*command* boot option. By specifying /bin/bash as the command to start, you can get a quick prompt on your machine without *exec*'ing *init* or going through any of the other steps in your system's normal startup process.

The shell that is started when you *exec /bin/bash* directly does not have job control (Ctrl-Z) and does not respond to interrupts (Ctrl-C), so be very careful what commands you run from this shell. Don't run any commands that do not automatically terminate or prompt for subcommands that enable you to exit and return to the shell.

If you're using the GRUB bootloader, press any key to interrupt the standard GRUB boot process, use the arrow keys to select the kernel you want to boot, and press the e key to edit the boot options for that kernel. Select the line containing the actual boot options (usually the first line), press the e key again to edit that command line, and append the command init=/bin/sh to the end of the command line. You can then press b to boot with those boot options. You should see a shell prompt in a few seconds.

If you're still using the LILO bootloader, you can do the same thing by entering the name of the boot stanza you want to boot (usually linux), followed by a space and the init=/bin/sh command. Again, you should get a shell prompt in a few seconds.

After getting a shell prompt, you should remount */proc* to make sure that commands such as ps (and anything else that uses the */proc* filesystem) work correctly. You can do this by executing the following command as root (or via sudo):

```
# mount -t proc none /proc
```

If you need to create files on your system (for example, if you're creating a file archive that you want to migrate to another system "just in case"), you must also remount your root filesystem in read/write mode, since at this early point in the boot process it is mounted read-only. To do this, execute the following command as root (or via sudo):

```
# mount -o remount,rw /
```

You can now execute commands such as the filesystem repair commands [Hack #89], start your Ethernet interface manually by executing */sbin/ifconfig* with a static IP address, or perform any other commands that you need to do in order to repair your current system or migrate data from it to another system.

Find Out Why You Can't Unmount a Partition

HACK
#92

If you can't unmount a disk because it's busy, you can use the lsof and fuser commands to find open files or pesky attached processes.

The popularity of removable drives and their usability for things such as backups [Hack #50] makes mounting and unmounting partitions a fairly common activity while a system is running. Another not-so-common but more critical sysadmin activity is the need to unmount a drive in an emergency, such as when one of your users has accidentally deleted his thesis or the source code for your next-generation product, or the disk begins getting write errors and you need to initiate recovery ASAP. In either case, it's truly irritating when you can't unmount a partition because some unknown process is using it in one way or another. Shutting down a system just to unmount a disk so that you can remove or repair it is clearly overkill. Isn't there a better way? Of course there is—read on.

Background

One of the most basic rules of Linux/Unix is that *you can't unmount a partition while a process is writing to or running from it*. Trying to do so returns an informative but fairly useless message like the following:

```
$ sudo umount /mnt/music
umount: /mnt/music: device is busy
umount: /mnt/music: device is busy
```

In some cases, terminating the processes associated with a partition is as easy as looking through all your windows for suspended or background processes that are writing to the partition in question or using it as their current working directory and terminating them. However, on multi-user, graphical systems with many local and remote users, this isn't always as straightforward as you'd like.

As progress toward an ultimate solution to this frustration, special-purpose Linux specifications such as Carrier-Grade Linux (CGL) require some "forced unmount" functionality in the kernel (*http://developer.osdl.org/dev/fumount/*), and the umount command includes a force (-F) option for NFS filesystems. That's all well and good, but those of us who are using vanilla Linux distributions on local disks still need a practical solution that doesn't require patching each kernel or killing a fly with a hammer through an immediate shutdown.

Recent versions of the umount command provide a -1 option to "lazily" unmount a filesystem immediately, and then try to clean up references to the filesystem as the processes associated with them terminate. This is certainly interesting and can be useful, but I generally prefer to know what's going on if I can't unmount a filesystem that I think I should be able to unmount. Your mileage may vary.

Linux provides two commands that you can use to identify processes running on a filesystem so that you can (hopefully) terminate them in one way or another: fuser (find user process) and lsof (list open files). The key difference between the two is that the fuser command simply returns the process IDs (PIDs) of any processes associated with the file or directory specified as an argument, while the lsof command returns a full process listing that provides a variety of information about the processes associated with its argument(s). Both are quite useful, and which you use is up to you. The next two sections show how to use each of these commands to help find the pesky process(es) that are keeping you from unmounting a partition.

The Open Source Development Lab's forced unmount page, referenced at the end of this hack, provides a cool but crude script called *funmount* that tries to automatically combine a number of passes of fuser with the appropriate unmount commands to "do the right thing" for you when you need to forcibly unmount a specified partition. It's worth a look.

Finding Processes That Are Using a Filesystem

The fuser command returns the PIDs of all the processes associated with the device or mounted filesystem that is specified as an argument, along with terse information that summarizes the way in which each process is using the filesystem. To search for all processes associated with a mounted filesystem or device, you need to specify the -m option, followed by the name of the filesystem or its mount point. For example, the following fuser command looks for processes associated with the filesystem mounted at */mnt/music* on my system:

```
$ fuser -m /mnt/music
/mnt/music:          29846c 31763c
```

Each process ID returned by the fuser command is followed by a single letter that indicates how the specified process is using the filesystem. The most common of these is the letter c, which indicates that the process is using a directory on that filesystem as its current working directory. In the previous example, you can see that both of the processes listed are using the filesystem as their current working directory.

Once you have this sort of output, you can use the grep command to search for each of the specified process IDs and see what they're actually doing, as in the following example:

```
$ ps alxww | grep 29846
0  1000 29846  7797 16 0  9992 2284 wait   Ss   pts/13  0:00 /bin/bash
4     0 29912 29846 16 0 24608 1364 finish T    pts/13  0:00 su
0  1000 31763 29846 16 0 10292 2480 -      S+   pts/13  0:00 vi playlist.m3u
0  1000 31789 30009 17 0  3788  764 -      R+   pts/14  0:00 grep -i 29846
```

By default, the fuser command returns all active processes. However, as we can (accidentally) see in the above process listing, there is also a terminated su process that is a child of the process that fuser identified, which could prevent us from unmounting the filesystem in question. To provide a more complete fuser output listing, you should generally run the fuser command as root (or via sudo), and also specify the -a option to ensure that all processes are listed, regardless of their states, as in the following example:

```
$ sudo fuser -am /dev/mapper/data-music
/dev/mapper/data-music: 29846c 29912c 29916c 31763c 32088
```

As you can see, fuser now picks up the process ID of the su process.

> If you're really in a hurry, you can also specify the fuser command's -k option, which kills any processes it finds. It's generally a good idea to try to find the processes in question and terminate them cleanly, but in some cases you may just want to kill the processes as quickly as possible (for example, when you're hoping to subsequently recover deleted files and want to prevent filesystem updates).

Listing Open Files

The fuser command returns PIDs that require subsequent interpretation to figure out which files they're actually using on the specified filesystem (though the status indicator appended to each PID gives you a quick idea of how each process is using the filesystem). In contrast, the lsof command returns more detailed information about processes that have open files on a specified filesystem, and may tell you everything that you need to know in one swell foop. For example, the following is the output of the lsof command on the same filesystem used in the previous examples:

```
$ lsof /mnt/music
COMMAND   PID USER  FD   TYPE DEVICE  SIZE NODE NAME
bash    29846  wvh  cwd   DIR  253,0    64  131 /mnt/music/test
vi      31763  wvh  cwd   DIR  253,0    64  131 /mnt/music/test
vi      31763  wvh   4u   REG  253,0 12288  133 /mnt/music/test/.playlist.
m3u.swp
```

The first column (COMMAND) shows each command that the system is running that is associated with the file, directory, or mount point that you specified as an argument. The last column (NAME) identifies the file or directory that each command is actually associated with. The FD column shows the active file descriptors associated with the process or, in the case of a shell or command, the fact that the shell or command is using the specified directory as its current working directory (cwd).

As with fuser, when run by a standard user the output of lsof shows only active processes. To get more complete output, you should generally run the lsof command as root (or via sudo), as in the following example:

```
$ sudo lsof /mnt/music
COMMAND   PID USER    FD   TYPE DEVICE  SIZE NODE NAME
bash    29846 wvh    cwd    DIR  253,0    64  131 /mnt/music/test
su      29912 root   cwd    DIR  253,0    17  128 /mnt/music
bash    29916 root   cwd    DIR  253,0    17  128 /mnt/music
vi      31763 wvh    cwd    DIR  253,0    64  131 /mnt/music/test
vi      31763 wvh     4u    REG  253,0 12288  133 /mnt/music/test/.playlist.
m3u.swp
```

You can see that the output of this instance of the lsof command picked up the suspended su process, and also identifies the *bash* shell associated with this process.

Unlike the fuser command, the lsof command doesn't provide an option to automatically terminate the processes it has located, but it provides a good deal more information to begin with. Once you know exactly what they're doing and are sure that it's safe to kill them, you can always quickly terminate each process manually from the command line in order to unmount the filesystem.

Summary

The fuser and lsof commands are useful additions to your Linux sysadmin toolset. fuser quickly delivers information about active processes and provides an option to automatically and instantly terminate processes associated with the filesystems or files that you specify as arguments, but its output requires subsequent interpretation (if you have time to play detective). The lsof command returns more detailed information about the associated processes (although additional interpretation may still be required), and can also display information about network-related files and sockets that may be open (see its manpage or FAQ for more details). However, it doesn't include an option to quickly terminate all of the processes in one go. In my experience, fuser is faster, but lsof provides a much richer spectrum of information. Each is useful at different times, depending on what you're looking for and how quickly you need to find (and perhaps kill) it.

See Also

- *http://www.osdl.org/lab_activities/carrier_grade_linux*
- *http://developer.osdl.org/dev/fumount/*
- *ftp://lsof.itap.purdue.edu/pub/tools/unix/lsof/FAQ*

HACK #93 Recover Lost Partitions

If you can't mount any of the partitions on a hard drive, you may simply need to recreate the partition table. Here's a handy utility for identifying possible partition entries.

Seeing messages like "/dev/FOO: device not found" is never a good thing. However, this message can be caused by a number of different problems. There isn't much you can do about a complete hardware failure, but if you're "lucky" your disk's partition table may just have been damaged and your data may just be temporarily inaccessible.

> If you haven't rebooted, execute the `cut lproc /partitions` command to see if it still lists your device's partitions.

Unless you have a photographic memory, your disk contains only a single partition, or you were sufficiently disciplined to keep a listing of its partition table, trying to guess the sizes and locations of all of the partitions on an ailing disk is almost impossible without some help. Thankfully, Michail Brzitwa has written a program that can provide exactly the help you need. His *gpart* (guess partitions) program scans a specified disk drive and identifies entries that look like partition signatures. By default, *gpart* displays only a listing of entries that appear to be partitions, but it can also automatically create a new partition table for you by writing these entries to your disk. That's a scary thing to do, but it beats the alternative of losing all your existing data.

> If you're just reading this for information and aren't actually in the midst of a lost data catastrophe, you may be wondering how to back up a disk's partition table so that you don't have to depend on a recovery utility like *gpart*. You can easily back up a disk's master boot record (MBR) and partition table to a file using the following dd command, where *FOO* is the disk and *FILENAME* is the name of the file to which you want to write your backup:
>
> ```
> # dd if=/dev/FOO of=FILENAME bs=512 count=1
> ```
>
> If you subsequently need to restore the partition table to your disk, you can do so with the following dd command, using the same variables as before:
>
> ```
> # dd if=FILENAME of=/dev/FOO bs=1 count=64 skip=446
> seek=446
> ```

The *gpart* program works by reading the entire disk and comparing sector sequences against a set of filesystem identification modules. By default, *gpart* includes filesystem identification modules that can recognize the following types of partitions: *beos* (BeOS), bsddl (FreeBSD/NetBSD/386BSD), *ext2* and *ext3* (standard Linux filesystems), *fat* (MS-DOS FAT12/16/32), *hpfs* (remember OS/2?), *hmlvm* (Linux LVM physical volumes), *lswap* (Linux swap), *minix* (Minix OS), *ntfs* (Microsoft Windows NT/2000/XP/etc.), *qnx4* (QNX Version 4.x), *rfs* (ReiserFS Versions 3.5.11 and greater), *s86dl* (Sun Solaris), and *xfs* (XFS journaling filesystem). You can write additional partition identification modules for use by *gpart* (JFS fans, take note!), but that's outside the scope of this hack. For more information about expanding *gpart*, see its home page at *http://www.stud.uni-hannover.de/user/76201/gpart* and the *README* file that is part of the *gpart* archive.

Looking for Partitions

As an example of *gpart*'s partition scanning capabilities, let's first look at the listing of an existing disk's partition table as produced by the *fdisk* program. (BTW, if you're questioning the sanity of the partition layout, this is a scratch disk that I use for testing purposes, not a day-to-day disk.) Here's *fdisk*'s view:

```
# fdisk -l /dev/hdb
Disk /dev/hdb: 60.0 GB, 60022480896 bytes
255 heads, 63 sectors/track, 7297 cylinders Units = cylinders of 16065 * 512
= 8225280 bytes
   Device Boot      Start         End      Blocks   Id  System
/dev/hdb1              1          25      200781   83  Linux
/dev/hdb2             26          57      257040   82  Linux swap / Solaris
/dev/hdb3             58        3157    24900750   83  Linux
/dev/hdb4           3158        7297    33254550    5  Extended
/dev/hdb5           3158        3337     1445818+  83  Linux
/dev/hdb6           3338        3697     2891668+  83  Linux
/dev/hdb7           3698        4057     2891668+  83  Linux
/dev/hdb8           4058        4417     2891668+  83  Linux
/dev/hdb9           4418        4777     2891668+  83  Linux
/dev/hdb10          4778        5137     2891668+  83  Linux
/dev/hdb11          5138        5497     2891668+  83  Linux
/dev/hdb12          5498        5857     2891668+  83  Linux
/dev/hdb13          5858        6217     2891668+  83  Linux
/dev/hdb14          6218        6577     2891668+  83  Linux
/dev/hdb15          6578        6937     2891668+  83  Linux
/dev/hdb16          6938        7297     2891668+  83  Linux
```

Let's compare this with *gpart*'s view of the partitions that live on the same disk:

```
# gpart /dev/hdb
Begin scan...
```

```
Possible partition(Linux ext2), size(196mb), offset(0mb)
Possible partition(Linux swap), size(251mb), offset(196mb)
Possible partition(Linux ext2), size(24317mb), offset(447mb)
Possible partition(Linux ext2), size(1411mb), offset(24764mb)
Possible partition(Linux ext2), size(2823mb), offset(26176mb)
Possible partition(Linux ext2), size(2823mb), offset(29000mb)
Possible partition(Linux ext2), size(2823mb), offset(31824mb)
Possible partition(Linux ext2), size(2823mb), offset(34648mb)
Possible partition(Linux ext2), size(2823mb), offset(37471mb)
Possible partition(Linux ext2), size(2823mb), offset(40295mb)
Possible partition(Linux ext2), size(2823mb), offset(43119mb)
Possible partition(Linux ext2), size(2823mb), offset(45943mb)
Possible partition(Linux ext2), size(2823mb), offset(48767mb)
Possible partition(Linux ext2), size(2823mb), offset(51591mb)
Possible partition(Linux ext2), size(2823mb), offset(54415mb)
End scan.

Checking partitions...
* Warning: more than 4 primary partitions: 15.
Partition(Linux ext2 filesystem): primary
Partition(Linux swap or Solaris/x86): primary
Partition(Linux ext2 filesystem): primary
Partition(Linux ext2 filesystem): primary
Partition(Linux ext2 filesystem): invalid primary
Partition(Linux ext2 filesystem): invalid primary
Partition(Linux ext2 filesystem): invalid primary
Partition(Linux ext2 filesystem): invalid primary
Partition(Linux ext2 filesystem): invalid primary
Partition(Linux ext2 filesystem): invalid primary
Partition(Linux ext2 filesystem): invalid primary
Partition(Linux ext2 filesystem): invalid primary
Partition(Linux ext2 filesystem): invalid primary
Partition(Linux ext2 filesystem): invalid primary
Partition(Linux ext2 filesystem): invalid primary
Ok.

Guessed primary partition table:
Primary partition(1)
   type: 131(0x83)(Linux ext2 filesystem)
   size: 196mb #s(401562) s(63-401624)
   chs:  (0/1/1)-(398/6/63)d (0/1/1)-(398/6/63)r
Primary partition(2)
   type: 130(0x82)(Linux swap or Solaris/x86)
   size: 251mb #s(514080) s(401625-915704)
   chs:  (398/7/1)-(908/6/63)d (398/7/1)-(908/6/63)r
Primary partition(3)
   type: 131(0x83)(Linux ext2 filesystem)
   size: 24317mb #s(49801496) s(915705-50717200)
   chs:  (908/7/1)-(1023/15/63)d (908/7/1)-(50314/10/59)r
Primary partition(4)
   type: 131(0x83)(Linux ext2 filesystem)
   size: 1411mb #s(2891632) s(50717268-53608899)
   chs:  (1023/15/63)-(1023/15/63)d (50314/12/1)-(53183/6/58)r
```

Doing the math can be a bit tedious, but calculating the partition size and offsets shows that they are actually the same. *gpart* found all of the partitions, including all of the logical partitions inside the disk's extended partition, which can be tricky. If you don't want to do the math yourself, *gpart* provides a special -c option for comparing its idea of a disk's partition table against the partitions that are listed in an existing partition table. Using *gpart* with the -c option returns 0 if the two are identical or the number of differences if the two differ.

Writing the Partition Table

Using *fdisk* to recreate a partition table can be a pain, especially if you have multiple partitions of different sizes. As mentioned previously, *gpart* provides an option that automatically writes a new partition table to the scanned disk. To do this, you need to specify the disk to scan and the disk to write to on the command line, as in the following example:

```
# gpart -W /dev/FOO /dev/FOO
```

If you're paranoid (and you should be, even though your disk is already hosed), you can back up the existing MBR before writing it by adding the -b option to your command line and specifying the name of the file to which you want to back up the existing MBR, as in the following example:

```
# gpart -b FILENAME -W /dev/FOO /dev/FOO
```

As mentioned at the beginning of this hack, a disk failure may simply be the result of a bad block that happens to coincide with your disk's primary partition table. If this happens to you and you don't have a backup of the partition table, *gpart* does an excellent job of guessing and rewriting your disk's primary partition table. If the disk can't be mounted because it is severely corrupted or otherwise damaged, see "Recover Data from Crashed Disks" [Hack #94] and "Piece Together Data from the lost+found" [Hack #96] for some suggestions regarding more complex and desperate data recovery hacks.

See Also

- "Rescue Me!" [Hack #90]

HACK
#94 # Recover Data from Crashed Disks
You can recover most of the data from crashed hard drives with a few simple Linux tricks.

As the philosopher once said, "Into each life, a few disk crashes must fall." Or something like that. Today's relatively huge disks make it more tempting than ever to store large collections of data online, such as your entire music collection or all of the research associated with your thesis. Backups can be problematic, as today's disks are much larger than most backup media, and backups can't restore any data that was created or modified after the last backup was made. Luckily, the fact that any Linux/Unix device can be accessed as a stream of characters presents some interesting opportunities for restoring some or all of your data even after a hard drive failure. When disaster strikes, consult this hack for recovery tips.

 This hack uses error messages and examples produced by the *ext2fs* filesystem consistency checking utility associated with the Linux *ext2* and *ext3* filesystems. You can use the cloning techniques in this hack to copy any Linux disk, but the filesystem repair utilities will differ for other types of Linux filesystems. For example, if you are using ReiserFS filesystems, see "Repair and Recover ReiserFS Filesystems" [Hack #95] for details on using the special commands provided by its filesystem consistency checking utility, *reiserfsck*.

Popular Disk Failure Modes

Disks generally go bad in one of three basic ways:

- Hardware failure that prevents the disk heads from moving or seeking to various locations on the disk. This is generally accompanied by a ticking noise whenever you attempt to mount or otherwise access the filesystem, which is the sound of disk heads failing to launch or locate themselves correctly.

- Bad blocks on the disk that prevent the disk's partition table from being read. The data is probably still there, but the operating system doesn't know how to find it.

- Bad blocks on the disk that cause a filesystem on a partition of the disk to become unreadable, unmountable, and uncorrectable.

The first of these problems can generally be solved only by shipping your disk off to a firm that specializes in removing and replacing drive internals, using cool techniques for recovering data from scratched or flaked platters, if necessary. The second of these problems is discussed in "Recover Lost Partitions" [Hack #93]. This hack explains how to recover data that appears to be lost due to the third of these problems: bad blocks that corrupt filesystems to the point where standard filesystem repair utilities cannot correct them.

If your disk contains more than one partition and one of the partitions that it contains goes bad, chances are that the rest of the disk will soon develop problems. While you can use the techniques explained in this hack to clone and repair a single partition, this hack focuses on cloning and recovering an entire disk. If you clone and repair a disk containing multiple partitions, you will hopefully find that some of the copied partitions have no damage. That's great, but cloning and repairing the entire disk is still your safest option.

Attempt to Read Block from Filesystem Resulted in Short Read...

The title of this section is one of the more chilling messages you can see when attempting to mount a filesystem that contained data the last time you booted your system. This error always means that one or more blocks cannot be read from the disk that holds the filesystem you are attempting to access. You generally see this message when the *fsck* utility is attempting to examine the filesystem, or when the *mount* utility is attempting to mount it so that it is available to the system.

A short read error usually means that an inode in the filesystem points to a block on the filesystem that can no longer be read, or that some of the metadata about your filesystem is located on a block (or blocks) that cannot be read. On journaling filesystems, this error displays if any part of the filesystem's journal is stored on a bad block. When a Linux system attempts to mount a partition containing a journaling filesystem, its first step is to replay any pending transactions from the filesystem's journal. If these cannot be read—voilà!—short read.

Standard Filesystem Diagnostics and Repair

The first thing to try when you encounter any error accessing or mounting a filesystem is to check the consistency of the filesystem. All native Linux filesystems provide consistency-checking applications. Table 10-2 shows the filesystem consistency checking utilities for various popular Linux filesystems.

Table 10-2. Different Linux filesystems and their associated repair utilities

Filesystem type	Diagnostic/repair utilities
ext2, ext3	*e2fsck, fsck.ext2, fsck.ext3, tune2fs, debugfs*
JFS	*jfs_fsck, fsck.jfs*
reiserfs	*reiserfsck, fsck.reiserfs, debugreiserfs*
XFS	*fsck.xfs, xfs_check*

Recover Data from Crashed Disks

The consistency-checking utilities associated with each type of Linux filesystem have their own ins and outs. In this section, I'll focus on trying to deal with short read errors from disks that contain partitions in the *ext2* or *ext3* formats, which are the most popular Linux partition formats. The *ext3* filesystem is a journaling version of the *ext2* filesystem, and the two types of filesystems therefore share most data structures and all repair/recovery utilities. If you are using another type of filesystem, the general information about cloning and repairing disks in later sections of this hack still applies.

If you're using an *ext2* or *ext3* filesystem, your first hint of trouble will come from a message like the following, generally encountered when restarting your system. This warning comes from the *e2fsck* application (or a symbolic link to it, such as *fsck.ext2* or *fsck.ext3*):

```
# e2fsck /dev/hda1
e2fsck: Attempt to read block from filesystem resulted in short read
```

If you see this message, the first thing to try is to cross your fingers and hope that only the disk's primary superblock is bad. The superblock contains basic information about the filesystem, including primary pointers to the blocks that contain information about the filesystem (known as inodes). Luckily, when you create an *ext2* or *ext3* filesystem, the filesystem-creation utility (*mke2fs* or a symbolic link to it named *mkfs.ext2* or *mkfs.ext3*) automatically creates backups copies of your disk's superblock, just in case. You can tell the *e2fsck* program to check the filesystem using one of these alternate superblocks by using its -b option, followed by the block number of one of these alternate superblocks within the filesystem with which you're having problems. The first of these alternate superblocks is usually created in block 8193, 16384, or 32768, depending on the size of your disk. Assuming that this is a large disk, we'll try the last as an alternative:

```
# e2fsck -b 32768 /dev/hda1
e2fsck: Attempt to read block from filesystem resulted in short read while
        checking ext3 journal for /dev/hda1
```

 You can determine the locations of the alternate superblocks on an unmounted *ext3* filesystem by running the mkfs.ext3 command with the -n option, which reports on what the *mkfs* utility would do but doesn't actually create a filesystem or make any modifications. This may not work if your disk is severely corrupted, but it's worth a shot. If it doesn't work, try 8192, 16384, and 32768, in that order.

This gave us a bit more information. The problem doesn't appear to be with the filesystem's superblocks, but instead is with the journal on this filesystem. Journaling filesystems minimize system restart time by heightening filesystem consistency through the use of a journal [Hack #70]. All pending changes to the filesystem are first stored in the journal, and are then applied to the filesystem by a daemon or internal scheduling algorithm. These transactions are applied *atomically*, meaning that if they are not completely successful, no intermediate changes that are part of the unsuccessful transactions are made. Because the filesystem is therefore always consistent, checking the filesystem at boot time is much faster than it would be on a standard, non-journaling filesystem.

Removing an ext3 Filesystem's Journal

As mentioned previously, the *ext3* and *ext2* filesystems primarily differ only in whether the filesystem contains a journal. This makes repairing most journaling-related problems on an *ext3* filesystem relatively easy, because the journal can simply be removed. Once the journal is removed, the consistency of the filesystem in question can be checked as if the filesystem was a standard *ext2* filesystem. If you're very lucky, and the bad blocks on your system were limited to the *ext3* journal, removing the journal (and subsequently *fsck*'ing the filesystem) may be all you need to do to be able to mount the filesystem and access the data it contains.

Removing the journal from an *ext3* filesystem is done using the *tune2fs* application, which is designed to make a number of different types of changes to *ext2* and *ext3* filesystem data. The *tune2fs* application provides the -O option to enable you to set or clear various filesystem features. (See the manpage for *tune2fs* for complete information about available features.) To clear a filesystem feature, you precede the name of that feature with the caret (^) character, which has the classic Computer Science 101 meaning of "not." Therefore, to configure a specified existing filesystem so that it thinks that it does not have a journal, you would use a command line like the following:

```
# tune2fs -f -O ^has_journal /dev/hda1
tune2fs 1.35 (28-Feb-2004)
tune2fs: Attempt to read block from filesystem resulted in short read
        while reading journal inode
```

Darn. In this case, the inode that points to the journal seems to be bad, which means that the journal can't be cleared. The next thing to try is the debugfs command, which is an *ext2/ext3* filesystem debugger. This command provides an interactive interface that enables you to examine and modify many of the characteristics of an *ext2/ext3* filesystem, as well as providing an internal features command that enables you to clear the journal. Let's try this command on our ailing filesystem:

```
# debugfs /dev/hda1
debugfs 1.35 (28-Feb-2004)
/dev/hda1: Can't read an inode bitmap while reading inode bitmap
```

```
debugfs:  features
features: Filesystem not open
debugfs:  open /dev/hda1
/dev/hda1: Can't read an inode bitmap while reading inode bitmap
debugfs:  quit
```

Alas, the debugfs command couldn't access a bitmap in the filesystem that tells it where to find specific inodes (in this case, the journal's inode).

> If you are able to clear the journal using the tune2fs or debugfs command, you should retry the *e2fsck* application, using its -c option to have *e2fsck* check for bad blocks in the filesystem and, if any are found, add them to the disk's bad block list.

Since we can't *fsck* or fix the filesystem on the ailing disk, it's time to bring out the big hammer.

Cloning a Bad Disk Using ddrescue

If bad blocks are preventing you from reading or repairing a disk that contains data you want to recover, the next thing to try is to create a copy of the disk using a raw disk copy utility. Unix/Linux systems have always provided a simple utility for this purpose, known as *dd*, which copies one file/partition/disk to another and provides commands that enable you to proceed even in the face of various types of read errors. You must put another disk in your system that is at least the same size or larger than the disk or partition that you are attempting to clone. If you copy a smaller disk to a larger one, you'll obviously be wasting the extra space on the larger disk, but you can always recycle the disk after you extract and save any data that you need from the clone of the bad disk.

To copy one disk to another using *dd*, telling it not to stop on errors, you would use a command like the following:

```
# dd if=/dev/hda of=/dev/hdb conv=noerror,sync
```

This command would copy the bad disk (here, */dev/hda*) to a new disk (here, */dev/hdb*), ignoring errors encountered when reading (noerror) and padding the output with an appropriate number of nulls when unreadable blocks are encountered (sync).

dd is a fine, classic Unix/Linux utility, but I find that it has a few shortcomings:

- It is incredibly slow.
- It does not display progress information, so it is silent until it is done.
- It does not retry failed reads, which can reduce the amount of data that you can recover from a bad disk.

Therefore, I prefer to use a utility called *ddrescue*, which is available from *http://www.gnu.org/software/ddrescue/ddrescue.html*. This utility is not included in any Linux distribution that I'm aware of, so you'll have to download the archive, unpack it, and build it from source code. Version 0.9 was the latest version when this book was written.

The ddrescue command has a large number of options, as the following help message shows:

```
# ./ddrescue -h
GNU ddrescue - Data recovery tool.
Copies data from one file or block device to another,
trying hard to rescue data in case of read errors.

Usage: ./ddrescue [options] infile outfile [logfile]
Options:
  -h, --help                 display this help and exit
  -V, --version              output version information and exit
  -B, --binary-prefixes      show binary multipliers in numbers [default SI]
  -b, --block-size=<bytes>   hardware block size of input device [512]
  -c, --cluster-size=<blocks> hardware blocks to copy at a time [128]
  -e, --max-errors=<n>       maximum number of error areas allowed
  -i, --input-position=<pos> starting position in input file [0]
  -n, --no-split             do not try to split error areas
  -o, --output-position=<pos> starting position in output file [ipos]
  -q, --quiet                quiet operation
  -r, --max-retries=<n>      exit after given retries (-1=infinity) [0]
  -s, --max-size=<bytes>     maximum size of data to be copied
  -t, --truncate             truncate output file
  -v, --verbose              verbose operation
Numbers may be followed by a multiplier: b = blocks, k = kB = 10^3 = 1000,
Ki = KiB = 2^10 = 1024, M = 10^6, Mi = 2^20, G = 10^9, Gi = 2^30, etc...
  If logfile given and exists, try to resume the rescue described in it.
  If logfile given and rescue not finished, write to it the status on exit.
  Report bugs to bug-ddrescue@gnu.org #
```

As you can see, *ddrescue* provides many options for controlling where to start reading, where to start writing, the amount of data to be read at a time, and so on. I generally only use the --max-retries option, supplying -1 as an argument to tell *ddrescue* not to exit regardless of how many retries it needs to make in order to read a problematic disk. Continuing with the previous example of cloning the bad disk */dev/hda* to a new disk, */dev/hdb*, that is the same size or larger, I'd execute the following command:

```
# ddrescue --max-retries=-1 /dev/hda /dev/hdb
Press Ctrl-C to interrupt
rescued:    3729 MB,  errsize:    278 kB,  current rate:   26083 kB/s
   ipos:    3730 MB,  errors:       6,  average rate:   18742 kB/s
   opos:    3730 MB
Copying data...
```

The display is constantly updated with the amount of data read from the first disk and written to the second, including a count of the number of disk errors encountered when reading the disk specified as the first argument.

Once *ddrescue* completes the disk copy, you should run *e2fsck* on the copy of the disk to eliminate any filesystem errors introduced by the bad blocks on the original disk. Since there are guaranteed to be a substantial number of errors and you're working from a copy, you can try running *e2fsck* with the -y option, which tells *e2fsck* to answer yes to every question. However, depending on the types of messages displayed by *e2fsck*, this may not always work—some questions are of the form Abort? (y/n), to which you probably do not want to answer "yes."

Here's some sample *e2fsck* output from checking the consistency of a bad 250-GB disk containing a single partition that I cloned using *ddrescue*:

```
# fsck -y /dev/hdb1
fsck 1.35 (28-Feb-2004)
e2fsck 1.35 (28-Feb-2004)
/dev/hdb1 contains a file system with errors, check forced.
Pass 1: Checking inodes, blocks, and sizes
Root inode is not a directory.  Clear? yes

Inode 12243597 is in use, but has dtime set.  Fix? yes
Inode 12243364 has compression flag set on filesystem without compression
support.  Clear? yes
 Inode 12243364 has illegal block(s).  Clear? yes
 Illegal block #0 (1263225675) in inode 12243364.  CLEARED.
Illegal block #1 (1263225675) in inode 12243364.  CLEARED.
Illegal block #2 (1263225675) in inode 12243364.  CLEARED.
Illegal block #3 (1263225675) in inode 12243364.  CLEARED.
Illegal block #4 (1263225675) in inode 12243364.  CLEARED.
Illegal block #5 (1263225675) in inode 12243364.  CLEARED.
Illegal block #6 (1263225675) in inode 12243364.  CLEARED.
Illegal block #7 (1263225675) in inode 12243364.  CLEARED.
Illegal block #8 (1263225675) in inode 12243364.  CLEARED.
Illegal block #9 (1263225675) in inode 12243364.  CLEARED.
Illegal block #10 (1263225675) in inode 12243364.  CLEARED.
Too many illegal blocks in inode 12243364.
Clear inode? yes

Free inodes count wrong for group #1824 (16872, counted=16384).
Fix? yes
 Free inodes count wrong for group #1846 (16748, counted=16384).
Fix? yes
 Free inodes count wrong (30657608, counted=30635973).
Fix? yes
[much more output deleted]
```

Once *e2fsck* completes, you'll see the standard summary message:

```
/dev/hdb1: ***** FILE SYSTEM WAS MODIFIED *****
/dev/hdb1: 2107/30638080 files (16.9% non-contiguous), 12109308/61273910
blocks
```

Checking the Restored Disk

At this point, you can mount the filesystem using the standard mount command and see how much data was recovered. If you have any idea how full the original filesystem was, you will hopefully see disk usage similar to that in the recovered filesystem. The differences in disk usage between the clone of your old filesystem and the original filesystem will depend on how badly corrupted the original filesystem was and how many files and directories had to be deleted due to inconsistency during the filesystem consistency check.

> Remember to check the *lost+found* directory at the root of the cloned drive (i.e., in the directory where you mounted it), which is where *fsck* and its friends place files and directories that could not be correctly linked into the recovered filesystem. For more detailed information about identifying and piecing things together from a *lost+found* directory, see "Piece Together Data from the lost+found" **[Hack #96]**.

You'll be pleasantly surprised at how much data you can successfully recover using this technique—as will your users, who will regard you as even more wizardly after a recovery effort such as this one. Between this hack and your backups (you do backups, right?), even a disk failure may not cause significant data loss.

See Also

- "Recover Lost Partitions" **[Hack #93]**
- "Repair and Recover ReiserFS Filesystems" **[Hack #95]**
- "Piece Together Data from the lost+found" **[Hack #96]**
- "Recover Deleted Files" **[Hack #97]**

Repair and Recover ReiserFS Filesystems
HACK #95

Different filesystems have different repair utilities and naming conventions for recovered files. Here's how to repair a severely damaged ReiserFS filesystem.

"Recover Data from Crashed Disks" **[Hack #94]** explained how to use the *ddrescue* utility to clone a disk or partition that you could not check the consistency of or read, and how to use the *ext2/ext3 e2fsck* utility to check and correct the consistency of the cloned disk or partition. This hack explains how to repair and recover severely damaged ReiserFS filesystems.

The ReiserFS filesystem was the first journaling filesystem that was widely used on Linux systems. Journaling filesystems such as *ext3*, JFS, ReiserFS, and XFS save pending disk updates as atomic transactions in a special on-disk log, and then asynchronously commit those updates to disk, guaranteeing filesystem consistency at any given point. Developed by a team led by Hans Reiser, ReiserFS incorporates many of the cutting-edge concepts of the time into a stable journaling filesystem that is the default filesystem type on Linux distributions such as SUSE. For more information about the ReiserFS filesystem, see its home page at *http://www.namesys.com*.

ReiserFS filesystems have their own utility, *reiserfsck*, which provides special options for repairing and recovering severely damaged ReiserFS filesystems. Like *fsck*, the *reiserfsck* utility uses a *lost+found* directory, located at the root of the filesystem, to store undamaged files or directories that could not be re-linked into the filesystem correctly during the consistency check. However, unlike with *ext2/ext3* filesystems, this directory is not created when a ReiserFS filesystem is created; it is only created when it is needed. If it has already been created by a previous *reiserfsck* consistency check, the existing *lost+found* directory is used.

Correcting a Damaged ReiserFS Filesystem

Though ReiserFS filesystems guarantee filesystem consistency through journaling, hardware problems can still prevent a ReiserFS filesystem from reading or correctly replaying its journal. Like inconsistencies in any Linux filesystem that is automatically mounted at boot time, this will cause your system's boot process to pause and drop you into a root shell (after you supply the root password). The following is a sample problem report from the *reiserfsck* application:

```
reiserfs_open: the reiserfs superblock cannot be found on /dev/hda2.

Failed to open the filesystem.

If the partition table has not been changed, and the partition is
valid and it really contains a reiserfs partition, then the
superblock is corrupted and you need to run this utility with
--rebuild-sb.
```

When you see a problem such as this, check */var/log/messages* for any reports of problems on the specified partition or the disk that contains it. For example:

```
Jun 17 06:48:20 64bit kernel: hdb: drive_cmd: status=0x51
                              { DriveReady SeekComplete Error }
Jun 17 06:48:20 64bit kernel: hdb: drive_cmd: error=0x04 { DriveStatusError }
Jun 17 06:48:20 64bit kernel: ide: failed opcode was: 0xef
```

If you see drive errors such as these, clone the drive before it actually fails
[Hack #94], and then attempt to correct filesystem problems on the cloned disk.
If you see no disk errors, it's safe to try to resolve the problem on the original disk. Either way, you should then use the following steps to correct ReiserFS consistency problems (I'll use */dev/hda2* as an example, but you should replace this with the actual name of the partition with which you're having problems):

1. If the disk reported superblock problems, execute the `reiserfsck -rebuild-sb` *partition* command to rebuild the superblock. You'll be prompted for the ReiserFS version (3.6 if you are running a Linux kernel newer than 2.2.x), the block size (4096 by default, unless you specified a custom block size when you created the filesystem), the location of the journal (an internal default unless you changed it when you created the partition), and whether the problem occurred as a result of trying to resize the partition. After *reiserfsck* performs its internal calculations, you'll be prompted as to whether you should accept its suggestions. The answer to this should always be "yes," unless you want to try resolving the problem manually using the *reiserfstune* application, which would require substantial wizardry on your part. Here's an example:

```
# reiserfsck --rebuild-sb /dev/hda2
reiserfsck 3.6.18 (2003 www.namesys.com)

[verbose messages deleted]

Do you want to run this program?[N/Yes] (note need to type Yes if you
do): Yes

reiserfs_open: the reiserfs superblock cannot be found on /dev/hda2.

what the version of ReiserFS do you use[1-4]
    (1)    3.6.x
    (2)  >=3.5.9 (introduced in the middle of 1999) (if you use linux 2.
              2, choose this one)
    (3)  < 3.5.9 converted to new format (don't choose if unsure)
    (4)  < 3.5.9 (this is very old format, don't choose if unsure)
    (X)    exit
1

Enter block size [4096]: 4096

No journal device was specified. (If journal is not available, re-run
with --no-journal-available option specified).
Is journal default? (y/n)[y]: y

Did you use resizer(y/n)[n]: n
rebuild-sb: no uuid found, a new uuid was generated (9966c3a3-7962-4a9b-
b027-7ea921e567ac)
```

```
Reiserfs super block in block 16 on 0x302 of format 3.6 with standard
journal
Count of blocks on the device: 2048272
Number of bitmaps: 63
Blocksize: 4096
Free blocks (count of blocks - used [journal, bitmaps, data, reserved]
blocks): 0
Root block: 0
Filesystem is NOT clean
Tree height: 0
Hash function used to sort names: not set
Objectid map size 0, max 972
Journal parameters:
    Device [0x0]
    Magic [0x0]
    Size 8193 blocks (including 1 for journal header) (first block 18)
    Max transaction length 1024 blocks
    Max batch size 900 blocks
    Max commit age 30
Blocks reserved by journal: 0
Fs state field: 0x1:
    some corruptions exist.
sb_version: 2
inode generation number: 0
UUID: 9966c3a3-7962-4a9b-b027-7ea921e567ac
LABEL:
Set flags in SB:
Is this ok ? (y/n)[n]: y
The fs may still be unconsistent. Run reiserfsck --check.
```

2. Try running the reiserfs –check *partition* command, as suggested. If
   you're lucky, this will resolve the problem, in which case you can skip
   the rest of the steps in this list and go to the next section. However, if
   the partition contains additional errors, this command will fail with a
   message like the one shown here:

```
# reiserfsck --check /dev/hda2
reiserfsck 3.6.18 (2003 www.namesys.com)

[verbose messages deleted]

Do you want to run this program?[N/Yes] (note need to type Yes if you
do): Yes
###########
reiserfsck --check started at Sun Jun 26 21:54:58 2005
###########
Replaying journal..
Reiserfs journal '/dev/hda2' in blocks [18..8211]: 0 transactions
replayed
Checking internal tree..

Bad root block 0. (--rebuild-tree did not complete)

Aborted
```

3. If the reiserfsck -check *partition* command fails, you need to rebuild
   the data structures that organize the filesystem tree by using the
   reiserfsck -rebuild-tree *partition* command, as suggested. You will
   also want to specify the -S option, which tells *reiserfsck* to scan the
   entire disk. This forces *reiserfsck* to do a complete rebuild, as opposed
   to trying to minimize its data structure updates. The following shows an
   example of using this command:

```
# reiserfsck --rebuild-tree -S /dev/hda2
reiserfsck 3.6.18 (2003 www.namesys.com)

[verbose messages deleted]

Do you want to run this program?[N/Yes] (note need to type Yes if you
do): Yes
Replaying journal..
Reiserfs journal '/dev/hda2' in blocks [18..8211]: 0 transactions
replayed
###########
reiserfsck --rebuild-tree started at Sun Jun 26 21:56:29 2005
###########

Pass 0:
####### Pass 0 #######
The whole partition (2048272 blocks) is to be scanned
Skipping 8273 blocks (super block, journal, bitmaps) 2039999 blocks will
be read
100%                            left 0, 9230 /sec
383 directory entries were hashed with "r5" hash.
Selected hash ("r5") does not match to the hash set in the super block
(not set).
    "r5" hash is selected
Flushing..finished
    Read blocks (but not data blocks) 2039999
        Leaves among those 2032
        Objectids found 390

Pass 1 (will try to insert 2032 leaves):
####### Pass 1 #######
Looking for allocable blocks .. finished
100%                            left 0, 225 /sec
Flushing..finished
    2032 leaves read
        1975 inserted
        57 not inserted
    non-unique pointers in indirect items (zeroed) 444
####### Pass 2 #######

Pass 2:
100%                            left 0, 0 /sec
Flushing..finished
    Leaves inserted item by item 57
```

```
Pass 3 (semantic):
####### Pass 3 #########
Flushing..finished
    Files found: 359
    Directories found: 25
    Broken (of files/symlinks/others): 2
Pass 3a (looking for lost dir/files):
####### Pass 3a (lost+found pass) #########
Looking for lost directories:              done 1, 1 /sec
Looking for lost files: Flushing..finished
    Objects without names 4
    Files linked to /lost+found 4
Pass 4 -                   finished
    Deleted unreachable items 23
Flushing..finished
Syncing..finished
###########
reiserfsck finished at Sun Jun 26 22:00:26 2005
###########
```

> Pass 3a in this sample output shows that some files were
> linked into the filesystem's *lost+found* directory. See the next
> section of this hack for information about those files.

4. Once this command completes, try manually mounting the partition
   that you had problems with, as in the following example:

   ```
   # mount -t reiserfs /dev/hda2 /mnt/restore
   ```

5. If the mount completes successfully, check the *lost+found* directory for
   recovered files (their naming conventions are explained in the next section):

   ```
   # ls -al /mnt/restore/lost+found
   total 179355
   drwx------   2 root root      144 2005-06-26 20:44 .
   drwxr-xr-x  27 root root     1176 2005-06-26 20:24 ..
   -rw-r--r--   1 root root 33745969 2005-06-26 20:24 350_355
   -rw-r--r--   1 root root 27046983 2005-06-26 20:24 350_356
   -rw-r--r--   1 root root 67049649 2005-06-26 20:24 350_357
   -rw-r--r--   1 root root 55630200 2005-06-26 20:24 350_358
   ```

If you experienced problems with one partition on a drive and saw disk errors
in the system log (*/var/log/messages*), you should also check the consistency of
all other data partitions on the disk using *reiserfsck* or the consistency checker
that is appropriate for any other type of filesystem you are using. You can list
the partitions on the disk and their types using the fdisk -l command, as in
the following example:

```
# fdisk -l /dev/hda

Disk /dev/hda: 60.0 GB, 60022480896 bytes
```

```
255 heads, 63 sectors/track, 7297 cylinders
Units = cylinders of 16065 * 512 = 8225280 bytes

    Device Boot      Start         End      Blocks   Id  System
/dev/hda1   *            1          13      104391   83  Linux
/dev/hda2               14        1033     8193150   83  Linux
/dev/hda3             1034        1098      522112+  82  Linux swap / Solaris
/dev/hda4             1099        7297    49793467+   f  W95 Ext'd (LBA)
/dev/hda5             1099        2118     8193118+  83  Linux
/dev/hda6             2119        3138     8193118+  83  Linux
/dev/hda7             3139        4158     8193118+  83  Linux
/dev/hda8             4159        5178     8193118+  83  Linux
/dev/hda9             5179        6198     8193118+  83  Linux
/dev/hda10            6199        7218     8193118+  83  Linux
```

Identifying Files and Directories in the ReiserFS lost+found

To explore a filesystem's *lost+found* directory, you must first mount the filesystem, using the standard Linux mount command, which you must execute as the root user. When mounting ReiserFS filesystems, you must use the mount command's -t reiserfs option to identify the filesystem as a ReiserFS filesystem and therefore mount it appropriately. Once the filesystem is mounted, cd to the *lost+found* directory at the root of that filesystem, which will be located in the directory where you mounted the filesystem. If this directory contains any files or directories, you're in luck—there's more data in your filesystem than just the standard files and directories it contains!

As with the *lost+found* directories used by other types of Linux filesystems, the entries in a ReiserFS *lost+found* directory are files and directories whose parent inodes or directories were damaged and discarded during the consistency check. You will have to do a bit of detective work to find out what these are, but two factors work in your favor:

- The names of the files and directories in the *lost+found* directory for ReiserFS filesystems are based on the ReiserFS nodes associated with the lost files or directories and their parents and are in the form *NNN_NNN* (*parent_file/dir*). Files and directories with the same numbers in the first portions of their names are usually associated with each other.

- The *reiserfsck* program simply re-links unconnected files and directories into the *lost+found* directory, which preserves the creation, access, and modification timestamps associated with those files and directories.

Aside from the different naming conventions used by the files in a ReiserFS *lost+found* directory, the process of identifying related files and directories is the same as that described in "Piece Together Data from the lost+found" [Hack #96]. See that hack for more information.

See Also

- "Recover Lost Partitions" [Hack #93]
- "Recover Data from Crashed Disks" [Hack #94]
- "Recover Deleted Files" [Hack #97]

Piece Together Data from the lost+found

fsck and similar programs save lost or unlinked files and directories automatically. Here's how to figure out what they are.

The *fsck* utility, created by Ted Kowalski and others at Bell Labs for ancient versions of Unix, removed much of the black magic from checking and correcting the consistency of Unix filesystems. No one wept many tears for the passing of *fsck*'s predecessors, *icheck* and *ncheck*, since *fsck* is far smarter and encapsulates a lot of knowledge about filesystem organization and repair. One of the coolest things that *fsck* brought to Unix filesystems was the notion of the *lost+found* directory at the root of a Unix filesystem. Though actually created by utilities associated with filesystem creation (*newfs*, *mkfs*, *mklost+found*, and so on, depending on the filesystem and version of Unix or Linux that you're using), the *lost+found* directory is there expressly for the use of filesystem repair utilities such as *fsck*, *e2fsck*, *xfs_repair*, and so on.

The idea behind the *lost+found* directory was to preallocate a specific directory with a relatively large number of directory entries, to be used as an electronic catcher's mitt for storing files and directories whose actual locations in the filesystem can't be determined during a filesystem consistency check. When a utility such as *fsck* performs a full filesystem consistency check, its primary goal is to verify the integrity of the filesystem, which means that filesystem metadata such as lists of free and allocated blocks, inodes, or extents (typically stored as bitmaps) are correct, all files and directories in the filesystem are correctly linked into the filesystem, directory and file attributes are correct, and so on. Unfortunately, preserving corrupted data is a secondary concern during filesystem consistency checking and repair. Inconsistent files or directories are usually simply purged during a filesystem consistency check, but the contents of directories that are purged may still themselves be consistent. When this situation occurs during a filesystem consistency check, the contents of such directories are automatically linked to existing (empty) entries in that filesystem's *lost+found* directory. On older Unix systems, the hard links to these "recovered" files and directories were given names corresponding to their inode numbers. On *ext2* or *ext3* Linux filesystems, the hard links to such files and directories are given names beginning with a hash mark (#) and followed by the inode number.

When you encounter a severely corrupted filesystem or recover one as part of a repair or recovery [Hack #94], you will almost always find files and directories in that filesystem's *lost+found* directory after *fsck*'ing the filesystem. Here are some tips on how to figure out what they contain, what files and directories they may have been, and how to put them back into the actual filesystem.

> This hack focuses on piecing things together for an *ext2* or *ext3* filesystem, but the procedure for identifying files and directories applies to other filesystems as well. For some ReiserFS-specific tips, see "Repair and Recover ReiserFS Filesystems" [Hack #95].

Exploring the lost+found

To explore a filesystem's *lost+found* directory, you must first mount the filesystem using the standard Linux mount command, which you must execute as the root user. Once the filesystem is mounted, cd to the *lost+found* directory at the root of that filesystem, which will be located in the directory where you mounted the filesystem. If this directory contains any files or directories, you're in luck—there's more data in your filesystem than just the standard files and directories it contains!

The entries in the *lost+found* directory are files and directories whose parent inodes or directories were damaged and discarded during the consistency check. You will have to do a bit of detective work to find out what these are, but two factors work in your favor:

- The names of the files and directories in the *lost+found* directory for an *ext2/ext3* filesystem are based on the numbers of the inodes associated with the lost files or directories.

- The *e2fsck* program simply re-links unconnected files and directories into the *lost+found* directory, which preserves the creation, access, and modification timestamps associated with those files and directories.

The first thing to do when exploring an *ext2* or *ext3* *lost+found* directory is to prepare an area on another disk to which you can temporarily copy files and directories as you attempt to reconstruct their organization. In this hack, I'll use the example */usr/restore*, but you can use any location. As you proceed with exploration and reconstruction, it is important not to modify the files in the *lost+found* directory in any way other than by copying them elsewhere, or you may lose helpful timestamp information.

Just to be safe, first redirect a long directory listing of the contents of the *lost+found* directory into a file in your restore area, as in the following example:

```
# cd /mnt/baddisk
# ls -lt > /usr/restore/listing.txt
```

This listing is a precaution against accidental modification of those files. Here's a section of the sample output from the *lost+found* directory from "Recover Lost Partitions" [Hack #93]:

```
# ls -lt
total 2116264
drwx------  3 root root     16384 2005-06-17 18:14 .
drwxr-xr-x  6 root root      4096 2005-06-17 18:14 ..
-rw-r--r--  1 wvh  users 48873341 2005-02-12 08:41 #11993089
-rw-r--r--  1 wvh  users 26737789 2005-02-12 08:41 #11993090
-rw-r--r--  1 wvh  users 27987253 2005-02-12 08:41 #11993091
-rw-r--r--  1 wvh  users 24691821 2005-02-12 08:41 #11993092
-rw-r--r--  1 wvh  users 25752913 2005-02-12 08:41 #11993093
-rw-r--r--  1 wvh  users 15258373 2005-02-12 08:41 #11993094
-rw-r--r--  1 wvh  users 16291065 2005-02-12 08:41 #11993095
-rw-r--r--  1 wvh  users 25151049 2005-02-12 08:41 #11993096
-rw-r--r--  1 wvh  users 27290257 2005-02-12 08:41 #11993097
-rw-r--r--  1 wvh  users    31643 2005-02-12 08:41 #11993098
-rw-r--r--  1 wvh  users     2751 2005-02-12 08:41 #11993099
-rw-r--r--  1 wvh  users     2670 2005-02-12 08:41 #11993100
-rw-r--r--  1 wvh  users 35270097 2005-01-28 05:29 #14811137
-rw-r--r--  1 wvh  users 39914258 2005-01-28 05:29 #14811138
-rw-r--r--  1 wvh  users 39709879 2005-01-28 05:30 #14811139
-rw-r--r--  1 wvh  users 58648049 2005-01-28 05:30 #14811140
-rw-r--r--  1 wvh  users 29533858 2005-01-28 05:30 #14811141
-rw-r--r--  1 wvh  users 27692066 2005-01-28 05:30 #14811142
-rw-r--r--  1 wvh  users 29308352 2005-01-28 05:30 #14811143
-rw-r--r--  1 wvh  users      564 2005-01-28 05:30 #14811144
-rw-r--r--  1 wvh  users      809 2005-01-28 05:30 #14811145
-rw-r--r--  1 wvh  users      156 2005-01-28 05:30 #14811146
drwxr-xr-x  2 lmp  users     4096 2005-01-22 21:46 #30507055
drwxr-xr-x  2 lmp  users     4096 2005-01-22 21:45 #30507031
-rw-r--r--  1 wvh  users 29523256 2005-01-18 05:21 #3063821
[much more output removed]
```

As you can see from this example, the files and directories in my *lost+found* directory are nicely grouped by date and inode number, and many of them were last modified on the same date. This is typical of partitions that are essentially written to once and then used as a source of data. In this case, the partition I lost was a repository for an online music collection for my server's users, consisting of audio files and associated files such as playlists and recording descriptions, so I have a good idea of how the files and directories were originally organized on the disk that went bad. The disk consisted of directories named by artist and date, each of which contained the recordings and associated files for the artist's performance on that date.

Recovering Directories from the lost+found

The first thing to do when exploring and recovering the contents of a *lost+found* directory is to copy out any directories that already contain related sets of files. You can then explore the contents of these directories at your leisure, putting the recovered files back into a live filesystem on your machine.

As you can see from the previous code listing, my *lost+found* directory contains two directories, *#30507055* and *#30507031*. Listing both of these shows the following:

```
# ls -l \#30507055 \#30507031

#30507031:
total 0

#30507055:
total 222380
-rw-r--r--  1 lmp users      915 2005-01-22 21:45 monroe1967-05-15d2.ffp.txt
-rw-r--r--  1 lmp users 11694266 2005-01-22 21:45 monroe1967-05-15d2t01.flac
-rw-r--r--  1 lmp users 14046056 2005-01-22 21:45 monroe1967-05-15d2t02.flac
-rw-r--r--  1 lmp users 21405678 2005-01-22 21:45 monroe1967-05-15d2t03.flac
-rw-r--r--  1 lmp users 10724376 2005-01-22 21:45 monroe1967-05-15d2t04.flac
-rw-r--r--  1 lmp users 19590818 2005-01-22 21:45 monroe1967-05-15d2t05.flac
-rw-r--r--  1 lmp users 13981201 2005-01-22 21:45 monroe1967-05-15d2t06.flac
-rw-r--r--  1 lmp users 13576225 2005-01-22 21:45 monroe1967-05-15d2t07.flac
-rw-r--r--  1 lmp users 12057959 2005-01-22 21:45 monroe1967-05-15d2t08.flac
-rw-r--r--  1 lmp users 15432553 2005-01-22 21:45 monroe1967-05-15d2t09.flac
-rw-r--r--  1 lmp users 19475592 2005-01-22 21:46 monroe1967-05-15d2t10.flac
-rw-r--r--  1 lmp users 13427860 2005-01-22 21:46 monroe1967-05-15d2t11.flac
-rw-r--r--  1 lmp users 16973390 2005-01-22 21:46 monroe1967-05-15d2t12.flac
-rw-r--r--  1 lmp users 12077969 2005-01-22 21:46 monroe1967-05-15d2t13.flac
-rw-r--r--  1 lmp users 26182260 2005-01-22 21:46 monroe1967-05-15d2t14.flac
-rw-r--r--  1 lmp users  6718719 2005-01-22 21:46 monroe1967-05-15d2t15.flac
-rw-r--r--  1 lmp users      405 2005-01-22 21:46 playlist.m3u
```

The directory *#30507031* is empty and can safely be ignored, but the directory *#30507055* seems to contain an intact collection of related files. Based on the filenames, I know that this is a live performance by the bluegrass artist Bill Monroe from May 15, 1967, and that it was created by the user *lmp*. (By the way, you will rarely be this lucky!) To preserve this directory, I'll recursively copy it to my restore area, giving it an appropriate name:

```
# cp -rp \#30507055 /usr/restore/monroe1967-05-15
```

Note the use of the cp command's -p option, to preserve user and group ownership and timestamps.

If I can't easily identify the contents of a directory in the *lost+found*, I generally copy it to my restore area, giving it a name based on the directory's timestamp. The inode number in the old filesystem is meaningless after a copy, but a visual clue for knowing when the directory was last updated may be useful when trying to figure out what it contains, especially if a project or system user or group owns the directory.

Recovering Recognizable Groups of Files

When recovering files that are essentially preorganized by their creation dates, I usually create recovery directories in my restore area based on the times-tamps and use this as a preliminary organizer when copying the files there. The previous code listing shows two groups of files, one created on Feb 12, 2005 (2005-02-12) and another created on January 28, 2005 (2005-01-28). I would thus create two corresponding directories and use wildcards to copy the associated files into those directories, as in the following example:

```
# mkdir /usr/restore/2005-02-12 /usr/restore/2005-01-28
# cp -p \#11993??? /usr/restore/2005-02-12
# cp -p \#148111?? /usr/restore/2005-01-28
```

Next, let's try to figure out what each of these directories actually contains. Change directory to one of the restore directories and examine its contents using the file command:

```
# cd /usr/restore/2005-02-12
# file *
#11993089: data
#11993090: data
#11993091: data
#11993092: data
#11993093: data
#11993094: data
#11993095: data
#11993096: data
#11993097: data
#11993098: JPEG image data, JFIF standard 1.01
#11993099: ASCII English text, with CRLF line terminators
#11993100: ASCII text, with CRLF line terminators
#11993101: ASCII English text
```

Looking at the text files in any directory usually provides some information about the contents of that directory. Let's use the head command to exam-ine the first 10 lines of each of the text files:

```
$ head *99 *100 *101
==> #11993099 <==
EAC extraction logfile from 8. February 2005, 23:22 for CD
Cheap Trick 1981-01-22d1t / Unknown Title

Used drive  : HP      DVD Writer 300n   Adapter: 1  ID: 1
Read mode   : Burst
Read offset correction : 0
Overread into Lead-In and Lead-Out : No

Used output format : Internal WAV Routines
                    44.100 Hz; 16 Bit; Stereo
```

```
==> #11993100 <==
EAC extraction logfile from 8. February 2005, 23:49 for CD
Cheap Trick 1981-01-22d2t / Unknown Title

Used drive  : HP        DVD Writer 300n    Adapter: 1  ID: 1
Read mode   : Burst
Read offset correction : 0
Overread into Lead-In and Lead-Out : No

Used output format : Internal WAV Routines
                     44.100 Hz; 16 Bit; Stereo

==> #11993101 <==
1981-01-22d1t01 Stop This Game.shn
1981-01-22d1t02 Go For The Throat (Use Your Own Imagination).shn
1981-01-22d1t03 Hello There.shn
1981-01-22d1t04 I Want You To Want Me.shn
1981-01-22d1t05 I Love You Honey But I Hate Your Friends.shn
1981-01-22d1t06 Clock Strikes Ten.shn
1981-01-22d1t07 Can't Stop It But I'm Gonna Try.shn
1981-01-22d1t08 Baby Loves To Rock And Roll.shn
1981-01-22d1t09 Gonna Raise Hell.shn
1981-01-22d2t01 Heaven Tonight.shn
```

This tells me that the first two files contain logfiles produced when ripping
audio from the CDs that originally contained these live recordings, while the
last (*#11993101*) contains a playlist for the files in the original directory.
Let's see if looking at more of one of the logfiles can tell us more about the
files in this directory:

```
$ head -20 *99
EAC extraction logfile from 8. February 2005, 23:22 for CD
Cheap Trick 1981-01-22d1t / Unknown Title

Used drive  : HP        DVD Writer 300n    Adapter: 1  ID: 1
Read mode   : Burst
Read offset correction : 0
Overread into Lead-In and Lead-Out : No

Used output format : Internal WAV Routines
                     44.100 Hz; 16 Bit; Stereo

Other options     :
    Fill up missing offset samples with silence : Yes
    Delete leading and trailing silent blocks : No
    Installed external ASPI interface


Track  1
    Filename G:\Cheap Trick\Cheap Trick 1981-01-22 Dallas, Tx(Reunion Arena)\
             1981-01-22d1t01 Stop This Game.wav
```

Hooray! This appears to be a live concert by the band Cheap Trick from January 22, 1981, recorded in Dallas. Let's verify that one of the files reported

as data actually contains consistent data that is in the lossless Shorten (SHN) format, as listed in the playlist file. We can do this using the shninfo command, which is part of the Linux Shorten command suite:

```
# shninfo *11993089
----------------------------------------------------------------------
---
file name:                        #11993089
handled by:                       shn format module
length:                           8:19.10
WAVE format:                      0x0001 (Microsoft PCM)
channels:                         2
bits/sample:                      16
samples/sec:                      44100
average bytes/sec:                176400
rate (calculated):                176400
block align:                      4
header size:                      44 bytes
data size:                        88047120 bytes
chunk size:                       88047156 bytes
total size (chunk size + 8):      88047164 bytes
actual file size:                 48873341 (compressed)
compression ratio:                0.5551
CD-quality properties:
  CD quality:                     yes
  cut on sector boundary:         yes
  long enough to be burned:       yes
WAVE properties:
  non-canonical header:           no
  extra RIFF chunks:              no
Possible problems:
  inconsistent header:            no
  file probably truncated:        n/a
  junk appended to file:          n/a
Extra shn-specific info:
  seekable:                       no
```

Another success! Unfortunately, there's no way to verify which of the recovered files is which of the files listed in the playlist, but let's see if we got all of the Shorten files that were in the original directory. We can do this in a number of ways, but the easiest is to count the number of lines in the playlist file and compare this number against the number of files in the recovered directory:

```
$ wc -l *101
18 #11993101
$
$ ls -l | wc -l
14
```

Unfortunately, this shows that the playlist file contains 18 entries, while there are only 14 files in the recovered directory, 3 of which are text files and 1 of which is a JPEG file. This means that we only recovered 10 of the files containing music in the original directory: the others apparently were located on disk blocks that had gone bad on the original disk or were otherwise inconsistent. Oh well—10 is definitely better than 0!

To complete the recovery process for this directory, I would rename the directory with something more meaningful than its creation date (perhaps *cheaptrick1981-22-01_dallas*) and then play the Shorten files one by one, renaming them once I recognized them.

Examining Individual Files

The end of the listing of our *lost+found* directory at the beginning of this hack showed one file, *#3063821*, that was not accompanied by files with similar inode numbers or timestamps. This means either that the file is the only one that could be recovered from a damaged directory, or that the file was located at the top level of the recovered filesystem but could not be relinked into the filesystem correctly.

Examining individual files in a *lost+found* directory is similar to examining a group of files. First, use the file command to try to figure out the type of data contained in the file, as in the following example:

```
# file \#3063821
#3063821: FLAC audio bitstream data, 16 bit, stereo, 44.1 kHz, 11665332
samples
```

Depending on the type of data contained in the file, you can use utilities associated with that file type to attempt to get more information about its contents. For text files, you can simply use utilities such as *cat* or *more*. For binary files in a nonspecific format, you can either make an educated guess based on the type of files that you know were stored on the filesystem, or you can use generic utilities such as *strings* to search for text strings in the binary file that may give you a clue to its identity. In this case, the file is a lossless FLAC audio file, so we can use the metaflac command's -list and -block-number options to examine the comments in the FLAC header that are stored in block number 2, and see if we can get any useful information:

```
# metaflac --list \#3063821 –block-number=2
METADATA block #2
  type: 4 (VORBIS_COMMENT)
  is last: false
  length: 254
  vendor string: reference libFLAC 1.1.0 20030126
  comments: 8
    comment[0]: REPLAYGAIN_TRACK_PEAK=0.64492798
    comment[1]: REPLAYGAIN_TRACK_GAIN=-5.84 dB
    comment[2]: REPLAYGAIN_ALBUM_PEAK=0.98718262
    comment[3]: REPLAYGAIN_ALBUM_GAIN=-4.77 dB
```

```
comment[4]: ALBUM=Old Waldorf SF
comment[5]: ARTIST=Pere Ubu
comment[6]: DATE=79
comment[7]: GENRE=Avantgarde
```

I am indeed lucky! The creator of this file was thoughtful enough to include comments, which identify this file as a recording by Pere Ubu, created in 1979 at the Old Waldorf in San Francisco. Unfortunately, the title isn't listed, but I can now play the file using *flac123* in the hopes of identifying it so that I can copy it to the */usr/restore* area with a meaningful filename.

Summary

The examples provided in this hack show a variety ways of examining and reorganizing files that were saved by the *e2fsck* program in a filesystem's *lost+found* directory. I was quite lucky in these examples (modulo the fact that I had filesystem consistency problems in the first place), since the disk that had problems contained a large number of sets of files that were for the most part organized in a specific way. However, you can use these same techniques to examine the contents of any *lost+found* directory—and even if you've lost many files and directories, remember that recovering anything is always much better than losing everything.

See Also

- "Recover Lost Partitions" **[Hack #93]**
- "Recover Data from Crashed Disks" **[Hack #94]**
- "Recover Deleted Files" **[Hack #97]**

HACK #97 Recover Deleted Files

Deleting a file doesn't make it lost forever. Here's a quick method for finding deleted text files.

Sooner or later everyone has an "oh no second" when they realize that they've just deleted a critical file. The best feature of old Windows and DOS boxes was that they used a simplistic File Allocation Table (FAT) filesystem that made it easy to recover deleted files. Files could easily be recovered because they weren't immediately deleted: deleting a file just marked its entries as unused in the file allocation table; the blocks that contained the file data might not be reused until much later. Zillions of utilities were available to undelete files by reactivating their FAT entries.

Linux filesystems are significantly more sophisticated than FAT filesystems, which has the unfortunate side effect of complicating the recovery of deleted files. When you delete a file, the blocks associated with that file are immediately returned to the free list, which is a bitmap maintained by each filesystem that shows blocks that are available for allocation to new or expanded files. Luckily, the fact that any Linux/Unix device can be accessed as a stream of characters gives you the chance to recover deleted files using standard Linux/Unix utilities—but only if you act quickly!

This hack focuses on explaining how to recover lost text files from partitions on your hard drive. Text files are the easiest type of file to recover, because you can use standard Linux/Unix utilities to search for sequences of characters that you know appear in the deleted files. In theory, you can attempt to undelete any file from a Linux partition, but you have to be able to uniquely describe what you're looking for.

Preventing Additional Changes to the Partition

As quickly as possible after discovery that a critical file has been deleted, you should unmount the partition on which the file was located. (If you don't think anyone is actually using that partition but you can't unmount it, read "Find Out Why You Can't Unmount a Partition" [Hack #92].)

In some cases, such as partitions that are actively being used by the system or are shared by multiple users, this will require that you take the system down to single-user mode and unmount the partition at that point. The easiest way to do this is cleanly is with the shutdown command, as in the following example:

```
# shutdown now "Going to single-user mode to search for deleted files..."
```

Of course, it would be kindest to your users to give them more warning, but your chances of recovering the deleted file decrease with every second that the system is running and users or the system can create files on the partition that holds your deleted file. Once the system is in single-user mode, unmount the partition containing the deleted file as quickly as possible. You're now ready to begin your detective work.

Looking for the Missing Data

The standard Linux/Unix *grep* utility is your best friend when searching for a deleted text file on an existing disk partition. After figuring out a text string that you know is in the deleted file, execute a command like the following, and then go out for a cup of coffee while it runs—depending on the size of the partition you're searching, this can take quite a while:

```
# grep -a -B10 -A100 -i fibonacci /dev/hda2 > fibonacci.out
```

In this case, I'm searching for the string "fibonacci" in the filesystem on */dev/hda2*, because I accidentally deleted some sample code that I was writing for another book. As in this example, you'll want to redirect the output of the grep command into a file, because it will be easier to edit. Also, because of the amount of preceding and trailing data that is actually incredibly long lines of binary characters, you will need to have several megabytes free on the partition where you are running the command.

The options I've used in my grep command are the following:

-a   Treats the device that you're searching as a series of ASCII characters.

-B*N* Saves *N* lines before the line that matches the string that you're looking for. In this case, I'm saving 10 lines before the string "fibonacci."

-A*N* Saves *N* lines after the line that matches the string you're looking for. In this case, I'm saving 100 lines after the string "fibonacci" (this was a short code example).

-i   Searches for the target string without regard to whether any of the characters in the string are in upper- or lowercase.

After the command finishes, start your favorite text editor to edit the output file (*fibonacci.out*, in our example) to remove preceding and trailing data that you don't want, as shown in Figure 10-3. Some such data will almost certainly be present.

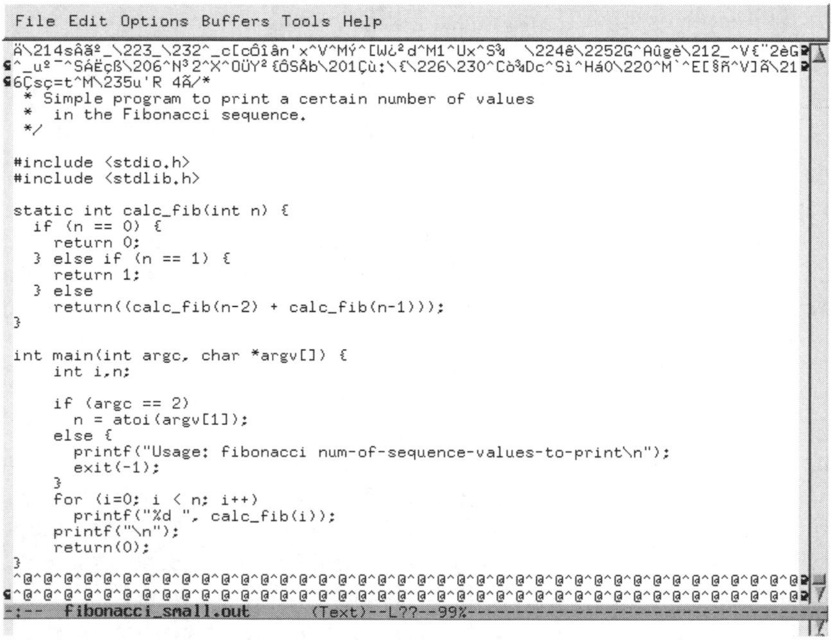

```
 File Edit Options Buffers Tools Help
Ä\214sÂã²_\223_\232^_c[côîân'x^V^Mý^[W¿²d^M1^Ux^S¾  \224ê\2252G^Aûgè\212_^V£"2èGⅢ
ⅢΛ
�Ⅲ_u²¯^SÁEçß\206^N³2^X^0ÜY² £ôSÅb\201Çù:\£\226\230^Cò¾Dc^Sì^Há0\220^M¯^E[§Ñ^VJÄ\21ⅢⅢ
ⅢⅢ6Çsç=t^M\235u'R 4ã/*
   * Simple program to print a certain number of values
   *  in the Fibonacci sequence.
   */

  #include <stdio.h>
  #include <stdlib.h>

  static int calc_fib(int n) {
    if (n == 0) {
      return 0;
    } else if (n == 1) {
      return 1;
    } else
      return((calc_fib(n-2) + calc_fib(n-1)));
  }

  int main(int argc, char *argv[]) {
      int i,n;

      if (argc == 2)
        n = atoi(argv[1]);
      else {
        printf("Usage: fibonacci num-of-sequence-values-to-print\n");
        exit(-1);
      }
      for (i=0; i < n; i++)
        printf("%d ", calc_fib(i));
      printf("\n");
      return(0);
  }
^@^@^@^@^@^@^@^@^@^@^@^@^@^@^@^@^@^@^@^@^@^@^@^@^@^@^@^@^@^@^@^@^@^@^@^@^@^@^@Ⅲ
ⅢΛ
Ⅲ^@^@^@^@^@^@^@^@^@^@^@^@^@^@^@^@^@^@^@^@^@^@^@^@^@^@^@^@^@^@^@^@^@^@^@^@^@^@^@Ⅲ
 -:--  fibonacci_small.out    (Text)--L??--99%--------------------------------Ⅱ
```

Figure 10-3. Recovered file shown in emacs

When the time it takes to edit and clean up the recovered file is weighed against the time needed to recreate the deleted file, you'll usually find it's worth the effort to attempt recovery. Once you're satisfied that you have recovered your file, you can remount the partition where it was formerly located and make the system available to users again—and be more careful next time!

See Also

- "Recover Lost Partitions" [Hack #93]
- "Recover Data from Crashed Disks" [Hack #94]
- "Repair and Recover ReiserFS Filesystems" [Hack #95]
- "Recover Lost Files and Perform Forensic Analysis" [Hack #100]

HACK
#98   Permanently Delete Files

Deleting a file typically just makes it harder to find, not impossible. Using a simple utility to write over files that you delete can help ensure that your data is gone for good.

We all store personal, secret, or potentially embarrassing data on our machines at one time or another. Whether it's last year's tax returns, instructions to your bank in the Cayman Islands, or a risque picture of your husband or wife, everybody has some data that they don't want anyone else to see, and no one keeps their computers forever. What do you do with your old machines? In business environments, they often simply get passed down the user food chain until they die. Are they wiped clean before each transfer? Rarely.

As we all know from the various Windows utilities that have been around for years to enable you to recover files (and from "Recover Deleted Files" [Hack #97] and "Recover Lost Files and Perform Forensic Analysis" [Hack #100]), just because you've deleted a file doesn't mean that it's actually gone from your disk. There's a good chance that the data blocks associated with any deleted file are still present on your disk for quite a while, and could be recovered by someone who was desperate or persistent enough.

You probably won't be surprised to hear that Linux, the OS of a thousand utilities, provides an out-of-the-box solution for truly deleting files. To recover a deleted file, you must reassemble the file, either by walking through the free list or by looking for the data that the file contained. The Linux *shred* utility makes files unrecoverable by overwriting all of their data blocks with random data patterns, meaning that even if you can piece a deleted file back together, its contents will be random garbage. The *shred* utility is part of the Linux *coreutils* package (the same package that brings you popular utilities such as *ls*, *pwd*, *cp*, and *mv*, which means that it is found at */usr/bin/shred* on almost every desktop Linux distribution.

Using the shred Utility

Using the *shred* utility to overwrite the contents of an existing file with random junk is easy. As an example, my online banking service enables me to download information about banking transactions in Quicken Interchange Format (QIF), which *gnucash* can import into my personal copy of my banking records. A snippet of one of these files looks like the following:

```
!Type:Bank
D10/08/2004
PWIRE TRANSFER FEE
N
T-11.00
^
D10/07/2004
PPAYPAL          INST XFER
N
T-217.20
^
D10/07/2004
PNAT CITY ATM   CASH WITHDRAWAL
N
T-240.00
^
D10/06/2004
PGIANT EAGLE IN, VERONA,PA
N
T-11.76
```

Assuming that I have a copy of one of these files (named, say, *EXPORT-11-oct-2004.QIF*) on my laptop from work, I'd really like to make sure that this data is wiped when I trade up to a newer machine and my old laptop goes to someone else. Rather than actually wiping the entire hard drive [Hack #99], I could simply use *shred* to overwrite and randomize this file, using the following command:

```
$ shred -n 3 -vz EXPORT-11-oct-2004.QIF
The output from this command looks like the following:
shred: EXPORT-11-oct-2004.QIF: pass 1/4 (random)...
shred: EXPORT-11-oct-2004.QIF: pass 2/4 (random)...
shred: EXPORT-11-oct-2004.QIF: pass 3/4 (random)...
shred: EXPORT-11-oct-2004.QIF: pass 4/4 (000000)...
```

The options I've passed to the shred command cause it to overwrite the file with three passes of random data (-n 3), be verbose (v), and write a final pass of zeros over the file after completing the random overwrite passes (z). If you don't specify the number of overwrite passes to perform, *shred*'s default behavior is to overwrite the file 25 times, which should be random enough for just about anyone.

Once this command has completed, let's look at the file again:

```
$ cat -v EXPORT-11-oct-2004.QIF | more
^@^@^@^@^@^@^@^@^@^@^@^@^@^@^@^@^@^@^@^@^@^@^@^@^@^@^@^@^@^@^@^@^@^@^@
^@^@^@^@^@^@^@^@^@^@^@^@^@^@^@^@^@^@^@^@^@^@^@^@^@^@^@^@^@^@^@^@^@^@^@
^@^@^@^@^@^@^@^@^@^@^@^@^@^@^@^@^@^@^@^@^@^@^@^@^@^@^@^@^@^@^@^@^@^@^@
^@^@^@^@^@^@^@^@^@^@^@^@^@^@^@^@^@^@^@^@^@^@^@^@^@^@^@^@^@^@^@^@^@^@^@
[much more similar data deleted]
```

As you can see, the contents of this file are gone.

In most cases, when shredding a file you would also use the -u option to tell *shred* to automatically truncate and delete the file after overwriting it, but I didn't use that option here so that I could demonstrate that the contents of the file are actually gone. One very cool thing about using *shred* is that it overwrites the file in place, so you're pretty much guaranteed that the contents of the file are irretrievably gone. Gee, I hope I imported that file into *gnucash*, now that I think about it....

See Also

- `man shred`
- [Hack #99]

 ### HACK #99 Permanently Erase Hard Disks

Before discarding old hardware, make sure you're not accidentally giving away proprietary or personal data.

Most government agencies—certainly the ones with three-letter names—have extremely stringent requirements for wiping hard drives before they discard old computing equipment. These requirements usually also extend to any contractors who have done work for them. Some security requirements are so stringent that disks must be destroyed, rather than simply erased, before the hardware can be discarded. The quickest and easiest way to do this (and the mechanism preferred by more militant sysadmins) is to take the disks in question to the local shooting gallery (guns, that is) and put a few rounds through them. For information on how to totally disable a disk using this mechanism, check out a recent copy of *Field & Stream*. However, if you prefer to erase a disk using software, read on.

Lest you think that finding embarrassing data on hard drives is simply anecdotal, I have some good experience with this myself. I collect old workstations, and I once bought an ancient, still-working Tektronix Unix system that I managed to hack into since I didn't have the install media for uTek. Once in, I did a bit of exploring and found that the system had apparently last been used as a node in a Bondage and Domination BBS. Now that was some interesting (and scary) mail!

Using shred to Wipe Hard Drives

"Permanently Delete Files" [Hack #98] introduced the *shred* utility, which is designed to overwrite the contents of specified files on a Linux system with random data. Thanks to the approach that Linux and Unix take to devices ("everything is a file"), you can also use *shred* to wipe a hard drive by specifying the base name of the drive as the name of the target file, as in the following example:

```
# shred -n 3 -vz /dev/drive-name
```

On most Linux systems, the first IDE hard drive is */dev/hda*, the first SCSI disk is */dev/sda*, the second IDE disk is */dev/hdb*, and so on. The command to wipe a primary IDE disk would therefore be:

```
# shred -n 3 -vz /dev/hda
```

If you're using *shred* to randomize the contents of one or more hard drives, you'll have to repeat your favorite shred command, specifying each drive as an argument. You can also let *shred* do its default 25 passes by excluding the -n 3 option on the command line, but this will take a *really* long time when wiping an entire hard drive. (If you have a very large disk, *shred* could conceivably still be running when the next edition of this book comes out!)

You'll have to be logged in as root in order to access the device directly, and you must also have booted from a disk other than the one you want to wipe. Because *shred* is part of the standard *coreutils* package, it is found on most rescue disks, in CD-based Linux distributions such as Knoppix, and in the Rescue Mode boot option for most Linux distributions.

Using Darik's Boot and Nuke

Another option when you want to completely erase a hard drive is to use a specialized boot floppy or CD that's designed for only that purpose. Darik's Boot and Nuke (DBAN) application (*http://dban.sourceforge.net*) is delivered in exactly that fashion and also supports an automated search-and-destroy mode that seeks out every hard drive in your system and does an extremely thorough job of overwriting the disks with random data. Because

DBAN is delivered as a boot disk and is designed to wipe disks (and only wipe disks), you should consider it to be the sysadmin's equivalent of a loaded gun. Be careful! Luckily, booting a system from a DBAN boot floppy or CD displays the screen shown in Figure 10-4, rather than simply beginning its search and destroy mission.

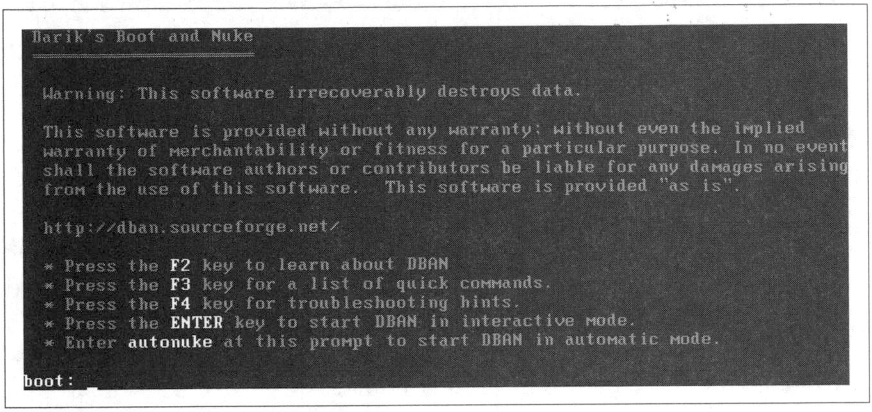

Figure 10-4. The DBAN boot screen

DBAN is provided as part of the System Rescue CD (*http://www.sysresccd. org*), but it must be started manually in that case. DBAN supports wiping IDE, SCSI, and SATA drives, and it even provides a variety of approaches to wiping your disks, as shown in Figure 10-5. To see this screen in DBAN, press F3 at the boot prompt. To select a specific wipe method, enter its name and press Return.

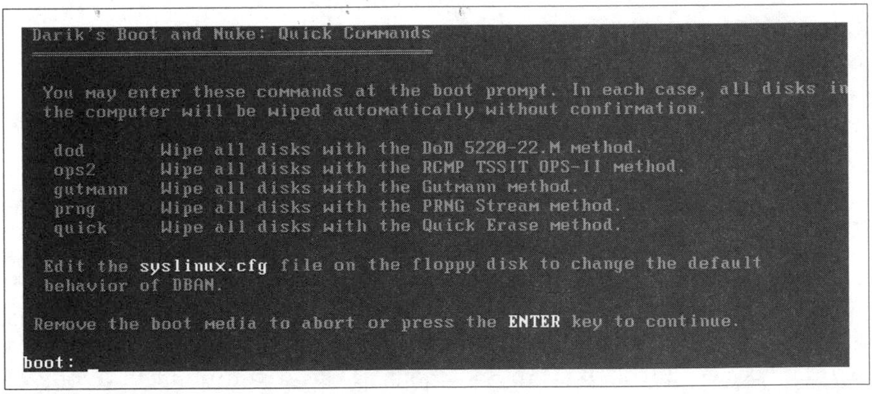

Figure 10-5. Wipe options in DBAN

DBAN is widely used by government agencies with stringent security requirements, such as the Department of Energy and the National Nuclear

Security Agency. For once, "good enough for government work" is a positive comment! DBAN can be your software hammer if you want to permanently erase a drive without physically beating it to death or shooting it. No software solution can beat physical destruction, and truly desperate people might still be able to recover something from a disk that was wiped with DBAN, but it's unlikely that the eBay purchaser of one of your old systems is going to spend the five- or six-figure dollar amount required to do so.

Summary

Wiping disks is always a good idea when you take a machine out of circulation, sell it, or recycle it. Make sure you do backups of anything you want to save first, of course! DBAN is my preferred solution for wiping disks, but make sure that you label the CD carefully and then hide it just in case some of your more curious offspring or friends decide to use it as a boot disk and press Return at its boot prompt. Tools such as DBAN and *shred* will do a great job of making sure that only the most compulsive and wealthy randoms could even hope to resurrect any potentially embarrassing data from your old systems.

See Also

- *http://www.sysresccd.org*
- *http://dban.sourceforge.net*
- DBAN FAQ: *http://dban.sourceforge.net/faq/index.html*
- "Permanently Delete Files" [Hack #98]

HACK 100   Recover Lost Files and Perform Forensic Analysis

The Sleuth Kit and Autopsy are designed for computer forensics, but they also provide a great suite of tools for helping you recover lost data.

Most people know forensics—the application of domain knowledge to legal questions—best from television shows like *Quincy* (for old people and TV Land fans) or *CSI* (for younger people). Computer Forensics, a science that's growing for a variety of reasons, tries to answer questions like "what the heck happened to my system?" "who hacked in here and what did they change?" and "how did my accountant get all my corporate funds into his Swiss bank account without my noticing?" Even if you don't have one of these specific problems, it's a downright interesting field. What self-respecting computer geek wouldn't like the opportunity to legally burst in somewhere, seize or clone disk drives, do his best to hack in and examine them, and get paid for it, too?

All fun aside, forensic analysis of computer data can save your company's data or bacon (or perhaps both) in court, as well as helping law enforcement officials track down the crackers and thieves who give real hackers a bad name. This hack provides an overview of The Sleuth Kit, the best-known open source software package for computer forensics, and Autopsy, which provides a web-based, graphical frontend to The Sleuth Kit and integrated support for other security and consistency-checking software. The Sleuth Kit (TSK) is based on an earlier collection of forensics tools known as The Coroner's Toolkit (TCT), which is available at *http://www.porcupine.org/forensics/tct.html*. The Sleuth Kit runs on Linux/Unix systems and can recover files and analyze data from NTFS, FAT, *ext2*, *ext3*, UFS1, and UFS2 filesystems.

Walking you through a complete forensic recovery session would require its own book, so the HOWTO portions of this hack will simply explain how to build and install both packages and how to use some of the tools in The Sleuth Kit to recover lost files more easily than you can with the mechanisms discussed in "Recover Deleted Files" [Hack #97].

Building and Installing The Sleuth Kit

The Sleuth Kit and the associated Autopsy package are not provided by default with most Linux distributions, but they're easy enough to build and install. If you're building The Sleuth Kit and Autopsy yourself for installation on your primary system, you can download the latest version of The Sleuth Kit from *http://www.sleuthkit.org/sleuthkit/download.php* and the latest version of Autopsy from *http://www.sleuthkit.org/autopsy/download.php*.

> One of the key concepts of forensic software is, of course, that you need to be able to run it from a safe, secure environment in order to analyze disks (or disk images) from other systems, so one of the best ways to get and use The Sleuth Kit and Autopsy is to get a bootable CD with these packages installed. My personal favorites are the Penguin Sleuth Kit (*http://www.linux-forensics.com/downloads.html*), the F.I.R.E. (Forensic and Incident Response Environment) CD (*http://fire.dmzs.com*), and, for BSD fans, the Snarl Bootable Forensics CD (*https://sourceforge.net/projects/snarl/*). Each of the CDs includes The Sleuth Kit and a variety of other forensics-related software.

You should always build and install The Sleuth Kit before building and installing Autopsy, because Autopsy's configuration process will ask you for the location of the installed TSK. The downloadable TSK source is provided as a gzipped tar file. To extract its contents and build the software (using

Version 2.02 as an example, which was the current version when this book was written), do the following:

```
$ tar zxvf sleuthkit-2.02.tar.gz
$ cd sleuthkit-2.02
$ make
```

The Sleuth Kit does not offer an install option, so I generally build it in */usr/ local/src* and then use sudo or become root to create a symbolic link from */usr/ local/sleuthkit* to */usr/local/src/sleuthkit-version*. I then add */usr/local/sleuthkit/ bin* to my path, and I'm good to go.

Building and Installing Autopsy and Related Software

The source code for Autopsy is also provided as a downloadable, gzipped tar file. You really only need to install Autopsy if you're interested in forensic analysis. If you're only interested in recovering files using The Sleuth Kit, that's most easily done from the command line (as of the time this book was written—things may have changed by the time you read this).

As mentioned earlier, Autopsy also integrates some other forensics software with the core capabilities provided by The Sleuth Kit—namely, a Reference Data Set (RDS) consisting of the digital signatures of known, traceable software applications, which includes hash values for many common hacking scripts and can thus be very useful when trying to determine how a system was hacked. These digital signatures are available from the National Software Reference Library (NSRL), a National Institute of Science and Technology (NIST) project, at the download page *http://www.nsrl.nist.gov/ Downloads.htm*. This page provides ISO images of four CDs, each of which provides signatures for a class of software:

- ISO 1 contains the signatures of non-English software.
- ISO 2 contains the signatures of common operating systems.
- ISO 3 contains the signatures of a huge amount of application software.
- ISO 4 contains the signatures of standard image and graphics files and formats.

These signatures are contained in the file *NSRLFile.txt*, which is itself contained in a ZIP file in each of the ISO images. You can produce one true signature file by downloading all of the ISOs, mounting them, and concatenating together all of the resulting files. You'll need 8 GB of free space when you're doing this, because the complete concatenated file is 4 GB in size! The following example uses RDS 2.9 as an example, which was the current version when this book was written. After creating the directory */usr/ local/nsrl*, do the following for each of the ISOs:

```
# mount -o loop RDS_29[ABCD].iso /mnt
```

```
# unzip /mnt/rds_29[abcd].zip NSRLfile.txt
# mv NSRLFile.txt NSRLFile.txt.[ABCD]
# umount /mnt
```

You can then concatenate them using the following command:

```
$ cat NSRLFile.txt.A NSRLFile.txt.B NSRLFile.txt.C NSRLFile.txt.D  >
NSRLFile.txt
```

You should then punt all of the *NSRLFile.txt.X* files, because you no longer need the individual versions.

You're now ready to build and install Autopsy. To extract the Autopsy source code and build the software (using Version 2.05 as an example, which was the current version when this book was written), do the following:

```
$ tar zxvf autopsy-2.05.tar.gz
$ cd autopsy-2.05
$ make
    Autopsy Forensic Browser Installation
perl found: /usr/bin/perl
----------------------------------------------------------------
Autopsy uses the grep utility from your local system.
grep found: /usr/bin/grep
----------------------------------------------------------------
Autopsy uses forensic tools from The Sleuth Kit.
           http://www.sleuthkit.org/sleuthkit/
Enter the directory where you installed it:
/usr/local/sleuthkit
  Sleuth Kit bin directory was found
  Version 2.02 found
  Required version found
----------------------------------------------------------------
The NIST National Software Reference Library (NSRL) contains
hash values of known good and bad files.
          http://www.nsrl.nist.gov
Have you purchased or downloaded a copy of the NSRL (y/n) [n] y Enter the
directory where you installed it:
/usr/local/nsrl
  NSRL database was found (NSRLFile.txt)
----------------------------------------------------------------
Autopsy saves configuration files, audit logs, and output to the
Evidence Locker directory.
Enter the directory that you want to use for the Evidence Locker:
/usr/local/evidence_locker
  /usr/local/evidence_locker already exists
----------------------------------------------------------------
Settings saved to conf.pl.
Execute the './autopsy' command to start with default settings.
```

You can then run the autopsy command via sudo or as the root user, because it needs root privileges in order to mount disk images, write to the evidence locker directory (unless you've set its ownership so that normal users can write there), and so on:

```
# ./autopsy
=============================================================================
                        Autopsy Forensic Browser
                     http://www.sleuthkit.org/autopsy/
                                ver 2.05
=============================================================================
Evidence Locker: /usr/local/evidence_locker
Start Time: Sun Sep 11 16:57:23 2005
Remote Host: localhost
Local Port: 9999
Open an HTML browser on the remote host and paste this URL in it:
    http://localhost:9999/autopsy
Keep this process running and use <ctrl-c> to exit
```

To begin using Autopsy, simply connect to the specified URL using a web browser. As mentioned earlier, stepping through a complete forensic recovery session using Autopsy could easily require its own book, but Autopsy is quite user-friendly in terms of walking you through each step of creating a unique directory (referred to as a "case") to hold the results of the forensic examination of a specific disk, disk image, or set of multiple disks or images. I've found Autopsy to be quite useful for identifying deleted files, such as those shown in Figure 10-6.

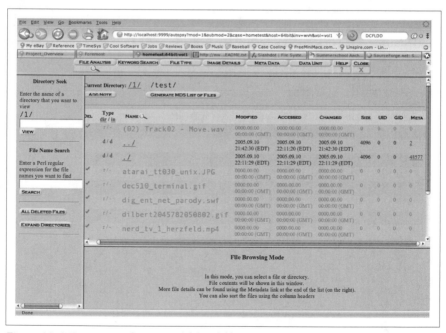

Figure 10-6. Browsing a directory of deleted files in Autopsy

Using The Sleuth Kit to Recover Deleted Files

The extent to which you can recover files using The Sleuth Kit (and therefore Autopsy) is completely dependent on the characteristics of the type of filesystem used on each disk or disk image that you're examining. *ext2* and *ext3* filesystems zero out inodes when the files associated with them are deleted, but the applications provided in The Sleuth Kit can simplify recovering any type of file whose contents you can uniquely identify. This can be problematic when trying to recover binaries, but it's great for text files.

The Sleuth Kit can analyze disks or disk images. To copy an existing partition or disk to a file for forensic analysis, run a command like the following via sudo or as the root user:

```
# dd if=/dev/disk-or-partition bs=1024 of=name-of-image-file conv=noerror
```

Once you have an image of the partition that contains the data you want to recover, make sure that */usr/local/sleuthkit/bin* is in your path, and follow the steps below to recover deleted text files. I'll look for the */etc/passwd* file in the sample image file *hd5_image_etc_files_deleted.img*. This is a clone of my system's root disk, in which I've deleted every text file in */etc*. (Good thing I only did that as an example!)

Looking for a deleted text file requires the following steps:

1. Use TSK's dls command to extract all of the unallocated space from the disk image into a single file, which expedites the process of searching for the file that you've deleted:

   ```
   $ dls hd5_image_etc_files_deleted.img > dls_output.dls
   ```

2. Next, use the standard strings command to search for all text strings in the output file produced by the previous step, and write that information to a file:

   ```
   $ strings -t d dls_output.dls > dls_output.dls.str
   ```

3. Use grep to search for a string that identifies the file you're looking for as uniquely as possible. I'll search for the string :0:0:, which shouldn't appear in too many files other than the */etc/passwd* file:

   ```
   $ grep ":0:0:" dls_output.dls.str
   130746025    (scsi0:0:0:0)
   130998233              if ( !strncmp( line, "PSPCAM", 6 )
   )root:x:0:0:root:/root:/bin/bash
   131698688 root:x:0:0:root:/root:/bin/bash
   150589440 root:x:0:0:root:/root:/bin/bash
   156106752 root:x:0:0:root:/root:/bin/bash
   176209920 root:x:0:0:root:/root:/bin/bash
   182677504 root:x:0:0:root:/root:/bin/bash
   187670528 root:x:0:0:root:/root:/bin/bash
   [snip]
   ```

4. The numeric value at the beginning of each line identifies the numeric byte offset for the string you're looking for in the file that contains text strings from the file containing unallocated blocks. Use the standard Linux dc (desktop calculator) command to divide this offset by the filesystem's block size (4096 for *ext2/ext3* filesystems, by default) in order to get the right value. I'm looking for the block/fragment that contains the string found in the third entry in the previous output, which is located at byte offset 131698688:

```
$ dc
131698688
4096 / p
32153
q
```

5. Next, use the dcalc command to convert the address from the unallocated block file into the address in the original disk image file:

```
$ dcalc -u 32153 hd5_image_etc_files_deleted.img
34152
```

6. Finally, use the dcat command to display the contents of the specified block in the fragment:

```
$ dcat hd5_image_etc_files_deleted.img 34152
root:x:0:0:root:/root:/bin/bash
bin:x:1:1:bin:/bin:/bin/bash
daemon:x:2:2:Daemon:/sbin:/bin/bash
lp:x:4:7:Printing daemon:/var/spool/lpd:/bin/bash
mail:x:8:12:Mailer daemon:/var/spool/clientmqueue:/bin/false
games:x:12:100:Games account:/var/games:/bin/bash
wwwrun:x:30:8:WWW daemon apache:/var/lib/wwwrun:/bin/false
ftp:x:40:49:FTP account:/srv/ftp:/bin/bash
nobody:x:65534:65533:nobody:/var/lib/nobody:/bin/bash
man:x:13:62:Manual pages viewer:/var/cache/man:/bin/bash
news:x:9:13:News system:/etc/news:/bin/bash
uucp:x:10:14:Unix-to-Unix CoPy system:/etc/uucp:/bin/bash
at:x:25:25:Batch jobs daemon:/var/spool/atjobs:/bin/bash
messagebus:x:100:101:User for D-BUS:/var/run/dbus:/bin/false
mdnsd:x:78:65534:mDNSResponder runtime user:/var/lib/mdnsd:/bin/false
postfix:x:51:51:Postfix Daemon:/var/spool/postfix:/bin/false
ntp:x:74:65534:NTP daemon:/var/lib/ntp:/bin/false
sshd:x:71:65:SSH daemon:/var/lib/sshd:/bin/false
haldaemon:x:101:102:User for haldaemon:/var/run/hal:/bin/false
gdm:x:50:15:Gnome Display Manager daemon:/var/lib/gdm:/bin/bash
^@^@^@^@^@^@^@^@^@^@^@^@^@^@^@^@^@^@^@^@^@^@^@^@^@^@^@^@^@^@^@^@^
@^@^@
^@^@^@^@^@^@^@^@^@^@^@^@^@^@^@^@^@^@^@^@^@^@^@^@^@^@^@^@^@^@^@^@^
@^@^@
^@^@^@^@^@^@^@^@^@^@^@^@^@^@^@^@^@^@^@^@^@^@^@^@^@^@^@^@^@^@^@^@^
@^@^@
^@^@^@^@^@^@^@^@^@^@^@^@^@^@^@^@^@^@^@^@^@^@^@^@^@^@^@^@^@^@^@^@^
@^@^@
[snip]
```

Voilà! If it looks like a password file and smells like a password file…

 Whenever I use this approach, I typically redirect the output of the dcat command into a file, which I can then edit to remove the trailing junk that you see at the end of the last example.

Had I been fumble-fingered enough to actually delete all the files in a real /etc directory, I'd also have to recover /etc/group, possibly /etc/shadow (depending on the authentication mechanism that the system uses), and /etc/fstab, but all of these could easily be recovered using the same approach.

Summary

The Sleuth Kit and Autopsy are powerful packages that do an incredible amount of work for you if you're trying to recover deleted text files and are basically essential if you're trying to do computer forensics work on the Linux platform.

A huge number of other open source packages that purportedly help recover deleted files are also available. One of the most promising of these is *Foremost* (*http://foremost.sourceforge.net*), which is open source but was written by two special agents in the United States Air Force Office of Special Investigations. (No, I'm not kidding.) Foremost uses file header and footer signatures and internal data structures to help identify binary files on a disk or in a disk image. It is currently being updated—the current version (1.0 Beta when this book was written) is hard-wired to accept specific file formats, but they're adding a flexible configuration, which is very promising for sysadmins who need to be able to recover binary files such as Microsoft Office documents, image files, and so on. If you've always wanted to get involved in open source software, this is a great project to start with.

See Also

- "Recover Data from Crashed Disks" [Hack #94]
- "Recover Deleted Files" [Hack #97]
- *File System Forensic Analysis*, by Brian Carrier (Addison Wesley)
- *Forensic Discovery*, by Dan Farmer and Wietse Venema (Addison Wesley)
- The Sleuth Kit: *http://www.sleuthkit.org/sleuthkit/*
- Autopsy: *http://www.sleuthkit.org/autopsy/*
- The Sleuth Kit's newsletter: *http://www.sleuthkit.org/informer/*
- The Coroner's Toolkit: *http://www.porcupine.org/forensics/tct.html*
- Foremost: *http://foremost.sourceforge.net*
- More forensics links: *http://www.sleuthkit.org/links.php*

Index

We'd like to hear your suggestions for improving our indexes. Send email to *index@oreilly.com*.

Colophon

Our look is the result of reader comments, our own experimentation, and feedback from distribution channels. Distinctive covers complement our distinctive approach to technical topics, breathing personality and life into potentially dry subjects.

The tools on the cover of *Linux Server Hacks, Volume Two* are hatchets, a type of ax. The hatchet is a single-handed striking tool used primarily to cut and split wood. Based on the wedge, one of the six simple machines of physics, the ax is one of the earliest man-made tools. It dates back from 100,000 to 500,000 years, but its simplicity and efficiency make it indispensable to this day.

Jamie Peppard was the production editor and proofreader for *Linux Server Hacks, Volume Two*. Rachel Wheeler was the copyeditor. Darren Kelly and Claire Cloutier provided quality control. Loranah Dimant, Jansen Fernald, and Lydia Onofrei provided production assistance. Johnna Dinse wrote the index.

Karen Montgomery designed the cover of this book, based on a series design by Edie Freedman. The cover image was created from an original photograph from the CMCD collection. Karen Montgomery produced the cover layout with Adobe InDesign CS using Adobe's Helvetica Neue and ITC Garamond fonts.

David Futato designed the interior layout. This book was converted by Keith Fahlgren from Microsoft Word to FrameMaker 5.5.6 using Open Source XML technologies. The text font is Linotype Birka; the heading font is Adobe Helvetica Neue Condensed; and the code font is LucasFont's TheSans Mono Condensed. The illustrations that appear in the book were produced by Robert Romano, Jessamyn Read, and Lesley Borash using Macromedia FreeHand MX and Adobe Photoshop CS. This colophon was written by Jamie Peppard.

Better than e-books

Buy *Linux Server Hacks, Volume Two* and access
the digital edition FREE on Safari for 45 days.

Go to www.oreilly.com/go/safarienabled
and type in coupon code 88EK-KEUD-SSXW-ZDDS-E3KR

Search
thousands of
top tech books

Download
whole chapters

Cut and Paste
code examples

Find
answers fast

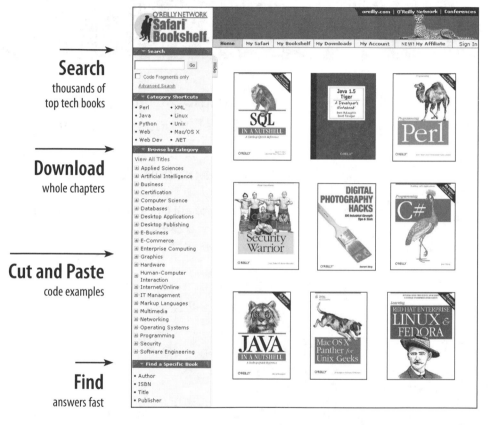

Search Safari! The premier electronic reference
library for programmers and IT professionals.